Archaeology's Footprints in the Modern World

Archaeology's Footprints
in the Modern World

Michael Brian Schiffer

THE UNIVERSITY OF UTAH PRESS

Salt Lake City

The Defiance House Man colophon is a registered trademark
of the University of Utah Press. It is based on a four-foot-tall
Ancient Puebloan pictograph (late PIII) near Glen Canyon, Utah.

21 20 19 18 17   1 2 3 4 5

LIBRARY OF CONGRESS CATALOGING-IN-PUBLICATION DATA

Names: Schiffer, Michael B., author.
Title: Archaeology's footprints in the modern world / Michael Brian Schiffer.
Description: Salt Lake City : The University of Utah Press, [2017] | Includes
    bibliographical references.
Identifiers: LCCN 2016034793| ISBN 9781607815334 (pbk. : alk. paper) | ISBN
    9781607815341 (ebook)
Subjects: LCSH: Archaeology—History. | Archaeology and history. | Social
    archaeology.
Classification: LCC CC165 S324 2017 | DDC 930.1—dc23
LC record available at https://lccn.loc.gov/2016034793

Cover photographs: top image is a detail of a mosaic from the House of Eustolios,
Kourion, photo by S. Rae (Flickr.com Creative Commons); the bottom image is
a panel in room 1 of the Bonampak murals showing musicians and dancers and
lavish use of the pigment Maya blue (Wikimedia Commons, photographer unknown).

Printed and bound by Edwards Brothers Malloy Inc., Ann Arbor, Michigan.

For Ethan Louie, Aliya Hannah, and their generation

Contents

Figures and Tables

Figures

Table

Preface

As the study of people and things in all times and all places, archaeology has many footprints in the modern world: our work affects governments at all levels, other sciences and humanities, and ordinary people. Although most people in industrial societies have some familiarity with archaeology—the discipline is, after all, a media darling—many contributions are obscure. *Archaeology's Footprints in the Modern World* addresses that situation. It brings a selection of contributions, including lesser-known ones, to a general audience to show that archaeology matters.[1] The book is for people who want to learn more about what archaeologists do and have done, and assumes that the reader has little knowledge of the subject. Together, the chapters in *Footprints* highlight archaeology's unique importance to the modern world.

Archaeologist is a somewhat odd profession—or, rather, calling. We use libraries extensively and work in laboratories, but much of our data comes from digging in the dirt. To learn about societies, past and present, we prioritize the study of material culture. We ferret out information from all pertinent sources and collaborate with colleagues from virtually all other disciplines. Because only we have access to the entirety of humankind's experience on this planet, our findings shed light on everything from human evolution in the deep past, to the prehistory of societies around the world, to present-day food waste and homelessness. The chapters that follow demonstrate how our unorthodox approaches have helped to produce new knowledge of lasting value.

I hope you will enjoy reading this book as much as I have enjoyed researching and writing it.

Many colleagues have contributed to this book by commenting on draft chapters, furnishing photographs, and suggesting sources; they are thanked individually in the chapter notes. Don D. Fowler and an anonymous reviewer made cogent suggestions, some of which I followed. I am especially grateful to Smithsonian curators Deborah J. Warner and Peggy Kidwell who helped to clarify my thinking and sharpen my arguments in Tuesday lunchtime discussions. Warner read the entire manuscript and, as usual, supplied persuasive comments and pruned my verdant prose. Annette Schiffer, wife, lover, and best friend, plowed through the chapters and gave much helpful advice.

Introduction

"Archaeologists don't do dinosaurs," declares the bumper sticker on a pickup truck laden with shovels and wheelbarrows. The statement merits a chuckle because most literate people have already learned from media that paleontologists do dinosaurs; archaeologists study human beings. Yet the media have a love for archaeological stories. Many finds lend themselves to such superlatives as "oldest," "largest," "richest," even "weirdest," all of which qualify as newsworthy. A field project in a challenging environment can also be framed as a heroic adventure. The enduring mysteries of Stonehenge, Egyptian pyramids, Machu Picchu, and the like furnish captivating story lines for television programs. Archaeological projects also provide settings for lavishly illustrated articles in popular magazines such as *National Geographic* and *Archaeology*. And cyberspace is populated by countless archaeological stories. Archaeology's vast footprints in the media stoke and satisfy widespread interest in what we do and what we have learned about human societies, past and present, from their material culture.

Because most young people would agree that archaeology is cool, there is a consistent demand for archaeology courses at colleges and universities. Hundreds of institutions have large departments of anthropology whose archaeologists offer courses that span the world. Smaller colleges may teach about local prehistory or historical archaeology. Many students who get a taste of archaeology as undergraduates acquire a lifelong interest in the discipline and its findings.

Archaeology's impact on modern societies reaches far beyond the media and college courses. Some footprints are little known to the general public, such as testifying in trials, advocating for homeless persons, and collaborating with Indian tribes. Other footprints are better known, such as debunking racist myths, excavating at major tourist attractions, and augmenting the historical record. This book presents a panorama of footprints, large and small,

FIGURE I.1. The Pantheon in Rome (Wikimedia Commons; Georg Schelbert, photographer).

shallow and deep. Each of the 14 parts focuses on one kind of footprint, such as Managing Cultural Resources and Expanding the Social Sciences. The three chapters in each part illustrate that footprint with varied case studies.

Here, I present a range of footprints in modern material culture and popular culture. Let us begin by strolling down the National Mall in Washington, D.C., from the Capitol to the Lincoln Memorial, seeking traces of the distant past in the present.

A grand edifice with an imposing dome, the Capitol typifies the Neoclassical Revival style, which liberally borrows architectural elements from ancient Greek and Roman buildings. The dome is a distant descendant of the one that caps Rome's two-millennia-old Pantheon (Figure I.1). Atop the Capitol dome is *Freedom*, a bronze woman peering eastward while standing on a small Greek temple. Perhaps most typical of the Neoclassical Revival style are the tall Doric, Corinthian, and Ionian columns on the Capitol's interior and exterior, as well as the triangle-shaped pediment, also a copy of the Pantheon's. Many other federal buildings in Washington, D.C., including the

FIGURE I.2. National Museum of the American Indian (author's photo).

White House, also embody this style, which evokes the great achievements of the classical civilizations and implies power and permanence.

In view of its evident meanings, the Neoclassical Revival style has been used widely throughout the United States in county courthouses, state houses, churches, colleges, libraries, museums, mansions, banks, even cemeteries. Elements of this style also abound in Europe, as in the columns on Buckingham Palace and the Palace of Versailles. At one time, both London and Paris even had their own Pantheon facsimiles.

Heading downhill from the Capitol we encounter the first of the Smithsonian Institution's many museums. On our immediate left is the National Museum of the American Indian (Figure I.2). This recent building (2004) was designed to evoke the majestic thirteenth-century cliff dwellings of the American Southwest, visually anchoring living Indians to their ancestors and signaling to everyone else—especially lawmakers in the nearby Capitol—that Indians have become a potent political force. The museum houses large collections of prehistoric artifacts from North, Central, and South America.

Resuming our stroll, we look across the mall to the National Gallery of Art, West Building, with its prominent Roman dome, pediment, and tall classical columns. Once again, the dome's interior is a dead ringer for that of the Pantheon. Holdings include a fair number of excavated objects, including Greek pottery and sculptures, South American gold ornaments, and Maya pottery and stone carvings. Exhibits of archaeological objects are common in art museums throughout the world, inspiring us to appreciate the pan-human impulses that created beautiful works in so many places distant from us in time, space, and culture.

The domed building immediately west of the National Gallery of Art is the National Museum of Natural History, whose exterior invokes the Pantheon with dome and columns. Like natural history museums in most countries, this one has archaeologists on its staff, possesses large collections of prehistoric artifacts from many countries, and exhibits not just high art and exotica but objects of everyday life from diverse cultures. A stellar exhibit includes casts of the important fossils that demonstrate human evolution.

Looking south across the Mall, we see bronze Joseph Henry standing before the "castle," the original home of the Smithsonian Institution. Today it houses administrative offices and a café. Joseph Henry, America's most esteemed physicist during the mid-nineteenth century, was the first Secretary of the Smithsonian and set it on a course to become a world-renowned research institution. The Smithsonian's earliest publication, which he personally edited, was archaeological: Squier's and Davis's *Ancient Monuments of the Mississippi Valley* (1848).[1] Henry also hired archaeologist Charles Rau and solicited ethnographic and archaeological artifacts. The Smithsonian's interest in American Indians and archaeology survived Henry's passing in 1878. By the turn of the twentieth century, it had become the leading institution of anthropological and archaeological research in the United States.[2]

Near the castle are several newer, partly subterranean Smithsonian art museums. The Arthur M. Sackler Gallery, in particular, displays many archaeological objects from East and South Asia. The art history books in its gift shop include prehistory, and, like many other art and natural history museums around the world, it also sells replicas and miniatures of archaeological finds. West of the castle is the Freer Gallery of Art whose eclectic collection includes archaeological ceramics.

Peering north beyond the mall, we can just make out a Neoclassical building that once housed the Post Office Department. Postage stamps are

FIGURE I.3. Postage stamps depicting artifacts and sites. *Clockwise from upper left*: vase, Greece; Chimu gold figurine, Peru; mask of King Tutankhamun, Egypt; Roman Aqueduct, Italy; Great Wall, China; cave painting, Lascaux, France, (author's collection).

a medium through which many countries, including Italy, Greece, Peru, and Egypt, celebrate their archaeological heritage by illustrating important sites and objects (Figure I.3). Archaeological sites have also been pictured on currency, such as the modern 5-euro note that depicts Pont du Gard, a 2,000-year-old Roman aqueduct in southern France.

Resuming our westward trek we arrive at the Washington Monument. At a height of 555 feet, it is the tallest obelisk in the world, as well as the tallest structure in Washington, D.C. *Ancient* obelisks are common in Europe because hundreds were robbed from their original sites in Egypt. Erected in plazas and other public spaces in England, Germany, Italy (see the obelisk at left in Figure I.1), and elsewhere, they stand as mute testimony to the engineering skills of ancient Egyptians and to the passions of the rich and powerful to possess genuine monuments of antiquity.

Our last stops are the Jefferson Memorial, which requires a slight southern detour, and the Lincoln Memorial. Both monuments are Neoclassical: the domed and column-rich Jefferson Memorial is modeled after the Roman Pantheon; the Lincoln Memorial is in the style of a Greek Doric temple. Thomas Jefferson, by the way, was smitten with classical architecture, which influenced his designs for Monticello, his home, and the University of Virginia, which he founded. The third U.S. president, Jefferson was also the first U.S. archaeologist. Not only did he excavate a prehistoric mound on his Virginia plantation but he also published his findings.[3]

Turning our attention away from National Mall, we find that the Neoclassical style exemplifies just one of many archaeological inspirations present in modern architecture. From reading books on the ancient Maya of Central America and viewing plaster models of Maya buildings at the 1892–93 Columbian Exposition in Chicago, famed American architect Frank Lloyd Wright became an admirer of this unique construction style, which includes stepped pyramids and carved stone elements. Wright designed commercial buildings and houses for wealthy Americans that incorporated Maya design features on the interior and exterior. His architect son, Lloyd Wright, was another devotee of the "Maya Revival Style." Lloyd Wright's most distinctive house, inspired by temple architecture, was built in Los Angeles for John Sowden in 1926 (Figure I.4).[4]

The iconic Egyptian pyramids are copied in modern buildings at many scales, from the enormous Luxor Hotel in Las Vegas (which also boasts a sphinx and an obelisk) to the more modest pyramids in the main courtyard of the Louvre in Paris. The pyramids have also spawned a cult whose believers insist that the pyramidal shape has supernatural powers, such as enhancing health and stimulating the libido. Cult members buy miniatures made of many materials so they can tap into "pyramid power."[5]

Miniature pyramids scarcely qualify as art, but artists do get design ideas from ancient sites and artifacts. Eighteenth-century painters sometimes depicted Greek and Roman ruins, evoking the romance of ancient civilizations. In recent times, Stonehenge has given rise to dozens of large installations,

FIGURE I.4. Exterior view of the living room of Lloyd Wright's Sowden House, Los Angeles, Maya Revival Style (courtesy of the Library of Congress).

including henges made of cars, inflatable plastic stones, and outhouses. Photoshopped and painted images are for sale online, along with miniatures for gardens and sandboxes.[6] Archaeological pottery, jewelry, and chipped-stone artifacts inspire artists working in many media. Painter Paul Gauguin made ceramic sculptures adapted from prehistoric designs, and Diego Rivera's murals and frescoes reference Mexico's rich archaeological heritage.[7]

Sites, artifacts, and archaeologists also appear in modern literature. The most successful mystery writer of all time, Agatha Christie featured archaeology in *Murder in Mesopotamia, Death on the Nile,* and *Death Comes at the End.* Married to archaeologist Max Mallowan, she also took part in digs and became a skilled ceramic analyst. Michael Crichton, author of science fiction thrillers *The Andromeda Strain, Congo, Jurassic Park,* and many others, earned an undergraduate degree in anthropology from Harvard. His novel *Timeline* includes archaeologists and historians.[8] Lyn Hamilton wrote an entire series of archaeological mysteries set in different parts of the work. The romance of ancient ruins also enters the occasional poem, as in Robert Browning's "Love among the Ruins," which extols love and ridicules the follies of ancient kings.

Although King Tutankhamun was not found in a pyramid, the discovery of his tomb in the Valley of the Kings by Howard Carter in 1922 set off a frenzy of newspaper and magazine coverage. Tut's resting place, the last pharaoh's tomb discovered, had lavish burial accompaniments including the renowned gold burial mask (Figure I.3, center row, right), sculptures of gods, elaborate wall paintings, ornate furniture, jewelry glittering in gems and gold, and other spectacular objects. Publication of these finds influenced many areas of popular culture from the 1920s to the present. Some museums today sell replicas, often miniatures, of objects found in Tut's tomb. And entrepreneurs never tire of making King Tut kitsch such as ballpoint pens, swimsuits, or even a cigarette case with the image of a 1920s flapper wearing only Tut jewelry (Figure I.5). As part of a comedy routine on television, Steve Martin wore Tut-inspired regalia.

King Tut also spawned The Mummy, a "horror" movie starring Boris Karloff (1932). This was one among many dozens of archaeology-themed movies that have graced the big screen and now videodisks.[9] The Indiana Jones movie series, beginning with Raiders of the Lost Ark (1981) and starring Harrison Ford, revised the field archaeologist's stereotype. No longer a cautious and mild-mannered scholar wearing a pith helmet, as in older movies, Indiana Jones wears a fedora and carries a bullwhip. The dashing and daring Jones overcomes herculean challenges while pursuing archaeological treasures of world significance. His exploits have little to do with real field archaeology, but the movies are entertaining and have won a smattering of Academy Awards. The Indiana Jones franchise also includes dozens of novels about new adventures, a television series, video games, children's literature, toys, and amusement park attractions.[10]

Many archaeological sites are themselves tourist attractions. On Indian reservations as well as on state and federal land, Arizona alone offers visitors more than a dozen prehistoric sites. Among these are the spectacular Casa Grande Ruins National Monument, a four-story adobe structure in the desert; the 700-room pueblo at Homolovi State Park; and, for hikers, Keet Seel and Betatakin, large cliff dwellings in Navajo National Monument.

Eastern states also have parks featuring prehistoric sites. The most impressive is Cahokia Mounds State Historic Site, located in Illinois just across

FIGURE I.5. A flapper wearing replicas of King Tutankhamun's jewelry (author's collection).

the Mississippi River from St. Louis. Once home to a community of more than 10,000 people, it features Monks Mound, the largest mound north of Mexico. Cahokia receives nearly a million visitors annually, almost as many as Stonehenge.

U.S. archaeological parks and monuments commonly have visitor facilities, displays, dioramas, educational programs, and even guided tours. Most also have informative websites and some, like Cahokia, have gift shops that sell archaeology books and replica artifacts. Many communities derive significant income from tourists who travel to sites and museums, buying curios and postcards, and spending money on food, lodging, and transportation. Beyond the U.S., entire countries benefit from such income. Cultural tourism is increasing because people in the growing and graying middle classes have the means to visit historical and archaeological sites at home and abroad.

The varied and often highly visible footprints of archaeology in popular culture ensure that most literate citizens have some acquaintance with our discipline. But archaeology also has many subtle and little-known footprints. The following chapters present a mix of archaeological contributions to modern societies, some of them obscure yet fascinating and important, such as the role archaeologists played in developing radiocarbon dating and in helping Indian potters create commercially viable styles. From the many case studies, I hope you will acquire a deeper understanding of what we do and why we do it and will come to appreciate that archaeology is as significant as it is cool.

I

Evaluating Myths, Sagas, and Legends

E VERY SOCIETY has stories or narratives—often known as myths, sagas, or legends—that recount its origins, migrations, significant people and their deeds, and the doings of supernatural beings. Such stories may also buttress ideologies and rationalize ongoing practices. In traditional societies, stories are passed from generation to generation through oral traditions; in literate societies, stories may also be written down and perhaps published. Often reflecting a society's morals and existential concerns, stories reflect and reinforce cultural values and also play psychological and social roles in the lives of believers, and so stories are perpetuated.

People may accept their society's stories without question, but archaeologists—as scientists—are a skeptical lot. We do not take stories at face value but treat them as hypotheses that may be evaluated on the basis of relevant evidence. Sometimes our research validates a story, other times it does not. Archaeological findings can become the focus of controversy, especially if they undermine traditional beliefs. Chapters 1–3 furnish intriguing examples of archaeology's role in evaluating stories.

The "lost races" myth arose in the United States during the nineteenth century. The landscape of the eastern United States is covered with thousands of earthen mounds, some of them quite large. Instead of attributing the construction of these mounds to Indians, Americans invented the myth of lost races. It was believed that Indians lacked the organizational and technical skills to build such mounds, and so Americans looked to groups such as the Phoenicians or Lost Tribes of Israel. At a time when the United States was waging wars against Indian tribes, taking their lands and forcing them onto reservations, the myth helped to justify racist practices. Yet, at the end of the century, Cyrus Thomas used archaeological and other lines of evidence to overturn the lost races myth, showing that in fact Indians had built the mounds.

Icelandic sagas are ancient family histories transmitted orally for two centuries and later written down. Scandinavians long believed the sagas demonstrated that Norsemen had reached North America, but others were skeptical. Using two sagas as guides, Helge Ingstad retraced what he believed was the route of Leif Ericsson from Greenland to the northernmost tip of Newfoundland. After years of searching, in 1960 Ingstad found a promising site, L'Anse aux Meadows, in northern Newfoundland. Archaeological excavations there confirmed the presence of Norse settlement in the New World at around AD 1000.

The Hebrew Bible describes King Solomon not only as a wise man but also an enormously wealthy one who possessed vast amounts of precious metals, including gold and copper. Although the legend of King Solomon's mines actually originated in a novel published in 1885 by H. Rider Haggard, it quickly attracted believers. In that tale, adventurers find Solomon's lost gold mine in sub-Saharan Africa. Entirely fictional, this legend is easy to dismiss because King Solomon would have had access to gold and other metals from neighboring societies much closer to Jerusalem. Recent archaeological excavations have identified, in the Faynan District of southern Jordan, extensive evidence of copper mining and smelting that took place during King Solomon's era. These mines were a source of Solomon's copper, which was made into bronze tools and decorative objects.

1

Debunking the "Lost Races" Myth

From Oklahoma to Virginia, from Minnesota to Louisiana, the eastern
United States is dotted with thousands of earthen mounds, the largest of
which—Monks Mound at the Cahokia site near East Saint Louis, Illinois—
reaches a height of 90 feet, and has a huge footprint. Like Monks Mound,
some were enormous; others stretched thinly over the landscape, as in the
case of Ohio's Great Serpent Mound; some contained burials or held the
remains of structures; some had both; some sites had a multitude of mounds;
and others had just one (Figure 1.1).

Beginning in the late eighteenth century, Euro-Americans began to
wonder who built the mounds. Interest intensified during the nineteenth
century. At the time, it was easy for Euro-Americans to believe that Indians
were "blood-thirsty savages," unable to create the organization and master
the skills needed to construct the mounds. Their lifeways, especially in the
eastern United States, were changing drastically. Many Indians now lived in
the most impoverished conditions, their numbers greatly reduced by warfare, introduced diseases, disruption of traditional subsistence activities, and
Euro-American appropriation of their lands. Some groups were still violently
resisting encroachments and relocations, occasionally with great success.

If Indians did not build the mounds, then other peoples, now vanished,
must have done so. Scholars trained in several disciplines, *but not yet archaeology*, offered varied candidates, including Egyptians, Norsemen, Aztecs,
Toltecs, and the Lost Tribes of Israel. In fact, what modern archaeologists
call the "moundbuilder myth" was actually a myth about "lost races": peoples

FIGURE 1.1. Grave Creek Mound, West Virginia (from Squier and Davis 1848).

who were more advanced, more civilized than American Indians, with kings, sophisticated religion and social organization, and highly refined crafts. Only such races, it was believed, could have built large towns with mounds. These lost races—pick a favorite—supposedly were driven out by the Indians *before* Europeans arrived.[1]

Gaining traction during the middle of the nineteenth century, the lost races myth captivated John Wesley Powell. Educated in the classics, Powell also had a strong interest in nature and the outdoors. In his mid-twenties he rowed his way down the tributaries of the Mississippi River, observing geological features and cataloguing and sometimes digging mounds he spied from his boat. As a Union soldier in the Civil War, Powell lost most of his right arm in the Battle of Shiloh.

Even while in uniform Powell managed to record and excavate mounds, but his belief in lost races was shaken by what he found near Nashville, Tennessee. There he unearthed glass beads and an iron knife, which led him to hypothesize that the mounds had been "constructed subsequent to the advent of the white man on this continent."[2]

After returning to civilian life, Powell taught at several universities in his home state of Illinois. Serving in these posts, he organized exploring

expeditions, studying by boat the geology of the Colorado River, and publishing his maps and descriptions, which were valuable assets to a U.S. government interested in learning more about the federal territories in the far
West. He also observed ruins in the Southwest and cultivated an interest in
living Indians. His first major book was *Introduction to the Study of Indian
Languages,* published in 1877.

In 1879 Powell organized the Bureau of Ethnology in the Smithsonian
Institution and was appointed its director. For the first appropriation, Congress directed the Bureau to spend 20 percent of its budget on investigations
"relating to mound-builders and prehistoric mounds."[3]

By this time, many scholars, including several founders of American
anthropology, had staked out opposing positions on the mound builders.
Ephraim G. Squier and Edwin H. Davis, whose 1848 report on their excavations of about 200 mounds in the Mississippi Valley was the Smithsonian's
first publication, believed that the mounds had been built by an ancient
race—probably from Mexico and regions to the south.[4] In contrast, Henry
Schoolcraft, the first great ethnographer of American Indians, believed that
Indians and their ancestors built them.

The scattered observations that scholars and antiquarians summoned in
support of their positions did not resolve the issue, but advocates of lost races
were more numerous. As Powell observed, "The theory that the mounds
and other remains of antiquity are referable to mythical vanished races has
always been the most popular."[5] To undermine the myth would require new
archaeological fieldwork in a wide-ranging project. Powell was in the enviable
position of having a government mandate and the resources to investigate
mounds throughout the eastern United States.

In 1881 Powell appointed fellow Illinoisan Cyrus Thomas to head up the
project. Thomas, like Powell, was a gifted polymath who had studied medicine and became a lawyer, county clerk, and school superintendent. In 1873,
Thomas accepted a professorial appointment in natural science at Southern
Illinois University; he was also Illinois's chief entomologist.

When tapped by Powell to lead the mound project, Thomas lacked
archaeological experience, but he firmly grasped the issues and evidence
needed to resolve them. Assistants did the actual fieldwork, made collections, and prepared reports for Thomas. On the basis of this work (and on
antiquarians' reports), Thomas had information on more than 2,000 mounds
in 22 states. Virtually every variety of mound was investigated, yielding a

huge artifact collection that was shipped to the Smithsonian. In Washington, Thomas pored over the reports, studied the artifacts, combed through previous publications, and over a decade fashioned a masterful synthesis. Although he had once embraced the lost races myth, he judged that the weight of new evidence overwhelmingly favored the view that Indians had built the mounds.

Thomas marshaled many lines of evidence to support this conclusion. Important information came from descriptions of historic Indian villages in the writings of early French, English, and Spanish explorers, travelers, and missionaries, as well as more recent ethnographic accounts. In area after area, strong similarities in the houses, defensive works, and even mounds of historic and prehistoric villages indicated that the same people had built both. Thomas's position was unequivocal: "As the historical evidence adduced shows beyond contradiction that the Indians of the southern portion of the country at the time they were first encountered by Europeans did erect mounds, construct walls of defense, and dig canals, the question of their ability to plan and to combine and control force for the construction of such works must be conceded."[6] In many areas, burial customs, engraved shell, stone smoking pipes, and other artifacts also exhibited strong continuities from prehistoric to historic groups. The most convincing evidence, however, was the occurrence in undisturbed mounds of European artifacts and materials. Among the finds were iron knives, glazed pottery, glass and ceramic beads, along with a gun barrel, a Catholic medal, a gunflint, an iron hatchet, and a copper kettle. These items showed that Indians were still building mounds after Europeans arrived.[7]

Summarizing the project's findings, Powell concluded that "the links of evidence connecting the Indians and mound-builders are so numerous and well established as to justify archaeologists in assuming that they were one and the same people."[8]

From the vantage point of the twenty-first century, we may wonder how such a seemingly outlandish myth could have been believed by so many well-educated people—including at first both Powell and Thomas. But in American society of the nineteenth century, the myth seemed obviously true because it reflected, and reinforced, a pervasive racism founded on the belief that race and societal level were closely related. Thus, some races, having a better hereditary endowment, were more "vigorous," "intelligent," "inventive," or "industrious" than others, and therefore capable of greater achievements. Indians in the United States were obviously an inferior race, so the mounds had to have been built by other peoples better endowed. Because the lost-races myth resonated with these common beliefs, it helped rationalize Euro-American policies and practices toward Indians, including land seizure, forced relocation, military campaigns, and coerced conversion to Christianity.

The lost-races myth was not a harmless fiction, but its expiration date—at least among scholars—had been reached, owing to Thomas's definitive report. When the U.S. government published his report in 1894, American archaeology was still in its infancy as a profession. Yet, this upstart discipline, through the support of the federal government, destroyed the myth and challenged the racism on which it rested. In the early twentieth century, American archaeology and Indian prehistory would rise on a nonracist foundation.[9]

2

Did the Norse Beat Columbus
to the Americas?

AFTER COLUMBUS'S EXPLOITS in the New World became widely known in Europe, scholars in many countries insisted that their own heroic navigator had discovered America before 1492. The maritime nations of England and Portugal, for example, made cases for priority in this discovery, yet none stuck. Claims and counterclaims persisted in the absence of definitive evidence; new contenders arose; but Columbus was not dethroned.

Scandinavians had long believed that their explorers had reached land beyond Greenland, but two centuries passed before they entered the fray in a more public way, arguing they had discovered the New World. The Dane Thomodus Torfaeus made the case in his book, *Historia Vinlandiae Antiquae.* Published in Latin—then a lingua franca—in 1705, Torfaeus drew upon two Norse sagas, family histories eventually written down about AD 1250.[1] *The Greenlanders' Saga* and *Eirik the Red's Saga* recounted Leif Ericsson's discovery of a new land around AD 1000. Drawing from earlier sagas that told of this land's existence, Ericsson set sail from Greenland, colonized earlier by the Norse.

The sagas describe Ericsson's voyage in some detail, including mentions of vegetation and geographic features of the coast he encountered. His journey included visits to lands he named Helluland and Markland and ended when Ericsson reached a place called Vinland, where the Norse established a short-lived settlement, a base for exploration. The geographical details enabled Torfaeus to speculate that Vinland was in Newfoundland. But how much weight could be placed on stories related from generation to genera-tion for more than two centuries before being written down?

Aware that the seemingly preposterous claim for Scandinavian priority would fall on deaf ears without hard evidence, Carl C. Rafn, who was pre-paring a book on the subject, attempted to verify Vinland's existence and location. Seeking evidence of Norse antiquities, he sent queries to histori-cal societies throughout eastern America. According to Harvard historian Samuel Eliot Morison, Rafn's inquiries provoked "a frenzied hunt for Norse artifacts and inscriptions."[2] Americans offered a host of candidates, especially monuments and stones with purported engravings in runic, the ancient Scandinavian script.

Rafn's influential but ponderously titled 1837 book, *Antiquitates Ameri-canae sive Scriptores Septentrionales rerum ante-Columbianarum in America*, included not only the Old Norse version of the sagas, but also translations in Danish and Latin; an English edition was published in 1838.[3] Accompanying the book was a map drawn on the basis of responses to his inquiries, "exhib-iting the discoveries of the Northmen in the Arctic Regions and America" during the tenth through thirteenth centuries. Hundreds of dots on the map, indicating find spots of purported Norse artifacts in the Canadian Arctic and on the Atlantic and Gulf coasts, suggest that Rafn took every claim at face value. Later scholars were more discerning: many of the alleged Norse artifacts, including the rune stones and monuments, were revealed as frauds, some obvious, others less so.

Owing to the rampant deceptions, many scholars dismissed out of hand further reports of Norsemen in America. Historian and founder of the Naval Academy, George Bancroft asserted in 1879 that there was "no clear historic evidence" that "Northmen" had ventured to America. He dismissed the Icelandic sagas as "mythological in form, and obscure in meaning."[4] Like Bancroft, many historians lionized Columbus, dismissing or ignoring the Scandinavian claims. Even so, some researchers in the United States and in Europe remained believers and championed Rafn's conclusions.[5] And, of course, visits by Norsemen remained popular lore at the local level, especially in New England, for they were a source of civic and regional pride.

Interest in the possible Norse discovery of America continued to stimu-late debates, generating shelves of books and exciting the public imagination well into the middle of the twentieth century. But, it must be emphasized here, no amassing of questionable rune stones, much less tiresome scholarly

arguments over the meaning of texts, could settle the matter. What was missing was evidence of Norse settlement sites, excavated and reported by archaeologists. Only carefully documented work with trowel and spade could
show that Vinland of the sagas was an actual place.

In the 1950s, Helge Ingstad, a Norwegian lawyer turned explorer, writer,
and ethnographer, became obsessed with locating Norse remains in America.
He was thoroughly familiar with the two major sagas as well as those of previous Norsemen who had traveled west and south from Greenland. Sailing
up and down the coast, comparing landforms, vegetation, and distances with
those mentioned in the sagas, Ingstad became convinced, as had Torfaeus
centuries earlier, that Vinland was on the island of Newfoundland. On a
visit to northernmost Newfoundland in 1960, he learned from a fisherman
about undisturbed ruins near a village called L'Anse aux Meadows. Searching
there, Ingstad spotted no surface artifacts but did see subtle traces in the
turf—mounds and possibly outlines of structures. Encouraged by what he
had seen, Ingstad raised funds and lined up personnel from Scandinavia for
a major field project. He put his archaeologist wife, Anne Stine Ingstad, in
charge of excavations.

Fieldwork began in the brief summer of 1961 and continued the next
two years, the last with support from the National Geographic Society. The
archaeologists uncovered traces of a very large building, several smaller ones,
and a probable steam bath that resembled Norse structures known from
Greenland and Iceland. Constructed of timber (which was not preserved)
and sod, the large structure measured 70 by 55 feet; it contained a central hall
with sleeping platforms and a firepit. In one hut, the archaeologists found
traces of ironworking, including iron fragments, rusted nails, charcoal, and
a stone anvil. Apparently, bog iron had been smelted and worked at this
location, most likely to provide nails for ship repair. Despite careful work
with trowels and brushes, few actual Norse artifacts were found; the most
notable were a spindle-whorl of soapstone, a bone needle, and a bronze
pin. Excavators also found a small number of Eskimo and Indian artifacts.[6]

The Ingstads were sure they had found a Norse site, but knew that it
would be a hard sell to skeptical researchers. After all, critics could argue that
Eskimos, Indians, or later colonists might have built the simple structures,
and a few Norse artifacts could always be explained away. In an inspired
move, the Ingstads invited three distinguished archaeologists—a Canadian
and two Americans—to authenticate the discovery.[7] After touring the site

and examining the artifacts, the experts unanimously concluded "the ruins could only be Norse."[8] The case was clinched by 10 radiocarbon dates that placed the site's occupation in the vicinity of the tenth and eleventh centuries, a perfect match with dates inferred from the sagas. And, significantly, the site lacked Colonial-period artifacts.

Writing in *National Geographic Magazine* in 1964, Helge Ingstad triumphantly proclaimed that "Here, on the northernmost tip of the island of Newfoundland, we had discovered the first proven remains of a Norse settlement in the Americas."[9] Additional evidence of Norse activities at L'Anse aux Meadows accumulated in the course of later excavations during the 1960s and 1970s sponsored by Parks Canada. More structures (for a total of eight) and Norse artifacts turned up along with evidence for millennia of native occupation nearby.[10] And new radiocarbon dates supported the site's original dating.[11]

Despite some initial doubts, the scholarly community accepted L'Anse aux Meadows as a Norse settlement, perhaps part of Leif Ericsson's very Vinland. Once the threshold of acceptance had been crossed, archaeologists revisited supposed finds of Norse artifacts in Indian and Eskimo sites in North America, finding some credible evidence. After an exhaustive search through old site reports, Canadian archaeologist Robert McGhee concluded, "The Norse probably contacted Indian populations in southern Labrador and Newfoundland, Dorset Palaeoeskimos in northern Labrador, and Thule Eskimos in Greenland and perhaps in the eastern Canadian Arctic."[12] He suggested that occasional contacts, consisting of trade and plundering, took place over several centuries.

The Icelandic sagas described real historical events that left identifiable archaeological traces. Even so, archaeologist Birgitta Wallace cautions against taking sagas literally: "The sagas are not straightforward accounts of actual events. Although they contain historical ingredients, situations have been compressed, localities conflated, and the identity of expedition members changed to suit the purposes of the recorder."[13] Yet despite distortions in the sagas, they were essential for Helge Ingstad's project, providing enough information to justify and sustain his efforts, though he achieved success only after years of searching.

In 1978, UNESCO named L'Anse aux Meadows a World Heritage Site. Today it is a Canadian National Historic site boasting a museum, reconstructions of Norse buildings, and activities exhibiting tenth-century Norse

FIGURE 2.1. Reconstructed Norse buildings at L'Anse aux Meadows, Newfoundland (Wikimedia Commons; Dylan Kereluk, photographer).

life (Figure 2.1). Visitors can tour the site that forced the revision of textbooks: knowledgeable writers now state categorically that Columbus was a latecomer to the New World—at least among Europeans. Be that as it may, the Norse visit was historically inconsequential, whereas Columbus's visit was not.

3

King Solomon's Mines

IT IS WRITTEN in the Hebrew Bible that the wise and wealthy King Solomon had 1,400 chariots and 12,000 horses to pull them, 300 concubines, and 700 wives. Such seemingly incredible claims raise doubts about whether King Solomon—son of David, builder in Jerusalem of the first temple, and ruler of a united Israelite kingdom with Israel in the north and Judah in the south—was an actual person. However, biblical scholars and many archaeologists believe that King Solomon was a historical figure whose life and exploits can be illuminated by scientific excavations and analyses. For example, recent work at the site of Khirbet Qeiyafa, in the Judean hills, has shown that an urban society, perhaps a kingdom or state, was already in existence in Judah by the tenth century BC.[1] Israelites of biblical times were not just tribal shepherds.

According to widely accepted chronologies tied to Egyptian calendrics, King Solomon reigned for 40 years, beginning around 967 BC. During that time, he strengthened colonial holdings established by David and developed far-flung trade networks that furnished his kingdom with precious metals, luxury goods, and wives. Solomon also built a magnificent palace, resplendent, like the temple, with gold lavishly employed in a grandiose throne, an altar, table, drinking vessels, and more. Other biblical passages refer to widespread use of copper for Solomon's temple. Archaeologists have found neither temple nor palace, but excavations cannot be done in sensitive locations where these structures were likely built, such as the Temple Mount in Jerusalem's Old City. Even so, archaeological studies of mining and metallurgy from the time of Solomon can contribute new information.

The tenth century BC, Solomon's era, was preceded by two centuries
that marked the beginning of the Iron Age in the "Holy Land," known to
archaeologists as the southern Levant. This region takes in Israel, Jordan,
the Palestinian Territories, southern Syria, Lebanon, and the Sinai Desert.[2]
Although Solomon purportedly possessed an abundance of precious metals,
the Hebrew Bible mentions no mines, and the Levant lacks appreciable deposits of silver and gold.

The legend of Solomon's lost mines originated in the English novel, *King
Solomon's Mines*, by H. Rider Haggard, published in 1885. In this adventure
story, explorers deep in sub-Saharan Africa, thousands of miles from the
southern Levant, eventually find a cave filled with diamonds and gold pieces
stamped with Hebrew characters. A bestseller in 1885, the book inspired
many movies that have perpetuated the legend with great effectiveness down
to the present day: Michael Crichton's *Congo* (1995) also features a search
for Solomon's African mines. Well beyond novels and films, the legend now
has a life of its own in the popular imagination.

In the century-plus that has passed since the publication of *King Solomon's Mines*, archaeologists have carried out many excavations in the Levant,
Egypt, and nearby regions. These projects have turned up artifacts indicating
that, around the time of Solomon's reign, the Israelite kingdom was part
of an interaction sphere involving Egypt and regions to the north and east
whose participants took part in warfare, trade, and exchange of mates. To
the extent that the acquisitive King Solomon did have loads of silver and
gold, these metals could have been obtained closer to home through this
expansive network. Perhaps gold and silver were acquired in trade from
gold-rich Egypt, Saudi Arabia, or Anatolia—the Asian part of Turkey, which
is known to have exported the precious metals. What we know for certain is
that there is no need to search for distant lost mines. The legend that King
Solomon had gold mines far south in Africa, whose locations are lost in the
mists of antiquity, began in fiction and remains there.

But copper mines are another story. Ironically, artifacts of copper and
bronze (whose major ingredient is copper) were more common in the Iron
Age than artifacts made of iron. The Hebrew Bible mentions both copper
and bronze, and archaeologists have found weapons, tools, and decorative
items of bronze in Israelite sites. Large deposits of copper ore are found in
the southern Levant, specifically in the nearby Faynan District of Jordan.
Researchers have known for more than a century that copper was mined and

smelted there prehistorically. Could Solomon have had copper mines in this area? To lay a foundation for answering this question, archaeologists must learn *when* the mining and smelting in the Faynan District took place. Even if copper had been exploited during Solomon's reign, the king may not have controlled the mines. Archaeological excavations in the past several decades have been addressing these issues.

The Faynan District includes several sites where processing of copper ore took place. Khirbat en-Nahas (KEN) is the largest of these at about 25 acres and includes towers, an immense fortress, and more than 100 buildings. Most impressive, however, are a dozen or so huge mounds that contain black slag, the discarded waste product of copper smelting. Domestic refuse and smelter debris have also been found in some mounds.[3]

Various researchers, visiting KEN sporadically for more than a century, have offered many conjectures as to when copper was being processed and by which groups. To help resolve these issues, the Edom Lowland Regional Archaeology Project (ELRAP), codirected by Thomas E. Levy and Moham-mad Najjar, began an intensive program of fieldwork and analysis in the late 1990s. Since 2002, the project has included major excavations at Iron Age mines, smelters, stratified deposits, fortresses, and more.[4] Among the most significant contributions is a chronology of stratified metallurgical activities across the Faynan countryside anchored by radiocarbon dating from several production sites.

Copper exploitation began during the Pre-Pottery Neolithic period.[5] Later, during the Early Bronze Age, a period of intensified production began around 2700 BC and ended around 1950 BC. Until the beginning of the Iron Age, around 1200 BC, Cyprus was the major supplier of copper to the Levant. About this time, however, many societies in the eastern Mediterranean collapsed, including the Mycenaeans, the Hittites, and Egyptians, which likely disrupted Cypriot metal production. Demand for the metal, especially by new local societies that arose in the southern Levant, may have led to the renewed exploitation of copper sources in the Faynan at KEN.[6]

Beginning in 2002, excavations in a structure, and especially in a strat-ified slag mound, yielded an abundance of charcoal samples suitable for high-precision radiocarbon dating. The dates fall entirely within the twelfth through the ninth centuries BC.[7] Four years later, the archaeologists placed a large excavation unit in a slag mound whose 35 strata reached a depth of 6.1 m. Radiocarbon-dated charcoal samples from many strata in that mound and from excavations in a variety of buildings showed that during the tenth and ninth centuries BC there was industrial production of copper at KEN.[8]

Although other areas of the site may contain traces of earlier production, it is significant that major activity occurred there during the reign of King Solomon. This could have been the location for Solomon's copper mines but such a determination is difficult. Levy and colleagues believe that the district was part of Edom, a kingdom also mentioned in the Hebrew Bible. Edom's progenitor, Esau, was the brother of Jacob—ancestor of the Israelites. According to a widely accepted Edomite chronology, however, Edom did not come into existence until several centuries *after* the major metallurgical activities had ceased at KEN. Levy and colleagues argue that the received chronology is incorrect and have revised it based on more than 100 radiocarbon dates. In their view, the kingdom of Edom developed before the tenth century.[9] Other researchers have disputed this revision and reaffirmed the original chronology.[10]

These chronological debates emphasize the uncertainties as to which kingdom—Israelite or Edomite—controlled the Faynan District. If the Edom polity arose centuries after the reign of Solomon, then during Solomon's time the Faynan District was perhaps part of the Israelite Kingdom. Even if the two kingdoms were contemporary, Edom may have been under Solomon's hegemony, as implied by the Hebrew Bible. With either scenario, the copper mines can be considered King Solomon's. And if Edom was master of the copper-producing region, its rulers could have established alliances with the Israelites, providing them with access to the mines or to copper, perhaps through trade.

Source analysis of finished bronze artifacts has contributed new information to this issue. Employing sophisticated chemistry techniques, source analysis compares the trace elements (usually in parts per million or billion) from finished artifacts with those in metal from likely mines. Researchers have shown with trace-element analysis that artifacts dating to Solomon's era contain copper from Faynan District.[11] If these two adjacent kingdoms were contemporary and very likely interacting, then it is safe to suggest that the Faynan District was the location of King Solomon's mines, in the sense that they supplied copper for Israelite artifacts, regardless of which group was in control.

The legend that King Solomon had a gold mine in sub-Saharan Africa does not withstand scrutiny. Not only did the legend begin in a Victorian novel but archaeological research indicates that Solomon almost certainly got precious metals by trading with other kingdoms in Egypt and southwestern Asia. In one sense or another, recent projects have shown that Solomon did have mines—*copper* mines. These were located in the nearby Faynan District of Jordan and may have been under the king's control. But the copper mines were not lost: researchers have known about them for more than a century. Unfortunately, there is less romance and adventure in nearby copper mines than in distant gold mines, and so the legend of King Solomon's lost African mines will probably live long in the popular imagination.

I thank Thomas E. Levy for his comments on an earlier draft and for furnishing references.

II

COMPLEMENTING
HISTORICAL EVIDENCE

ALTHOUGH CLASSICAL ARCHAEOLOGISTS have for centuries studied the material remains of the ancient Greek and Roman civilizations, only in the mid-twentieth century did archaeologists in large numbers begin to investigate artifacts and sites created in more recent times, particularly in Western Europe and the Americas. Today, historical archaeology, which researches the material remains of peoples who also created written records, is a dynamic and well-developed discipline with advanced degree programs and practitioners in many nations.

The need for historical archaeology of recent periods—even the early twenty-first century—is not obvious, but this discipline developed for good reasons. The written materials of any society, such as business and governmental records, letters and diaries, newspapers, magazines, and books, were created to convey timely information to contemporaries, not to enlighten posterity. As a result, written materials often lack evidence to answer the kinds of questions that modern archaeologists, especially anthropological archaeologists, ask about past human behavior. Further, the available evidence is often irrelevant, incomplete, inaccurate, or contradictory. In addition, many people are poorly represented in historical materials because they were silent, as in underclasses and enslaved peoples, or others spoke for them. And many documents have not survived owing to discard processes, wars, vandalism, fires, and floods.

The archaeological record also has limitations, but in favorable cases it complements the historical record, enabling the creation of a more complete and accurate account of past events and lifeways. Historical archaeology is, above all, newsworthy, with widespread reach in books, journal articles, and websites. Projects continually make their way into the media and popular culture. Today, no person can speak *knowledgeably* about the historical past if pertinent archaeological findings have been overlooked, as shown by the case studies in chapters 4–6.

A fascinating project of maritime archaeology is the recovery and excavation of the American Confederacy's submarine, *H. L. Hunley*. The *Hunley*
was the first submarine to sink a ship during combat, but it disappeared after
using a spar torpedo to destroy the Union ship *Housatonic*. Not surprisingly,
the mystery of the *Hunley's* fate has generated a huge and largely speculative
literature whose authors have had to labor without adequate records of the
submarine's construction, fitting out, and last voyage. Found essentially intact and not far from the *Housatonic's* resting place, the *Hunley's* find-spot
negated several scenarios about its disappearance. Meticulous excavation
of the submarine's interior has also provided a wealth of new information
about its technology and crew.

The discovery and excavation of the remains of an eighteenth-century
pottery factory in Yorktown, Virginia, led to an important revision of the
industrial history of the American Colonies. Before this find, it was believed
that British policy preventing large-scale factory production of ceramics had
been effective. In fact, William Rogers, the "poor" potter of Yorktown, as he
was described in official Colonial documents, was a successful entrepreneur
and industrialist whose stoneware and earthenware pottery was sold wholesale and shipped to other cities and colonies. The excavations revealed much
about his factory's capacity, technology, and the kinds of vessels it produced,
augmenting a sparse and misleading historical record.

Nuclear archaeology deals with sites and artifacts related to nuclear
weapons and other nuclear technologies. In recent decades, archaeologists
have done work on the Nevada National Security Site. In the decades after
World War II, this vast expanse of desert witnessed a host of secret Cold
War, nuclear-related activities, including tests of almost 1,000 bombs and
nuclear-thermal reactors and engines for powering rockets (Project Rover).
Although there are records of these activities, many remain classified. Archaeological surveys have documented abundant remains of bomb tests and
structure complexes associated with Project Rover. In one case, a building
still contains many artifacts and facilities used during the 1950s and early
1960s in testing reactors. The archaeological reports by Colleen M. Beck
and her colleagues at Nevada's Desert Research Institute furnish unique
information about the material culture and landscapes of some fascinating
and expensive Cold War projects.

4

The Confederate Submarine, *H. L. Hunley*

UNTIL RECENTLY, mariners set sail to ports near and far without knowing whether they would return. Ferocious storms, poorly charted coastlines, mechanical failures, hostile humans, and submerged obstacles all took a heavy toll on merchant and military vessels. Lighthouses, foghorns, and buoys made sailing safer, but ships still sank annually by the hundreds. In addition to wrecks and vessels scuttled in wartime, many ships at the end of their lives were deliberately sunk because the hulks could not be reused effectively.[1] As a result, the archaeological record of ships is abundant and varied, extending from Bronze Age merchant vessels to nuclear-powered submarines.

Survey and excavation of ships is the bailiwick of nautical archaeology, also known as maritime archaeology. Some projects begin with historical accounts of a lost ship, yet others begin when a wreck or hulk is found serendipitously. In both cases, the historical and archaeological records usually provide complementary evidence about the vessel.

Historical evidence about a specific ship may be plentiful, especially after the late seventeenth century in the West. Archaeologists scour the archives of governments, shippers, insurance companies, and newspapers for information about a ship's name and ownership and, for each voyage, date and port of departure, people aboard, cargo, armaments, and intended route and destination. Yet unless a ship ran aground in a populated area or had survivors, historical records can be thin regarding the circumstances leading to her demise. For noteworthy ships, this information vacuum encourages people to fashion stories about what happened.

With evidence from a ship's actual remains, archaeologists may be able to discount some stories or, on occasion, learn how the vessel came to its final resting place. Archaeologists may also recover evidence that augments or contradicts historical records, such as construction details, unreported cargo, and unrecorded modifications to the ship's hull, rigging, and propulsion system. Sometimes there is gritty detail about the lives of the people aboard, including personal possessions, items of food and recreation, and human remains.

Perhaps no wreck illustrates these possibilities better than the *H. L. Hunley*, the first submarine to sink a surface vessel in combat—an event that occurred during the American Civil War. The *Hunley* was not the first submarine or even the first Confederate submarine, but intense curiosity about the aftermath of the brief encounter between the *Hunley* and the USS *Housatonic* in 1864 has sired numerous stories.

Desperate to break the Union blockade of Southern ports, the Confederacy resorted to developing and deploying unconventional weapons, including mines (then called "torpedoes"), semi-submersibles, and submersibles. Privately, Horace L. Hunley of New Orleans and other entrepreneurs designed a submarine, enlisted investors hoping to land bounties for sinking Union ships, and had the vessel built by the Park & Lyons machine shop in Mobile, Alabama, maker of steam engines and boilers as well as earlier submarines. In this case, power came from men crouching in her damp and cramped interior, arduously turning cranks to drive the propeller. No original plans of the submarine survive, only a photograph, paintings, and imperfect recollections of one *Hunley* builder written down about 40 years later.

Called the *Fish Boat*, the submarine was sent by rail to Charleston, South Carolina, a port guarded by several Union vessels, including the USS *Housatonic*, a new "sloop of war." After her arrival, the Confederate Navy commandeered the *Hunley* and tested her seaworthiness. The tests did not go well.

The first trial of the *Fish Boat*, soon renamed the *H. L. Hunley*, was performed with the hatches open. The wake from a passing steamer overwhelmed the vessel; she rolled over and drowned the five-man crew of volunteers. After she was salvaged, Hunley himself commanded the second test, but it also failed, as the vessel dove but never resurfaced. All eight men aboard perished. Although the cause of the submarine's catastrophic failure was not discovered, the Confederate Navy once again raised the *Hunley* and made her seaworthy.

A crew of malnourished volunteers, commanded by Lieutenant George E. Dixon, trained hard in the dead of winter for what would become the submarine's last voyage.[2] The *Hunley* was outfitted with a spar torpedo—essentially a bomb at the end of a long, forward-extending pole—whose mode of detonation was unrecorded. The Confederacy produced several kinds of torpedoes; some were set off by contact with the target, others remotely by rope or electricity.

On February 17, 1864, on calm seas, the killing machine departed after nightfall from Breach Inlet at the north end of Sullivan's Island. Cruising stealthily just below the surface, she reached the *Housatonic* anchored 4 miles from shore. As she came within about 100 yards of the Union ship, John K. Crosby, Officer of the Deck, spotted the *Hunley* and sounded an alarm. She was greeted with pistol and musket fire that probably did no damage, but the *Housatonic's* big guns remained silent. Reaching the ship's stern, the *Hunley* placed the torpedo below the waterline. It detonated and set off the warship's huge powder magazine. The *Housatonic* sank in a few minutes, taking five sailors with her.

Survivors, who had climbed the rigging, did not see the submarine again, and she never returned to shore. Later, Union Lieutenant Commander W. W. Churchill dragged a large area around the *Housatonic* but found no trace of the rebel vessel.

Decades later, bestselling novelist Clive Cussler was hunting lost ships. Attracted by nautical mysteries, he founded the National Underwater and Marine Agency (NUMA), a nonprofit foundation "dedicated to preserving our maritime heritage" through archaeological investigation.[3] NUMA, which had been searching on and off for the *Hunley* since 1980, claimed success in May 1995. After legal issues were resolved (the federal government owned the *Hunley* but gave South Carolina permanent possession), NUMA disclosed the ship's location to the federal government, and the National Park Service (NPS) was charged with investigating the site.

The NPS Submerged Cultural Resources Unit conducted the survey jointly with the U.S. Naval Historical Center and the South Carolina Institute of Archaeology and Anthropology. In addition, the project received contributions from a host of companies that supplied state-of-the-art technologies and personnel. The survey grappled with several questions: was the wreck found by NUMA in fact the *Hunley*? What was its present condition? And how could it best be preserved?

The site was mapped in detail using several techniques for remotely sensing what lies beneath the sea's surface, including magnetometry, side-scan sonar, and sub-bottom profiling. A coring tool, obtaining samples at regular intervals, showed that the wreck, almost 1000 feet seaward of the *Housatonic*, was buried under 3 feet of sediment. A test excavation using a dredge reached the hull and exposed features known to have been present on the *Hunley*, including fore and aft hatches. Cussler was right: the wreck could only be the *Hunley*.

Tests indicated that the hull's riveted iron plates were in good condition: the ship had been buried rapidly, and was largely protected from corrosion by coral and other encrustations.[4] This finding supported the recommendation that the *Hunley* be raised and preserved. After all, if left on the bottom, she would soon become the target of looters and souvenir hunters.

The *Hunley*'s excellent condition immediately brought several stories of her demise into question. Obviously, she was not destroyed by the explosion, since there was no evidence that the hull had buckled or was breached. Nor had she left the scene for a distant port or been carried out by the tide, only to sink somewhere else.[5]

The next stage of the project—raising the *Hunley*—required a huge team of contractors and archaeologists. While she was held firmly in place, the surrounding sediments were slowly removed. Secured by a specially designed harness and truss furnished by Oceaneering International, the 23-ton vessel was lifted out of the water by crane on August 8, 2000, and placed aboard a barge.[6]

To house the *Hunley* and all of the equipment required for her study and preservation, the 46,000-square-foot Warren Lasch Conservation Center was built. With contributions raised by "Friends of the *Hunley*," along with federal and state funds, the Center fast became one of the best-equipped archaeological laboratories in the world. Transported to the Center, the *Hunley* arrived in her harness and truss and was lowered into a 90,000-gallon tank of fresh water. During excavation of her interior, the ship would be kept as wet as possible to prevent further deterioration.

Robert Neyland, on loan from the Underwater Archaeology Branch of the Naval Historical Center, oversaw the recovery project, and nautical archaeologist Maria Jacobsen of Texas A&M University directed the excavation; conservation was in the hands of Paul Mardikian.[7] Confident that the

FIGURE 4.1. Working inside the Confederate submarine, the *H. L. Hunley* (courtesy of the Naval Historical Center).

hull would retain its integrity, the excavators cautiously drilled out the rivets from several topside iron plates to access the ship's contents.

The interior was filled with silty sediments that had filtered in through several small openings, probably within a few decades after she sank. Working on scaffolds because the vessel was still partially submerged during the workday, archaeologists removed the wet sediments in thin layers and screened them several times. The excavations progressed to the point where the archaeologists had enough room to work inside the ship (Figure 4.1). The recovered artifacts were cleaned and conserved. Human remains went to the Center's morgue.

Work began in 2001 and continued until 2004 when the *Hunley* had been emptied of everything except its mechanisms. The latter revealed a sophisticated submarine with a joystick-like control for the rudder, levers to adjust the pitch of the "fins" that raised and lowered her in the water, a mercury depth gage, and differential gears and flywheel that coupled the crankshaft to the propeller. In addition, more than 2 tons of pig iron ballast was spread on the bottom of the hull.[8] Some damage to the propeller shroud and several small holes nearby suggested that the *Hunley* might have been dealt a glancing blow by another vessel before sinking.[9] Alternatively, before being buried, she could have been damaged by ship anchors, dredging, or Churchill's dragging operation. Other holes in the hull resulted from corrosion and erosion.[10]

Artifacts found in the *Hunley* included shoes, leather belts, clothing fragments, smoking pipes, and canteens, as well as a pocketknife, wallet, small corked bottle, lantern, iron wrench, oil can, binoculars, and the ship's compass. Highly varied buttons indicated that the men had not been issued uniforms. Near the remains of Lieutenant Dixon were his gold ring, diamond brooch, gold watch, silver suspender buckles, brass vest buttons, and a $20 gold piece that he carried for good luck.[11] The coin was misshapen, confirming the story that it had saved his life when he was struck by a musket ball in the battle of Shiloh. By the time Dixon took command of the *Hunley*, however, the coin's magical powers had apparently dissipated.

The crew's eight skeletons, each one pieced together in the laboratory, yielded a wealth of information about the men, including age, height, and diseases such as herniated discs. An analysis of diet history, based on ratios of stable isotopes such as strontium measured in teeth and bone, showed that four men "were born in North America," while the other four were likely born in northern Europe.[12] Casts were made of the skulls, and their faces were reconstructed.

After thorough analysis and recording, the bones of each man were carefully wrapped, sealed in a copper coffin, and then enclosed in a period-appropriate wooden coffin. On April 17, 2004, "a military Honor Guard of Civil War re-enactors escorted the caskets on horse-drawn caissons to Charleston's Magnolia Cemetery."[13] They were interred near the graves of the *Hunley*'s earlier star-crossed crews.

That the sailors had died at their cranking stations, as shown by the locations of their bones, permits several inferences. Perhaps the *Hunley* was already resting on the bottom, which precluded escape because water pressure might have prevented the hatches from being opened. Had the ship been on the surface and the men been aware of a problem, they might have rushed the hatches.

An intriguing scenario of the *Hunley*'s last hours fits most of the available evidence. Tests conducted by Lieutenant Dixon had shown that the ship could stay submerged for about two-and-half hours with a full crew before exhausting the air supply.[14] Perhaps, after the blast, Dixon moved the *Hunley* a few hundred yards seaward, hiding on the bottom to avoid the Union ships converging on the *Housatonic* and waiting for the incoming tide to reduce the rigor of the return trip. Greatly fatigued by the hour-plus sprint to the *Housatonic* and excited by the kill, the men would have been breathing hard. If the *Hunley* had stayed too long on the bottom, the sailors might have run out of oxygen long before Dixon's two-and-half-hour dive limit, gradually and helplessly succumbing to anoxia.[15]

Another scenario, championed by historian Tom Chaffin, has it that the *Hunley* was drawn into a vortex caused by the *Housatonic*'s descent.[16] In this case, the vessel might have been sent irreversibly to the bottom. This scenario is supported by a recent finding.[17] The torpedo at the end of the iron spar was not detachable. Thus, when the *Hunley* rammed the *Housatonic* and the torpedo exploded, the two ships were less than 20 feet apart. However, this explains neither the lack of major damage to the *Hunley*'s hull nor its later burial 1000 feet seaward of the doomed Union ship.

Although the recovery and excavation of the *Hunley* and the analysis of her structure and contents have furnished much new information about the ship's construction, mechanisms, mode of operation, and crew, the archaeological project may never provide an ironclad answer to why she did not return to Breach Inlet.

I thank J. Jefferson Reid for comments on this chapter.

5

The "Poor" Potter of Yorktown, Virginia

FOUNDED IN 1691, Yorktown, Virginia, is a settlement on the York River that played a decisive role in the Revolutionary war. Although the British occupied Yorktown and built defenses, a larger force of French and American troops surrounded the town and attacked. On October 19, 1781, British General Charles Cornwallis surrendered 8,000 men to General George Washington. So ended ground hostilities in Britain's former colonies. Today, Yorktown is a tourist attraction that features restored Colonial structures, the Yorktown battlefield, and museums.

While under British rule, Yorktown and other Colonial towns were part of a mercantile system. Colonies were expected to export to the mother country raw materials such as tobacco, timber, and sugar; in turn they would import manufactured goods such as iron tools, ceramics, and glassware. To maintain this system, England enacted laws and administrative policies that discouraged, and sometimes prohibited, certain kinds of manufactures in the Colonies. But the Colonists largely ignored these edicts, established factories, and concealed their activities from London.

As historical archaeologist Ivor Noël Hume remarked, "Factory operators, and even the Colonial governors went to considerable lengths to play down the importance of manufacturing projects and even to keep them out of the records altogether."[1] Thus, historical records hold only tiny hints of the vast amount of manufacturing that actually took place. Fortunately, traces of these activities abound in the archaeological record. And so it was at Yorktown, where archaeologists encountered the remains of one of the

FIGURE 5.1. Artist's conception of the Yorktown potter's large kiln (from Barka, Ayres, and Sheridan 1984).

Colonies' largest unrecorded pottery factories. Their work changed "existing conceptions about the history of technology and industry in colonial America," especially in the Southern Colonies.[2]

The first traces of the Yorktown pottery factory came to light accidently in 1957.[3] Digging a utility trench under Main Street, workers ran into a thin layer of earthenware and stoneware vessel fragments.[4] Although the pottery could have been made anywhere, perhaps even imported from England, the deposit also contained saggar fragments. A saggar is a ceramic container, usually a lidded box or cylinder, that holds vessels during firing, isolating them from the kiln's fuel. The saggar fragments strongly suggested that pottery had been made *nearby*. A decade later, an immense deposit of "wasters"—flawed vessels and fragments discarded by the potter—was discovered, clinching the case for local manufacture.

Finally, in 1970, testing in the vicinity of the waster pit under a modern garage encountered the remains of a huge, well-preserved kiln (Figure 5.1).[5] Rectangular in floor plan, the wood-fired kiln had a capacity of 310 cubic feet for stacking vessels and saggars.[6] Beyond demonstrating that pottery had been made at Yorktown in vast quantities, these finds held a surprise: the

stoneware—a kind of pottery fired at high temperature and very durable—
was "as good as any made in England."[7]

The historical record presented a different picture. In reports to England's
Board of Trade, William Gooch, lieutenant governor of Virginia, described
a "poor potter" who made only coarse earthenware. Year after year, Gooch
reported that this enterprise was of "little consequence" and did not threaten
ceramic imports from England.[8] On the basis of these reports, historians
would have learned nothing about the scale of pottery production or the
range and quality of the wares.

In a multistage project funded mainly by the National Park Service, historical archaeologists located and excavated the remains of a smaller kiln, the
main workshop and other structures, and several pits filled with wasters. A
date on one pottery fragment indicated that production had begun by 1720,
suggesting that the factory may have been the earliest producer of stoneware
in the Colonies.

Preliminary historical research identified the factory owner as William
Rogers. To learn about Rogers's life and his pottery business and to augment
the archaeological finds, Edward Ayres launched an uncommonly thorough
search for historical evidence. The major goal was to "learn more about the
pottery factory, its operation, its workers, and its customers."[9] In this project,
as in so many others, history would be archaeology's handmaiden.

In principle, the most reliable historical materials would have been
Rogers's personal papers and business records, but neither survived. Instead,
the most useful historical resources were York County records for the period 1700 to 1750. Researchers pored over wills, probate records, deeds, and
administrative and court documents, recording every reference to Rogers
and his associates as well as to pottery and pottery sales. They also examined
manuscript collections in Virginia libraries for letters, family papers, and so
forth. Ayres searched microfilm copies of the Public Record Office in England for information about Rogers's business activities. And in newspapers
from Virginia and nearby colonies, he sought ads for the factory's wares. Yet,
such prodigious efforts yielded only tidbits of useful information. Rogers
himself remained elusive, his factory a phantom.

William Rogers was likely born in England, perhaps to a family of brew-
ers. He arrived in Yorktown around 1710 and set up a brewery; the following year he purchased two adjacent lots.[10] During the next quarter century,

Rogers established many enterprises. He was not only a brewer but also "a merchant, manufacturer, ship owner, planter and contractor," and possessed additional properties in and around Yorktown, including a store and a waterfront warehouse.[11] In the 1730s he was a wealthy and respected member of Yorktown's middle class, whose prosperity depended largely on the labor of indentured white servants and enslaved Africans. At his death in 1739, Rogers owned more than two dozen slaves, and slaves may have been the factory's core work force.[12] By this time, Yorktown, though it only had a few hundred residents, was a busy port, receiving dozens of vessels annually from England.

The historical record holds only the occasional hint about Rogers's pottery business.[13] One find was the ledger of a local trader, John Mercer, who recorded that in 1725 he purchased hundreds of earthenware vessels from Rogers for just over £12.[14] Yorktown shipping records for 1725–35 indicate that exports of earthenware and stoneware exceeded imports, which hints at a substantial local industry.[15] The 1730 shipping records noted that the sloop *William and John*, owned by Rogers, set sail for Maryland with a cargo that included earthenware.[16] Mercer's ledger and the shipping records pertain to *wholesale* transactions, another indication that the factory was thriving and its products reaching far beyond Yorktown. In the "Inventory and Appraisal of William Rogers's Estate" much pottery is listed, including 312 quart mugs, 720 pint mugs, 132 milk pans, and 6 chamber pots. These quantities implicate a large-scale enterprise.[17] After Rogers's death, an ad in the *Virginia Gazette* shows that the factory, then being operated by his son-in-law, Thomas Reynolds, was still active.[18]

Nowhere in the historical record is there a word about the pottery factory itself, details of manufacture processes, or a list of the entire range of vessels produced. But the archaeological excavations were able to resolve these issues.

Even before the kiln and factory were discovered, Hume had offered inferences on the basis of the pottery that had already been found, including refuse from Yorktown's Swan Tavern.[19] This site yielded stoneware ale tankards with a swan decoration, clearly made for the tavern. The stoneware was slipped and "salt-glazed," meaning that during firing salt had been shoveled into the kiln, which combined with the clay and produced an orange-peel-like glaze. Great variation in the tankard handles indicated to Hume that several people of different skill levels had made and applied the handles.

Although the best-made stonewares rivaled those of European makers, many were underfired, overfired, off color, or had a very mottled appearance. But the potters exercised uniformly high skills in forming vessels on the wheel.

The wasters and other pottery from the factory site yielded an inventory of vessel forms and furnished information on manufacture processes.[20] Employing many illustrations, the archaeologists showed how the vessels were made and also described use of the kilns, whose design most resembled seventeenth- and eighteenth-century kilns excavated in London.[21] There were 16 lead-glazed, earthenware forms, including basins, bowls, and crocks of several sizes, as well as porringer, platter, colander, and birdhouse bottle. Stoneware was made in at least seven forms: mug (tankards), pipkin, bottle, storage jar, bowl, crock, and chamber pot. Several forms were present in different sizes. Significantly, by making these varied forms, the factory could meet essentially all of the Colonists' utilitarian pottery needs.[22] And exports were important, as sherds of Rogers's wares have been found as far north as New England.

Thanks to the fieldwork of historical archaeologists, Rogers's pottery vessels and their manufacture processes, as well as several factory structures, are now known in detail.[23] These investigations have documented a successful industrial enterprise that promoted self-sufficiency in ceramics and was allowed to flourish under the benign governorship of Gooch. This was precisely the sort of industrial activity that London feared most because it threatened the mercantile system. Attempts to suppress Colonial economic ventures eventually helped to foment the Revolution, whose hostilities on land ended with Washington's triumph at Yorktown, once home to the "poor potter." The discovery of Rogers's factory, along with archaeological studies of other phantom factories, has promoted significant revisions of Southern Colonial history.

6

Nuclear Archaeology in the Nevada Desert

IN 1938 AUSTRIAN PHYSICIST Lise Meitner and her German colleague Otto Hahn showed that certain radioactive elements spontaneously fission into daughter elements and liberate energy. This momentous but unexpected discovery of nuclear fission excited scientific communities around the world. Physicists in Germany, the United Kingdom, and the United States also recognized an ominous possibility: nuclear fission could be harnessed in a bomb that would convert a minute amount of matter into an enormous amount of energy, as per Einstein's famous equation ($E=mc^2$). The destructive power of an atomic bomb was almost too immense to contemplate.

Fearing that Germany was developing an atomic bomb, Einstein and others urged the United States to build one first and use it to end the war. In 1942, President Roosevelt authorized a top-secret project to do just that in collaboration with the United Kingdom. The administrative head of what became known as the Manhattan Project was General Leslie Groves, an engineer who had supervised construction of the Pentagon. The scientific director was J. Robert Oppenheimer, a brilliant nuclear physicist at the University of California, Berkeley. Under this odd couple's leadership, the Manhattan Project took shape in a remote area of northern New Mexico called Los Alamos, which rapidly became a small city. The goal was to produce two bombs that could be dropped on Germany. If all went well, one bomb would use uranium-235 to be produced at Oak Ridge, Tennessee. The other would use plutonium to be generated at the Hanford plant in Washington State.

Far more than $1 billion (in early 1940s dollars) was spent on the Manhattan Project, which eventually produced the bombs but not in time to punish an already-defeated Germany. Confident that the uranium bomb would work, Los Alamos researchers did not test it before dropping it on Japan. However, there was less certainty about the plutonium bomb and its devilishly complicated detonator; and so it had to be tested first at home. After being hoisted atop a tower, the plutonium bomb was set off in July 1945 in southern New Mexico. Code-named Trinity, the explosion excavated a large crater and turned desert sand into pieces of green, mildly radioactive glass known to mineral collectors as trinitite. To discourage collecting, the government filled the crater and prohibited unauthorized entry. Although the Trinity site is a National Historic Landmark on the White Sands Missile Range, it is open to tourist visits only one or two days a year.[1] Trinity was the first and last nuclear test at this location.[2]

At the beginning of the Cold War in the immediate postwar period, nuclear bombs were tested in lagoons at the Bikini and Kwajalein atolls in the Pacific. These explosions measured the effects of above- and below-water blasts on a variety of American, Japanese, and German warships and on the living animals they contained.[3] Not surprisingly, these atoll locations had logistical, security, and weather problems, and forced the removal of hundreds of native islanders who could never return home. Searching for a more appropriate site, the Atomic Energy Commission settled on a vast U.S. Air Force property in the desert of southern Nevada. Now called the Nevada National Security Site, the area hosted the detonation of almost 1,000 nuclear weapons and the testing of other experimental nuclear technologies.

Although many billions of dollars were spent on such secret projects during the height of the Cold War, ordinary Americans still have little knowledge of the activities carried out there, much less what remains of them on and in the ground. Fortunately, archaeology has begun to penetrate the shroud of secrecy surrounding the material culture of these nuclear projects.

Because no bomb tests have been carried out since 1992, the government has contracted with Nevada's Desert Research Institute (DRI) for cultural resource surveys on the Nevada National Security Site. Pioneers of nuclear archaeology, UC Berkeley-trained archaeologist Colleen M. Beck and her colleagues have been conducting surveys and recording remains of nuclear-related activities. Research includes investigations of atmospheric and underground nuclear blasts, experiments to assess radiation effects on materials and structures, and tests of nonweapon technologies. Beck emphasizes that these investigations furnish "an opportunity to document a class of historic constructions that, for the most part, are either unique or limited to only a few locations in the world."[4]

For underground tests, bombs were placed near the ends of horizontal or, more commonly, vertical bore holes. At several blast sites, the archaeologists recorded a crater, towers, foundations, and assorted electrical cables.[5] One blast site was accompanied by an amazing number of support facilities. Known as the Rainier Event, in 1957 it was "the first fully contained underground nuclear explosion in the world."[6] At the Rainier site, the DRI archaeologists described and photographed 21 structures and 20 features inside and outside the horizontal tunnel complex, including railroad tracks, fuel tank, high voltage area, electrical panel, communication trailer, compressor station, generators, and the drill holes.

Although some sites of atmospheric tests had been cleaned up and reused, many structures remain, as in one area of Frenchman Flat where the crew recorded 157 structures. Among the frequent features were "metal stanchions embedded in square cement blocks" at ground zeroes. These stanchions supported towers to which bombs were tethered.[7] Researchers also found underground bunkers as well as metal towers that held instrumentation.[8] Beck notes that the earliest bunkers suffered blast damage, but later ones were more robust.

Perhaps the most curious remains were those of the "Japanese Village," a cluster of Japanese-style houses, fitted with dosimeters, which measured the radiation-shielding effects of structures. The project aimed to provide Japanese biomedical researchers with information about the likely long-term effects of radiation exposure from the Hiroshima and Nagasaki blasts. The archaeologists found and recorded the wood-frame skeletons of several surviving structures.[9]

Although nuclear weapons testing created an abundant archaeological record in the Nevada desert, one nonweapon project left behind a treasure trove of intact concrete buildings along with some original contents. Project Rover ran from 1955 to 1973 at a cost of $1.45 billion when the United States and the Soviet Union were competing for preeminence in rocketry and space-exploration technologies.[10] The project's expected product was a nuclear-thermal engine capable of propelling a rocket.

Already envisioned during the late 1940s, the basic operating principles of a nuclear-thermal engine are simple.[11] Because a nuclear reactor's core generates a massive amount of heat, it can raise the temperature of hydrogen flowing through it to more than 2,000 degrees C. When liquid hydrogen is pumped through the reactor's hot core, it vaporizes immediately, expands enormously, and escapes through a nozzle producing great thrust.

Much optimism surrounded Project Rover. Calculations showed that such an engine might cut travel time or permit a heavier payload than engines fueled by chemical reactions. And unlike the solid-fuel chemical engines of the time, a nuclear-thermal engine could in principle be started, stopped, and restarted. However, the engine would also spew radioactive gas, so it could not serve as a rocket's first stage.

Although a nuclear engine's basic operating principles are simple, embodying them in functioning hardware turned out to be difficult. Project Rover spawned a vast array of new apparatus and kinds of structures, which included four massive building complexes at the Nevada National Security Site.

Project Rover's earliest stage, about 1959–64, was called Kiwi, referencing New Zealand's flightless bird, for these reactors would be earth-bound and only used to tweak reactor designs. The Phoebus stage, lasting from about 1965 to 1968, created a generation of powerful and sophisticated engines.[12]

Reactors and engines were designed and built at Los Alamos and, especially in later years, at contractors' facilities. Testing took place in an area of the Nevada National Security Site called Jackass Flats. DRI archaeologists, assisted by an architect, architectural historian, and professional photographer, recorded the four structure complexes and their contents, in some cases before anticipated decontamination and demolition.

The earliest structure, named R-MAD (Reactor Maintenance and Disassembly), was built in 1958 for the Kiwi project and was in relatively good condition when the DRI crew visited. R-MAD contained "offices, shops, restrooms, assembly and disassembly bays, hot cells, viewing galleries, and work stations." Much original equipment survived, including electronics-intensive control rooms and workstations, the heating and cooling system, and a cavernous hot room with equipment for disassembling the highly radioactive reactors after testing.[13] The researchers described and photographed R-MAD inside and out and crafted a generously illustrated report that includes historic photographs and floor plans. On April 8, 2010, R-MAD was demolished.[14]

Phoebus activities took place mainly in a new facility, E-MAD (Engine Maintenance and Disassembly), opened in 1965. E-MAD and ancillary structures contained much original equipment, including giant manipulator arms

FIGURE 6.1. Moving the Phoenix 2A nuclear engine, 1968 (courtesy of Los Alamos National Laboratory).

in the disassembly area, the master control center with electronics, several rooms with control panels, and a machine shop with tools.[15] There was also a locomotive and special rail car for transporting completed engines to and from the test cell 2 miles away (Figure 6.1).

The DRI crew also surveyed Test Cells A and C, where reactors and engines underwent testing and periods of high-power operation. Test Cell A consisted of the main building and more than a dozen support structures, including a bunker, tank farm, and an enormous dewar (vacuum flask) for holding liquid hydrogen. The DRI report contains room-by-room artifact inventories, descriptions of the architecture and remaining equipment, maps and drawings of the entire complex, and stunning photographs. This complex is remarkable, essentially a time capsule that has revealed many on-the-ground details about the first reactor tests.

Built in 1961, Test Cell C was larger and had expanded capabilities. During its lifetime, Test Cell C underwent many additions and modifications, in part to handle newer reactor and engine designs. After Project Rover ended, the U.S. Geological Survey reused Test Cell C for the Yucca Mountain Project, and in the 1990s the military used it "to practice infiltration and urban warfare tactics."[16] The survey of Test Cell C focused on the main structure where, despite later uses, some Project Rover equipment remained.[17]

Engine tests at Test Cells A and C were conducted next to the main buildings. However, the possibility of an explosion from a runaway reactor, plus the dangers of radioactive exhaust, required that the tests be operated remotely. The Remote Control Point, a building complex almost 2 miles away, received data from instruments in the test cells, conveyed by cables through a tunnel. These precautions paid off. In one test, turbulence caused parts of the reactor core to be ejected, spewing radioactive materials and contaminating the immediate area. Fortunately, no one was hurt.[18]

Throughout its existence, Project Rover was about research and development, with no firm applications agreed to by federal agencies, Congress, and presidents from Eisenhower through Nixon. Some advocated it as the third stage of a Saturn V rocket; others suggested that it could be used in a spacecraft for ferrying people and supplies between an earth-orbiting space station and a lunar base.[19] None of these proposed missions led to a consensus by decision-makers. With no definite mission, strained budgets at the height of the Vietnam War, and the availability of powerful chemical engines, Project Rover was terminated in 1973 before an engine could be tried out on a rocket.

The Nevada National Security Site also includes the notorious Area 51, where some people believe the U.S. government has squirreled away the body of a space alien recovered from a crash site near Roswell, New Mexico.[20] Ironically, the top-secret activities that took place at the Nevada National Security Site, as in the testing of nuclear bombs and Project Rover, were almost as bizarre as keeping a supposed alien in cold storage.

The historical record of the nuclear-related projects is extensive, yet access to many documents is still restricted. The books and articles written on the basis of available documents provide incomplete information about the material culture of these projects and their archaeological aftermath. Fortunately, these projects left behind a rich archaeological record that Colleen M. Beck and her colleagues at DRI have been investigating and recording. Their studies not only complement historical accounts but also preserve disappearing evidence: like R-MAD, many sites are slated for decontamination and destruction, despite their historical significance. Without archaeological surveys of these remains, our understanding of the material culture and landscapes of these fascinating and expensive Cold War projects would remain hidden behind the gates of the Nevada National Security Site.

I thank Colleen M. Beck for providing reports of nuclear archaeology.

III

Enhancing Cultural Tourism and Heritage Awareness

FOR CENTURIES, travelers, adventurers, curiosity-seekers, and people on the "grand tour" have visited impressive archaeological sites such as the Giza pyramids of Egypt, the colosseum of Rome, the Parthenon of Athens, and Stonehenge. Prior to the late twentieth century, cultural tourism was available mainly to people of ample means; now it can be enjoyed by the middle classes in many countries. Cultural tourists travel to take part in structured experiences focused on archaeological sites that celebrate heritage, both at home and abroad. It has also become big business: more than a million people visit some sites annually, and cultural tourism in some countries provides an important income stream. Not surprisingly, governments around the globe are investing resources to enhance such tourism and heritage awareness.

There are many approaches to transforming an archaeological site into a place that materializes heritage, ranging from partial excavation and display of the preserved parts to total reconstruction of a building formerly without surface remains. Structures may also contain artifact displays or be accompanied by a museum.

Heritage sites usually convey ideological messages, which can become highly contentious.[1] For example, at the home of an early American president should the slave quarters be reconstructed or should visitors be spared knowledge of the living conditions of enslaved Africans? In ideal cases, archaeologists are consulted when these decisions are made. In any event, archaeological (and sometimes historical) investigations unearth the evidence needed to design reconstructions and museum displays.

George and Martha Washington's Virginia plantation, Mount Vernon, features reconstructions of eighteenth-century buildings, including slave quarters, blacksmith shop, and a distillery. Producing rye whiskey, the distillery was one of Washington's little-known yet very successful enterprises. Although the distillery records survived, the building itself did not. Mount

Vernon archaeologists located its remains and excavated the entire footprint, revealing construction details as well as placement of internal features such as furnaces that heated the stills. The archaeological finds along with historical evidence made it possible to reconstruct the distillery. Today, tourists can view its operations and, on occasion, buy its pricey products.

Kourion is a large site on the island of Cyprus founded by Greeks around the eleventh century BC. Its later Roman occupation was brought to a close in the fourth century AD by a massive earthquake. Archaeological excavations have taken place there since the 1930s, revealing houses of the elite, an amphitheater, and the Temple of Apollo. The remains of one sumptuous house, that of a certain Eustolios, is protected by a roof, and elevated ramps enable tourists to see the stunning mosaic floors. The reconstructed amphitheater invites tourists to watch performances of Classic Greek plays. In the 1980s archaeologist David Soren's excavations in the "earthquake house" revealed a touching death scene of a mule and young girl crushed by stuctural debris. Although the earthquake house was partially reconstructed, the Cyprus Department of Antiquities ignored archaeological inferences and roofed the house's largest room with an entirely modern tile design.

Stonehenge has been for many centuries a magnet for tourists and researchers. Early antiquarians and then archaeologists have tackled the many mysteries of the big stones. Detailed maps, excavations among the stones, and archaeological surveys of the surrounding countryside have solved some mysteries. Construction episodes have been dated, sources of the stones have been pinpointed, and techniques of erecting and joining the stones identified; Stonehenge has also been situated in a dynamic regional system. But why it was built and remodeled and how it was used over time all remain controversial issues. Recently, the site's immediate environment has been given a makeover to enhance the tourist experience: noisy roads have been rerouted or eliminated, and the bucolic surroundings now host grazing sheep. A new visitor center at some distance from the stones contains attractive exhibits that enable tourists to see excavated artifacts and learn about the latest finds and interpretations.

7

Mount Vernon and George Washington's Whiskey Distillery

AFTER HIS SECOND TERM as president ended in 1797, George Washington returned to Mount Vernon, the plantation that had been in the Washington family since 1674.[1] Facing the Potomac River just south of Alexandria, Virginia, the Mount Vernon mansion was the headquarters of a large and diversified enterprise, including a gristmill and distillery. After George and Martha died, however, the new owners failed to maintain the estate. By the mid-nineteenth century, the mansion had fallen into disrepair and many outbuildings were in ruins.

Sailing on the Potomac River in 1853, Mrs. Robert Cunningham noticed that the first president's home was in terrible shape. She was a South Carolinian who had been born in Alexandria, Virginia, and whose father and grandfather belonged to the same church as George Washington.[2] Disturbed by the sight, she impressed upon her daughter, Ann Pamela Cunningham, the urgency of saving it for the country. The younger Cunningham learned that the property was owned by a great-grandnephew of George who offered to sell 200 acres, including the mansion, for $200,000.

To coordinate fundraising efforts, Cunningham founded the Mount Vernon Ladies Association of the Union, the country's first organization dedicated to historic preservation.[3] She recruited a national network of preservation-minded women—"Lady Managers"—who helped the Association secure funds to buy the property. Beyond saving the mansion, the Association's goal was to preserve it so that Americans could see where the great general and statesman had lived and died. By the early twentieth century,

the Association's goals embraced restoration of the plantation to 1799, the
year of Washington's death. Today, the Association operates Mount Vernon
as a tourist attraction and a center for research on Washington's life as one
of Virginia's wealthiest planters and entrepreneurs.

During his long tenure at Mount Vernon, Washington increased the
holdings to about 8,000 acres, which included five farms: Mansion, Muddy
Hole, Dogue Run, Union, and River. In addition to the mansion, gardens,
and fields, the Mansion Farm had about two dozen buildings. Of these, 12
structures near the mansion, along with the stable and the Washingtons'
tombs, survived into the twentieth century but required restoration. Many
other important structures were essentially gone, including the greenhouse/
slave-quarter complex, blacksmith shop, and coach house. And, about three
miles away, at the Gristmill complex, the mill itself, miller's cottage, cooperage, and whiskey distillery no longer stood.

The Association has pursued a long-term program of restoration and
reconstruction. Perhaps aware of the excavations at Jamestown and Colonial
Williamsburg, the Association recognized that before reconstructing a vanished structure, archaeology could help discern its footprint and construction details; excavations might even turn up artifacts and features related
to its use.

The first intensive archaeological investigations at the Mansion Farm
began in 1931 under the direction of Morley Jeffers Williams, a landscape
architect and Harvard professor.[4] He uncovered traces of four outbuildings
razed by Washington during a major renovation in 1775 and several structures
erected after Washington's death. Williams was a careful excavator who documented his work with photographs and detailed drawings but left Mount
Vernon in 1939 before completing his program.

Two years later, Walter M. Macomber, an architect who had worked
at Colonial Williamsburg, excavated at the sites of the greenhouse/slave-
quarter complex, furnishing useful information for their restoration. The
greenhouse, incidentally, had heating ducts below the floor that allowed
Washington's exotic plants to survive in winter.

Macomber's excavations at the blacksmith shop embroiled him in a
battle with the Association. He believed that the structure had been built
on a brick foundation, but his interpretations of the archaeological evidence
left Association officials unconvinced. Given the uncertainties about major

construction details, the Association decided not to restore the blacksmith shop at that time. Macomber was miffed by this decision and quit.

The Association resumed archaeological work in the mid-1980s, contracting with Virginia's Historic Landmarks Commission for a survey of Mount Vernon as well as test excavations. Under the direction of Alain C. Outlaw, the Blacksmith Shop was revisited. Some work was also done at several other sites, including a refuse-rich cellar in the slave quarter.

In 1987, the Association established an in-house archaeology program staffed with professionals. The Archaeology Department defined its mission as research "aimed at providing information helpful in refining the organization's restoration and educational efforts."[5]

In the Archaeology Department's first project, excavations were resumed on the oft-probed remains of the Blacksmith Shop. It turned out that Macomber's inferences were flawed: the structure was not supported by a brick foundation but by timbers.[6] The new findings, including traces of two corner posts, at last furnished crucial evidence for restoring the Blacksmith Shop and ended decades of dispute.

Esther White, who became Director of the Archaeology Department in 1994, led an ambitious project at the site of Washington's whiskey distillery, a little-known but significant enterprise.[7] Historical research showed that the distillery, with 50 wooden mash tubs (hogshead barrels) and five stills, was an industrial-scale operation—perhaps the largest in the United States at that time.

In 1797, Washington hired a new plantation manager, Scottish immigrant James Anderson. He was also an experienced distiller and hatched the idea for the distillery, which Washington agreed to fund. At this time, the elder statesman was trying to simplify Mount Vernon's diversified enterprises. Those enterprises included fishing, growing grains, making flour, raising cattle, and providing stud services. Washington sought to create greater cash flow while lessening dependence on enslaved workers. A profitable whiskey distillery might contribute to these goals.

After being housed briefly in the cooperage, the distillery was enlarged and moved to a new stone building measuring 75 by 30 feet. It was immediately profitable, producing 11,000 gallons in 1799 that yielded about £600. But it consumed so much corn and rye that some grain had to be bought from outside sources. In the end, the distillery reduced neither the complexity

of Mount Vernon's operations nor the need for slaves. After Washington's
death, the distillery limped along until 1814, when it burned. Afterwards,
the masonry was scavenged for nearby houses, and the structure's remains
entered the archaeological record.

In 1932 the state of Virginia purchased the Gristmill complex. The gristmill and miller's cottage were excavated and reconstructed. Although the
distillery was partially excavated, plans for restoration were dropped because
temperance advocates were hostile to the idea, refusing to call attention to—
or even acknowledge—Washington's close association with whiskey.[8] When
the Association received the property from Virginia in 1997, it revived the
vision of a reconstructed distillery, perhaps one that could actually exhibit
whiskey-making processes.

As archaeologist Eleanor Breen noted, distilling processes were well represented in industry manuals of the early nineteenth century.[9] These works
pinpoint the major processes and their associated features: fermenting grains
in mash tubs set on a vibration-free surface, heating the fermented mash in
copper pots with a furnace, capturing the alcohol-rich gas and running it
through a condensation coil, packaging the resultant liquid in barrels, and
then storing the barrels on site for later transport.

Complementing information in the manuals were "weekly work reports,
ledgers, and other documents specific to George Washington's Distillery."[10]
These yielded insights into actual practice, such as labor requirements, grain
consumption, and whiskey production. Esther White calculated the ingredients in Washington's rye whiskey—his primary product—on the basis of
grain quantities consumed by the distillery: 60% rye, 35% corn, 5% malted
barley.[11]

The rich historical information inspired optimism that the Association
could eventually rebuild the distillery building, furnish it with period-
appropriate equipment, and operate it effectively. Missing from the documents, however, were essential details about the building's construction,
locations of features such as furnaces and stills, and the know-how for actually making whiskey. And there was a lack of comparative archaeological
material. After surveying the property, locating the distillery, and conducting
test excavations, the archaeologists concluded that the site was reasonably
well preserved and could be reconstructed—after extensive excavation.

Grants from the Distilled Spirits Council of the United States and the
Wine and Spirits Wholesalers of America supported large-scale excavations

from 2001 to 2005.[12] The project unearthed the entire footprint of the distillery building as well as adjacent areas—a total of 4,500 square feet. A vast body of evidence was generated for the proposed reconstruction.[13]

As for the structure itself, intact foundations around 3 feet thick were identified on the south and west sides. A single course of masonry survived on the south side, revealing rough-shaped sandstone blocks mortared in a wall 2 feet thick. Workers also found part of a masonry partition that had divided the building into two sections. The smaller section, 15 feet wide, was subdivided by a wooden partition, probably into a storage area and office. A paved area of stone and bricks on the floor seems to have been the foundation for the stairway leading to a second floor where grain was stored and several workers lived. By spatially plotting the artifacts recovered from a looter's trench, the archaeologists approximated the location of the upstairs living quarters.[14] Another portion of the main floor was paved with large cobbles to create a stable surface for the mash barrels.

With the exception of a few tiny metal pieces, no distillation equipment was found. After all, the valuable copper stills and condensation coils would have been salvaged after the fire or scavenged later. But the archaeologists did find remains of distillation-related features. Two furnaces, each of which heated two stills, were represented by brick foundations showing evidence of prolonged burning. A burned area lacking brick was interpreted as the trace of a furnace that had heated a lone still. The stills' locations were confirmed by the discovery of part of the "plumbing" system that provided water for the wooden tubs holding the condensation coils. Although the intake troughs left no trace, the excavators did find five subfloor drainage troughs that led outside from the stills. Supplying hot water for cooking the mash required a separate steam boiler and furnace. Evidence of this feature consisted of a large burned zone and brick impressions adjacent to the likely location of the mash barrels.

Despite ample historical and archaeological evidence, the distillery's reconstruction required the working out of hundreds of details. Deciding on these details—sometimes just educated guesses—engaged archaeologists, historians, historical architects, and distillers in many discussions.[15] Carpenters and masons executed the final design, which was paid for by "leaders of the liquor industry" eager to set the record straight about Washington and alcohol.[16] Some design compromises were made to comply with local regulations, such as providing an elevator to reach the second story, heating

FIGURE 7.1. Reconstructed furnace and distillation apparatus, Mount Vernon, Virginia (photo by the author).

the steam boiler with electricity, and using smaller stills to make room for fire-brick insulation (Figure 7.1).[17] In addition, a large part of the second story is devoted, not to storage, but to a museum that includes many large displays of images and texts prepared by archaeologists.

Even with the building and equipment in place and the ingredients known, making whiskey with eighteenth-century processes required trial runs under the guidance of master distiller David Pickerell. Failures eventually gave way to success, as the Mount Vernon workers acquired the necessary know-how.[18] The happy result was a functioning distillery, although its capacity was much below that of the original—owing to the smaller stills and the arduous labor required. No reconstruction can perfectly replicate the past, but the one at Mount Vernon is a good facsimile of an eighteenth-century distillery.

The building was dedicated by Prince Andrew, Duke of York, on September 27, 2006, and opened to visitors the following spring, accompanied by a barrage of media coverage, orchestrated by the liquor industry. Media attention continues to this day.

At the first public offering of Mount Vernon rye, 470 bottles sold briskly at $85 each. In a 2014 holiday sale, two varieties were available in 375-ml bottles: George Washington's Straight Rye Whiskey, aged two years, $185; and George Washington's Rye Whiskey, unaged, $95.[19] Opinions about the taste of the unaged liquor range from "swill" to a "spirit brimming with notes of fresh grain, peppery spice and a touch of dried herbs."[20] Contradictory opinions about the product aside, the Mount Vernon distillery lets tourists see a unique reenactment of late eighteenth-century processes for making rye whiskey, which materializes a little-known facet of George Washington's wide-ranging activities.

Mount Vernon archaeologists continue to embark on new projects, expanding our knowledge of the Washingtons' material life and those of their employees and slaves. As in the case of the distillery, all restorations, reconstructions, and museum exhibits are as authentic as possible, built on a foundation of rigorous historical and archaeological research. Not surprisingly, the carefully interpreted workings of America's most famous plantation attract droves of domestic and foreign tourists—around a million annually.

I thank Mount Vernon archaeologists Esther White, Eleanor Breen, and Luke Pecoraro for sharing information and insights, and showing me the gristmill and distillery. Esther White provided comments on an earlier draft.

8

Kourion, a Roman Town in Cyprus

ABOVE EPISKOPI BAY, on the southwestern coast of Cyprus, lies the ancient site of Kourion. Founded by Greek settlers around the eleventh century BC and dominated by a succession of empires, including the Persian and Egyptian, Kourion finally fell under Rome's hegemony in the first century AD. Kourion was a prosperous Greco-Roman city-kingdom until a massive earthquake destroyed it in the fourth century. Parts of the sprawling city were resettled and Christianized, but much of Kourion remained buried except for a large amphitheater and clusters of columns indicating collapsed structures. Beneath the surface is an unusually intact record of life and death in a Roman city, somewhat comparable to Pompeii—the clichéd "moment frozen in time."

Although several authors of antiquity had mentioned Kourion, archaeologists did not "discover" the site until the mid-nineteenth century and conducted no major excavations. In the 1930s and 1940s, a team from the University of Pennsylvania Museum (UPM) exposed and identified many structures, some of which have well-preserved mosaic floors of great beauty and cultural significance. Leading the UPM team were J. F. Daniel and George McFadden, the latter a wealthy enthusiast and patron of archaeology. In Episkopi, the modern village closest to Kourion, McFadden built a large house that served as a base of operations and later became the Episkopi Museum.

The UPM's excavations included extensive work at the Sanctuary of Apollo (a multistructure complex that includes the Temple of Apollo Hylates), the amphitheater, the House of Achilles, and the stadium. Also

FIGURE 8.1. Mosaic floor in the house of Eustolios, Kourion, Cyprus (Wikimedia Commons; Wknight94, photographer).

excavated were a Christian basilica and the House of Eustolios, both of which had post-earthquake occupation.[1] Later excavations by M. Loulloupis uncovered, among other finds, the House of the Gladiators. The houses' evocative names derived from images and inscriptions in the mosaics. For centuries, visitors had passed through Kourion, but after these archaeological discoveries and their interpretations were publicized, Kourion became one of Cyprus's most important tourist attractions.

Catering to the growing tourist traffic, the Cyprus Department of Antiquities embarked on an ambitious program of restoration, reconstruction, and public display of the more spectacular finds. First to be tackled, in 1961, was the amphitheater, which became a venue for Greek and Shakespearean plays, as well as other activities that continue to this day. The house of Eustolios, which boasts stunning mosaic floors, was too large for reconstruction, and so a roof was erected over most of it (Figure 8.1). From an elevated walkway, visitors can view the wall stubs and mosaics. Owing to the mosaics' images and inscriptions, the house of Eustolios, named for the wealthy Christian who built it, is a modern shrine to early Christianity. The Temple of Apollo was partially reconstructed on the basis of David Soren's excavations in the 1970s.

Beginning with his work on the Temple of Apollo, Soren became hooked on "seismic archaeology," especially intrigued by the possibility that Kourion "is a moment in time frozen and preserved, like a snapshot."[2] Reading through field diaries from the UPM project, he learned that the excavators had found two human skeletons, whom they named Romeo and Juliet, pinned to the floor by structural debris and caught in an eternal embrace. Perhaps other finds would be as fascinating.

The UPM project also recovered many Roman coins, the latest of which was dated to AD 365. Roman coins do not bear calendar dates, per se, but include the heads of Roman rulers, inscriptions, and traces of the mint. Numismatists have correlated these features with historical records and fashioned a coin chronology. When emperors had short reigns, as in the case of Valens, whose visage is on the latest Kourion coins, the date can be fixed precisely—in this case 365.[3] If the sample of coins is large enough, it can be inferred that the earthquake occurred at or shortly after this date. Fastening on 365, Soren scoured the writings of antiquity, seeking to link Kourion's destruction to an earthquake of known date described by ancient chroniclers.

In the writings of Ammianus Marcellinus, Soren learned about an earthquake that struck the eastern Mediterranean on July 21, 365, causing a tidal wave that killed many thousands of people. Soren hypothesized that this was the quake that destroyed Kourion. His hypothesis did not fare well at first, for most archaeologists believed that Kourion had been destroyed earlier in the century. Convinced that his hypothesis was correct ("I knew I was right; all I needed was a little excavational luck.") Soren set to work raising funds and securing a permit for excavations to begin in 1984.[4] His applications were well received because, regardless of when the quake occurred, Kourion's sealed deposits with human remains presented a unique opportunity to learn about daily life and health in a fourth-century Greco-Roman city.

With funding and the precious permit in hand, Soren and his multidisciplinary team set up camp at the Episkopi Museum. The first task in the field was to relocate UPM's Trench III, which had exposed Romeo and Juliet. Surely, similar deposits would lie nearby and hold additional surprises. A map made by the UPM project's architect provided the crucial information, and Trench III was found on the *first day* of fieldwork. So far, Soren was enjoying "excavational luck."

Expanding Trench III, the crew encountered room after room of a large house, laden with artifacts and more quake victims. One room, used as a makeshift stable, held another heart-rending death scene. A 13-year-old girl had been tending to a mule when the quake struck; both mule and girl were crushed and buried by masonry debris. Soren made the most of this find because publicizing the discovery could help attract more funding and perhaps ensure renewal of the permit. The University of Arizona, then his home institution, issued press releases that led to articles in dozens of newspapers across the country including the *New York Times*. Continued funding and permits were forthcoming.

Soren, my colleague at Arizona, invited me to join his Kourion crew in 1985, and I agreed to participate. When I arrived, excavation was already underway in Room 8, part of a large structure called the "Earthquake House."[5] Immediately visible in Room 8 was a baulk (a vertical section of the original deposit that could be studied after the rest of the room had been excavated). The baulk contained a jumble of roof and wall debris, including mud brick, limestone blocks, odd pieces of cement and mortar, nails, and ceramic roof tiles—most them shattered.

Soren mentioned that there was interest in reconstructing at least part of the house, especially Room 8, and perhaps turning it into a museum. Accordingly, he tasked me with inferring the roof's appearance, its completeness, and whether the house had more than one story. The deposits in the baulk indicated the lack of a second floor, but did not answer the other questions; perhaps the roof tiles could. It was necessary to approach these like any pottery assemblage, making inferences on the basis of measurements of whole tiles, counts of fragments, and traces on the tiles' surfaces.

Tiles there came in two varieties: immense flat ones (53.5 cm by 45.0 cm) and long, narrow curved ones (ca. 52 cm long). Patterns of mortar traces as well as impressions in mortar fragments indicated how the tiles had been arranged on the roof. Covered with vertically overlapping flat tiles, the roof originally rose from two sides to a peak. The ridge at the top was heavily mortared and covered by a line of curved tiles. Curved tiles also covered the horizontal joins of adjacent flat tiles.

To learn if Room 8 had been completely roofed, the number of flat tiles had to be estimated. The lower right and lower left corners of broken flat tiles were counted, and the counts agreed closely (268 and 275). Taking into

account the roof's pitch as well as the vertical overlaps of flat tiles, I concluded that the roof had been fully tiled.[6]

Employing these inferences about the roof as well as plan drawings and
the artifacts found in Room 8, artist David Vandenberg fashioned a cut-away
painting of the room, showing both the interior and roof, that was reasonably
faithful to the archaeological findings.[7]

After Soren's excavations at Kourion ended in 1987, the Cyprus Department of Antiquities reconstructed Room 8. However, the roof departed
greatly from Vandenberg's painting. Instead of employing large flat tiles and
long curved tiles, as had the original builders, the restorers used only short
curved tiles in the modern overlap-underlap pattern. Perhaps they were un-
willing or unable to commission manufacturers to mold tiles in unfamiliar
sizes and shapes.

Archaeologists are conflicted about reconstructions and restorations.
On the one hand, these places enhance the tourist experience by translating
our inferences into the tangible expression of a structure's appearance in its
prime, as in Kourion's amphitheater. On the other hand, Room 8 at Kourion
demonstrates that the translation process may be imperfect. Restorations
and reconstructions may not be authentic in details that archaeologists insist
are important. Although the rebuilt roof of Room 8 was entirely modern in
design, tourists—if they bothered to look at the roof—might view the restoration favorably. And when the audience in Kourion's amphitheater attends
the performance of a Greek tragedy, they care not whether the restoration
is accurate but are captivated by the feeling of being transported back to
the time of Aeschylus or Euripides. To spur tourism, government agencies
around the world continue to authorize reconstructions and restorations,
and archaeologists continue to carp about inaccuracies.

After reconstruction, Room 8 underwent additional changes. It first became a mini-museum, displaying artifacts and skeletal remains recovered
from the Earthquake House. At some point, however, the room was closed to
the public and its contents transferred to the Kourion Museum in Episkopi.
Room 8 is now used for storage.[8]

And what about Soren's hypothesis that Kourion's destruction took place
in AD 365? His project found around 200 more coins, whose latest dates
are consistent with the original hypothesis. Some geologists now propose
that the Kourion quake actually took place a decade or two later, yet I find
Soren's arguments and archaeological evidence persuasive.[9] Regardless

of the fate of this hypothesis, Soren's broader conjecture—that Kourion's undisturbed deposits hold a wealth of evidence of daily life—was amply confirmed during the project's four field seasons. Not only did he expose the Earthquake House with its many artifacts of daily life and skeletons but nearby he also found and partially excavated an outdoor market.

Despite the loss of the onsite display of finds from the Earthquake House, Kourion is now an official archaeological park and offers tourists satisfying displays of excavated structures. According to the Cyprus Tourism Organisation, Kourion is "The most impressive archaeological site on the island."[10] This judgment finds support in independent travel guidebooks, including *Frommer's Cyprus Day by Day*.[11]

I thank David Soren for helpful discussions.

9

The World Heritage Site of Stonehenge

A UNIQUE CLUSTER of big stones on the Salisbury Plain in southern England, Stonehenge has entranced tourists for centuries. In 1698, Frenchman Henri Misson de Valbourg wrote in his travelogue of the British Isles that Stonehenge "is worth a Man's while to go a great Journey to see."[1] Samuel Johnson in 1783 noted, "When you enter the building and cast your eyes around upon the yawning ruins, you are struck into an extatic [sic] reverie."[2] Even Americans were impressed. Writing to his wife Olivia, in 1873, Samuel Clemens (Mark Twain) observed that Stonehenge "is one of the most mysterious & satisfactory ruins I have ever seen."[3]

Visitors to Stonehenge have long asked questions such as: who built it and when? Where were the big stones quarried and how were they shaped, transported, and erected? And, of course, why was Stonehenge built, and what did people do there?

An inquisitive visitor of earlier times might have sought answers in the writings of antiquarians. Learned men and enthusiasts, antiquarians documented and investigated sites of historical and archaeological interest. In the era before professional archaeology, antiquarians were archaeologists in all but name, and many of their publications remain useful. Antiquarians mapped Stonehenge many times, excavated among the stones, recorded neighboring sites and features, and pored over old manuscripts trying to identify the builders. At the end of the nineteenth century, antiquarian ideas about Stonehenge were summarized for tourists in John Sprules's book, *The Visitor's Illustrated Pocket-Guide to Stonehenge and the Salisbury Plain*.[4]

During the twentieth century, many professional archaeologists excavated at Stonehenge and surveyed its surroundings, answering several questions in more detail but posing new ones. This stream of information has
contributed to the publication of over 100 books, many aimed at the general
reader. Thus, the would-be tourist may now consult myriad works before
traveling to Stonehenge. But be forewarned: significant mysteries remain. As
Julian Richards remarked, "Stonehenge will always keep some of its secrets."[5]

Stonehenge is a "persistent place."[6] Once sanctified by construction of the
first ritual architecture, Stonehenge possessed an attraction for later peoples
seeking to exploit its specialness. Over the course of five millennia, many
groups carried out varied ceremonial activities of social and religious significance. That is why the early questions now have multiple answers. After
all, Stonehenge—the site—had a complex life history. Piecing together that
life history is especially challenging because of the many changes wrought
by remodeling, deterioration, vandalism, earlier excavations, re-erection
of some stones, and stone robbing. Despite the obstacles, archaeologists,
building on the findings of antiquarians, have made progress.

Stonehenge's first builders have not been firmly identified.[7] Antiquarians
offered many hypotheses: Danes, Romans, Phoenicians, Celts, and others.
Quite a few came to believe—correctly—that the ruins predated the Roman
conquest of Britain. Working in the early eighteenth century, William Stuke-
ley asserted that the builders were Druids. He became a Druid himself and
revitalized interest in conducting ceremonies at the site, which are still performed. Most archaeologists believe Stonehenge was the work of indigenous
Britons but probably not Druids.

It is difficult to discriminate among, and assign dates to, specific construction and remodeling events, and so interpretations abound. However,
the earliest henge, an earthwork, is well dated to about 2950 BC. With antler
tools, the indigenes—whatever their identity—dug a circular earthwork
about 300 feet in diameter, consisting of a ditch banked on both sides. This
henge was associated with 56 large, equally spaced holes that held stone or
wooden posts, animal bones that dated several centuries earlier, and later
the cremated remains of at least 60 individuals. The earthwork henge was
apparently a place for interring persons of high social standing.

Bronze Age people using Beaker pottery refurbished the ditch, perhaps
at about 2500 BC, and aligned its entrance with the rising sun of midsummer.
These "Beaker Folk" also erected five immense trilithons using sarsen

stones (sandstone) hauled from Marlborough Downs, 20 miles away. A trilithon consists of two uprights, the largest weighing more than 40 tons, capped by a lintel. How the stones were transported is unknown, but many prehistoric groups were able to move large stones. After arrival, the stones were modified by a technique more akin to woodworking than stone masonry. To join the lintels to the uprights, the builders used hammerstones to shape tenons on uprights and to make mortise holes in lintels. The uprights were eased into a prepared pit and then tilted into final position. Experiments have shown that the lintels could have been raised gradually with levers on a growing platform of logs.[8]

The trilithons were set a short distance apart in a horseshoe pattern. From within the horseshoe, the rising sun is visible at the open end during midsummer. In addition, the sun at Winter Solstice can be seen through a gap in the uprights. In traditional societies throughout the world, agricultural and ceremonial cycles are tied to the seasons, and that is why many peoples built structures to observe the solstices. Stonehenge served, at the very least, as a monumental solar calendar for some peoples, a gathering place to celebrate the change of seasons.

Inside the trilithons, the Beaker Folk placed another horseshoe, this one of so-called bluestones. A circle of bluestones, surrounding the trilithons, consisted of 29 complete stones and a fractional one, which may correspond to the lunar month of 29.5 days. By marking off the days, a priest could use the stone circle to predict the arrival of the new and full moon. Composed of several kinds of igneous rocks, the bluestones were smaller than the trilithons' sarsens, but the largest still weighed five tons. Bluestones were quarried in the Preseli Hills in Wales, about 150 miles away; part of the journey was likely by raft.

Having been brought from a great distance, the bluestones were clearly special. Archaeologists Timothy Darvill and Geoffrey Wainwright have proposed that they might have been imbued with healing properties, attracting the afflicted from as far away as the continent.[9] Other archaeologists disagree. Michael Parker Pearson, for one, insists that Stonehenge was always a distinctive burial place, the stones symbolizing the dead.[10] Despite growing knowledge of Stonehenge's life history and of the societies occupying the Salisbury Plain, many social interpretations remain in flux.

A few centuries later, the bluestones were rearranged, and a continuous circle of sarsens was added surrounding all earlier stones. Shaped by pounding, the curved lintels were mated to uprights by mortise-and-tenon joints, and adjacent lintels were joined by tongue and groove.

Artifacts from later periods, as in carvings of Bronze Age weapons on several sarsens, assorted pottery, and Roman coins, show that activities were still taking place at the monument for millennia, probably intermittently. In addition, Stonehenge was in most times part of a regional system consisting of villages, fields and pastures, barrows (tombs), flint quarries and workshops, and other henges. Fleshing out this dynamic regional system and Stonehenge's changing roles in it through time are matters of ongoing research.

Although prospective tourists can read in many books about the findings of archaeological research at Stonehenge and its landscape, until recently many visitors had a less-than-stellar experience. The visitor center was small and rather pathetic, with few amenities. Even more troubling, the encounter was disturbed by vehicles rumbling along the A303, a national highway only 700 feet away. The visual experience was also marred by a closer regional road, the A344, that led from A303 past the stones to the visitor center and parking lot, literally a stone's throw from the stones. Belatedly affirming the obvious, a committee of Parliament proclaimed Stonehenge a "national disgrace."[11] Although some visitors were satisfied with their experience, Stonehenge did not meet modern standards for a world-class tourist destination.[12]

Agitation for improvements gained momentum after UNESCO, in 1986, designated Stonehenge and 2,600 hectares around it a World Heritage Site. Two years earlier, Stonehenge had been placed in the stewardship of English Heritage, a quasi-governmental organization dedicated to preserving important historical and prehistoric properties. Fortunately, much of the Stonehenge landscape, incorporating hundreds of sites, had long been owned by the National Trust. Beginning in late 1980s, then, these organizations offered plan after plan to improve the tourist experience but ran into obstacles owing to conflicting interests among dozens of stakeholders, changing ideas about which modifications would be appropriate, and lack of financing for major improvements.[13] An important concern was ensuring that the monument, its environment, and related sites were preserved in the face of increasing visitation.

Despite the glacial progress in crafting a workable plan, English Heritage continued developing and distributing resource materials for tourists that incorporated archaeological findings. In 1987, it published a handsome guide with color images that summarized current knowledge. The author was R. J. C. Atkinson, a distinguished British prehistorian who had excavated at Stonehenge between 1950 and 1964.[14] The most recent edition of the guide was written by Julian Richards, whose other works on Stonehenge have also been published by English Heritage, including a Teacher's Kit.[15] The well-illustrated kit contains lesson plans, answers to basic questions, and a glossary. Available in English and French versions, the kit's rich content informs teachers about archaeology in general and Stonehenge findings in particular. English Heritage also published a brochure for professors and students of tourism studies.[16] Of course, today's prospective tourist will turn first to the Internet. English Heritage's Stonehenge website is artfully constructed, easy to navigate, and informative.[17] It boasts that Stonehenge is "one of the wonders of the world and the best-known prehistoric monument in Europe."

Bournemouth University in collaboration with English Heritage prepared a comprehensive Archaeological Research Framework. Largely written by Timothy Darvill with contributions from nearly a dozen specialists, this impressive work reviewed the history of research, assessed the archaeological resources, presented a detailed synthesis on Stonehenge in its landscape through time, established research needs, and set priorities.[18] Following this framework, English Heritage sponsored several archaeological projects whose findings are being incorporated into tourist materials.

Although messy politics and dicey economics held sway for many years, the government directed English Heritage to oversee the creation of a revised management plan that might reflect a consensus among stakeholders and conform to World Heritage Site guidelines. A comprehensive plan was published in 2009 and, with government support, parts of it have been implemented.[19] The A303 has been rerouted, the old visitor center dismantled, the A344 eliminated, and the nearby landscape returned to pasture. Nothing now disturbs the serenity of the scene save, perhaps, a blustery rain and the bleating of sheep.

On December 18, 2013, English Heritage opened a new visitor center about a mile from Stonehenge and beyond sight of the stones. With its modern cafeteria, gift shop, and museum, the center enables tourists to eat well, purchase hundreds of Stonehenge-branded items, and learn about the latest archaeological findings and interpretations. To reach the stones, visitors can walk or ride the tram, which deposits them at the foot of a path leading to the

FIGURE 9.1. Tourists pose for pictures at Stonehenge, England (author's collection).

monument. Walking the path that encircles the stones, tourists can view the landscape in all directions and photograph Stonehenge from every vantage point. And, with the stones in the background, tourists take pictures that can be uploaded almost immediately to social media (Figure 9.1).

The museum is itself a special place befitting a World Heritage Site. Upon entering, the visitor first passes through a space on whose semicircular walls is projected a panoramic view of Stonehenge as if one were standing in the middle of the trilithon horseshoe. The dramatic images show seasonal changes and a solstice that even jaded archaeologists may enjoy. Next comes a large room with display cases that exhibit, by time period, about 300 artifacts from Stonehenge and its environs. The artifacts are creatively mounted and accompanied by informative labels. Against one long wall is projected a busy timeline of activities that occurred on the Stonehenge landscape. There is also an exhibit of early books on Stonehenge, open to pages with drawings.

Stonehenge is a source of immense pride to Britons and is one of the most visited archaeological sites in the world, drawing half its visitors from abroad. However, when viewed without benefit of archaeological inferences and interpretations, the site is just a jumble of large stones. Although the stones do inspire awe and curiosity, by themselves they tell us nothing about their past lives. Happily, antiquarians and archaeologists have made much sense of this jumble, and English Heritage has furnished their findings to tourists—about one million annually.

I thank Timothy Darvill and Sara Lunt for arranging our visit to Stonehenge in December 2013.

IV

COLLABORATING WITH COMMUNITIES

T HROUGHOUT THE DISCIPLINE'S early history, archaeologists did fieldwork without interacting much with descendant communities. When excavating in a foreign country, for example, U.S. and Western European archaeologists commonly took the artifacts home. This made analysis easier but it was difficult for descendant peoples to appreciate their own heritage. The situation was so bad that some countries forbade fieldwork by foreigners.

This rude awakening caused many archaeologists to rethink their ethics and relations with living peoples. Now it is expected that every project will involve collaboration with relevant communities. The "ideal" field project today has a local archaeologist as the co-principal investigator, hires local students and researchers, collaborates on analyses and publications, and uses various media to present the findings to pertinent publics. In some cases, an archaeologist will help build a country's or a tribe's infrastructure for teaching and research. In advance of any project, negotiations determine the nature of the collaboration.

The Levi Jordan Plantation is located in southern Texas and consists of a dilapidated mansion and the ruins of slave-tenant cabins. Ignoring the mansion, archaeologist Kenneth L. Brown excavated in the slave-tenant cabins, unearthing a rich artifact assemblage. A major part of this project was engagement with descendants of the plantation's residents, black and white. Conducted by Carol McDavid, interviews with descendants elicited diverse views that crosscut both black and white groups about the desirability of revisiting slavery in public presentations of the plantation's archaeology. An advisory committee with an equal number of blacks and whites (plus Brown) was tasked with making plans for the public presentations. Regrettably, the advisory committee's influence was diminished when the State of Texas acquired the plantation site. Even so, McDavid constructed an interactive website that has served as a model for other archaeological projects.

The Ozette site is located on the reservation of the Makah Nation on the Olympic Peninsula of Washington state. Occupied for millennia, a portion of Ozette, still in use just before European contact, was threatened by erosion. The tribe called in Richard Daugherty, an archaeologist at Washington State University, to assess the situation. What he found at Ozette was extraordinary: a cornucopia of well-preserved organic materials, from house posts to wooden boxes to delicate leaves. With the encouragement of the tribe, he undertook an ambitious excavation project that not only employed some Makah students but also helped to inspire a cultural revival. The Makah built a conservation center and museum staffed by tribal members, some trained by Daugherty. The museum's Ozette exhibits showcase many spectacular artifacts and include a wooden-plank longhouse built to prehistoric specifications. Archaeologists and members of the Makah tribe have enjoyed a close collaboration because their interests converged on illuminating the traditional lifeways of the ancestors.

Cambridge-trained Thurstan Shaw, a pioneer of Ghanaian and Nigerian archaeology, solved the mystery of the bronze sculptures first found at the site of Igbo–Ukwu in the 1930s. His later excavations, at the invitation of Nigerian officials and employing an all-Nigerian crew, showed that these sophisticated objects were crafted by indigenous Nigerians more than a millennium ago. However, Shaw's most important contribution was to build an infrastructure so that Nigerians could do their own archaeology. He founded the Department of Archaeology at Ibadan University, taught there until his retirement, and inspired some students to become archaeologists. He also established journals for reporting West African archaeology, published a book for a general audience, and through the meticulous reporting of the Igbo-Ukwu project set high research standards. Nigerians honored him repeatedly and, after his passing in 2013, attended a weeklong celebration of his life at Cambridge University.

10

The Levi Jordan Plantation Project

IN FIELD PROJECTS TODAY, archaeologists have an ethical, and sometimes legal, obligation to collaborate with communities, including nearby residents and descendants of the historic or prehistoric group they are studying. Most communities, however, are not socially homogeneous, and so their members may respond differently to archaeological inferences and interpretations. This situation can present a special challenge when planning a project's public presentation, such as an on-site exhibit, news release, or website. In the Levi Jordan Plantation Project, involving descendants of both slaves and slaveholders in eastern Texas, archaeologists gained experience engaging with socially diverse communities.

Throughout the American South, hundreds of antebellum plantation mansions have been restored and stocked with period furnishings. Glorifying a planter, his family, and life in the Old South, these places are now tourist destinations, many of them listed on the National Register of Historic Places. Until recent decades, mansion guides and tourist brochures may have mentioned slavery but had little to say about how the oppressed people really lived; after all, slave life is poorly represented in historical records. Fortunately, we can learn much about slavery and its aftermath from archaeological evidence because, ideally, artifacts and their distributions reflect actual activities.[1]

Inspired by the Civil Rights Movement and the growth of historical archaeology in the United States, archaeologists began excavating in and around slave cabins and workshops. One of the pioneers was Charles H. Fairbanks, who taught at the University of Florida and began excavating

slave cabins in the late 1960s in Georgia and Florida.[2] Since then, dozens
of similar projects throughout the South have yielded a wealth of insights
about slavery and the roots of African-American culture.[3]

In highly publicized projects, archaeologists have been digging in the
slave quarters of plantations once owned by famous Americans, including
George Washington (Mount Vernon), Thomas Jefferson (Monticello), and
Andrew Jackson (The Hermitage). Plantations of less prominent people have
also been excavated. One of these is the Levi Jordan Plantation. Started in
1848, it is located in Brazoria County, south of Houston, Texas, about 15 miles
from the Gulf of Mexico. Across more than 2,200 acres, Jordan grew cotton
and sugar, and processed sugar cane in his mill for nearby plantations. The
large enterprise relied on a large labor pool: according to the 1860 U.S. census, the plantation had 141 slaves, living in 29 cabins.[4] In the postwar period
when many freedmen stayed on the plantation and became tenant farmers,
cattle ranching assumed greater economic importance.

After Jordan's death in 1873, the plantation was run briefly by his grandsons and then leased for more than a decade. Around 1890, four great-
grandsons divided the plantation.[5] During much of the twentieth century,
the house and other structures were neglected as Jordan descendants, in the
Martin and McNeill families, feuded amongst themselves.[6]

In the 1980s, Jordan descendants still owned the house and nearby buildings, including the slave-tenant quarters. One of the Martins, willing to have
the plantation's story told in its entirety, enabled University of Houston archaeologist Kenneth L. Brown to conduct excavations. In 1986, Brown began
a project that would last more than two decades, digging mainly in the slave-
tenant quarters, which had been occupied until 1890 or 1891.[7]

In a curious reversal of common nineteenth-century construction practices, the plantation house, which survived and has been restored, was built
of wood; while the slave cabins were built of brick, though only the lowest
courses remained in a foundation trench. Excavation showed that the slave
cabins were unusual in another respect: individual spaces or cabins had been
created by partitioning the interiors of eight rectangular buildings.

The cabins yielded even more surprises. A wealth of floor-associated artifacts, many still useful, suggested that the residents abandoned their homes
in haste. The historical record supports this inference: during the turmoil
surrounding the division of the property around 1890, the tenant farmers
apparently were evicted. After the tenants left, the buildings were padlocked

and allowed to deteriorate. The wooden floors, elevated a few inches above the ground, gradually rotted, and the artifacts on them moved downward, joining others that had previously fallen between the floorboards. Bricks from the walls were scavenged in 1913, creating a debris layer that protected the underlying artifacts from further disturbance. That the cabin area was never plowed also helped preserve the rich artifact assemblages.[8]

During excavation the crew peeled away the debris layer in one-foot squares, exposing the floor artifacts and plotting their exact locations. This information permitted Brown to identify individual cabins inside the brick structures as well as specific activity areas. In addition to the glass, ceramics, and animal bones indicating food storage and consumption, tools found in the cabins suggested specialized pursuits, perhaps even occupations, including carpenter, blacksmith, hunter, lead shot maker, and seamstress.

One cabin yielded freshwater mussel shells, blanks of freshwater and marine shells, tools for drilling them, and a carved shell cameo.[9] Brown inferred that this cabin had been the living quarters and workshop of an "African craftsman" who made buttons. Because other cabins contained handmade shell buttons, Brown suggested that residents of the quarters had acquired them from the African craftsman.

Another cabin contained bird skulls, bases of five iron kettles, chalk pieces, an animal's paw, a brass tube made from bullet casings, doll parts, nails, "fake" metal knives, and others. Ethnographic sources from West Africa and Cuba suggested that this assemblage was "the ritual 'tool kit' of a traditional West African and African-American healer/magician."[10] Brown inferred that divination employed white powder (the chalk) that the magician spread on a tray (the kettle bases) and manipulated to produce interpretable symbols. The brass tube and other artifacts likely had been used in curing ceremonies. In the ethnographic cases, divination and curing were closely related; the ritual specialist in this cabin probably performed both kinds of rites. In West Africa and in Cuba, however, these rites were carried out with much more "elaborate and symbolically decorated items." Perhaps on the Jordan plantation these expressions of African-American spiritual life were being suppressed and so were practiced "underground."[11] Since 1990, when these findings were published, numerous plantation excavations have also brought to light artifacts of African-American spiritualism, indicating that West African beliefs and practices persisted widely in the Americas.

Many descendants of the plantation's residents live in the nearby small towns of Brazoria, West Columbia, and Sweeny. After his project was well underway, Brown hired Carol McDavid, one of his graduate students, to assess the feasibility of collaborating with descendants to create "public presentations of the archaeology." She advocated an "inclusive" approach involving collaboration with both blacks and whites. McDavid was curious about how the people "viewed their own histories, and their places in those histories."[12] She also wanted to know how the public interpretation of archaeology would affect existing social divisions. Would airing controversial issues lead to healing or discord in the modern social order that was still segregated and dominated by whites?

A southern white woman, McDavid made exploratory trips to the area in 1992 and 1993, and followed them up with formal interviews. She also took part in community meetings, made public presentations, and took advantage of informal encounters. McDavid cast her net widely, seeking the views of "the descendants of Levi Jordan, the descendants of the African Americans who lived on the site, other European American and African-American members of the surrounding region, community leaders, local educators, people interested in history and archaeology, academics who study history and archaeology, and others."[13] She did, however, ignore white supremacist groups believed to be active in the area.

Members of the Martin family had owned the plantation when the tenants were evicted. Aware of this event, some Martin descendants wanted "the whole truth" to be told and supported the archaeological work, but others did not want their past to be exposed.[14] To deal with such conflicts, as well as others revealed by McDavid's ethnographic work, two Jordan descendants and Kenneth Brown in 1993 set up a nonprofit corporation, the Levi Jordan Plantation Historical Society, to coordinate the plantation's public archaeology. With the exception of Brown, all members of the corporation's board were to be local.

Formal interviews with African Americans at first did not go well. People were polite, but McDavid found that arranging appointments was very difficult. She sensed that African Americans were reluctant to share their views with her and finally learned why. It was not her skin color. Rather, blacks felt burned by previous community projects because their input was solicited only after most plans had already been made.[15] By emphasizing that "inclusiveness" was not tokenism under a new name, McDavid eventually gained their trust, and they began to express their views.

Like Jordan descendants, some blacks didn't want to "stir all that slavery stuff up again"; others hoped that interpretations would be "nonpolarizing." There was also some support for the idea of putting "archaeology into history curricula in local schools." It was suggested that the "ugly parts of history had to be included" but handled gently so that they could even be understood by children.[16] As for Black History Month, some said that "maybe it would be better if black history was studied all year, not just in February."[17]

Obtaining the views of white people presented fewer problems. Some worried that a public interpretation would only be about black history. Whites, while acknowledging that their ancestors were not always saints, also wanted "better" stories to be told, such as "the friendships that sometimes developed between black and white plantation residents, and stories about the courage and fortitude of the women in the planter's family."[18] One McNeill descendent believed that public interpretation could contribute to healing on both sides.

In short, McDavid learned that among both whites and blacks there was a wide range of views. Even so, there seemed to be general agreement that people could learn about everyone's history, throughout the year, from public interpretation of the site.

The Levi Jordan Plantation Historical Society appointed a Board of Directors consisting of seven members: three whites, three blacks, and Kenneth L. Brown. The board's composition made inclusiveness a reality and emphasized that power over decision-making was shared. A mission statement included the following: "The primary mission... is to preserve and interpret the archaeologies and histories of *all* the people who lived and worked on this plantation after its inception in the mid-19th century."[19]

But before plans for on-site exhibits could be finalized, the plantation became the property of the Texas State Historical Commission. As a result, the Jordan Historical Society lost its decision-making powers. Now it merely advises a state bureaucracy.[20] As of mid–2015, the plantation is a State Historic Site still "under development and only open to the public on a limited basis and by appointment."[21] There is some hope that future on-site exhibits will present interpretations of the archaeology from diverse perspectives.

The major vehicle for public interpretation is a website, authorized by the Jordan Historical Society and put together by Carol McDavid in 1998. It seeks to help visitors "learn more about how people talk about archaeology and history on the Internet."[22] The site allows "the descendants of the original residents of this plantation... to conduct critical dialogues with archaeologists, with each other, with people elsewhere—and with 'the past.'" Thus, visitors can furnish corrections, new information, and their own interpretations. As she emphasizes, the website is less presentation than conversation.[23]

One of the most interesting pages presents several interpretations of the abandonment of the slave-tenant quarters, delicately negotiating a sensitive subject. Recall that Kenneth Brown originally concluded that the floor artifacts and historical evidence indicated that the tenants had been forcibly removed. Although this interpretation may be substantially correct, further historical research, as well as comments from descendants, raised additional possibilities. Some families abandoned their cabins before 1890 because the ranching economy required fewer laborers.[24] A few families may have bought their own farms and moved away. And in the hostile environment of Jim Crow laws and white supremacists—including some Jordan descendants—families may also have fled in fear for their lives.[25]

McDavid's website offers several uncontroversial messages about archaeology in general: (1) evidence may be interpreted in many ways, from many perspectives; and (2) interpretations can change when new evidence becomes available. A less obvious message is that the archaeologist is no longer *the* authority on the past, as his or her inferences and interpretations may be disputed—and alternatives offered—by any interested party. Some archaeologists are uncomfortable here because, *taken to extremes*, inclusiveness undermines archaeology's hard-won standing as a science. It might be asked, for example: would the inclusiveness philosophy require that public presentations of human evolution be accompanied by creationist and ancient-astronaut stories?

That the on-site interpretation of the plantation is now in the hands of a state agency is surely a disappointment to the archaeologists and the local communities. Even so, the founding of the Jordan Historical Society, with its diverse board, was an impressive accomplishment that fostered communication across lines of race and social class. And Brown's excavation project and McDavid's website remain models that inspire other archaeologists who seek to collaborate with socially diverse communities.[26]

I thank Kenneth Brown and Carol McDavid for reading a draft of this chapter.

11

The Ozette Site and the Makah Indian Nation

IN THE FAR NORTHWESTERN reach of Washington's Olympic Peninsula, where the rainforest meets the Pacific Ocean, is the 47-square-mile reservation of the Makah Nation, a tribe with around 2,000 members. The Makah once lived in five villages; the southernmost one, Ozette, was very large and very old. Now an outlier of the main reservation, Ozette was abandoned in 1917 but not forgotten, even as the U.S. government forced its residents to move to the town of Neah Bay. From generation to generation, Makah people handed down stories about Ozette, including one that told of a great landslide that buried part of the village.[1] Did this compelling tale recount a real event in Makah history?

The answer came in 1970. In February, a big storm swept over the coast, eroding an area above the beach near the abandoned village. Beneath an old landslide, pounding waves exposed wooden houses along with their original contents, including items not seen in modern times. The wealth of unusual artifacts rapidly attracted looters who made away with pieces of the Makah past. After confirming that looting was taking place, Edward E. Claplanhoo, Chairman of the Makah Nation, contacted an acquaintance, Richard Daugherty, an archaeology professor at Washington State University. A few years earlier, Daugherty had done a field school at a 2,000-year-old part of Ozette, but did not find houses full of artifacts.

After visiting the revealed Ozette, Daugherty could see that the site was in immediate danger from further erosion and looting. With the invitation and encouragement of the Makah Tribal Council, Daugherty geared up an excavation project that would last 11 years, much of it funded by the National

Park Service. Given the risk of looting and Ozette's remoteness, the project built a camp next to the site. The crew worked year round, despite sometimes cold and stormy weather; but when the skies cleared, the archaeologists could delight in the sight of a breathtaking seascape.

The composition of the Ozette crew changed from year to year, but regularly included Makah high school and college students. The students brought "a sense of historical continuity to the excavation," sharing details about their traditional lifeway with the non-Makah and conveying "a respect for the connections between the past and present." Touched by these encounters, several Anglo archaeologists became advocates for tribal interests.[2]

Because this part of the site had suffered a catastrophic end, Ozette has been called an American Pompeii, but that doesn't do it justice. What makes Ozette so special (and what Pompeii lacks) is the abundance of items made from normally perishable plant materials, such as planks and posts for houses, whaling equipment, looms and blankets, clothes and masks, baskets and mats, bows and arrows, and wooden boxes and bowls. Ozette's unusual preservation occurred because the site was completely saturated with water and covered with a protective layer of mud from the landslide, sustained by the area's 100-plus inches of annual rainfall. With Ozette's riches in mind, archaeologists excavating ordinary sites in the Pacific Northwest, which stretches from southern Alaska to northern California, are painfully aware that the stone, bone, and shell artifacts they recover vastly underrepresent the range of things that past peoples used daily.

Radiocarbon dating indicates that Ozette's destruction took place sometime between AD 1500 and 1700, before contacts with Europeans, which began about 1790. Thus, Ozette was a time capsule whose study would be of great interest to archaeologists. More importantly, Ozette could also give the Makah people glimpses of their ancestors' lifeway before it was affected by European diseases, loss of territory, competition with Anglos for resources, new technologies and trade patterns, and government restrictions. Happily, both archaeologists and the Makah tribe wanted to learn what life had been like in the seaside village. This convergence of interests fostered a mutually satisfying collaboration.

Wresting artifacts from a wet and sticky clay-silt matrix would not be easy. When waterlogged wood and textiles are first exposed, they appear to be in good condition because they retain their original shapes. A wooden box looks like a box and a basket looks like a basket, but these items are very fragile and easily damaged if touched by trowel or shovel. Daugherty and his crew learned that flowing water was a better excavation tool. With pipes dipping into the sea, high-pressure pumps, and hoses stretching to the site, the crew washed away the 6- to 10-foot layer of mud covering the cultural deposits. When the cultural layer was reached, the crew switched to a low-pressure, fine spray that gently separated the artifacts from the clay and from each other. This technique promoted the recovery of material "as incredibly fragile as the alder and twinberry leaves and as minute as shavings left by a woodworker."[3]

Unless waterlogged artifacts are kept constantly wet or treated with preservatives, they will warp and disintegrate. Thus, immediately after recovery, wood and textiles were given first aid in the camp laboratory, a process called conservation. They were first washed in water and then immersed in a preservative solution for a month or longer depending on size. Treated artifacts were carried by helicopter to Neah Bay for "final stabilization, storage and analysis." Not only did several Makah students work in the Neah Bay lab, but tribal elders also visited often to view the finds. They identified some items and discussed their uses.[4]

In addition to a half million seeds, the Ozette excavations recovered "over 55,000 tools and tool fragments; more than 15,000 house planks, poles, and posts from buried houses; and over 1 million bones and shells," all belonging to the Makah Nation.[5] This massive collection presented a big storage challenge. The National Park Service or a university museum might have curated the artifacts off-reservation, a common practice in earlier decades. However, when archaeological collections are held and displayed in distant museums, descendant communities find it difficult or impossible to maintain a close connection to the materials, much less influence how they are interpreted to the public. The situation changed in the 1960s, as tribes became more politically active and pushed to establish museums—now more than 100—so that they, not outsiders, could control the exhibits and messages.[6] Following this trend, and no doubt encouraged by the archaeologists, the Makah kept possession of their history by curating the Ozette collections in their own facility.

While fieldwork was under way, the tribe secured a grant from the federal Economic Development Administration to build a museum and cultural center in Neah Bay. Opened in 1979, the Makah Museum, which includes the Makah Cultural and Research Center, is owned and operated by the tribe and staffed entirely with tribal members. Makah students who took part in excavations at Ozette and other archaeological projects on their reservation became the first generation of Makah researchers and cultural specialists.[7] With support from the tribe, along with grants from the National Endowment for the Humanities and private foundations, the tribe built a new storage facility and dedicated it in 1993.[8]

Doing justice to such large and varied collections required the work of many researchers. Daugherty chose them with care, parceling out the analyses to specialists, including his doctoral students at Washington State. Analyses began in the temporary quarters, but once the Ozette collections came to the Makah Museum, Anglo researchers were given workspace and access to facilities. The close collaboration among Anglos and museum staff yielded impressive results. In the museum's exhibits and in dozens of publications, Ozette provides the most comprehensive picture of life in a late prehistoric coastal village anywhere in the Pacific Northwest.

Studies of the faunal and floral assemblages, recovered from houses and exterior trash, showed that the Ozette villagers enjoyed a diverse diet dominated by meat and fish. This is not surprising because the village's prime location gave access to marine and rainforest resources, including migratory whales and birds, and allowed year-round occupation. The abundant refuse from meals indicated consumption of whales, seals, sea otters, salmon, halibut, rockfish, herring, ducks, geese, clams, crabs, and many others. Deer and elk taken in the forest above the village, along with plants gathered there, also contributed to the diet.[9] But by far, the majority of the diet was whale meat and oil.[10]

Material technologies such as wood, basketry, and bone also loomed large in the deposits, but, like other tribes of the Northwest Coast, the Makah made no pottery. When studying the artifacts, the specialists had to recreate—or model—the knowledge of environmental resources that enabled the Makah ancestors to make and use their technologies.

Janet Patterson Friedman was given a daunting assignment: do the first study of Ozette's diverse wood technology.[11] She fastened on two major questions. First, did the artisans choose a specific wood for each kind of artifact? Second, if they did, what knowledge guided these choices? To answer the first question, Friedman examined each artifact (often under a microscope), identified the species from which it was made, and tabulated the results. She learned that wood choices were highly patterned, as certain species were preferred for each artifact type.

FIGURE 11.1. Makah basket weavers, ca. 1910 (Wikimedia Commons, Asahel Curtis, photographer).

In answering the second question, Friedman concluded that the artisans knew a great deal about the properties and performance characteristics of different wood species, as indicated by their effective choices. An example is red alder, a lightweight hardwood that can be easily carved and has a pleasing grain; it is also odorless and tasteless and takes a high polish. On the basis of this knowledge, the ancient Makah made their bowls and trays—some with carved decorations—from red alder and other woods. Such woods were well suited for the handsome Makah food and oil containers. Friedman repeated this process for the 10 most common kinds of wood, and so approximated the Makah's detailed technological knowledge. Today, Makah artisans apply that same knowledge when making Ozette-inspired wooden crafts for tourists.

Sometimes archaeologists benefited from technological knowledge that tribal elders possessed and were happy to share. For example, several Makah women aided Dale Croes's early study of Ozette basketry by telling him about the uses of different baskets, and they also taught him basket weaving (Figure 11.1).[12]

Jeffrey E. Mauger analyzed the house remains: eight were initially identified and three were completely excavated.[13] Because wooden planks, posts, rafter beams, and other parts were present, he was able to reconstruct the structures' appearance, dimensions, and construction techniques. Built of planks, these rectangular "longhouses" were large (some exceeded 1,500 square feet) and contained windows, benches, carved panels, partitions, fish-drying frames, and so forth. Analyses of such features and interior artifact distributions indicated that several families lived in each house.

Drawing on Mauger's architectural study, the Makah built on the beach a traditional longhouse according to prehistoric specifications. Later, the structure was taken apart and rebuilt inside the museum, where it is a focal point of the permanent exhibit.[14]

In her review of tribal museums, Smithsonian anthropologist JoAllyn Archambault discussed how the tribe wanted to show "the close relationship between Makah culture and the environment." The exhibits of Ozette artifacts, organized around the seasonal activities of hunting, gathering, and fishing, display the technologies that each employed. There is an emphasis on the sea, to which the Makah "are oriented...as a source of livelihood and spiritual identity." The objects, she continued, "are beautifully displayed, and there is an immediacy about the exhibit made possible by the preservation of organic materials."[15] A plaque at the gallery entrance acknowledges tribal members for contributing to the exhibit's conception.

Writing with anthropologist Patricia Erikson in 2005, Janine Bowechop, Executive Director of the Makah Cultural and Research Center, noted that "tribal museums and cultural centers can serve as a tool to reclaim practices based upon traditional values; they also can serve as a base for conducting research whose ethics and design are relevant to community needs."[16] That is why this center also includes the Makah Language Program, Archives and Library Department, Makah Education Department, and Tribal Historic Preservation Office.[17]

Activities of the center's divisions help to educate young tribal members about traditional elements of their culture such as language, wood carving, and basketry. Archambault points out that the center "has played a significant role in the cultural revitalization of the Makah."[18] According to Greig Arnold, the museum's first director, "*Without the site and the museum,* we'd still dance our dances and sing our songs...but everything is much more meaningful now. It brings our past and our culture into a much sharper focus."[19]

12

Thurstan Shaw and Nigeria's Enigmatic Bronzes

IN 1939 ISAIAH ANOZIE, a resident of Igbo–Ukwo in southeastern Nigeria, was digging a cistern at home when he came upon something surprising: a large cache of exquisite bronze sculptures. The lively and intricate forms included snail shells (Figure 12.1), gourds, bowls, staff-heads, braziers, sword scabbards, a pot stand, and a small human face with an incised pattern resembling the traditional scarified faces of Igbo men.

Before Anozie had given all the finds to his neighbors, a British colonial officer, J. O. Field, purchased the remaining sculptures and presented them to the Nigerian Museum in Lagos. In an illustrated report in the journal *Man*, Field noted that the sculptures had been made using the lost-wax (*cire perdue*) process.[1]

The lost-wax process enables the manufacture, in metal, of the most complex objects that an artist can imagine. In the simplest version of the process, an artist's impression of a shell or human face is first sculpted in beeswax or similar substance from which a mold is made.[2] The mold consists of a mixture of sand, a small amount of fine clay, and water packed closely around the wax sculpture, inside and out, except for tubular channels that permit the escape of air and the entry of molten metal. After drying, the mold is placed in a kiln whose heat hardens it and burns out the wax. Liquid metal is poured into the mold and allowed to cool. Finally, the mold is gently chipped away to free the object—a one-of-a-kind sculpture.

The makers of the Igbo–Ukwu bronzes were highly skilled artists, probably occupational specialists in a complex society apparently out of place in

FIGURE 12.1. Snail-shaped bronze vessel from Igbo–Ukwu, Nigeria (Wikimedia Commons; Ochiwar, photographer).

a tropical forest. Although many African societies worked metals, including iron and copper, none made anything like the sculptures that Mr. Anozie discovered. And so their age and cultural origins were mysteries. Field guessed that the sculptures were less than a century old because some pieces retained traces of textiles.[3]

In much of the Western world at that time, sub-Saharan societies—in so-called darkest Africa—were thought to be static and primitive, their peoples incapable of high cultural and technological achievements.[4] These racist beliefs were even held by some colonial-period archaeologists who asserted that the sophisticated Igbo–Ukwu bronzes must have been made by more "progressive" peoples, perhaps in North Africa. Such explanations were over-turned, eventually, by British archaeologist Thurstan Shaw. His excavations at Igbo–Ukwu, beginning in 1959, showed that the "progressive" peoples responsible for the bronzes and other ornate artifacts were none other than indigenous Nigerians in Igboland.[5] The finding sent a shock wave through the scholarly world that still reverberates today.

Trained in anthropology and archaeology at Cambridge University, Shaw was no stranger to the prehistory of West Africa. During the years 1937–44 he taught at Achimota College in the Gold Coast, a British colony that in 1957 became the independent Republic of Ghana. While at Achimota, he excavated Bosumpra Cave, which produced a long sequence of prehistoric remains, and at the historic site of Dawu. These sites are pillars of modern Ghanaian archaeology. In 1945, he returned to Cambridge with his malaria-stricken wife but unable to land a university position in wartime England went to work for the Institute of Education.[6]

In the late 1950s, as Nigeria approached independence from England, the Nigerian Antiquities Department determined to solve the mysteries of the bronze sculptures. Seeking an archaeologist to excavate at Igbo–Ukwu, they turned to Shaw. With facilities and funds furnished by the Antiquities Department, he assembled an all-Nigerian crew and, in 1959, began excavations in Isaiah Anozie's compound. There, under a wall, Shaw's team unearthed the rest of the bronze cache found two decades earlier, including gourd-shaped bowls, bronze scabbard with iron blade, and ornaments in the shape of animal heads.[7]

Excavations in a neighboring compound turned up a spectacular burial. Traces of wood along with iron clamps and nails indicated that the body, seated on a ceremonial stool, had been placed in a timber-lined chamber. Although the bones were in poor condition, they were accompanied by a spectacular array of bronze sculptures, including a headdress and a leopard's skull on a staff. The burial assemblage also contained ivory tusks and 100,000 trade beads made of glass and carnelian. Shaw conjectured that this find was the burial of a "priest-king."[8] A few years later, Shaw excavated again at Igbo–Ukwu and found a cache pit containing bronzes, pottery, and swords. In total, the three excavation areas yielded 165,000 beads—which someone had to count—as well as 685 bronze objects, hundreds of ornate ceramic items, and other artifacts.

Shaw's excavations began to solve the mysteries of the bronzes, but his inferences were not immediately embraced. In contradiction to racist views, Shaw felt "sure that the bronzes are of indigenous African workmanship." And, by referring to the burial as a "priest-king," which alludes to an institution of the modern Igbo (*Eze Nri*), he implied but did not claim that the bronzes had been made by ancestors of the Igbo, one of Nigeria's major ethnic groups.[9]

At first, Shaw doubted that radiocarbon dating would be applicable because, like Field, he believed the site to be fairly recent—the "sixteenth or seventeenth century is most likely."[10] But he admitted that this was a guess and called for more work. Even so, Shaw did send some Igbo–Ukwu samples to a radiocarbon laboratory. The results were stunning: four of the five

dates—one on wood from the stool in the burial chamber and four on charcoal samples—clustered in the ninth century A D. These dates were strong
evidence that the bronzes had been made a millennium before, an inference
that Shaw had no trouble accepting. There was, however, a fifth date that
fell in the fourteenth or fifteenth century, which he regarded as an anomaly.

Shaw published a comprehensive report on his excavations.[11] The two-
volume work met the highest archaeological standards, furnishing abundant data on the artifacts and their find-spots along with more than 500
illustrations. Not only did this work lay the foundation for future research,
but it also provided a cornucopia of evidence that critics could use to attack
Shaw's dating.

Babatunde Lawal, a Nigerian art historian, wrote a scathing critique.[12]
Lawal suggested that the fifth date might be the only correct one, the other
four being the real anomalies. He also insisted that the textile fragments
could not have survived during a millennium of burial. And, employing a
fallible logic (complex forms follow simple ones), Lawal maintained that the
Igbo–Ukwu bronzes must have been made *after* the less sophisticated brass
objects crafted by other West African groups.

Reluctantly entering the fray, Shaw refuted Lawal's claims.[13] A review
of the stratigraphic evidence permitted Shaw to conclude that the charcoal
yielding the fourteenth-fifteenth-century date could have moved downward
from an overlying—and later—deposit. What's more, four consistent dates
cannot be easily explained away, certainly not by Lawal's claim that radiocarbon dating needed to be "perfected." As for the preservation of textile
fragments, Shaw noted that perishable materials, such as textiles, sometimes
survive in the presence of copper-containing artifacts because the corrosion
products are toxic to decay organisms. Finally, flawed art-historical logic does
not trump strong archaeological evidence.

The increased pace of archaeological research in the newly independent
countries of Africa after the 1960s yielded much evidence consistent with
Shaw's dating of Igbo–Ukwu. Archaeologists came to agree with Shaw that
the makers of Igbo–Ukwu bronzes lived much earlier than anyone had
suspected.[14]

Recent projects also support Shaw's belief that the bronze technology
was not an import. In 1997, a large international team headed by Paul T. Craddock of the British Museum compared lead isotopes (and other elements)
in tiny samples of the bronzes with samples of potential source materials

from several mines. This study showed that *local* mines yielded the copper and lead in the bronzes, "thereby confirming their indigenous design and technology." Craddock and colleagues also suggested that the Igbo–Ukwu curtailed or ended the crafting of bronze sculptures "in the face of imports of brass from across the Sahara, brought by Arab traders in ever increasing quantities from the 11th and 12th centuries."[15]

Shaw was deeply invested in contributing to the countries where he worked and did so through collaboration and outreach at many levels. Unlike many colonial-period archaeologists, Shaw neither departed for a distant home after a field season ended nor shipped the finds to an English museum, for he was committed to living and working in Africa. In addition to teaching at Achimota College for eight years, he held a position in the Anthropology Museum in Accra, capital of Ghana. In Nigeria, he was appointed as the first archaeology professor at the University of Ibadan in 1960, where he later founded the Department of Archaeology. He taught at Ibadan until retiring in 1974. By teaching Nigerians about their own country's archaeology, he inspired some students to take up the profession, including two members of his 1959 crew. And he also co-authored a handful of articles with Nigerian archaeologists.[16]

To provide outlets for the abundance of new research findings, Shaw established the *West African Archaeological Newsletter* and the *West African Journal of Archaeology*. In 1977, he published *Unearthing Igbo–Ukwu* in Nigeria, a book for the general public that discussed the project and also told of the many difficulties faced during fieldwork. One reviewer predicted that, as Shaw intended, "This book will be widely used in schools and universities in Africa and beyond."[17]

Writing recently about Shaw's professional positions in Ghana and Nigeria, Susan Keech McIntosh observed that his "approach to building archaeological infrastructure was straightforward and remarkably effective: meticulous excavation and recording to establish key sites and sequences, public outreach through lectures and publications, and conscientious attention to building institutional and intellectual capacity." In short, Shaw "laid the foundations of Ghanaian and Nigerian archaeology" by invitation from—and collaboration with—West Africans.[18]

Nigerians, especially the Igbo, were well aware of the depth of Shaw's commitment to their past. In 1972, he received the traditional title of *Onu N'ekwulu Ora Igboukwu*, spokesman for Igbo Ukwu. He was honored again in 1989 with "the chiefly title *Onuna Ekwulu Nri* and *Onyafuonka* of Igboland, a truly extraordinary honour."[19]

Shaw passed away in 2013 at the age of 98. In celebration of his life and works, a weeklong memorial event took place at Cambridge University, where in 1968 he had received a Ph.D. for his early work in Ghana.[20] The attendees, including dozens of Africans, were welcomed by Colin Renfrew and Graeme Barker, past and present directors of the McDonald Institute of Archaeology. The week was filled with lectures and seminars that highlighted Shaw's collaborations with West Africans. Among those attending were Igbo–Ukwu chiefs as well as the traditional ruler, His Royal Highness *Igwe* Martin N. Ezeh. Also present were many government officials and archaeologists including Zagba Narh Oyortey, Executive Director of the Ghana Museums and Monuments Board; Mallam Yusuf Abdallah Usman, the Director General of the National Commission for Museums and Monuments in Nigeria; and representatives of the Igbo–Ukwu Development Union.[21] On the last day, there was a Quaker funeral in the chapel of Sidney Sussex College, followed by a parade through downtown Cambridge led by West Africans in colorful garb playing traditional musical instruments.[22]

Ghanaians and Nigerians hold Thurstan Shaw in the highest regard, and with good reason. After all, he did make monumental contributions to their prehistory. But, more importantly, he was instrumental in building the infrastructure that enabled West Africans to do their own archaeology.

I thank Pamela Jane Smith, historian of archaeology and widow of Thurstan Shaw, for furnishing comments and information.

V

Pursuing an Activist Agenda

WE LIKE TO THINK of science, in the abstract, as being politically neutral. However, researchers across the academy know that many science projects have political motivations, implications, or consequences. Archaeology's projects are no different. Some archaeologists have explicitly embraced an activist agenda, conducting a project that seeks to benefit a group or cause. The group could be a country, tribe, community, or social class; the cause could be reducing food waste or promoting the adoption of green technology. Activist archaeology is relatively recent, but many earlier projects did have a political agenda, often unstated.

Randall H. McGuire is the chief exponent of what he calls "involved archaeology." An involved archaeology is one with projects that serve the interests of both scholars and present-day communities. Putting this philosophy into practice, McGuire and colleagues excavated at the Ludlow Massacre site. The site holds the remains of the tent camp occupied by striking coal miners and their families. In 1914, the Colorado National Guard destroyed the camp, resulting in the deaths of women and children. McGuire and colleagues brought to light tangible evidence of this dark episode, hoping to remind modern Americans of the sacrifices that organized labor made to improve workers' lives. The project revealed much about daily life in the tent camp preceding the massacre and, through excavations at the company town of Berwind, also about lifeways before and after the strike. Findings were publicized in many media, including newspaper articles, a traveling exhibit, and educational packets on labor history for Colorado public schools.

Homelessness is a persistent issue in many communities. Several archaeologists have approached homelessness as a lifeway amenable to study. Larry J. Zimmerman's project documented the material culture of homeless people in Indianapolis solely through observations of their camps. His findings suggested several simple ways to improve lives, such as not bulldozing homeless camps, providing can openers when donating canned goods, and furnishing services without religious coercion. Zimmerman's project and policy recommendations attracted much favorable publicity in national media. In Bristol, England, John Schofield and Rachael Kiddey's project required fieldworkers to interact with homeless people and involve them in the archaeological project to document decades of camps on Turbo Island. The project created good will between archaeologists and homeless people, and a few of the latter rejoined mainstream society.

I took up the question: why did electric cars of a century ago fail to become mass-market products? If this failure could be explained, perhaps a new generation of electric cars could avoid the same fate. The early electric car was a niche product that appealed to wealthy urbanites, especially women, because it was the ideal city car. The gasoline car appealed to men because it could tour in the country. Many wealthy families bought both kinds of cars so they could enjoy all car-related activities, but middle-class families could afford only one car and chose gasoline. The explanation for this pattern focuses on the patriarchal structure of American families: men made this decision because they were the "breadwinners" at that time and favored their own activities. The findings of this project appeared in *Taking Charge: The Electric Automobile in America* (1994), which received much media attention.

13

Remembering the Ludlow Massacre

ON THE EAST SLOPE of the Rocky Mountains in the coal country of south-central Colorado is an archaeological site that organized labor holds sacred. In the fall of 1913, near Ludlow, workers on strike against the Rockefeller-owned Colorado Fuel and Iron Company established a tent colony of 1,200 residents after being evicted from company housing. On April 20, 1914, the Colorado National Guard assaulted the colony with machine guns and then burned it down (Figure 13.1). Although organized violence against striking workers had a long history in the United States, this time the outcome was different: among the 21 people who died were two women and 11 children. Articles in newspapers and magazines recounted the horrific events and told Americans about the inhumane conditions of life in the coalfields. These revelations led, eventually, to the enactment of laws supporting organized labor.[1]

In the following decades, labor unions grew in number and influence, and promoted a vast expansion of the American middle class. At the peak of union membership during the 1950s and early 1960s, an assembly-line worker at a General Motors or Chrysler plant could support a family, afford a modest house, and even buy the Chevrolet or Plymouth he helped assemble. However, union membership has declined drastically ever since, and in many industries the surviving unions have lost much of their bargaining power. Explanations for this trend vary, but automation, outsourcing, off-shoring, moving factories to right-to-work states, unfavorable court decisions, and right-wing demagoguery against organized labor all played roles—and still do.

FIGURE 13.1. Ruins of the Ludlow Colony, Colorado, 29 April 1914 (courtesy of the Library of Congress, Bain Collection).

The site of the Ludlow Massacre is properly regarded as a sacred place, for it was a turning point in labor's struggles to improve workers' lives. It remains a potent symbol of the supreme sacrifices made along the way. Two years after purchasing the massacre site in 1916, the United Mine Workers of America (UMWA) erected a handsome granite monument nearby portraying a mineworker and his wife holding a small child. Inscribed on the monument are these simple but poignant words: "In memory of the men, women and children who lost their lives in freedom's cause at Ludlow, Colorado, April 20, 1914." Each year in June, hundreds of UMWA members and miners' descendants arrive in Ludlow from around the country to take part in services recalling the 1914 tragedy.

Randall H. McGuire, grandson of a Colorado union man, descendant of miners who participated in the strike, and author of *A Marxist Archaeology* and *Archaeology as Political Action*, is the foremost American spokesperson for creating an "involved" discipline.[2] An involved archaeology is one that serves not only scholarly interests but also the interests of present-day communities, including people whose ancestral sites we excavate. In his field projects, McGuire puts this philosophy into practice, seeking to "make archaeology matter in the modern world."[3] He collaborated with like-minded Colorado archaeologists, Dean Saitta and Philip Duke, to form the Ludlow Collective and undertake a major excavation project.

Because the massacre site is hallowed ground, excavations were seemingly unthinkable. In two years of planning, however, the Ludlow Collective worked hard to gain the confidence of UMWA leaders, assuring them that the archaeologists were "sympathetic to the goals of the union movement."[4] Once convinced that the archaeologists shared their political goals, the UMWA leaders embraced the project. Not only did they permit the project to proceed but members of Local 9856 and its Women's Auxiliary, from nearby Trinidad, Colorado, helped to establish the Colorado Coalfield War Archaeology Project.

Coalfield "War" emphasizes that the Ludlow Massacre and its aftermath—destruction of coal company property and murder of some employees—was in fact an eruption of class warfare. "Class warfare" is now used metaphorically by the right wing to deride progressive attempts to highlight the ever-increasing economic inequality prevalent in the United States. But from the late nineteenth well into the mid-twentieth century, class warfare described episodic, violent clashes between workers and the agents of wealthy corporations, whether company thugs or state and federal troops.

A major goal of the project, shared by archaeologists and union members, was to remind Americans of this history by unearthing tangible evidence of the violence that occurred so long ago at Ludlow.[5] The archaeological finds would complement an abundance of historical information scattered in archives around the country, including federal investigative reports, personal papers of major figures on both sides, diaries, company papers, photographs, as well as many books by historians.

The project also had the scholarly goal of learning whether post-strike reforms were effective. To supply comparative data, excavations were slated for Berwind, a company town lived in before, during, and after the strike. Another major goal was to learn about the everyday life of families in the tent colony through excavations at the massacre site. A project of this size and complexity was going to be expensive, but the Ludlow Collective succeeded in piecing together funds from the Colorado Historical Society, Colorado Endowment for the Humanities, Binghamton University, University of Denver, and others. Fieldwork proceeded from 1998 to 2002 by students enrolled in the University of Denver archaeological field school.

The massacre site was first gridded into 30-meter squares, and visible features such as tent outlines were recorded. Information was entered into an AutoCAD file, which could be updated throughout the project. Also completed early on was a map of the abandoned town of Berwind. There, the remains of structures were recorded and artifact samples obtained from yards, privies, and dumps. The archaeological evidence indicated that sanitation and infrastructure, such as electrification, improved after the strike. More surprising was a change in household organization and subsistence strategy. Pre-strike deposits held tin cans and large cooking and serving vessels, suggesting that families were taking in boarders to make ends meet on inadequate wages. After the strike, when the coal companies frowned on boarders, these large vessels disappeared. Because wages were still low, women had to augment their family's diet by raising small stock and canning at home, as indicated by animal bones and canning jars.[6]

At the massacre site, some privies, trash-filled pits, communal dumps, tent outlines, and cellars were excavated. Among the many artifacts recovered were plain and decorated ceramics, food and condiment cans, jars, and bottles, domesticated animal bones, liquor bottles, medicine bottles, cosmetics containers, and children's toys and shoes. There were also stove fragments, the remains of iron beds, and artifacts indicating membership in churches, fraternal clubs, and organizations such as the Knights of Columbus.[7] The cellars were well constructed and had been used for storage and everyday activities. Despite the ethnically diverse, largely immigrant population, there was no evidence of ethnic precincts, for the strike had created a working-class solidarity among families that transcended cultural and ethnic differences. Despite the lack of income, diets were varied, including beef and pork as well as canned goods probably supplied by donations. There was also evidence that the strikers had been armed with rifles, shotguns, and other weapons.[8]

McGuire and colleagues dutifully reported their findings in scholarly publications, and then went much further. In practicing involved archaeology, they used the project to educate various audiences about working class history, including the general public, field school students, teachers, public school students, and especially working class families.[9]

During the excavations, hundreds of visitors were given tours of the site and learned about the events that had taken place there. Interviews with reporters led to coverage in all major newspapers in Colorado. One of the archaeologists' most creative moves was to construct a portable exhibit that circulated among union halls throughout the United States. They also designed a 30-panel interpretive kiosk from which visitors, venturing to the site from Interstate 25, could learn about the strike and massacre, the archaeological project, and Ludlow's importance in today's labor struggles.

The project reached young people of Colorado through the public schools. These efforts included the design of educational packets and programs, a curriculum on Colorado labor history for middle school students, and training institutes for teachers.

While the archaeological project was still in the field, steelworkers from Locals 2102 and 3267 in Pueblo, Colorado, struck the Colorado Fuel and Iron Company, the very same company (in name, that is) that precipitated the strike in 1913. Twice the archaeologists spoke to appreciative groups of striking steelworkers, presenting the archaeological findings and underscoring the significance of the events that occurred nearly a century earlier. The strikers, seeking to end forced overtime and preserve collective bargaining, wielded the Ludlow Massacre as a powerful symbolic weapon. Explicitly making the connection to Ludlow, they set up a tent camp—named Camp Ludlow—near the headquarters of Oregon Steel, which owned Colorado Fuel and Iron Company.[10] Comprehending the symbolism, Oregon Steel changed its subsidiary's name to Rocky Mountain Steel and eventually yielded ground to the steelworkers, settling the strike in 2004. It was a small victory for organized labor, but one showing that representations of the past can contribute to the exercise of power in the present—the main pillar of McGuire's "involved" archaeology.[11]

Not everyone believed that the people who made the supreme sacrifice at Ludlow for workers' rights should be honored. Vandals damaged the granite monument, but it has been restored. And in the wake of the archaeological project, interest grew in preserving the massacre site. With McGuire's input on the nomination form, in 2009 the Ludlow Tent Colony Site became the only place of labor struggle to become a National Historic Landmark.

I thank Randall H. McGuire for comments on an earlier draft.

14

Advocating for Homeless People

WHEN DOING FIELDWORK in cities, historical archaeologists sometimes come upon the camps of homeless people. A few archaeologists have used this encounter as a springboard to launch a research project. One such is Larry J. Zimmerman, who seeks to understand the material life of homelessness in order to influence public policy. Although other social scientists have contributed many insights into homelessness, Zimmerman has taken an archaeological tack, focusing on the material life of homeless people. In his view, homelessness can be framed as an alternative lifeway amenable to research and improvement. The goal is not to eliminate homelessness but to make the lives of the people a little better by investigating "the strategies homeless people rely on in order to access resources critical for their survival."[1]

In surveys of a historic mansion's abandoned gardens in St. Paul, Minnesota, Zimmerman and his crew found traces of homelessness, including cooking debris, alcohol bottles, sleeping bags, clothing, and sheltered areas where people slept. The deposits also had some depth, reaching back to the 1940s.[2] Contrary to stereotypes, the observed patterns showed that homeless people, like everyone else, "do indeed have material culture; they acquire it and use it, protect and keep some of it, and dispose of the rest."[3] In fact, homeless people forge a somewhat precarious lifeway in the face of environmental and governmental adversity.

After moving to Indianapolis, Zimmerman learned that this city had more than 2,000 homeless people, clustered in areas where shelters and resource areas for panhandling and obtaining food and beverages were accessible. Collaborating with Jessica Welch, one of his students who had been homeless for a time, he conducted a preliminary survey to get an idea of the kinds of places frequented by homeless people and the kinds of material culture that they used, saved, and deposited. Zimmerman and Welch also pilot-tested photo documentation techniques.

On the basis of this preliminary survey, they defined three kinds of sites.[4] A *route* site lacked evidence of sleeping or camping, but graffiti, food, human waste, and clothing indicated a brief human presence. *Short-term* sites sometimes had cardboard or plastic sheets used in simple shelters, as well as traces of eating but not always cooking. *Camp* sites, used more intensively and long term, exhibited a wide range of activities and artifacts, including prepared sleeping areas of cardboard or even more substantial structures, hearths, cooking-related items such as cans, dishes, and pots, and a host of other objects. In camps, the archaeologists also observed cached items, suggesting that the owner's return was anticipated. Many sites were still being used at the time of the survey, and that is why the recording techniques were photography and notetaking.

This preliminary information furnished the foundation for designing a much larger and more systematic survey. Zimmerman and Welch selected a study area of about one square mile east of downtown that included two shelters, railroad tracks, highways, and vacant lots and structures. They divided the area into five blocks, which in turn they divided into quadrants. Using pedestrian survey, the field crew walked over the quadrants as thoroughly as possible, avoiding areas of restricted access and those that appeared dangerous. Because the project sought to identify patterns of material culture and space use on the ground, fieldwork was done when homeless people were apt to be away from their camps. In the event of accidental encounters, crewmembers avoided conversation beyond greetings.

The survey yielded 61 sites and a wide range of material culture, which allowed Zimmerman to augment the list of items associated with the site types. Alcohol containers were present on all sites, but drug paraphernalia were sparse. Food packaging was common, including cans, the remains of fast-food meals, and plastic cups. Discarded clothing and shoes and various reading materials occurred on short-term and camp sites, as did tiny containers of toothpaste and hair-care products—the latter mostly unopened. Zimmerman learned that churches donate these personal hygiene products, collected from parishioners who had been urged to bring the products home after stays in motels and hotels. Toothpaste can be used without much water, but hair-care products require a generous supply, which homeless camps lack. Camps sometimes contained unopened food cans or ones that had exploded or been opened by battering. Well-meaning people apparently donate canned foods but neglect to provide openers.

Camps were often located in areas of natural shelter, such as under bridges or in a building; they appeared to be semipermanent and were apparently used by several people who, in effect, formed a small community. Plastic garbage bags held the caches, placed in concealed areas. The archaeologists did not open the caches but learned that they usually contain personal items such as important documents, medications, spare clothing, and family items. In some cities, political pressures have led to the brutal destruction of homeless camps and the disposal of all contents. The loss of caches is devastating, for personal items may be a homeless person's only link to a past life. Responding to these purges, homeless people have sued cities and, in the case of Fresno, California, have received substantial compensation for property loss.[5]

Zimmerman and his student Courtney Singleton discovered that blogs written by homeless people, presumably when they had access to computers in public libraries or shelters, were a rich source of information on the experiences of daily life.[6] Singleton also experimented with ways to document daily change in camps.

About the same time that the Indianapolis project began, Martha T. Valado was doing dissertation research on homelessness in Tucson, Arizona. Trained as an archaeologist, Valado obtained some information on the material culture of homeless people but focused on their use of space. Her main source of information, in addition to observations of camps (Figure 14.1), was interviews with 60 homeless people in order to learn, for example, how they adapted to urban policies designed to exclude them from occupying public and private spaces. These restrictive policies, she concluded, are "not only ineffective but also exacerbate the problem of homelessness."[7] Valado enumerated the strategies and tactics people employ to work around spatial restrictions such as building a street-level support system for sharing useful information and other resources.[8]

Valado's research took an activist turn: a commitment to understanding the homeless people from their perspective and helping them if possible. Thus, her dissertation became a case study in applied anthropology. Recently,

FIGURE 14.1. Homeless camp in Tucson, Arizona (courtesy of Martha T. Valado).

she co-edited a book that explores ethical issues in doing homelessness research.[9]

Zimmerman, instead of promoting applied anthropology or applied archaeology, advocates "translational research." This term comes from the biomedical sciences and means taking research findings from laboratory to clinic. Translational research also implies that the research is designed with potential applications in mind. Conducting translational research, he argues, is "one way for archaeology to become relevant."[10] This can be achieved by collaborating with homeless people to frame research problems that help solve *their* problems. Although calls for relevance in archaeology began many decades ago, Zimmerman has added an activist twist: "To be useful requires recognition that archaeology is political, that it is acceptable to have a political agenda and that it is OK to be activist."[11] These words resonate today among many archaeologists.

The Indianapolis project, with input from once-homeless Welch, identified material patterns of homelessness that could be translated into policy recommendations and "might prove useful in providing better provisioning to homeless people" *outside shelters.*[12] At the very least, they suggest, archaeologists can evaluate assumptions about material life made by the self-serving "homeless industry"—churches, shelters, foundations, and government agencies—and offer some simple and low cost solutions.[13] Churches and shelters can supply things useful in camps such as can openers, reading materials, and perhaps amusements; they should avoid donating ill-fitting clothing and grooming products that will simply be discarded. Bible pages used for toilet paper along with blogposts indicated that homeless people loathe being proselytized. In shelters, provisions and services should be furnished free of religious coercion. And city officials can refrain from bull-dozing camps and destroying personal possessions.

Zimmerman has publicized the project's preliminary results and recommendations. A press release from his university was picked up by many newspapers in the United States and abroad. And he gives invited talks at various universities on the archaeology of homelessness. Even *Archaeology* magazine, which reaches a large nonprofessional audience, published a brief description of the project.[14] He and Welch also wrote articles for *Anthropology News* and *Historical Archaeology,* which reach professionals.[15] Zimmerman's project has been recapped in *Anthropology News* and is also the subject of many blogs. Finally, in the Central Public Library in Indianapolis, there was an exhibition of project photographs entitled "What does homelessness look like?"[16]

Invited to lecture at a day shelter in Vancouver, British Columbia, Zimmerman presented the project's findings to more than 100 homeless people, and they responded with positive comments. He also listened to their stories, learning in one instance that some people preferred their unconventional lifeway: "We aren't homeless. We are home free. No mortgage, no rules. All I have to do is find a warm place to sleep and food."[17]

The high visibility of Zimmerman's research in popular media and professional venues inspired others to embark on similar projects. In Bristol, England, archaeologists John Schofield and Rachael Kiddey took the next step by collaborating with homeless people.[18] Their crew actively sought conversations, came to know many homeless people by their street names, and obtained permission to take and publish photographs. A unique component of this project was the "participatory" dig they did with homeless volunteers on Turbo Island, which had witnessed many decades—perhaps centuries—of homeless occupation.

The Bristol project has had many unpredictable and positive consequences such as forging "links between homeless and non-homeless people, links that can be strengthened and perhaps act as a necessary spark for beginning the process of rehabilitation, at least for some people."[19] The participants in the dig developed favorable attitudes toward archaeology and archaeologists and took part enthusiastically. They especially appreciated opportunities to share their experiences, in some cases waxing nostalgically about friends and communities in their past. Because the archaeologists were nonjudgmental, the participants gained greater self-esteem and a few even rejoined mainstream society.[20]

Beyond documenting a marginal urban lifeway and supplying policy recommendations, archaeologists are helping to give homeless people a voice—sometimes a face—in the scholarly literature and popular media. Homeless people may now be seen as individuals and families embedded in a network of material, spatial, social, and institutional relationships. When worked skillfully, this network provides access to resources and thus enables survival. The projects discussed here suggest that empathetic interventions based on an archaeological understanding of the material culture of homelessness can result in modest improvements in peoples' lives.

I thank Larry J. Zimmerman and Trenna Valado for commenting on this chapter.

15

Promoting the Electric Car Revival

DURING THE LATE 1980S, there were hints in the media that electric automobiles, which had enjoyed a brief heyday at the turn of the twentieth century, might soon make a comeback. Having grown up in smoggy Los Angeles at the beginning of the environmental movement in the 1960s, I looked forward to the arrival of a new generation of electric cars that promised no tailpipe emissions, at the least. But what happened to that first generation of electric cars? Perhaps an archaeologist's answer to this question might influence automobile makers, helping them to avoid previous mistakes.

At the beginning of this project, a search through books on automobile history turned up several generalizations about early electric cars. These sources, along with a few modern articles in scholarly journals, reported that electric cars were made mainly from the mid-1890s to the late teens. In explaining the electric car's failure to persist, the authors listed—among other alleged shortcomings—the slow speed and short range permitted by the batteries.[1] The flaws were supposedly fatal and allowed cars with internal combustion engines fueled by gasoline to triumph in the marketplace.

Because electric cars are quintessentially an *electrical* technology, it was necessary to consult sources—overlooked by automobile historians—that reported developments in electrical science and technologies. *Electrical World* and *Scientific American* were searched for articles about electric cars and batteries in the period 1890–1920. Information was also sought in publications of the *National Electric Light Association*.

These sources suggested that the rise and fall of the early electric car was not a smooth curve. Lead-acid batteries in the *earliest* electrics did have a limited range on one charge—about 25–35 miles, and failed quickly. Consumers rapidly shunned electric cars, causing some manufacturers to go under and sales for the remaining ones to slump. However, from 1908 to 1910 new battery designs came to market, including more powerful and durable lead acid-batteries along with Edison's alkaline nickel-iron battery; both types enabled a range greater than 100 miles. These developments helped to revive commercial interest because electric cars, most of which had closed-coach bodies for all-weather travel, were now generally regarded as a perfected technology. Such findings raised doubts about the automobile historians' conclusions.

Tellingly, automobile historians did not distinguish between early and late electric cars, treating the entire product type as a single technology destined to fail. Nor did they take note of the new batteries that stimulated a revival in manufacturing and sales. A different approach was needed, one free from the assumption that gasoline cars were inherently superior. By taking into account all relevant evidence, such an approach might reveal what happened to the first generation of electric cars.

An approach well suited for tackling this problem is behavioral archaeology, which privileges the study of people-artifact interactions in concrete activities—anywhere, anytime.[2] In applying this approach, it would be necessary to learn about (1) which companies made electric cars and when; (2) the "automobiling" activities in which the cars took part; (3) the cars' performance characteristics (behavioral capabilities) in automobiling activities; and (4) whether these activities had social-class and gender correlations.

An exhaustive catalog of all U.S.-made automobiles provided quantitative data for discerning patterns and trends in electric car production.[3] Figure 15.1 plots the number of companies that made electric cars during the years 1894–1942. It confirms that, although dozens of electric car makers ended production in the years 1900–05, after 1908 many firms *began* production. This pattern is further supported by Figure 15.2, which displays the number of companies that made their *first* electric car in a given year. Clearly, a second spurt of commercialization followed the advent of better batteries; and electric power companies at this time began to promote electric cars because they could potentially consume large amounts of off-peak current when batteries were being recharged overnight.

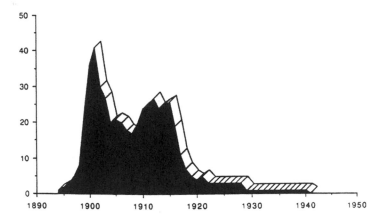

FIGURE 15.1. The number of U.S. companies producing electric cars, 1894–1942 (from Schiffer 2011).

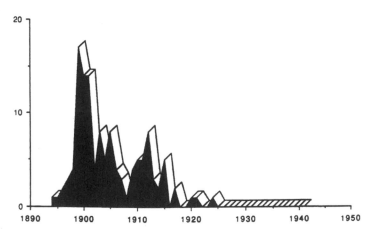

FIGURE 15.2. The number of U.S. companies producing their first electric cars in each year, 1894–1942 (from Schiffer 2011).

Figures 15.1 and 15.2 undermine the automobile historians' traditional explanations. If the battery technology was fatally flawed throughout the entire first generation of electric cars, then why did dozens of new companies bring such vehicles to market after 1908? Manufacturers should have avoided electric cars, but instead embraced them. Moreover, if electrics were such poor performers, why did consumers continue buying them well past the mid-teens?

Magazine articles made it possible to identify the major automobiling activities and their associations with gasoline and electric cars. The patterns were strong: gasoline cars were favored for "touring," that is, taking long, adventure-filled drives in the country; electric cars were used for running errands and traveling to social activities in town. This conclusion was documented in a "threshold performance matrix," a behavioral tool for comparing competing technologies on the basis of performance characteristics relevant to each kind of activity.[4]

The performance matrix (Table 15.1) shows that gasoline cars excelled in touring but were mediocre urban performers, whereas electric cars were quite suitable for urban travel but for touring were nonstarters. Given the horse-pace urban speed limits of the teens, around 8–12 mph, an electric car powered by the new batteries could cruise town all day long on one charge. Finally, magazine articles, advertisements, and even technical publications indicated that automobiling activities were highly gendered: touring was a man's domain; traveling in town was mainly a woman's (Figure 15.3). In addition, social class strongly affected car purchases. These patterns laid the foundation for creating an alternative explanation.

The performance matrix implies that the decision to buy a gasoline or electric car was not a choice between functionally equivalent vehicles. If a family bought only one car, some of its automobiling activities would become difficult or impossible. Thus, to enable *all* automobiling activities, many of America's wealthiest families bought both kinds of cars. The Henry and Clara Ford family had a stable of gasoline cars, including a Rolls Royce and a succession of Detroit electrics, the latter driven mainly by Clara. Thomas and Mina Edison also had "his" and "her" automobiles—gasoline and electric respectively. Despite Ford's association with gasoline cars and Edison's with electrics, both families bought cars that, together, enabled the entire range of automobiling activities. But because buying and maintaining any car was expensive, only very wealthy families could employ the two-car solution.

Middle class families of the time almost exclusively bought gasoline cars, clearly prioritizing touring activities over travel in town. Why did these families favor a leisure activity pursued mainly by men? The answer implicates the structure of middle-class families in early twentieth-century America. In the traditional Euro-American patriarchal family, men were the "breadwinners," and so could decide which activities in certain realms to favor and then choose the technologies that enhanced those activities. Middle-class men, captivated by touring and aware that ownership of a touring-capable car had become a status symbol among their peers, enhanced their leisure activities

TABLE 15.1. A Threshold Performance Matrix for Gasoline and Electric Automobiles, ca. 1912*

Activity	Performance Characteristic	Gasoline	Electric
Touring	Range of 100+ miles	+	–
	Top speed of 40–60 mph	+	–
	Ease of fueling, recharging	+	–
	Ruggedness	+	–
	Economy of operation and maintenance	–	–
	Reparability in country	+	–
	Can indicate owner's membership in the group "tourists"	+	–
	Can indicate owner's wealth	+	+
Running errands in town	Range of 50–100 miles	+	+
	Speed of 12–20 mph	+	+
	Ease of starting	–	+
	Ease of driving	–	+
	All-weather capability	–	+
	Reliability	–	+
	Economy of operation and maintenance	–	–
	Ease of fueling, recharging	+	+
	Can indicate owner's wealth	+	+
	Can indicate owner's social position	+	+
Traveling to social functions in town	Range of 50–100 miles	+	+
	Speed of 12–20 mph	+	+
	Ease of starting	–	+
	East of driving	–	+
	All-weather capability	–	+
	Reliability	–	+
	Economy of operation and maintenance	–	–
	Ease of fueling, recharging	+	+
	Cleanliness of operation	–	+
	Quietness of operation	–	+
	Can indicate owner's membership in the "horsey set"	–	+
	Can indicate owner's wealth	+	+
	Can indicate owner's affinity for "high culture"	–	+

Entries represent an approximation of how these performance characteristics were judged. A plus (+) indicates that the car exceeded the threshold value of that performance characteristic; a minus (–) indicates that the car fell short of the threshold value.
*Adapted from Schiffer 2011:153

FIGURE 15.3. Ad for 1916 Ohio Brougham targeting urban women (from *Literary Digest*, 25 November 1916, p. 1427).

and advertised their social competence by buying, displaying, and talking about gasoline cars. Occasionally they might have used them for touring.

The electric car of the teens was not a technical failure, but a successful upper-class niche product. Only in the late nineteen-teens, when most gasoline cars came with electrical starting and lighting systems and many had enclosed bodies, did they become capable city vehicles. And so the electric cars' niche market declined to near zero.

The findings of the electric car project were reported in *Taking Charge: The Electric Automobile in America* (1994), a book written for a general, nonscholarly audience and published by the Smithsonian Institution Press.[5] The hope was that it would be read widely, discussed, and might exert some influence on the electric car's second coming. The major lesson in *Taking Charge* is that social, cultural, and economic factors play a role alongside technical factors in explaining the "failure" of the early electric car. In fact, the electric car's only failure was in not "trickling down" to the middle class. It could have been otherwise. We can imagine that if middle-class men had not been enamored with the idea of touring, if men and women had equal power to decide automobile purchases, or if women had independent incomes, perhaps electric cars of the nineteen-teens would have found a market of millions—though unable to tour.

The last chapter of *Taking Charge* argues that such nontechnical factors were vastly different at the *end* of the twentieth century than they were at its beginning, paving the way for a sustained revival of electric cars. There were major changes in middle-class families, so obvious they were taken for granted: increased incomes and purchasing power made it possible to buy multiple cars; and many women had a significant say in major purchases because they worked outside the home.

Another change was that many Americans were born after World War II and had grown up green, exposed in schools and the mass media to the plight of the planet. It was suggested that they were predisposed to buy an electric so long as it was effective for their travel activities. In the U.S., several small companies were already offering capable commuter electric cars, and major manufacturers had formed a battery consortium and were building prototype electric vehicles. Still, electric cars were not expected to tour anytime soon.

The possibility of developing touring-capable batteries in the immediate future was discounted in view of the high bar set by modern gasoline cars—at least 500 miles on a charge. Shoring up the charging infrastructure was mentioned as a way to solidify interest in electric cars, and token efforts were proposed, such as installing charging stations in some parking lots, especially in California. Although the book was circumspect in forecasting the success of a new generation of electric cars, it transparently promoted this environment-friendly technology, advocating the commercialization and adoption of the vehicle that, for a century, had been "the car of the future."

The book received widespread publicity and provoked reactions, both positive and negative. In several scholarly reviews, writers dismissed its explanation for the "failure" of the early electrics and ridiculed its forecasts.[6] However, historians Gijs Mom and Robert A. Kirsch accepted *Taking Charge's* basic findings, built on them by digging even more deeply into archival materials, and in their books fashioned sophisticated histories of early electric cars and trucks.[7]

Taking Charge was favorably reviewed in the *Los Angeles Times* and *USA Today*, and I was interviewed by several radio stations and a Canadian TV station. The Northeast Sustainable Energy Association invited me to give a talk at their 1995 meeting, which was published in their proceedings.[8] And an invited article appeared in *Potentials*, a magazine of the Institute of Electrical and Electronics Engineers aimed at engineering students and young professionals.[9] Another paper explored the cultural sources of erroneous beliefs about electric car history.[10] During the 1990s many web sites about the past or future of electric cars employed information and images from *Taking Charge*. As of mid-2015, the book can still be found in over 700 libraries worldwide.[11]

A few years after the book came out, an engineer at General Motors familiar with *Taking Charge* called me with a historical question. After answering him, I asked how he happened to know about the book. It seems that several copies were circulating there. Whether *Taking Charge* influenced the decisions of carmakers is probably unanswerable. Regardless, the book was an archaeologist's attempt to bring the past to bear on the electric car's future at a time when many people were discussing the same subject in print and on the air. Today, the electric car in its many incarnations—battery-only, hybrid, and plug-in hybrid—is a familiar sight in many American cities.

VI

Reviving Ancient Technologies

M ANY AN ARCHAEOLOGIST has admired the ingenuity and skills that went into making and using ancient technologies. Some archaeologists have envisioned how such a technology might find a place in the modern world, and a few have even tried to revive a technology. Yet, introducing an old technology into a new societal context is fraught with unforeseen challenges that good will and optimism cannot always overcome. Not surprisingly, archaeological efforts to revive ancient technologies have had mixed results, as shown in chapters 16–18.

Don E. Crabtree succeeded in replicating an ancient Mesoamerican technique for making long, thin blades of volcanic glass (obsidian). Through his flintknapping field schools, Crabtree taught the technique to many archaeologists. Crabtree and several of his students believed that obsidian or even glass blades could be effective as scalpels and urged surgeons to try them out. Controlled trials on animals and operations on people, including Crabtree, did not produce consistent evidence that obsidian blades were superior to steel scalpels. Even so, some surgeons were pleased with the new tools. Independently, archaeologists Errett Callahan, J. Jeffrey Flenniken, and Payson D. Sheets attempted to commercialize obsidian or glass scalpels; but for various reasons all efforts failed in the end. Still, some flintknappers continue to supply a few surgeons with obsidian blades.

The Andean high plateau around Lake Titicaca, in Bolivia and Peru, is a marginal region for agriculture. Peasant farmers grow a variety of crops but rely on erratic rainfall and must fallow their fields for long periods. However, archaeologists have documented 1,200 km^2 of "raised fields" in this region that were in use between about AD 500 and 1150. Seeking to understand how this ancient agricultural technology worked, Clark Erickson (in Peru) and Alan L. Kolata (in Bolivia) excavated and refurbished some raised fields. They became convinced that this technology was effective and would allow *continuous* cropping and more productive agriculture, and so encouraged outside groups to fund larger experiments with local communities. At first the refurbished fields produced wonderful yields, but after a few years nematode infestations caused yields to drop sharply, and most fields were abandoned. Additional reasons for the failure to revive raised field agriculture on a large scale include the increasing availability of wage labor that seemed preferable to a labor-intensive type of farming.

With the encouragement and support of archaeologists, two skilled potters in the American Southwest raised their craft to an art that commanded critical respect and attracted customers from around the world. Nampeyo was a potter in the Hopi village of Hano in northern Arizona. Encouraged by archaeologist J. Walter Fewkes, she painted prehistoric designs on her pots and eventually developed a distinctive style—Sikyatki Revival—that enjoyed great commercial success. Maria was a potter living in San Ildefonso Pueblo in northern New Mexico with her husband Julian, who worked on an excavation project directed by archaeologist Edgar L. Hewitt. With the support of Hewitt through several New Mexico institutions, Maria and Julian developed distinctive decorative styles that were widely acclaimed in the art world. Potters in other pueblos adopted prehistoric models and went on to achieve much artistic success. Moreover, sales of their works, like those of Nampeyo and Maria, provided significant income for their families.

16

Chipped Stone Scalpels

OPERATING ON THE human body with cutting tools is a practice that began millennia ago.[1] Incisions in soft tissues, such as the scalp, were made with the sharp edge of a freshly chipped (or knapped) piece of stone, often chert or flint. The sharpest stone of all is obsidian, a natural glass formed by rapidly cooling, silica-rich lava. Wherever obsidian occurred, native peoples knapped it into knives and other implements. The Aztecs and Maya used obsidian blades for many activities, most notoriously for human sacrifice, removing the heart from a living victim.

These blades were astonishing tools. Some were more than eight inches long, less than an inch wide, and only a few tenths of an inch thick. And for centuries, their manufacture techniques were mysterious. As many archaeologists can testify, close inspection of the blades and blade cores, which abound in the Aztec and Maya areas, yields few clues about how they were made. This problem fascinated Don E. Crabtree, who had taught himself flintknapping and founded a summer field school to pass these skills to archaeology students. Crabtree, affiliated with the Idaho State Museum, set out to learn by experiment how the ancients of Mesoamerica had made these tools.

Drawing on an imprecise description of an Aztec knapper at work, written almost four centuries earlier by Juan de Torquemada, a Spanish friar and missionary in Mexico, Crabtree eventually devised a workable technique employing a "chest crutch." The chest crutch was a long wooden tool, shaped like a capital T, with a copper tip attached to the bottom. He placed the obsidian core in a wooden clamp resting on the ground. Standing on the clamp, Crabtree positioned the copper tip near the edge of the core's flat top, and then he gradually leaned on the crutch with his chest. Depending on where he placed the copper tip, he could predictably push off long blades with a triangular or trapezoidal cross-section from the core.[2]

Crabtree learned through vivid experience that obsidian blades are sharper than any metal knife and cut cleanly; best of all, the wounds heal quickly with little pain and scarring. Reflecting on his findings, he suggested that surgeons would be well served if they used obsidian scalpels for certain operations, though they might be "accused of reverting to cave man tactics."[3] The potential of obsidian blades for surgery was a take-away lesson for readers of Crabtree's 1968 article and for many archaeologists who had participated in his flintknapping field school.

While visiting their doctors, some archaeologists no doubt passed along Crabtree's suggestion, including Crabtree himself who convinced Dr. Bruce Buck to give obsidian blades a try. Buck operated with the delicate scalpels on volunteers, often other physicians, and on Crabtree's lung and heart, making half the skin incisions with obsidian, the other half with steel. Remarking on his handiwork, Buck noted, "The obsidian knife was indeed sharper, and healing of the two extremities of the incision was identical."[4] Another archaeologist who went under the obsidian knife was Bruce Dahlin, a Mayanist. During a lung operation in 1980, Dahlin's surgeon used an obsidian blade to make the first cut.[5] The operation went well and Dahlin lived for three more decades. The blades for Dahlin's operation came from fellow Mayanist Payson D. Sheets, who learned obsidian knapping from Crabtree.

Human trials were performed in 1976 by dermatologists Michael J. Scott and Michael J. Scott Jr. They used an obsidian blade for half the incision and a steel scalpel for the other half. Concluding, "The obsidian portion consistently healed equal to or superior to that of the steel blade," they recommended obsidian for use in "specialized plastic or dermatologic surgery."[6] They obtained their blades from archaeologist Richard D. Daugherty of Washington State University. Daugherty himself underwent surgery using an obsidian scalpel he had made, which left "an almost imperceptible scar."[7]

Because anecdotes and opportunistic human trials are not the gold standard of clinical testing, some physicians turned to experiments on animals. Crabtree's surgeon, Bruce Buck, conducted the first comparison of wound healing on rabbits. Incisions about an inch long were made with obsidian and steel scalpels. After 14 days, the wounds were examined for strength and other properties. Despite their identical appearance, the obsidian-produced scars were stronger, though under microscopic examination the wounds were indistinguishable. Even so, Buck believed that obsidian blades would be advantageous for delicate work in soft tissues, such as "microvascular surgery and fine plastic work on thin skin."[8]

Acknowledging that obsidian blades have a sharper edge than steel scalpels, surgeon Joseph J. Disa and colleagues experimented on 40 laboratory rats. They made two incisions about 3 inches long, one with an obsidian scalpel, the other steel. Over a period of six weeks, the surgeons and a pathologist monitored the healing process by testing the strength of the wound, measuring scar width, and observing inflammatory cells. In the first few weeks, the obsidian cuts were doing better, with less inflammation, but by the end of the test period all differences had disappeared. The authors concluded that their study did not "unequivocally support the anecdotal observations in humans" and recommended human trials.[9] They failed to mention, however, that reduced inflammation in the first week would probably mean less discomfort for a human patient.

During the early 1980s, several archaeologists tried to commercialize chipped stone scalpels. Working independently, they employed three different strategies, but all used the Stone Age technology reinvented and disseminated by Crabtree to make what they believed would be a beneficial and perhaps profitable product. Their efforts garnered a swarm of largely favorable publicity in highly visible newspapers and magazines, including *The Washington Post* and *Science 81*.[10] Especially significant was an article in *American Medical News*, a publication of the American Medical Association, that contained glowing endorsements of obsidian scalpels by several surgeons.[11] And, at the instigation of archaeologists, there were more surgeries. The stage was set for the dramatic triumph of a revived technology.

Errett Callahan was one of the most skillful flintknappers in the world. Although largely self-taught, he had also studied with Crabtree and other archaeologist-knappers. Callahan and several friends formed a company, Aztecnics, to sell obsidian blades. Their slick brochure, "The Alternative Edge," addressed surgeons and listed the advantages of obsidian in the operating room. Obsidian blades, they maintained, are sharper than steel, cannot be accidentally magnetized, are "non-absorbant [sic] and non-corrosive."[12] Although Aztecnics was not a successful business, Callahan periodically sold

blades to surgeon Lee A. Green, then of the University of Michigan Medical
School, and also supplied them for the rat experiments.

Undeterred by the failure of Aztecnics, Errett Callahan found another
way to commercialize his craft through a second company, Piltdown Pro-
ductions, Ltd., in Lynchburg, Virginia. Until his retirement around 2006,
Callahan's one-man company sold his replicas of prehistoric artifacts as well
as whimsical obsidian knives. The knives are stunning, award-winning works
of art, sold mainly to knife collectors.[13] Callahan signed and dated each object—more than 9,000—so that they could not be mistaken for the originals.
Callahan is also the author of many books on chipped stone technologies,
which are very popular among members of flintknapping clubs across the
United States, some of whom sell their products on eBay.

Another attempt to interest surgeons in obsidian blades was made by archaeologist J. Jeffrey Flenniken who, after Don Crabtree's passing in 1980, ran
the flintknapping field school. Instead of creating a company to sell blades,
Flenniken supplied them to medical equipment companies to distribute
them for trials.[14] Despite an initial flurry of interest and some lucrative contracts, no company actually brought his blades to market. The device makers
told him that obsidian blades lacked approval of the U.S. Food and Drug
Administration. And so ended another effort to commercialize obsidian
scalpels.[15]

The most ambitious attempt to bring Stone Age technology into the
operating room was by University of Colorado archaeologist Payson D.
Sheets, mentioned earlier as the one who supplied blades for Bruce Dahlin's
surgery.[16] Sheets believed that obsidian might not be homogenous enough
to yield blades of consistent quality. He turned to glass, whose chemical
composition and mechanical properties could be controlled, and developed a bronze mold for making cores that could be clamped for flaking. The
distinctive feature of the cores, as they came from the mold, was fluting on
two opposite sides, giving the appearance that the core had already yielded
blades. This "pre-flaking" enabled the indenter to be positioned precisely.
Sheets also invented a machine that could do the actual flaking.

After experimenting for several years, Sheets applied for a U.S. patent,
which he received on March 3, 1987 (No. 4,647,300). Collaborating with a
surgeon and a business professor, Sheets formed a Colorado corporation,
Fracture Mechanics, Ltd., to which he assigned his patent. The company
leased the patent to two New York investment bankers who bought a firm

in Europe to handle the product. Unfortunately, the bankers became over-extended when they also tried to cover the Asian market by buying a company there. The bankers abandoned the project, left the country, and the hard-won patent eventually expired. Nothing more came of Sheets's effort.[17]

Despite promising experiments on animals, successful operations on people, and widespread and largely favorable publicity, glass and obsidian scalpels were not generally adopted. Cautions expressed at the time, even by enthusiastic surgeons, suggest several factors—still relevant today—that discourage adoption of the "new" technology:

1. the ultra-thin cutting edge is easily damaged by lateral movement in the incision or contact with bone and connective tissue;
2. conventional scalpels are sterilized by the manufacturer, but obsidian ones may require sterilization at the place of use;
3. a bare blade cannot be grasped easily and so a haft, or extra chipping to blunt the part touching the hand, is necessary; either way, the surgeon must develop a new grip and new motions;
4. they are appropriate only for soft tissue;
5. at around $10, they would be more expensive than ordinary stainless steel blades (.50 each) but cheaper than diamond scalpels ($800 or more);
6. the blades' demonstrated advantages mainly benefit the patient, which may not matter to hospitals and surgeons except in certain kinds of cosmetic surgery.

Given these diverse factors, it is a tribute to the salesmanship of the archaeologists that so many surgeons were willing to try the blades on dozens, perhaps hundreds, of human patients. And some surgeons are still using them: according to a 2008 blogpost, surgeons were buying obsidian scalpels from an unidentified "Blademan."[18] In addition to scalpel sales by anonymous knappers and the many blade-based knives sold by hobbyist flintknappers, Fine Science Tools sells small obsidian blades mounted on wooden hafts for $78.50.[19] A person at the company told me that they are mainly bought as gags for presentation to graduating medical students.

17

Raised-Field Agriculture in the Andes

NESTLED IN THE ALTIPLANO (high plateau) of the Andes and straddling the border between Bolivia and Peru is Lake Titicaca, the largest body of fresh water in South America. The lake lies at an elevation of 3,800 m, where maize (corn) and many other New World crops cannot grow. Seemingly, the region is unsuitable for human habitation, much less the development of a complex society. Yet, between about AD 500 and 1150, there thrived in this arid, frost-prone environment the Tiwanaku state, whose traces include lively polychrome pottery, structures of closely fitted sandstone blocks adorned with carvings, and the unique Gate of the Sun.

In addition to the urban center of Tiwanaku and many prehistoric village sites, there is a culturally modified landscape consisting of elongated earthen platforms surrounded by canal networks. Such landscapes occur elsewhere in the New World, including present-day Colombia, Venezuela, Ecuador, and the Valley of Mexico; in the latter, the Aztec heartland, the platforms and canals remained in use after European contact. Early visitors to the Valley of Mexico erroneously called them "floating gardens" because the platforms or mounds, with their lush crops, appeared to be floating above the canals. The Lake Titicaca basin contains an estimated 1,200 km² of raised fields.[1]

Although the altiplano has been continuously inhabited since before the founding of Tiwanaku, in recent centuries no one farmed the raised fields. And, until a few decades ago, no archaeologist investigated them. That neglect ended with growing interest in traditional agriculture and its ecological underpinnings. Beginning in the 1980s, archaeologists Clark Erickson (working in Peru) and Alan L. Kolata (in Bolivia) independently carried out large-scale projects on raised fields in the Titicaca basin. In addition to surveys and excavations, Erickson and Kolata did experiments to learn how the raised fields worked as an agricultural technology. As Erickson remarked, "archaeology may be the only way to understand these technologies."[2]

Armed with the new knowledge their researches furnished, Erickson and Kolata modeled the construction, use, and maintenance of raised fields, which suggested that this abandoned technology had some advantages over dry farming (where rainfall is the only water source) and so might be put back into production. The vision inspired archaeologists to promote efforts to revive or "rehabilitate" the raised fields for the benefit of present-day inhabitants.

The altiplano is a challenging environment for farming, given its flooding, droughts, hailstorms, and killer frosts.[3] In modern times, the staple crop is a frost-resistant but bitter variety of potato. Also cultivated are quinoa, cañahua, fava beans, and several native roots as well as introduced crops including barley and oats.[4] These days, farmers do not plant on and around the ancient raised fields because this low-lying area is swampy and susceptible to seasonal flooding. Yet, prehistoric farmers indeed created large tracts of raised fields there and apparently cultivated them for long periods.

To learn when the raised fields were built and used, archaeologists placed trenches across a sample of fields and adjoining canals. The entire area today is one of low relief, suggesting that the fields themselves have eroded. This was not the case: fields retained nearly their original form, but the canals were filled with wind- and water-laid sediments.[5] In Bolivia, a large sample of radiocarbon dates indicated that the fields were used mainly during Tiwanaku times.[6]

Although highly variable in both width and length, the fields provided—in principle—good conditions for plant growth, furnishing moisture to roots while preventing waterlogging. Researchers predicted other favorable characteristics of raised fields, but only experiments with rehabilitated field systems could shed light on how they really worked.

Archaeologists rebuilt and operated raised-field systems in Peru and Bolivia and monitored their performance. The findings were very promising.[7] During the day, the sun raised the temperature of canal water. At night, this water created a slightly warmer microenvironment for plants, perhaps reducing the severity of frosts and lengthening the growing season. By storing

FIGURE 17.1. Raised fields near Lake Titicaca (Wikimedia Commons, courtesy of
FAO/Alipio Canahua).

water, canals also buffered variability in flooding and rainfall. The nutrient-
rich "muck" at the bottom of the canals, when scooped up and applied to the
fields, was an excellent fertilizer. In contrast to the modern villagers' fields,
which require crop rotation and long-term fallowing after just a few years,
raised fields, the archaeologists suggested, might be continuously cropped.[8]
In the first two years of use, the experimental fields produced bumper potato
crops, and other crops also thrived.

Encouraged by these experiments, the archaeologists sought outside
funding to help farmers rehabilitate many more fields. And they were successful: millions of dollars flowed into rehabilitation projects.[9] Alan Kolata's
colleague, Oswaldo Rivera, codirector of the project and director of the
National Institute of Archaeology in Bolivia, established a nongovernmental
organization (NGO), the Fundación Wiñaymarka. The foundation obtained
international funding, lobbied community leaders, and distributed illustrated
brochures to the farmers.[10] Eventually, farmers in 55 communities took part
in the project and rehabilitated almost 100 hectares of fields (Figure 17.1).[11]
In Peru, Erickson's experiments were carried out at first on a small scale in
the community of Huatta; promising results led to a large expansion of the

program to nearby communities.[12] By 2000, outside funding enabled the Peruvians to refurbish as many as 2000 hectares of raised fields.[13]

There were several reasons for the success in obtaining international support for these "development" projects.[14] During the 1980s, shortcomings of the so-called green revolution were becoming evident. As promised, newer crop varieties had impressive yields, but there was a drastic tradeoff when industrial practices were transferred to developing countries. Large, mechanized farms required constant and expensive inputs of fertilizer, petroleum fuels to operate equipment, and sometimes herbicides and pesticides. These inputs, along with the need to maintain tractors, irrigation pumps, and other equipment, chained communities to international markets, making them dependent on others and susceptible to capricious fluctuations in crop prices. Such "advanced" farming systems also increased pollution and contributed to growing debt for both farmers and developing nations. Not surprisingly, profits accrued not to local farmers but to middlemen and international bankers.

Calling attention to these problems, some scholars had pronounced the green revolution a sham, a veritable Trojan Horse, and urged the return to local, sustainable agriculture using traditional—that is, *appropriate*—technologies that supposedly would not despoil the environment.[15] Some development organizations took notice and responded favorably to proposals for such systems.

Erickson and Kolata embraced the academic critique of the green revolution and pitched raised-field agriculture as an attractive alternative that would operate, more or less autonomously, at the local level. Clearly, there was no need for tractors and costly inputs. In reconstructing and operating raised-field systems, farmers used only hand tools: in Peru, the "Andean footplow, hoe, clod breaker, and carrying cloths"; in Bolivia, "picks, shovels, mattocks, and wheelbarrows."[16] And the raised-field systems supplied their own fertilizer. In practice, this mode of farming seemed to hew closely to the ideals of sustainable agriculture. Further, to encourage participation, the development organizations gave farmers incentives in the form of seeds, tools, sometimes wages, and supplementary food, although Erickson, perhaps in a moment of doubt, pondered the fate of the fields "if these incentives are withdrawn."[17]

The projects received favorable publicity in mass media, which sometimes emphasized the roles played by archaeologists.[18] But after the photographers had gone, the archaeologists had moved on to new projects, and the incentives had ended, farmers had to decide for themselves whether this "new" system was worth maintaining, as Erickson surmised.

In 1996, cultural anthropologist Lynn Swartley conducted a study in Wankolla, one of many Bolivian communities on the altiplano that had rehabilitated raised fields. She found that "by 1996 all of the fields constructed by the NGO, Fundación Wiñaymarka, were abandoned."[19] Writing in 2005 about Peru, archaeologist Matthew Bandy observed, "Few if any raised fields remain in production today."[20]

Setting out to explain the farmers' decisions, Swartley interviewed farmers, NGO workers, and others. She learned that farmers had taken advantage of opportunities to augment their household's economy with earnings from wage labor outside the community; after all, the bitter potatoes they grew had no market as a cash crop, and there was convenient public transportation to jobs in La Paz, Bolivia's capital.[21] Many men lived only part of the week or part of the year in Wankollo, creating a shortage of labor needed to keep the raised fields going. With wages, a family could buy supplementary foods and other commodities. And, although households continued to do dry farming, the fields were all plowed with oxen or a rented tractor, which eliminated a labor-intensive activity.[22]

The availability of outside wage labor was not the only factor working against raised-field agriculture. Swartley also learned that the new fields failed to meet expectations regarding yields and continuous cropping. Yields were bountiful in the first and sometimes second year but fell off greatly by the third and fourth years.[23] Bandy assembled evidence showing that *continuous* cropping of potatoes in the Lake Titicaca basin is doomed to failure: native nematodes (parasitic worms that attack roots) will reach a certain density and then greatly reduce productivity. Even on raised fields, then, fallowing and crop rotation are mandatory. But farmers apparently did not turn to these strategies, which they used routinely on their dry fields. Bandy's analyses, which factor in the necessity of fallowing and crop rotation, also suggest that raised fields are, in general, more labor intensive than dry fields for a given yield.[24]

Why, then, were so many raised fields built during Tiwanaku times? Following economist Ester Boserup's intensification model, Bandy suggests that, as the Tiwanaku state's population grew, elite persons enticed farmers, through feasting and the provision of craft items, to build and cultivate raised fields despite the added workload.[25] Properly managed, raised fields enabled the cultivation of otherwise unusable land, thus generating a food surplus to support growing numbers of state functionaries and occupational specialists, including potters, goldsmiths, and the celebrated stone carvers and masons.

Despite abandoning their new fields, the modern farmers interviewed by Swartley did not regard the project as a failure: they cited bountiful harvests in the first years, along with the many incentives. Community members believed that they had enjoyed benefits without suffering ill effects. And they were able to continue cultivating their dry-farmed fields.[26]

The raised-field projects were plausible attempts to help the peasant farmers of the Lake Titicaca basin, but wage labor—and the cornucopia of purchases it enabled—proved to be a more powerful draw than the supposed subsistence autonomy that promoters of raised fields promised. Even so, it is possible that, in areas where access to wage labor is difficult, farmers whose other fields are marginally productive may still cultivate raised fields using crop rotation and fallowing.

The tantalizing possibility that this agricultural technology from the past could be useful in the present remains very much alive. Scholars from several disciplines recently collaborated on a review of raised-field agriculture and concluded that many more experiments are needed. But they also suggested that raised fields can still contribute to a form of sustainable agriculture.[27]

18

Ancient Pots and Modern Potters
in the American Southwest

MANY INDIAN TRIBES in the United States today make and sell hand-built pottery, but the American Southwest boasts the forms and decorative styles that most appeal to the tastes of tourists and art collectors. Moreover, after the railroad arrived in northern New Mexico and Arizona in the 1880s, commerce between tribes and other states accelerated, and the Southwest produced two ceramic artists who achieved international fame. Like some celebrities, these artists are known by single names: Nampeyo and Maria.

Both potters became renowned for their technical skills as well as creative designs alluding to ancestors' wares. Those designs are still made today by the hands of descendants and followers. Early on, archaeologists played roles helping Nampeyo and Maria establish their designs and reputations.

Jesse Walter Fewkes was a marine biologist at Harvard who became fascinated with Indians, ancient and modern.[1] Turning to anthropology in the early 1890s, he observed ceremonies at several Pueblo Indian villages. He was especially captivated by the Hopi, who lived on isolated mesas in the high desert of northeastern Arizona and retained a largely traditional lifeway. Drawing on his observations and those of other anthropologists, Fewkes published dozens of papers on Hopi myths and rituals.

In 1895, having been hired by the Bureau of American Ethnology in Washington, D.C., Fewkes excavated at the Hopi ancestral site of Sikyatki, just a few miles from First Mesa villages, hoping to support his theories on Hopi clan migrations. The excavations turned up pottery vessels of striking appearance. Eventually called Sikyatki Polychrome, the bowls and jars have a polished yellow-orange surface with lively decorative motifs delicately painted in red and dark brown or black.

Fewkes compared Sikyatki vessels with those still made by Hopi women for everyday use: "The best examples of ceramic art from the graves of Sikyatki, in texture, finish, and decoration, are, in my judgment, superior to any pottery made by ancient or modern Indians north of Mexico.... Among the Hopi themselves the ceramic art has degenerated, as the few remaining potters confess."[2] One of these potters was Nampeyo, a resident of Hano, a village on First Mesa. Even before Fewkes started excavations, Nampeyo, already an exceptional potter, had begun collecting and copying designs from pottery fragments she found at ancestral sites. But Fewkes's excavations at Sikyatki and a year later at Old Cuñopavi disgorged hundreds of whole vessels that inspired new design possibilities.[3] Fewkes let Nampeyo and her husband Lesou draw copies of the vessels' decorations. With some tweaking and translation into three-dimensional pots, these designs would energize a "Sikyatki Revival" whose products, made by many Hopi potters, are well known to archaeologists and Indian art lovers.[4] So faithful were Nampeyo's replicas that some were sold as originals to unsuspecting tourists, collectors, and museums.[5]

Whether direct copies of prehistoric vessels or, later, novel applications of the Sikyatki style, Nampeyo's stunning wares were an immediate commercial success (Figure 18.1).[6] Walter Hough in 1896 bought some of her early Sikyatki Revival vessels for the U.S. National Museum in Washington (part of the Smithsonian Institution). The nearby Keams Canyon trading post also offered Nampeyo's pots to tourists and traders. In 1905, the Fred Harvey Company, which owned a string of hotels along the Santa Fe Railroad, hired Nampeyo to demonstrate pottery-making for tourists at their Grand Canyon location. Soon her pots were being sold in the gift shops of every Fred Harvey hotel from New Mexico to California, clearly branded as Nampeyo's work. By 1910, Nampeyo was a celebrity potter, known in the art world as an extraordinary talent. Today, one can find a wealth of diverse Nampeyo pots in numerous public and private collections around the globe along with Sikyatki Revival pottery made by many Hopi potters.

Fewkes's role in the Sikyatki revival was minor, but the extent of his assistance to Nampeyo hardly matters, for this example teaches us something more general. That is, the archaeological remains themselves—*whole* Sikyatki Polychrome vessels—became Nampeyo's models for developing

FIGURE 18.1. Hopi potter Nampeyo and some of her pots, 1900 (courtesy of the National Archives, Records of the National Park Service).

the distinctive revival style still employed by modern Hopi potters. Using prehistoric materials as models for revivals or replicas has taken place, and continues to occur, in many societies around the globe, with and without the direct help of archaeologists.

In contrast to Fewkes's slight involvement with Nampeyo, Edgar Lee Hewett and other anthropologists took a very active role in the development and promotion of Maria's pottery.[7] Like Fewkes, Hewett was essentially self-trained in archaeology, but he did earn a doctorate, at long distance, from the University of Geneva on the basis of his early fieldwork in the Southwest.[8] He was also a prolific builder of institutions in northern New Mexico as first director of the School of American Archaeology (now the School for Advanced Research), first director of the Museum of New Mexico, and first head of the Department of Archaeology and Anthropology at the University of New Mexico. These institutions enabled Hewett to conduct archaeological research and teaching, lobby for the protection of New Mexico sites, and promote local Indian artists.

Maria and her husband, Julian, lived in San Ildefonso Pueblo, about 18 miles northwest of Santa Fe. Pottery made at San Ildefonso in the late nineteenth century was of indifferent quality, aimed mainly at undiscriminating tourists. Maria learned to make pottery as a youth and was soon recognized as possessing exceptional skill, even demonstrating her craft at the St. Louis World's Fair in 1904; but she was not yet an innovator.

In 1907, Hewett hired Julian to assist in excavations on the Pajarito Plateau, not far from San Ildefonso. Impressed, Hewett gave him watercolors, paper, and brushes and urged him to paint traditional pueblo scenes. Julian rapidly developed into an artist of great distinction; his paintings (and, later, commissioned murals) are known for their fine linework, intricate elements, and sensitive composition.

During the field season of 1908, Maria visited Julian in Hewett's camp and became interested in the black-on-cream pottery being unearthed. Taking advantage of the opportunity, Hewett encouraged Maria to decorate her bowls with prehistoric designs, but Maria was not a painter. Encouraged by Hewett and supported for several years by the Museum of New Mexico, she and Julian teamed up: Maria made the vessels and Julian decorated them with ancient designs. These were polychrome vessels whose form and decoration were executed with superior skill compared to then-current San Ildefonso wares, and they were quickly appreciated as art.

A few years later, after numerous experiments, Maria and Julian began making polished black pottery, which was also made at San Ildefonso and nearby Santa Clara Pueblo. In polishing a pot, the potter uses a rounded stone with an almost mirror-like smoothness. Rubbing the stone on the still-moist pot gives the surface a sheen. Maria polished the pots quickly and precisely, and discovered that the sheen was best retained if the pots were fired at a fairly low temperature. When dried, the pots were a shiny brown, but they turned black during firing in a reducing (oxygen-starved) atmosphere, which Maria created by smothering the fire at its hottest with ash and cow pies.

But the pottery for which Maria and Julian are best known is a polished black ware decorated with a matte (dull) black paint. After many experiments, Maria and Julian perfected this iconic ware in 1921. Owing to its immediate commercial success, black-on-black pottery was soon being copied by other pueblo potters and is still made today at San Ildefonso and several nearby pueblos.

Beginning in 1911, Maria and other Pueblo Indian potters displayed their wares at the Palace of the Governors in Santa Fe, bypassing traders and selling pots directly to the public. The institutions that Hewett built also became outlets for Indian arts and crafts. The Museum of New Mexico bought some of the finest wares. In 1922, Hewett, Kenneth Chapman (an artist-archaeologist), and others organized an annual "Indian Fair" in Santa Fe. To elevate the quality of arts and crafts, the Indian Fair required participants to use traditional methods of manufacture as well as native clays and pigments. Promoters and connoisseurs on both coasts flocked to Santa Fe, returning with pots that would grace the homes of discerning collectors of Indian art. Today, the "Indian Fair" thrives as the "Indian Market."

Both Hewett and Chapman strove to convince potters that greater labor invested in creating fine art, as opposed to cheap tourist trinkets, would be handsomely rewarded.[9] And it was. By one estimate, Maria's pottery earned for her household around $2,000 in 1924, a handsome amount for that time and place. By 1936, 20 potters were at work at San Ildefonso, and the total contribution of arts and crafts to the pueblo's annual income reached more than 60 percent.[10]

Potters in other New Mexico pueblos, seeking similar commercial success, also began painting prehistoric design elements on their pots.[11] At Acoma Pueblo, for example, Lucy Lewis employed motifs of ancient Mimbres black-on-white pottery. Continued by Lewis's descendants and neighbors, these wares remain popular.[12]

Although the Pueblo pottery revival rested on the artistic brilliance and productivity of Nampeyo, Maria, and other potters, commercial success also reflected strong demand for their wares. In the late nineteenth and early twentieth centuries, many upper-middle-class Americans were lured to the Southwest by the Santa Fe Railroad whose posters, booklets, and ads, some crafted with the collaboration of anthropologists, romanticized the Southwest, particularly its exotic Indians and their artifacts.[13] At the same time, participants in the Arts and Crafts movement—Anglo women especially—condemned the mediocre products of factory production, praised the virtues of preindustrial handicraft and the individual artisan, and promoted Pueblo Indian products.[14] Whether bought in a Fred Harvey shop, Indian Fair in

Santa Fe, or New York gallery, a Sikyatki-like jar, black-on-black wedding vase, or Mimbres-style water jar was a token of a traditional culture made by a person not a machine.

A final few words are needed about the potters' reasons for participating in global markets and transforming household craft items into commercial art. Even the isolated Hopi were already participating in markets by 1875, and many New Mexico pueblos, especially San Ildefonso, had been involved much earlier. Indians altered their traditional crafts to appeal to Anglo tastes—whether high art for connoisseurs or curios for traders—because the income from sales was important for survival. The Hopi had a precarious existence, subject to occasional famines after repeated crop failures. At San Ildefonso, Anglos and Spanish-Americans had encroached on tribal farmland, making it difficult for many Indian families to practice subsistence agriculture.[15] Given these conditions, the potters of Hopi, San Ildefonso, and other pueblos chose to supplement their household incomes with pottery sales, submitting to—yet influencing—the dictates of the art world.

VII

MANAGING CULTURAL RESOURCES

THROUGH LEGISLATION dating back to 1906, the U.S. government has gradually recognized its responsibility to protect cultural resources. To comply with what is now a tangle of laws and regulations, American governments at all levels conduct archaeological studies that furnish information for managing cultural resources. These resources include historical properties and archaeological artifacts and sites. Although some governments do the archaeology themselves, many contract for cultural resource management (CRM) studies with outside consulting companies, a number of which specialize in archaeology.

In order to specify the work that needs to be done—such as a survey in advance of road construction—and to evaluate and make use of consultants' reports, governments also employ their own archaeologists. Thus, many federal agencies have staff archaeologists, as do some cities, counties, and tribes. Government archaeologists may influence the treatment of archaeological resources, deciding whether to avoid sites on a road project or excavate them, for example. Some "in-house" archaeologists have built programs that not only furnish timely information for managing resources but also ensure that projects contribute to history and prehistory.

The federal effort actually consists of hundreds of local agencies that have developed individualized CRM programs. The Bureau of Land Management and U.S. Forest Service, for example, collaborated on a series of archaeological "overviews" or reports that synthesize existing information and help agency archaeologists guide future work. Although military bases were slow to comply with federal legislation, a 1990 law provided funds for archaeological investigations relating to Department of Defense activities. Some bases have hired archaeologists and taken a very active role in CRM, such as the exemplary program of the Army's White Sands Missile Range. Surveys on White Sands supplemented by historical information have identified, for example, significant launch complexes and other features associated with the testing of German V-2 rockets seized after World War II.

Relations between American Indian tribes and archaeologists were often strained in the past. Indians witnessed sacred places being damaged and ancestors being unearthed and removed to distant museums. For several reasons, including new federal legislation, this situation began to improve. Florida's Seminole Tribe, taking full advantage of new federal legislation giving tribes great autonomy over their cultural resources, established a CRM program, the Tribal Archaeology Section (TAS). The TAS conducts surveys, assesses the significance of sites, excavates when necessary, and interviews community members. In this way, Seminole archaeology seamlessly integrates the interests of archaeologists and tribal members. A recent project documented the Red Barn and detailed its local and national significance. The Red Barn played an important role in the Tribe's cattle industry, and it was also a meeting place where the Seminole tribal government took shape, leading to federal recognition in 1957.

Some cities also have CRM programs, as in Alexandria, Virginia. Citizen interest in the city's history and archaeology catalyzed the establishment in 1975 of the Alexandria Archaeology Commission, which became Alexandria Archaeology. As director of Alexandria Archaeology, Pamela Cressey established a CRM program called "community archaeology," which involves citizen participation in fieldwork and artifact analysis. In the Alexandria Archaeology Museum, volunteers process archaeological finds and answer questions from visitors. An education program includes teacher workshops and lesson plans for schools as well as internships and a summer field school. A major responsibility of Alexandria Archaeology is to administer the city's CRM legislation, which ensures that archaeological resources are assessed in advance of land-modification projects. Alexandria Archaeology's community approach to CRM has become a model for other cities.

19

Federal Agencies and
Cultural Resource Management

BEFORE 1906, anyone could dig in ruins on federal land and sell the booty with impunity. But in that year, at the urging of activist archaeologists, Congress passed the Antiquities Act, which requires that excavation permits be issued only to qualified researchers. In the same spirit and year, Congress established Mesa Verde National Park, home to hundreds of Pueblo ruins including the famed Cliff Palace. These moves were followed in the 1930s and 1940s by laws that authorized salvage (emergency) archaeology in river basins about to be flooded after dam construction and that established the National Park Service's Interagency Archaeological Salvage program.[1]

The Historic Sites Preservation Act of 1966 set up the National Register of Historic Places, specifies criteria for eligibility based on a site's significance, and requires federal agencies to consider the effects of their activities on Register-eligible sites. This law also creates a role for states by tasking a state historic preservation officer to help assess the eligibility of sites for the Register. Together, these and other federal laws led to much salvage archaeology but not to a comprehensive policy of cultural resource management (CRM).[2]

Around 1970, two new laws brought about a sea change in the way the federal government treats archaeological resources. The National Environmental Policy Act (NEPA) of 1969 mandates that federal agencies, in advance of a land-modification project, gather information on the nature, extent, and significance of any resources that the project might directly or indirectly affect.[3] NEPA also applies to corporate projects such as power lines that need federal permits. The law did not mention *archaeological* resources, but they were soon included in regulations and in the "environmental impact statements" that NEPA requires.[4] NEPA's immediate effect was to spur an enormous number of archaeological surveys, testing activities, and in some cases excavations.[5] Because information on archaeological resources must be acquired and evaluated before construction may begin, NEPA promotes *management* rather than salvage; after all, a project that threatens significant sites may be redesigned or terminated.

The second landmark law contributing to a management approach was Executive Order 11593, issued by President Nixon in 1971. Federal agencies were to become stewards of cultural resources, protecting and preserving them. It required landholding agencies to inventory their cultural resources and determine which are eligible for the National Register; the complete inventory was to be finished by July 1, 1973. This provision was spectacularly unrealistic because no archaeological survey can be complete: some sites are tiny, deeply buried, or covered in leaf litter—and surveys that thoroughly cover thousands of square miles are prohibitively expensive. Although no agency met the deadline, the Executive Order also fostered limited surveys in search of Register-eligible sites.

NEPA and Executive Order 11593 led to a vast increase in the number of archaeological projects, many of them contracted at first with universities and museums, but in later years the bulk of the business has gone to environmental consulting firms, which together employ thousands of archaeologists. With the exception of the National Park Service, however, most federal agencies in 1970 had one or two staff archaeologists at most and so were at a disadvantage in specifying work needed and evaluating contract reports. Thus, during the 1970s, federal agencies began to hire archaeologists in large numbers. The U.S. Forest Service, for example, employed one archaeologist in 1968; a decade later there were 74.[6]

Despite gaps, inconsistencies, and unrealistic provisions, this patchwork of laws—and others enacted in the following decades—enables federal agencies to craft innovative CRM programs. Respecting the spirit of the laws, an archaeologist working for a national forest, national park, or district of the Bureau of Land Management (BLM) can customize a program in response to local needs and conditions. Not surprisingly, programs vary greatly among federal agencies and even among local offices of a single agency. To illustrate this variation, I turn to two examples of federal CRM in practice, one from the BLM and the other from the Department of Defense.

The BLM is the largest federal landholding agency, governing more than 400,000 square miles, mainly in 12 western states. Although surveying all of its lands is impossible, the BLM contracted for small-scale surveys such as those in advance of proposed powerlines. But the BLM lacked sufficient background information for assessing the significance of sites found on these surveys. Faced with the same problem, the U.S. Forest Service collaborated with the BLM on a novel strategy. In Arizona and New Mexico, where both agencies have huge landholdings, they divided the states into large regions and contracted with archaeologists to prepare "overviews"—a synthesis and evaluation of previous projects in each region along with recommendations for future work. Because the overviews covered entire regions—not just BLM or Forest Service lands—they became the cornerstone of an enlightened CRM program.

In 1979, Chris Kincaid, the BLM's Phoenix District Archeologist, hired Randall H. McGuire and me to prepare the overview for southwestern Arizona, an arid and poorly known area. Prehistorically, this region witnessed many millennia of occupation, including parts of the Patayan and Hohokam archaeological cultures.

As a common type of project, overviews have many uses.[7] Agency archaeologists new to an office can rapidly become familiar with the region's prehistory. Overviews also allow contractors to learn about an area's previous research, field conditions, and so on before bidding on projects. Academic archaeologists and graduate students also consult overviews when designing their own research.

With these uses in mind, our comprehensive overview discussed the natural environment and its changes, reviewed the ethnographic literature on Native American groups living in the region, inventoried previously recorded sites, summarized the methods and findings of earlier projects, and synthesized the area's prehistory with attention to changing cultural adaptations.[8] The overview also contained bonus chapters, including a topical index to the region's archaeological reports, an evaluation and revision of the major Hohokam chronologies, and Michael Waters's report on Patayan ceramics.

District Archeologist Kincaid was especially eager to obtain advice for designing *cost-effective surveys of large areas* on the order of tens or even hundreds of square miles. Because such areas cannot be surveyed completely, they require some version of probability sampling, such as random selection of survey units from an arbitrary grid. Not only would these surveys help to satisfy the spirit of Executive Order 11593, but they were also required by NEPA if the BLM proposed to transfer a large tract of land to state or private ownership. And so we devoted a long chapter to problems of surveying in southwestern Arizona where sites tend to be small and occur at low density (fewer than 10 per square mile).[9] To ground our recommendations in real data, we did a comparative analysis of previous large-scale surveys in the region and in the greater American Southwest. We found that surveying in areas of low site density costs thousands of dollars per discovered site because fieldworkers spend most of their time crossing barren ground. And the number of sites found, perhaps a few dozen, is usually too small to permit reliable description and assessment of the resources.

Our suggestion was to supplement probability sampling with relatively inexpensive techniques to raise the yield of sites, such as surveying in the vicinity of any site encountered in a survey unit (because sites tend to occur in clusters) and searching near springs, sources of chippable stone, and so on.

As it turned out, the BLM participated in few large land exchanges after our report was completed in 1982; nor did the agency have funds to conduct large surveys solely for inventory purposes. However, the remainder of our report did supply—and still does—information for contractors, academics, and BLM archaeologists.[10] While the BLM–Forest Service overview series was an inspired strategy, the overviews quickly became dated and should have been revised at least once a decade. Unfortunately, most—including ours—have not.

Although the Department of Defense was slow to accept its responsibilities under CRM legislation, it eventually hired archaeologists at many bases, and the Navy established an Underwater Archaeology Branch. Surprisingly, surveys on most bases, even bombing ranges, have recorded many sites in relatively good condition because there was little looting.

The Department of Defense complained that it could not comply with environmental and historic preservation legislation because of insufficient funds. In 1990, Congress responded by establishing the Legacy Resource Management Program, which furnishes funds on a project-by-project basis for preserving "natural and cultural heritage."[11] This legislation authorizes archaeological investigations, particularly of sites and artifacts related to activities of the Department of Defense.

An early applicant for these funds was the Army's White Sands Missile Range. Located in an arid, sparsely populated part of southern New

Mexico, White Sands was the major testing ground for Army, Navy, and Air Force missiles during and after World War II. The Legacy Program funded a demonstration project to generate a list of Register-eligible Cold War sites of the period 1942–64.

In 1993, the Army awarded the project to Human Systems Research (HSR), a consulting company based in New Mexico.[12] Codirected by archaeologists Peter L. Eidenbach and Richard L. Wessel, the project searched the historical records of base activities, conducted interviews, field-checked sites, and consulted information in the White Sands Missile Range Museum.

Thousands of missiles of every conceivable type were launched at White Sands, many requiring construction of specialized facilities. The most significant launch sites were associated with Operation Paperclip. In this clandestine operation, the U.S. government reconstituted Germany's V-2 rocket program. In the last year of World War II, some 1,500 of these highly capable rockets rained down on England alone—especially London—causing much damage and over 7,000 deaths. The V-2 was clearly a must-have technology for the United States. And so, immediately after the war ended, 118 German scientists and engineers, along with parts for about 100 rockets, other equipment, and 12 tons of documents, were brought to the United States. Although the Germans were housed at Fort Bliss in nearby El Paso, Texas, the launch complexes, which included "isolated launch pads, blockhouses, test sites, and instrument stations," were erected at White Sands.[13] HSR recorded these structures in the field and compared them to original engineering drawings.

The archaeologists documented more than four dozen Cold War-related sites. Because of excellent preservation and its role in the V-2 project, Launch Complex (LC) 33 was deemed especially significant. Construction of LC-33 began in mid–1945, making it the oldest major U.S. launch complex (Figure 19.1).[14] Sixty-seven V-2 rockets were sent aloft from LC-33, as well as several modified, U.S.-built missiles.[15] This complex includes a missile storage facility, two blockhouses, gantries, and concrete pads. Many facilities—especially the gantries—retain their integrity. LC-33 is now on the National Register.

HSR's report makes available, in minute detail, the history of early Cold War rocketry in the U.S. and invites further research into the base's rich archaeological record. This CRM project helped the White Sands Missile Range fulfill its obligations under the Legacy Resource Management Program, which *partially* met the requirements of the Historic Sites Preservation Act of 1966 and Executive Order 11593.

FIGURE 19.1. Launch Complex 33, White Sands Missile Range, New Mexico (courtesy of Library of Congress).

Legacy Program projects are narrowly aimed at military-related sites and so need to be supplemented by other programs. Accordingly, in recent decades, Fort Bliss in Texas, Vandenberg Air Force Base in California, Luke Air Force Base in Arizona, and other Department of Defense facilities have put in place programs that address earlier historic and prehistoric resources. Some of the resulting projects have identified millennia of Native American occupation. These findings have led to better-informed management and to major revisions of local and regional prehistory.

Federal management of archaeological resources has come a long way since 1906. Landholding agencies, including military bases, now include CRM as a prominent element of their mission statements and are striving to satisfy the spirit of federal legislation with customized programs. Although the vast majority of prehistoric sites on federal lands remain undiscovered, most agency officials no longer authorize land-modification projects or approve permits without first preparing or obtaining an environmental impact statement with input from an in-house archaeologist. And on federal lands, looters caught in the act are prosecuted.

20

Tribal Archaeology

The Seminole Indians of Florida

MANY AMERICAN INDIANS have been hostile to archaeologists, and with good reason. According to treaties, tribes are independent nations, but in the twentieth century they were actually wards of the U.S. government under the jurisdiction of the Bureau of Indian Affairs and, in archaeological matters, the National Park Service. As such, tribes were largely powerless to resist archaeological excavations on their reservations, even when a federal undertaking, such as a dam, threatened significant sites.

Many Indian villages contain human burials. Not surprisingly, tribal members regard excavation of such places as desecration of their ancestors. Worse indignities sometimes followed: once in a museum, bones might be stored in a box, damaged in laboratory tests, or displayed without regard to the wishes of descendant groups. And there were additional aggravations when archaeological inferences contradicted traditional beliefs, such as when a tribe first occupied its territory or whether its ancestors engaged in cannibalism.

For acquiescence in what Bruce Trigger described as "imperialist" archaeology, a tribe received little in return, perhaps a public-relations lecture and copies of a jargon-filled report that engaged research questions of interest only to the archaeological community.[1] Relatively few archaeologists thought to ask if tribal members had questions about their own past that an excavation or survey might answer.[2]

For several reasons, relations between tribes and archaeologists began to improve during the latter decades of the twentieth century. First, Congress enacted the Native American Graves Protection and Repatriation

Act (1990), which required that museums receiving federal funding return human remains and grave goods to the pertinent tribe. The law also required *consultation with any tribes anywhere* that might claim a cultural affiliation with a project's archaeological resources. Second, there was an increase in tribal autonomy, which often included the creation of a cultural resource management (CRM) program. To mesh these programs with federal laws, many tribes appointed Tribal Historic Preservation Officers with the same powers and responsibilities as state historic preservation officers, including handling consultation requests.[3] And third, archaeologists admitted that many past practices were unjustifiable, perhaps unethical; the discipline would have to change, and it has.[4] On tribal and public lands, archaeologists excavate burials only in emergency situations; and archaeology has become a collaborative enterprise that serves both tribes and researchers.[5] Even so, overcoming decades of hostility means that archaeologists must repeatedly show that their work has value to the tribe that employs them.

Because reservations vary in occupational history, size, and environment, and tribes vary in culture, population size, governance, and wealth, approaches to CRM also vary.[6] Some tribes allow projects initiated by outside archaeologists; others do not. Some tribes are relative newcomers to their reservations; others have a millennia-deep prehistory. Some tribes hire an archaeological consultant to assist the Tribal Historic Preservation Officer; others build a comprehensive in-house archaeology program. Among the 500-plus Indian groups recognized by the U.S government, there are 500-plus approaches to CRM, including indifference.

The Seminoles of southern Florida, a business-savvy tribe of about 4,000 members, developed a multifaceted CRM program with historical archaeology at its core. The tribe consists of the descendants of small groups, mainly of Creek (Muscogean) heritage, who remained in Florida after the decades-long Seminole Wars ended in 1858. Waged by the U.S. Government, the conflicts forcibly moved most Florida Seminoles to Oklahoma where they joined the multitude of Creeks already relocated from other southeastern states. Scattered groups of no more than a few hundred Seminoles resisted the onslaughts by hiding in remote areas of southern Florida, including the Everglades, where they lived for decades in poverty.[7]

To improve their economic situation, Seminoles in the twentieth century sold handicrafts, traded with Anglos and others, and eventually established a prosperous cattle industry. The tribe received federal recognition in 1957 and today occupies six noncontiguous reservations scattered from Tampa to Miami: Tampa, Big Cypress, Brighton, Immokalee, Ft. Pierce, and Hollywood. In recent decades the Seminoles established a tax-free smoke shop, opened the country's first high-stakes bingo parlor, built hotels and casinos, and acquired the Hard Rock corporate brand. Several reservations have tourist attractions such as a replica village, museum, swamp tour, and alligator wrestling.

The Tampa Reservation owes its very existence to a serendipitous archaeological find. In 1983, parking lot construction in downtown Tampa encountered multiple human burials that archaeologists identified as Seminole. After careful retrieval, the remains were reburied about 7 miles away in an 8.5-acre plot given to the tribe for that purpose by the federal government.[8] A cultural center and bingo palace were built there and, later, a hotel and casino—all without disturbing the burials. James E. Billie, then tribal chairman, observed that "it seemed providential that the bones of the tribe's ancestors reached out throughout the years to lend a financial hand to their long-suffering descendants."[9]

Somewhat later, the Florida Division of Historic Resources began to examine archaeological resources on the Big Cypress Reservation. This modest project identified and assessed 31 historic and prehistoric sites. In 1992, a grant from the National Park Service funded the Seminole Heritage Survey, which turned up additional historic sites that deeply impressed influential members of the tribe. Quoting from the report, Billy L. Cypress—a highly educated Seminole and first Executive Director of the Ah-Tah-Thi-Ki Seminole Indian Museum (opened in 1997)—noted, "It was obvious from the results of that survey that many of these sites had not been known to tribal members, and that this information was not only important to supplementing tribal history but to effectively manage reservation lands in regards to proposed land improvements and developments."[10]

These early projects were carried out for the Seminole Tribe by the Archaeological and Historical Conservancy, a nonprofit organization based in Florida. As the Seminoles began expanding tribal housing, agriculture, and several businesses, they decided to develop in-house capabilities for archaeological research. The Tribe applied to the National Park Service to establish a Tribal Historic Preservation Office whose activities would include surveys to comply with federal legislation. The application was approved and the office was established in 2001. Located on the Big Cypress Reservation, the office is headed by the Tribal Historic Preservation Officer, an archaeologist, and is composed of 16 professionals in five sections.

The Tribal Archaeology Section (TAS), consisting of the Tribal Archaeologist and six Field Technicians, is tasked with "conducting archaeology by following the tenets and wishes of the Seminole Tribe."[11] The TAS surveys are part of an ongoing program: before a ground-disturbing activity is allowed to take place, sites are identified and assessed regarding eligibility for the National and Tribal Registers of Historic Places. In addition to conducting surveys, excavations when necessary, and archival research, the TAS interviews community members to obtain stories about each project area. In this way, archaeological and community perspectives are both included in reports. Working for an entrepreneurial tribe with many ongoing development projects, the TAS staff stays very busy.[12]

The Archaeometry Section designs databases using geographic information systems and, in the field, locates buried features using nondestructive techniques such as ground-penetrating radar.[13] The Compliance Section responds to requests for consultation—thousands annually—on construction projects throughout Florida and much of the southeastern United States, the tribe's ancestral region. The Collections Section manages the preservation and analysis of artifacts and historic documents. And buildings of historic significance to the tribe are recorded in the field and researched by the Architectural History Section, headed by Carrie Dilley.[14]

One of the signature projects of the Tribal Historic Preservation Office is a study of the Red Barn, an agrarian structure located on the Brighton Reservation near the northwest corner of Lake Okeechobee (Figure 20.1). Employing archival records, interviews, and field observations, Dilley documented in great detail the Red Barn's construction, use, and current condition. The barn was built in 1941 with funds from the U.S. Civilian Conservation Corps—Indian Division. Containing 13 horse stalls, two storage rooms, and a loft running the entire length of the building, the barn once housed horses, saddles, and hay. It continued in use until the early 1960s, and then was left to the mercy of the natural environment. Hurricane Wilma in 2005 destroyed its roof but it was replaced. Although the siding was in rough shape, the structure's wooden framework retained its integrity, making the barn ripe for restoration.[15]

Drawing on Dilley's work, the Tribal Historic Preservation Office nominated the Red Barn to the National Register, which is administered by the

FIGURE 20.1. Red Barn on the Brighton Seminole Indian Reservation, before restoration (Wikimedia Commons, Ebyabe photographer).

National Park Service. Because old red barns abound in the United States, many of them in stellar condition, the nomination form had to argue persuasively for the Red Barn's significance to the Seminoles and, by extension, to the nation. It turned out that the Red Barn jumpstarted the Seminole cattle industry, which helped lead the tribe to economic independence. And as the nomination form states, "It was more than just a horse barn—it was the center of community activity for the Brighton Reservation." In family reunions and tribal meetings there, the modern Seminole government took shape. "The Red Barn at Brighton fostered a sense of community togetherness that ultimately led to solidarity for the entire Seminole tribe."[16] The National Park Service agreed that this red barn was special and listed it on the National Register.

Stabilization of the Red Barn was completed in 2013, and wooden siding is no longer falling from the frame. To mark this milestone, the Tribal Historic Preservation Office and other tribal organizations hosted a celebration, an event attended by several hundred Seminoles and visitors. Plans are in the works to restore it completely.

The Architectural Section's historical, ethnographic, and field recording helped reveal the Red Barn's pivotal role in the creation of the modern

Seminole tribe. Once a decaying old structure known to few Seminoles, the Red Barn is now widely appreciated as a nationally recognized heritage site that represents critical events of the tribe's mid-twentieth-century history.

Most sites identified by the Archaeology Division lack the storied history of the Red Barn, but the ongoing discovery of other sites fills historical gaps and helps the Tribe manage its cultural resources. These surveys also furnish information to outside archaeologists who study Seminole history and pre-history throughout southern Florida.[17] Archaeological survey in southern Florida is beset by challenging field conditions, including sites situated on wooded islands in the midst of swamps. Reaching and recording sites in such tough environments requires expensive and almost heroic feats of fieldwork, and so the archaeological record of southern Florida, especially the interior, remains poorly known. The only major exceptions are development-related surveys along the Florida coasts, scattered academic studies, *and* the work of the Seminole Tribal Historic Preservation Office, including reports associated with Everglades Restoration.[18]

To share information with the archaeological community, the Tribal Historic Preservation Office presented a symposium at the 2013 meeting of the Southeastern Archaeological Conference. Most papers focused on tribal CRM issues but several described archaeological techniques and findings of interest to Seminole specialists. In a new project, Carrie Dilley completed an ethnoarchaeological study of *chickees*, the traditional Seminole wood-framed, thatched-roof house. The *chickee* project report was published as a book in 2015.

Owing to its wealth, the Seminole tribe can support a Tribal Historic Preservation Office having impressive capabilities for archaeological and historical research. Clearly, the Seminoles have established a high standard for tribal CRM that features fruitful collaboration between archaeologists and the tribe, yielding benefits to both.

I thank Paul Backhouse, Seminole Tribe Historic Preservation Officer, for helpful discussions and comments on a draft of this chapter. Carrie Dilley provided information about the Red Barn project.

21

Archaeology in the City of Alexandria, Virginia

EVERY AMERICAN CITY has abundant cultural resources, but only a few have developed comprehensive and effective cultural resource management (CRM) programs. One of the few is Alexandria, Virginia, whose CRM program has become a model for other cities. Founded in 1749, Alexandria has a long history of European settlement as well as a prehistory reaching back more than 10 millennia. It also has many residents, white and black, interested in their city's colorful past. And from 1977 to 2012 it had Pamela Cressey as the first City Archaeologist.

In the eighteenth and nineteenth centuries, Alexandria was an important port town on the Potomac River, trading in tobacco, grains, slaves, and so forth. Although the town was part of the original 10-mile square of Washington, D.C., that straddled the river, Virginia later concluded that the state received few of the anticipated benefits. At Virginia's request, the parcel including Alexandria was returned (retroceded) to the state in 1847. During the Civil War, Union troops occupied Alexandria, which experienced an influx of escaped slaves. To this day, immigrants from around the globe make their homes in Alexandria, a prosperous and ethnically diverse city.

The first archaeological project to take place in Alexandria was the excavation and partial restoration of Fort Ward, an installation established during the Civil War as a part of a Union defensive ring around the federal city. Interest in this effort was sparked by Dorothy Starr, a local historian who convinced the city council to conduct excavations. A crew headed by archaeologist Edward Larrabee did the work, which involved careful "reading" of soil profiles to identify subtle features of the earthen fort.[1]

Shortly after these excavations ended, Alexandria's "Old Town," with its abundant eighteenth- and nineteenth-century structures, was subjected to urban renewal. Many city blocks were slated for demolition, but in 1965, after work began in a six-block section, it became apparent that beneath the old buildings was a vast archaeological trove of wells, privies, and architectural remains. Abandoned wells and privies have always been prime places for dumping trash, such as glass bottles, pottery, food waste, toothbrushes, and other personal items, all of which are evidence for activities that occurred in nearby structures. Alarmed by the destruction, citizens encouraged the Smithsonian Institution to mount a "salvage" excavation. In a salvage (or "rescue") excavation, advance planning and research design are not feasible; the task is to stay ahead of the bulldozers, collecting and recording artifacts. A laboratory to process the finds was set up in the old Torpedo Factory by the waterfront where weapons had been produced between 1918 and 1945.

The Smithsonian project was overseen by Malcolm Watkins, with the actual fieldwork under the direction of Richard Muzzrole. They were assisted by a large corps of enthusiastic volunteers that included "local residents, city officials, college students, and high school students."[2] After the Smithsonian's involvement ended in 1971, the work was supported by the Committee of 100, a group of Alexandria citizens, each of whom donated $10 per month toward the project. In 1973, the city council picked up the funding.

Apart from furnishing a marvelous collection of well-preserved eighteenth- and nineteenth-century artifacts, the archaeology project yielded an important lesson: Alexandria residents were interested in their city's past and were eager to preserve it. In fact, citizen entreaties to save historic buildings ended the urban renewal project after the first six blocks had been demolished. Citizens also advocated the establishment of an entity to ensure that archaeology would continue.

In response, the city council set up the Alexandria Archaeological Commission in 1975. Members of the Commission are still selected by the City Council and represent diverse stakeholders ranging from the Chamber of Commerce to history enthusiasts. The Commission's responsibilities include setting "goals and priorities for the City's program; [it also] acquires, preserves, and displays all the artifacts found. It works with federal, state and local governments, private foundations, citizens, area schools, and colleges."[3] Citizen input is also encouraged at monthly public meetings.

By creating the Alexandria Archaeology Commission, the city took an important step toward establishing a CRM program that could precede and encompass all development projects because salvage, alone, is not cultural resource *management*. Such a program would require archaeologists to be involved in the planning process, recommending and carrying out research-oriented investigations whose results could potentially influence development decisions. There would be no need to dodge bulldozers.

The city's next move, in 1977, was to hire an archaeologist. The first city archaeologist was Pamela J. Cressey. She presided over a small but dedicated research staff, an operation that would eventually be called Alexandria Archaeology. The archaeologists and some of their collections were housed in the Torpedo Factory, where they can be seen today amidst three stories of upscale artist studios. Cressey put in place many outreach activities that involved citizens in projects. Supervised volunteers provided free labor and in return gained experience in fieldwork and analysis, as well as the satisfaction of having helped to preserve Alexandria's past.

But there was still a problem: companies planning to build a condominium complex, expand a warehouse, add a buried tank to a gasoline station, and so forth could do so without concern for archaeological resources. And the pace of development was outstripping the ability of volunteers and the staff of Alexandria Archaeology to keep up.

The City Council remedied that situation in 1989 by adopting the Archaeological Resource Protection Code, which applies to any proposed undertaking that could disturb the ground except for single-family dwellings. When proposing a project, the developer now consults with Alexandria Archaeology to learn whether the construction site contains known or potentially significant archaeological resources. If the assessment leads to a positive finding, the developer puts together a "preliminary site plan" consisting of "an archaeological evaluation report and a resource management plan" prepared by professional researchers.[4] The management plan specifies activities that can range from historical research, to monitoring during construction, to a full-scale excavation that includes analysis, conservation and curation of artifacts, and report preparation. This rigorous process furnishes archaeological input at a project's earliest stage when design changes may still be made to reduce archaeological impacts. When impacts cannot be prevented, there is usually time to conduct a well-designed excavation.

If archaeological services are required, the developer contracts with a qualified consulting company that performs the work and writes a report. Instead of allowing such reports to become part of the obscure "gray literature," which is difficult even for other researchers to access, Alexandria Archaeology maintains an online topical index to all contract reports, most of which can be downloaded for free.[5] There is also an online public summary that presents, with images, the project's results in the context of city history.

The activities of Alexandria Archaeology, including enforcement of the Archaeological Resource Protection Code, depend on community participation. Accordingly, with input from citizens and staff, Cressey adopted a multifaceted approach to public archaeology encompassing a museum, volunteers, education program, summer camp, field school, and heritage trail. An overarching goal "has been to conduct archaeology *with* the public, not only *for* the public."[6]

Founded in 1984, the Alexandria Archaeology Museum, with its large glass windows, is especially inviting. Here, visitors can meet archaeologists, talk to volunteers processing finds, and view interesting artifacts on display. There are over 100 volunteers, many of whom are members of the Friends of Alexandria Archaeology, which publishes a newsletter and contributes to the Museum's varied research and outreach activities.

The education program consists of teacher workshops along with lesson plans for elementary schools, secondary schools, and adults. One lesson includes an activity sheet that encourages students to relate historic documents from the eighteenth-century Gadsby's Tavern to artifacts recovered from the tavern's courtyard. Another lets participants pore over census records, maps, and artifacts from a site in the Hayti neighborhood founded by free blacks during the early nineteenth century. Educators (and others) can also arrange tours of Gadsby's Tavern Museum, Alexandria Black History Museum, Freedom House Museum, and other places of historic interest.[7]

In support of the Archaeology Museum's research activities, students aged 12–15 may take part in a summer camp to gain experience in excavation and artifact processing. A summer field school in historical archaeology is offered to college students through George Washington University. In 2014, field school excavations continued at the Shuter's Hill plantation site, focusing on an area linked to enslaved African Americans. The Museum also provides internship opportunities.

The 23-mile-long Heritage Trail wends its way through Old Town and the far reaches of Alexandria. It may be traversed by foot or bike and is divided into 10 segments of varying lengths. A handsome and well-illustrated guidebook written by Cressey herself discusses stops along the trail, calling attention to their historical significance.[8]

A strong CRM program depends on the systematic growth of information about the past to inform its decisions.[9] Yet compliance with the Archaeological Resource Protection Code could lead to the disjointed accumulation of information, dependent on where developers placed their projects. To avoid this problem, contractors are required to explain how their projects will add to the knowledge of Alexandria's past. In addition, to help fill information gaps, answer pressing research questions, and increase the program's visibility, Alexandria Archaeology designs and carries out its own excavations. Thus, the field school at Shuter's Hill Plantation seeks a better understanding of African-American life in the eighteenth and nineteenth centuries—a continuing theme of Alexandria Archaeology.[10]

The most compelling example of Alexandria's "community archaeology" is the identification and preservation of an African-American cemetery, which the federal government established during the Civil War for escaped slaves.[11] Before the Freedmen's Cemetery was abandoned in 1869, more than 1,700 people, including hundreds of children, were buried there. A 1997 article in the *Washington Post* alerted Alexandrians that the Woodrow Wilson Bridge project, a major reconstruction of Interstate 95, likely threatened the Freedmen's Cemetery, whose exact location and condition were unknown.

Concerned citizens formed the Friends of Freedmen's Cemetery, publicizing the cemetery's plight and collaborating with Alexandria Archaeology to advocate its preservation. Test excavations and further historical research pinpointed the cemetery's location under a gas station and adjacent land and identified many graves. With federal assistance, the city of Alexandria purchased the land, removed the gas station, and established the site as a memorial. Archaeological testing located about 700 burials, but none was excavated.

The Freedmen's Cemetery was rededicated on May 12, 2007.[12] The memorial, which opened in 2014, contains the newly marked graves, an interpretive plaza with bas-reliefs and text, and bronze tablets with the names of the interred. The preservation of the Freedmen's Cemetery indicates to Alexandria's African-Americans—22 percent of the population in 2010, including some descendants of people buried there—that their heritage is valued. The connection is emphasized in a special marker on the bronze tablets that names living descendants, 140 of whom attended the ceremony marking the opening of the memorial.

Readers may wonder if Alexandria's community approach to CRM is transferable to other cities and towns. Obviously, Alexandria's well-educated and wealthy population, located in the Washington metropolitan area, was primed to appreciate the value of preserving the city's past. Even developers have accepted their responsibilities under the Archaeological Resource Protection Code without appreciable pushback. Although other American cities may lack some of these favorable conditions, one fact looms large: the vast number of local museums, preserved buildings, and monuments in every state, in towns large and small, testifies to Americans' interest in preserving and celebrating their own past. It may take only a few passionate people to catalyze action for historic preservation and cultural resource management.

As Pamela Cressey showed, archaeologists can build on citizen interest, working with city officials, residents, and other stakeholders, to rally support for creating or expanding a CRM program and setting preservation goals. And, in the spirit of the Alexandria model, CRM programs have been established in several cities, including Boston, Massachusetts, and St. Augustine, Florida, both of which have long, rich archaeological records of Indian and European occupation.[13] Although there are few other "city archaeologists" per se, many U.S. cities (and counties) have historic preservation or cultural resource departments whose responsibilities may include the protection and preservation of archaeological resources.

I thank Lance Mallamo, Director of Historic Alexandria, for helpful discussions. I am grateful to Pamela Cressey who commented extensively on an earlier draft.

VIII

Participating in Judicial and Diplomatic Processes

ARCHAEOLOGISTS ARE OFTEN found digging in sites, analyzing artifacts in a laboratory, or even writing at a computer. Some can also be found preparing reports for attorneys, authenticating antiquities, giving depositions, and testifying in courtrooms. That is because our unique expertise about the archaeological record and prehistory may be relevant in certain legal and diplomatic contexts. When testifying as expert witnesses, archaeologists may provide evidence relevant to a native group's claims about traditional patterns of land use or help to convict looters and dealers in stolen antiquities.

After decades of ignoring Indian petitions for land compensation, in 1946 Congress established a commission to resolve about 600 claims. Hearings were much like trials, with a panel of commissioners rendering judgment on the basis of presentations by the plaintiffs (a tribe) and the defense (U.S. government), both sides represented by attorneys. The case discussed in chapter 22 is that of the California tribes, which focused on traditional patterns of land use. Hearings went from 1949 to 1956, with a decision in 1959. Anthropologist Ralph Beals testified for the government, claiming that much tribal land had not actually been used. Countering Beals's testimony, archaeologist Robert F. Heizer took pains to document how tribes used supposedly vacant land—even at very high elevations—to obtain resources. The commission ruled in favor of the Indians, but the total compensation was a pittance. This case points to ethical issues that may arise when scholars provide expert testimony in a judicial proceeding.

In the United States, federal antiquities laws do not protect sites and artifacts on private land, but the Archaeological Resources Protection Act (ARPA) of 1979 contains a noteworthy exception. It is a violation of that act if the looter hadn't obtained a landowner's permission to dig and then transported the spoils across a state line or international border. Looting of an important Hopewell mound in Indiana, owned by General Electric, led to a precedent-setting case in which five for-profit looters, including one big-time dealer, Arthur J. Gerber, were arrested and convicted under ARPA because they did not have permission to dig and had taken the artifacts to Kentucky. Archaeologists played crucial roles in this case: James Kellar inventoried more than 2,000 looted artifacts and affirmed their significance; Mark F. Seeman visited the site, interviewed the looters, examined the artifacts, prepared a report, and testified in Gerber's sentencing hearing. Four looters were convicted and given token sentences without jail time; however, Gerber was sentenced to a year in jail. Appealing his conviction, ultimately to the Supreme Court, Gerber's sentence and this use of ARPA were upheld.

Wealthy collectors, especially in industrialized countries such as the United States, create a strong demand for fine pottery, jewelry, sculptures, and other archaeological objects regarded as art. To meet the demand, looters and smugglers are active in many countries that have an especially rich archaeological heritage, including Egypt, Mexico, and Peru. To help stem the destruction of sites, UNESCO in 1970 adopted a convention urging countries to establish and strengthen their antiquities laws. In the spirit of the UNESCO convention, the U.S. Congress enacted a law restricting the import of stolen artifacts. When responding to a request from another country to return stolen property, an 11-member Cultural Property Advisory Committee, which in 2014 included three archaeologists and was headed by an archaeologist-attorney, investigates and makes a recommendation. If the committee determines in favor of the country's claim, then enforcement follows from the U.S. Customs and Border Protection Agency. To build the case against looters of prehistoric artifacts or Americans dealers, Customs consults with archaeologists. Chapter 24 discusses fascinating cases in which archaeologists were able to authenticate the antiquities and their countries of origin.

22

California Indians v. United States

WHEN OLD WORLD adventurers and colonizers first set foot in North America, they found Indians living in forests, prairies, swamplands, and deserts—just about everywhere. This posed a problem for the Europeans who wanted to settle that land and exploit its resources. They solved the problem by encroachment on Indian territories, conquest and genocide, and, especially in eastern North America, forced resettlement of survivors in less desirable regions. After an Indian group had ceded a large part of its territory to Euro-Americans, the appropriated lands were given legal status in treaties that favored, and were routinely violated by, national governments.

In the nineteenth century, some Indian nations or tribes (the latter is a somewhat artificial construct) began to press their claims to the U.S. government, seeking compensation for lands taken, some lost even before there was a United States. However, Congress and the Court of Claims were generally unsympathetic to Indians, who were still being subjugated and displaced, and so they settled few claims. During the twentieth century, the pace of claims accelerated and touched new cultural sensibilities, as more and more people began to acknowledge the country's atrocious treatment of its first inhabitants. As a result, pressure mounted on Congress, especially from anthropologist John Collier, Commissioner of Indian Affairs from 1933 to 1946, to establish a process for dealing with these festering grievances.[1]

To assess treaty-related claims, Congress established the United States Indian Claims Commission in 1946.[2] Tribes were given until 1952 to present claims, which resulted in 176 groups submitting 370 petitions—600 claims in all. Three commissioners decided cases in an adversarial setting—trials in all but name—with attorneys representing the plaintiff (a tribe) and defendant (the government). The life of the commission was to be five years, but the huge caseload and many lengthy hearings required a reluctant Congress to extend the commission's life several times and add two commissioners. When the commission was finally disbanded in 1978, unresolved cases went to the Court of Claims.

According to Congress and earlier court decisions, a tribe had to demonstrate title to its land on the basis of "exclusive tribal use and occupation from 'time immemorial.'"[3] Most cases hinged on a tribe's ability to show that it had been consistently using its territory, seasonally or continually, and that this use was central to its economy.[4] Resolving these issues clearly called for academic expertise, and so attorneys for the tribes employed cultural anthropologists and archaeologists to acquire and assemble relevant evidence, prepare reports, and testify as expert witnesses. Likewise, in defending the government, the Department of Justice hired expert witnesses from anthropology and archaeology. Attorneys on both sides used their academic consultants to help craft strategies, questions, and counterarguments.

Evidence about land use and territories from historical documents, ethnographies, and archaeological reports was often inconclusive and had to be interpreted through the lens of anthropological theories, which sometimes figured in contentious exchanges between attorneys and witnesses. The hearings also brought out differences between Euro-American modes of land ownership and traditional Indian patterns of land use and tenure.[5] These issues were sharply debated in many cases, but the tribes of California furnish a fascinating and especially important example.[6]

California had the largest number of culturally and linguistically distinct Indian groups of any state. There are more than 50 tribes, some consisting of smaller groups or "tribelets," speaking many languages, some of which are mutually unintelligible.[7] Before Europeans arrived, all tribes practiced only hunting and gathering, usually moving their villages annually to take advantage of seasonally available resources such as acorn harvests inland and fish and shellfish on the coast. In Southern California there were also desert dwellers.[8]

Despite the tribes' considerable ethnic and ecological diversity, their claims were consolidated into a single case, *The Indians of California v. The United States of America*. This was done for administrative convenience, but a few tribes were displeased and pressed their cases independently. In any event, the consolidated case dragged on for many years during the 1950s, involving numerous hearings, hundreds of exhibits, and thousands of pages of transcripts.[9] During litigation in this case, both sides hired authorities on California Indians and anthropological theory.

Because the government could not return lands to a tribe, except in a very few cases, its primary defense strategy was to reduce the amount of potential compensation. This amount was tied to the value of the land in 1848, when the United States wrested California from Mexico.

The government's chief expert witness was UCLA anthropologist Ralph L. Beals, a specialist in Latin American societies, who led a team of distinguished anthropologists including Harold E. Driver and Julian H. Steward. Beals advanced the so-called ecological theory of "land use and occupancy" for estimating the percentage of a territory that could provide the "greater part" of a tribe's subsistence.[10] By subtraction, one calculated the amount of land *not* being used or occupied. According to the theory, the tribe's loss of this supposedly unused, unoccupied land (in other words, the greater fraction of its territory) required no government compensation.

Alfred L. Kroeber was appointed chief expert witness for the Indian side. At the time of the hearings, Kroeber, retired from UC–Berkeley since 1946, was probably the most renowned American anthropologist. He had carried out ethnographic fieldwork among many California tribes; had written the *Handbook of the Indians of California*; and had even done some archaeology. In short, Kroeber's knowledge of California Indians and their history was second to none. In an early hearing, he put on a masterful performance advocating Indian territorial claims and then endured 10 days of cross-examination.[11] Later, despite being in his late 70s and having suffered a heart attack, he helped to prepare the cross-examination of Beals as well as the rebuttal to his testimony.[12] Attorneys for the plaintiffs chose Robert F. Heizer, a professor at UC–Berkeley, as the rebuttal witness. Heizer was the state's leading archaeologist and was also well versed in the ethnography of California Indians. Already sworn in during a previous hearing, Heizer took the stand and was questioned first by Mr. Foster, the Indians' attorney.

Foster asked if Beals's "ecological theory" was appropriate for determining land use and occupancy in 1848. Heizer replied no, and then elaborated. He acknowledged that ecological analysis could indicate how a group achieved basic survival. However, in his calculations, Beals assumed that a group exploited only one type of environment. This was misleading, according to

Heizer, because many tribes had territories and patterns of resource use that crosscut environmental types. In one example among many, he reported that the Coast Yuki consist of 11 tribelets, each of which "owns" strips of land along the ocean *and* inland, giving them access to several resource zones that were occupied seasonally. The use of multiple environmental zones, Heizer emphasized, was "typical of California Indians."[13]

Heizer emphasized that the "ecological approach," by focusing on major subsistence resources found only in a small fraction of a tribe's territory, contradicts well-documented patterns of land use. These theoretical calculations in turn led—conveniently for the government—to a vast underestimate of the percentage of territory needed to support the tribe's way of life. Worse still, it treated Indians as animals who care for nothing more than "getting enough to eat."[14] Heizer also noted that Beals's approach ignored secondary subsistence resources and every other use of a territory, which might include procurement of "salt, hides, furs, medicinal plants, marine shells used for ornaments and money…, stone from which various sorts of implements were made, basketry materials, [and] clay for pottery."[15] Territories were also crisscrossed by trails and dotted with sacred places.

After presenting his examples of territory use, Heizer was asked, "Do you know of any sizable areas in California which were not used by the Indian?" He immediately answered, "No," and then supplied archaeological examples.[16] Southern Sierra Miwok villages were situated in the foothills of the Sierra Nevada mountain range, most of them below 4,000 feet in elevation. Farther up the slopes, between 5,500 and 7,800 feet, a limited archaeological survey had found more than 25 sites, some "very large." Apparently, the Miwok had conducted activities well beyond their "home range," a circle ten miles in diameter around a village.[17] Heizer introduced additional archaeological surveys done at high elevations, which also found evidence of Indian occupation and use.[18] One survey covering five square miles above timberline (ca. 9,000 feet) found five probable hunting camps. He added that a survey in Yosemite National Park discovered dozens of sites above 9,500 feet. These examples showed "that the higher elevations of the Sierra, which are classed as areas of little or no use by the defendant, were in fact much used by Indians."[19]

In cross-examination, the government's attorney, Mr. Barney, asked Heizer what the Indians were doing at high elevations in Yosemite. Heizer replied that they hunted mountain sheep, fished, and collected plants.[20] In answer to questions about the ownership of territories, Heizer reiterated that groups owned land up to the crest of the Sierras and used the higher elevations seasonally. After some back-and-forth about group boundaries and the interpretation of "exclusive use," Barney homed in on the percentage of a territory that was unused or valueless according to Beals's calculations. Heizer reiterated that these mechanistic calculations were unrealistic.

Rendering their decision in favor of the Indians, the commissioners rejected the government's use of Beals's calculations and the "ecological theory" on which they were based. The commissioners asserted, "The Indian groups in California moved about their respective domains gathering wild foods as they ripened or captured available game, and during a normal season would visit and the use the whole territory to which they asserted ownership."[21] No doubt Kroeber and Heizer had influenced the commissioners' thinking because the decision was, in effect, a synthesis of the arguments they had presented in testimony.

More than a decade after the hearings ended, Beals acknowledged the ethical dilemmas that confront academics serving as expert witnesses in an adversarial proceeding.[22] The government's expert witnesses were fully aware of how Indians used their territories, which they had documented in the background reports prepared at government expense. However, as Beals admitted, "Not only I but the entire research staff over time became unconsciously biased toward the defendant's needs: the government became 'our' side." He further admitted that the ecological theory "was not derived solely from scientific considerations but was heavily influenced by the needs of the defense."[23] Likewise, one can also detect places in Heizer's testimony where he had gone beyond the evidence to fashion conclusions that favored the Indians' case, such as his claim that high elevations were "much" used.

In an ideal world, "good expert witnesses reach the same conclusions based on the same facts, whether they testify for a plaintiff or a defendant."[24] But "expert" witnesses, as opposed to ordinary witnesses, are given great latitude to express knowledgeable opinions and theoretical interpretations. Thus, in the *real* world, expert witnesses, no matter how highly respected and conscientious, disagree because they mold their opinions to fit the claims of the side that paid for their research and testimony *and* coached them on what to say. Given that the character of expert witness testimony is known by all (except for the very naïve or idealistic), why do distinguished scholars become involved in controversial cases that may cause ethical distress?

In this case, persuasive government attorneys convinced Beals that less-qualified people would be hired if he didn't take part.[25] Such threats, perhaps made by both sides, brought some anthropologists on board, as did the prospect of helping the long-suffering plaintiffs. And we cannot ignore pecuniary interest, as there would be money for participating in the proceedings. Kroeber, for example, received a $500 signing bonus and generous daily stipend.[26] Finally, the hearings gave academic masters of esoteric subjects the opportunity to influence public affairs.

Although testimony was shaded in favor of one side or the other, expert witnesses and their research teams obtained vast amounts of evidence from primary sources on almost every Indian group in the United States. These sources included old travel accounts, family documents, missionary records, early ethnographies, government records, oral histories, and archaeological surveys. The resultant reports, many written by archaeologists, remain a valuable resource on Indian history and prehistory and helped to formalize the discipline of ethnohistory.[27] And, significantly, the Indians' "side of American History has finally been told with voluminous documentation."[28]

In the hundreds of cases considered, the commissioners favored the tribes in more than 60 percent of the rulings and awarded them a total of $818 million. Setting the amount of an award to an individual tribe was a messy process because of "offsets" that were subtracted from the total compensation, such as federal investments in infrastructure on tribal land.[29] After lengthy negotiations, in 1963 the California tribes were awarded $29.1 million (minus $2.6 million in lawyers' fees) for the loss of 64 million acres, which amounted to less than 50 cents an acre.[30] In addition to the financial settlements and good uses to which the Indians presumably put the money, the Commission's activities helped to raise the tribes' "legal consciousness."[31] Since then, Indians around the country have employed political action and legal processes with much success.

23

Antiquities Acts and the Looting of the GE Mound

WHAT IS OFTEN called the Hopewell culture thrived over large parts of the midwestern and eastern United States from about 200 BC to AD 500. Really an interaction sphere, Hopewell tied together many culturally diverse groups that lived in substantial villages, built mounds in many shapes and sizes, and took part in far-flung exchange networks that circulated mica, obsidian, catlinite (pipestone), native copper, and other exotic materials. Skilled artisans fashioned these materials into pipes, delicately chipped spear points and knives, and copper celts; they also made handsome pottery for domestic and ceremonial uses.[1]

Not surprisingly, avid collectors are willing to pay premium prices for choice Hopewell objects. Carved catlinite pipes, for example, are offered on the Internet for $1,500 to $2,500, and a well-made spear point of a desirable material may cost hundreds of dollars.[2] This situation vexes archaeologists because the looters who feed the voracious collector market have damaged Hopewell sites and reduced any potential to yield new information about the lives of these peoples.

Antiquities laws protect Hopewell sites on federal and state lands, but no laws prevent landowners from unearthing—even selling—prehistoric and historic artifacts from their own land. Thus, looters who dig on private property with the landowner's permission are damaging sites *legally*. There is, however, one significant exception buried deeply in the Archaeological Resources Protection Act of 1979 (ARPA), as follows:

No person may sell, purchase, exchange, transport, receive, or offer to sell, purchase, or exchange, in interstate or foreign commerce, any archaeological resource excavated, removed, sold, purchased, exchanged, transported, or received in violation of any provision, rule, regulation, ordinance, or permit in effect under State or local law.[3]

With the help of archaeological studies and testimony, this provision of the law resulted in the arrest and conviction of looters who dug in a Hopewell mound on private land. The case set an important precedent.

On the northern bank of the Ohio River near Mount Vernon, Indiana, there is an enormous, loaf-shaped Hopewell mound on property owned by the General Electric Company (GE). Once measuring about 395 feet by 165 feet, the site had been marked on a U.S. Soil Conservation Service map, but was not generally known to archaeologists before extensive looting began in 1988.[4] Although an archaeologist had done a cursory survey there in advance of a road project, he wrongly concluded that the elevated area was a natural feature. The road project was permitted to proceed.

During quarrying of fill dirt for the road, construction equipment intruded the mound. The workers recognized the mound as an archaeological feature, which would become known as the GE site or the Mount Vernon site. Contrary to regulations, the workers did not report the site to authorities. What's more, the heavy-equipment operator who discovered the mound's true nature, John William Way, was an artifact collector and also the first looter. Not only did he transport the artifacts across the Ohio River to his Kentucky home, but he also sold them for $6,000 to Arthur J. Gerber, big-time dealer and organizer of shows where Indian antiquities were bought and sold.

To continue the digging, Gerber recruited two other looters, John D. Towery and Danny G. Glover of Kentucky, who removed many more commercially valuable artifacts, which were then transported across state lines in Gerber's vehicles. In all, the looters dug out thousands of artifacts, leaving behind a devastated site and desecrated human remains. Another collector, Randall R. Hansen, whose business card stated, "Have Shovel, Will Travel," also dug there, took his plunder across state lines, and attempted to sell it.[5]

Rumors about rampant looting of Hopewell artifacts from the mound reached Curtis H. Tomak, an archaeologist with the Indiana Department of Highways. On his first visit, Tomak observed the destruction already wrought by a season of energetic digging. He alerted GE managers, who took measures to protect what remained of the mound. In the fall of 1988, Tomak conducted test excavations in the mound's disturbed areas. With a small number of test pits, he confirmed that looting (as opposed to just earth-moving) had recently taken place, documented the mound's rich artifact yield, and attested to its great archaeological significance.[6]

The occurrence of recent looting was ironclad evidence that state laws had been violated because GE had not given anyone permission to dig there. Through an intermediary, Tomak alerted Ray White, Chairman of the Council of Miami Indians in Indiana, who in turn notified the U.S. Department of Justice that artifacts from the site might have been taken across state lines and sold in violation of ARPA. Other Indian tribes weighed in as well, urging law enforcement agencies to punish the vandals and recover the stolen artifacts. Even though enforcement of antiquities laws generally has a low priority in the United States, the FBI stepped in and mounted a thorough investigation.

A break in the case came when a looter who had kept his booty in Indiana was charged with trespass. He returned the ill-gotten goods, agreed to perform community service, and cooperated with authorities by naming Gerber and other GE Mound looters.[7] He also submitted to an interview about the site with archaeologist James Kellar, who had been hired by GE. In the meantime, pleas to the public for return of the artifacts were somewhat successful, as more than 2,000 items were turned in. Kellar inventoried these artifacts, which included pearl and shell beads, decorated leather objects, copper-covered wooden artifacts, three copper celts, and more than 1,900 pieces of chipped stone.

Eventually the FBI acquired enough information to arrest and indict under ARPA the five for-profit looters. Four of them admitted to trespass and theft of private property, which cinched conviction under ARPA. The men returned the artifacts in exchange for token fines and wrist-slap sentences. In a plea bargain, Gerber—the antiquities dealer and looting organizer—admitted his role and was fined $5,000. He also had to return the artifacts and suspend commercial activities for three years, pay a fine to release his impounded vehicles, and serve a year in prison.[8]

Contributing to the harshness of Gerber's sentence (relative to the other looters) was the testimony of archaeologist Mark F. Seeman, an authority on Hopewell and professor at Kent State University. At the request of Larry A. Mackey, the U.S. Attorney prosecuting the case, Seeman examined the recovered artifacts, visited the site, interviewed the looters, and prepared a report on his findings. As the only prosecution witness in Gerber's sentencing hearing, Seeman summarized his report, testifying that the mound was "one of the very largest Hopewell mounds ever constructed," whose artifacts held valuable evidence on Hopewell religion and burial practices.[9] He also estimated that a professional excavation of the GE Mound would have cost around $1 million. (In ARPA cases, such estimates are the basis for calculating *archaeological*—as opposed to commercial—value of cultural resources.[10]) There were also looters and dealers who testified on Gerber's behalf. They offered bizarre justifications for his actions, claiming, for example, that trespassing wasn't really wrong and that Gerber was actually preserving the artifacts—none of which moved the judge.

Gerber sought relief from his conviction in federal appellate court, where his case was supported by briefs from several collector and dealer organizations. On the government's side were briefs filed by reputable archaeology and historic preservation organizations. The three-judge panel concluded that the arguments backing Gerber were specious. In rejecting the appeal, they also affirmed that the section of ARPA under which he was convicted was on solid legal footing. When his petition to the Supreme Court was denied, Gerber went to prison.

The FBI returned the stolen GE Mound artifacts to General Electric, their legal owner. In consultation with Native American groups, mainly out-of-state, GE decided in a highly secretive process to rebury all artifacts and human bone fragments near the site. The move sounds drastic, and to many archaeologists and some Indians it is. After all, reburial precludes use of the artifacts for enhancing heritage awareness, prevents further analyses, and hastens deterioration of items such as leather and wood. It also undermines preservation laws because "it gives credence to the claims of Gerber and others, who justify looting by saying that without their efforts artifacts would never be saved and available for study."[11] Such objections, however, carried little weight with General Electric. After all, human remains were involved and the artifacts had most likely taken part in burial rituals. In May, 1994, Native Americans reburied the artifacts in a ceremony on GE property near the mound.[12]

With the support of archaeological findings and testimony, this case set an important precedent by showing that ARPA could be used to prosecute looters who unearthed artifacts illegally from private property and took them out of state. But for looters and their apologists, the GE Mound case has become a *cause célèbre*, an example of flagrant government overreach and—remarkably—an attack on private property rights, raising the specter that "all private collections will be confiscated."[13] Yet, looters fail to acknowledge that they can easily avoid arrest under ARPA if they obtain a landowner's permission to dig and keep their finds. As U.S. Attorney Larry A. Mackey noted years later, "the prosecution vindicated GE's property rights."[14]

Although looters and their customers returned thousands of artifacts (but certainly not all), the lack of information on their original locations in the mound prevented archaeologists from making *fine-grained* behavioral inferences about, for example, burial practices. Even so, Tomak, Kellar, and Seeman managed to wrest from the artifacts a number of general inferences regarding the site's centrality in the Hopewell interaction sphere. As a result, the GE Mound has come to occupy a place among the most significant Hopewell sites.[15]

24

The International Antiquities Trade

THROUGHOUT THE "DEVELOPING" world and beyond, looters damage sites and supply stolen antiquities to collectors, dealers, and museums. It is estimated that between 1940 and 1968, "100,000 holes were dug into the Peruvian site of Batan Grande." In Pakistan, a survey of one northern district "showed that nearly half the Buddhist shrines, stupas and monasteries had been badly damaged or destroyed by illegal excavations."[1] In countries such as Egypt, looting has been going on for millennia, but by the mid-twentieth century the insatiable demand for antiquities had fostered a worldwide crisis.[2]

In response, the United Nations Educational, Scientific and Cultural Organization (UNESCO) in 1970 adopted a convention on means for "prohibiting and preventing the illicit import, export and transfer of ownership of cultural property." Countries are expected to protect their heritage by passing laws and setting up organizations to oversee preservation efforts. Significantly, the convention invites a country whose cultural patrimony is being threatened to petition another country for help in stopping illegal commerce in its antiquities. And the international community is exhorted to take measures for "the control of exports and imports" of stolen artifacts.[3]

By mid-2014, 127 countries had ratified the UNESCO convention, though they came on board slowly. Not surprisingly, major sources of supply—countries in Africa, the Middle East, Latin America, and around the Mediterranean—ratified the convention during the 1970s. But the main consumers did so only recently: the United Kingdom (2002), Japan (2002), France (1997), and Germany (2007). The United States, a huge market for looted artifacts, ratified the convention in 1983.

Owing to the UNESCO convention, countries have passed and strengthened antiquities laws. These laws regard antiquities removed without a government permit as stolen property. Many countries have established an antiquities bureau, and a majority have one or more national museums.[4]

In implementing the UNESCO convention, the United States enacted the Convention on Cultural Property Implementation Act (CPIA) in 1983, which restricts imports of illegally exported archaeological and ethnological objects.[5] The act authorizes the president to sign a memorandum of understanding (MOU) with a country petitioning for such restrictions. To advise the president on the merits of each petition, the act established a Cultural Property Advisory Committee (CPAC).

CPAC consists of 11 presidential appointees: two museum representatives, three experts in "international sale…of cultural property," three members of the general public, *and* three professionals in "archaeology, anthropology, ethnology, or related areas."[6] CPAC evaluates each request, assessing whether it meets the criteria listed in the law. It then writes a report containing findings and a recommendation as to whether the United States should enter into an MOU with the requesting nation. The report is submitted to the Assistant Secretary of State for Educational and Cultural Affairs to whom the president has delegated his authority under the CPIA. If the Assistant Secretary decides favorably, then the MOU's specific provisions are finalized in bilateral negotiations.

CPAC reports are classified and its meetings, except for a public portion, are closed. But the MOUs are available online from the Department of State.[7] By 1997, more than a decade after the act went into effect, just five countries had negotiated MOUs, and in mid-2014 only 15 MOUs were in force. The small number of MOUs results from a lack of petitions submitted.

The three subject-matter experts on CPAC in 2014 were all distinguished archaeologists.[8] CPAC's chair at this writing is Patty Gerstenblith, appointed by President Obama in 2011. Filling one of the public slots, she is an archaeologist, an attorney, and the Distinguished Research Professor of Law at DePaul University. Gerstenblith earned a Ph.D. in art and anthropology from Harvard, specializing in the Middle Bronze Age of Syria–Palestine, and a law degree from Northwestern University. When most people switch careers, they rarely look back. Not so Gerstenblith. Archaeology and the law are her "two loves," and she combines these in a unique specialty focused on art, cultural heritage, and the law.[9] On these matters, she is the go-to person in the United States.[10]

When considering a request for an MOU, the archaeologists on CPAC are able to influence public policy by expressing concern for preserving antiquities in their original contexts. Recently, an MOU was signed with Belize, a small Central American country whose long and rich archaeological record is being ravaged. Belize's abundant Mayan ruins are magnets for looters because they contain objects of high value in the art world. By 1983, an estimated 59 percent of the country's Mayan sites had been damaged.[11] Signed in 2013, the MOU commits the U.S. to restrict the importation of any archaeological object that lacks a government-issued export permit, or that left Belize after the MOU's effective date, and to return any such objects. The Belizean government agrees to publicize its heritage protection laws to discourage looting and to "continue its efforts to prevent the illegal sale and export of archaeological objects, especially at ports of transit and shipment."[12]

MOUs are effective in stirring the U.S. to take action against importers of stolen or illegally exported antiquities, but CPAC has no police powers. Enforcing import bans and restrictions is the duty of the U.S. Customs and Border Protection Agency. In 2007, Customs officials received a tip that Peruvian antiquities were being smuggled in by Jorge Ernesto Lanas-Ugaz, arriving by air from Peru, which was one of the earliest countries to have an MOU with the United States. At the airport in Houston, Texas, inspectors found a ceramic figure and several bowls that they suspected were pre-Columbian. Lanas-Ugaz had no export license for these objects, but that was not enough to make a case against him; the government needed to authenticate the objects' age and place of origin, and this determination obviously required archaeological expertise.

Customs employs forensic specialists in laboratories around the country, but lacks in-house archaeologists.[13] Consulted by Customs officials, archaeologists at the American Museum of Natural History in New York confirmed the artifacts' authenticity. After a warrant was obtained, authorities searched Lanas-Ugaz's Houston home where they found hundreds of Peruvian antiquities, their identities confirmed by Smithsonian Institution archaeologists.

A U.S. citizen, Lanas-Ugaz pleaded guilty to "one count of knowingly and fraudulently importing into the United States merchandise that is against the law to sell, and receiving stolen goods." He was given three years' probation and fined $2,000. Clearly, archaeological consultants were essential for this conviction, but they are not named in the Customs press release. In 2009, federal agents returned the Lanas-Ugaz stash of 334 artifacts to the Peruvian government.[14] Although the MOU worked as intended, his sentence was rather light for someone who had also sold Peruvian antiquities on the Internet.[15]

As helpful as the MOU was in this case, it did not provide the legal basis for the arrest and prosecution itself; this authority is vested in the National Stolen Property Act.[16] On the books for many decades but seldom applied to antiquities, the law makes it a crime to knowingly transport, acquire, or dispose of stolen property worth more than $5,000 that has been taken across state lines or the U.S. border.

The first significant antiquities case, litigated in the late 1970s, resulted in what is known as the McClain Doctrine, which established that the United States recognizes a foreign government's ownership of antiquities so long as that country has a law clearly claiming such ownership.[17] Thus, artifacts taken without permission after that country's law was enacted are considered stolen property by the U.S. government.

In a more recent case, a prominent New York antiquities dealer, Frederick Schultz, was indicted for violating the National Stolen Property Act. He had been trying to sell high-end antiquities smuggled out of Egypt. One of them—a stone head of pharaoh Amenhotep III—had been disguised as a gaudy tourist trinket. Schultz was convicted and in June, 2002, was sentenced to a $50,000 fine and 33 months in prison.[18] He fought the conviction, taking the case to the U.S. Court of Appeals, Second Circuit. His appeal was supported by organizations representing antiquities dealers, art dealers, and professional numismatists; also signing on to Schultz's side was Christie's, the well-known auction house. Despite the formidable massing of interested parties as well as capable counsel who offered a large array of legal arguments, the three-judge panel found his claims "without merit" and upheld the conviction a year later.[19] Because of the wide range of issues raised by Schultz's counsel, all decisively rejected by the appeals court, the case greatly strengthened the National Stolen Property Act for prosecuting traffickers in stolen antiquities.

In *U.S. Cultural Diplomacy and Archaeology*, Christina Luke and Morag M. Kersel argue that the U.S. government employs archaeology as a diplomatic strategy, aiming to cultivate a positive image of the United States by showing concern for the cultural heritage of other countries. This strategy took a more definite shape after the disastrous frenzy of looting of sites and museums that followed the 1991 Gulf War and intensified after the 2003 start of the Iraq War.[20] The strategy is implemented not only by negotiating MOUs and prosecuting antiquities smugglers and dealers but also by providing grants to other countries for building fences around sites, installing security systems in museums, inventorying collections, creating databases, stabilizing a monument's façade, and so forth."[21] American archaeologists participate in these efforts as consultants.

Despite the progress made since 1970, looting continues at an alarming pace.[22] Apparently, reducing the international trafficking in antiquities requires more than enlightened public policy and rigorous law enforcement. In many source countries, impoverished locals do the digging, hoping to find salable objects to help support their families. Ironically, in grinding out a living, these people are damaging their own cultural heritage. Prodded by archaeologists, some countries are experimenting with ways to employ local residents in occupations other than looting, such as guarding sites or working at authorized excavations. But the greatest unsolved problem is how to reduce demand for antiquities by citizens in wealthy countries.

IX

DOING FIELDWORK
IN A FORENSIC CONTEXT

A NECESSARY ADJUNCT to law enforcement and other agencies, forensic archaeology has become an important specialty. The archaeologist brings to an investigation techniques such as resistivity surveying for finding graves. For recovering, recording, and studying traces of the burial process, techniques range from pollen analysis to evaluating shovel marks on the walls of a pit. Forensic archaeology is not for the squeamish, but it is necessary and important work that only archaeologists are qualified to do.

The first case we consider is a murder investigation in England. A woman was reported missing by a neighbor who suspected that her husband had killed her. Forensic archaeologist John R. Hunter searched the house but found nothing of interest. In the garden area, he carried out a soil resistivity survey, which identified two areas of anomalous electrical resistivity. One anomaly turned out to be a pit that showed promise because it contained flecks of clay indicating that the pit's original excavation had penetrated more than 40 cm into the subsoil (a natural layer). Half under a concrete patio, this pit was excavated in several stages after the concrete was removed. Under a layer of slate slabs, Hunter encountered a partially decomposed woman's body with a rope around her neck. He excavated the body with considerable care and produced evidence so compelling that the husband accepted a plea deal and was sentenced to prison.

Forensic archaeologists also locate and excavate mass graves. A grave in Serniki, Ukraine, holds the remains of hundreds of victims of Nazi Germany's program to exterminate the Jewish population. The impetus for this excavation was the arrest of a Ukrainian living in Australia who was later tried as a war criminal for his alleged participation in the Serniki massacre, an event some people recalled during postwar interviews. A search of archival records produced no definitive evidence of the massacre, so prosecutors sought tangible evidence of the murders in the form of a mass grave. Australian archaeologist Richard Wright was hired to carry out the investigation, and he found the grave. Archaeologists exposed and recorded 553 partially decomposed victims, most of whom had been shot in the head. Cartridge casings made in Germany indicated that the massacre probably occurred in 1941 or 1942. Having unearthed definitive evidence of the massacre, Wright testified at the trial, but the prosecution was unable to prove the suspect's participation.

The U.S. military's Central Identification Laboratory recovers the remains of service personnel lost in America's wars. During the Vietnam War, a reconnaissance plane disappeared en route from Thailand to North Vietnam. Searches in Vietnam failed to turn up a crash site, but inquiries in Laos led to a site on whose surface were pieces of an American aircraft. Survey and excavation confirmed that the parts came from the missing plane. Recovery of duplicate life-support equipment showed that the pilot and navigator had accompanied the plane to the ground. Although villagers had removed materials from the site, archaeologists were able to recover three small fragments of human bone. DNA testing on a tiny piece of femur confirmed that it belonged to one of the airmen.

25

Solving a Murder
in the Midlands of England

IN JANUARY 1968, criminologist Thomas O. Murton took over as Superintendent of Cummins Prison in Arkansas where, reportedly, a warden had murdered and buried many inmates. Murton believed the reports but was reluctant to dig for bodies. Feeling heat from worldwide press coverage, however, he put a crew to work where, according to an inmate's assertion, bodies were buried.

Conditions were wretched, as heavy rains had soaked the ground, and the fieldwork was conducted in the dead of winter by inmates. Although several bodies were recovered, the excavation was a fiasco, with potentially important evidence lost or destroyed.

This embarrassing outcome could have been avoided because Arkansas at the time had a statewide program, the Arkansas Archeological Survey, which could have been consulted on how to conduct a professional excavation.[1] But the Cummins Prison case was hardly unique. Although forensic anthropologists—specialists in analyzing bones, teeth, and other tissues—had been sporadically employed in criminal investigations during much of the twentieth century, forensic *archaeology* was essentially unknown in the 1960s.[2]

In 1976, an article in its own journal alerted the forensic sciences community to the contributions archaeologists might make.[3] The authors, including a forensic anthropologist-physician and an archaeologist, drew attention to horror stories such as the Cummins Prison case and specified basic requirements for the proper handling of grave excavations. Two years later, forensic anthropologists advocated the use of archaeological techniques in the *FBI*

Law Enforcement Bulletin.[4] No longer was there any excuse for law enforcement agencies to repeat debacles such as the Cummins Prison "excavation."

Archaeologists, too, had to be alerted to the importance of participating in forensic investigations. Writing in *American Antiquity*, the major professional journal, Brenda Sigler-Eisenberg in 1985 made the case: "Although forensic archaeology is in its infancy, I suggest that with increased support and participation by forensically trained professional archaeologists significant contributions will be made to the criminal justice system." In retrospect, it seems obvious: when archaeologists excavate graves in a forensic context, they often recover evidence that illuminates the sequence of events surrounding the process of burial. And because such evidence may play a crucial role in trials, prosecutors and police investigators began requesting the participation of archaeologists.

Forensic archaeology deals with the discovery and excavation of gravesites along with the recovery and analysis of associated evidence such as vegetation cover, insect parts, pollen, traces of original excavation tools, and sediments and other pit contents. During the late twentieth century, forensic archaeology grew rapidly as a recognized specialty allied with the criminal justice system. It now boasts a host of textbooks, handbooks, and informative case studies.[5] Archaeologists have influenced criminal investigations by introducing rigorous techniques of searching for, excavating, and recovering evidence from graves.[6]

When working on a police investigation, the archaeologist becomes part of a team—usually led by a law enforcement officer—that may include a forensic anthropologist, crime-scene investigators, forensic pathologist, and other specialists. The forensic context requires that the recovery of evidence and recording procedures meet the highest standards of modern archaeology. And it is essential that the chain of custody of evidence be preserved so that the archaeologist's court testimony, if required, will hold up under cross-examination. Although the forensic context implies that all cases ought to end up identifying a murderer, sometimes the archaeologist's work eliminates a suspect.

The most influential forensic anthropologist in the United States is William Bass III, longtime professor at the University of Tennessee, who began his career in archaeology.[7] He is best known for the "Body Farm," a plot of land he established in 1971 near the University's Medical School. There, human and animal corpses are buried and allowed to decay under natural conditions. Using sensors and test excavations, Bass and students monitor the processes of decomposition. Among other contributions, research at the Body Farm has vastly improved time-of-death estimates. In the classroom and at the Body Farm, Bass trained a cadre of forensic anthropologists. Many now work in Tennessee counties and elsewhere in the United States, introducing archaeological techniques into criminal investigations. Bass himself has consulted on more than 1,000 cases in Tennessee.[8]

Forensic archaeology is also well developed in England, where the Universities of Bournemouth, Bradford, and Birmingham offer it as a specialization. At Birmingham, John R. Hunter, Professor of Archaeology (now emeritus) and senior author of a major textbook on forensic archaeology, has assisted on many cases and enjoys a sterling international reputation.[9] One of his cases provides an example of archaeological practice in a forensic context.[10]

In 1994, Hunter was called to assist in a possible case of murder from the Midlands of England. A person had reported to the police that the woman living next door had disappeared in 1978, leaving behind her husband and two children. The neighbor also reported that the husband had been digging a fishpond in a secluded area of the garden at about the time the woman disappeared. Why it took more than a decade for the neighbor to report her suspicions is unknown, but despite the delay, the report triggered a search for the missing woman. The husband claimed that she had run off with a lover, though there was no trace of her in public records after 1978. Now suspecting foul play, the authorities began a search in which forensic archaeology would play the major role.

A search warrant for the man's house and garden was obtained, but no body was found in the house. If present at all, the body would have to be in the garden area, whose archaeological investigation required knowledge about soils. Excavating a pit in the garden, Hunter was able to expose the nature and depth of bedrock or subsoil (sediments undisturbed by human activity), which turned out to be yellow clay at a depth of 40 cm below the existing ground surface. This information might help to identify disturbances such as a burial pit: yellow clay in the fill of a pit would indicate intrusion into the subsoil.

The narrow garden area abutted a concrete patio and contained lawns, flowerbeds, vegetable garden, and the fishpond. Hunter judged that resistivity surveying was the technology of choice for seeking human remains there.

With probes inserted at 50-cm intervals throughout the area of lawn and ex-posed soils, he measured the resistance of subsurface materials to the passage of electrical current. Computer processing of the resistivity data generated a map displaying several anomalies (areas of higher or lower resistivity) that could have been caused by human or natural disturbances.

The first anomaly seemed promising because its dimensions, about 2.5 m by 1 m, hinted at a large burial pit. However, a small test trench placed across the anomaly's width reached the clay subsoil at a depth of 40 cm, indicating that it was not a burial pit because no cultural deposit could lie below this level.

The second anomaly appeared at the edge of the concrete patio, but only part of it was showing, about 0.5 m across. Close inspection of the surface revealed flecks of yellow clay. Hunter reasoned that when this likely pit was originally excavated into subsoil and then refilled, garden soil and the telltale clay became mixed. This highly suggestive evidence called for removal of the patio so that the entire disturbance could be mapped and, if necessary, excavated.

After the concrete had been broken up and removed and the exposed ground cleaned off, it was possible to discern the outlines of a pit measuring about 2 m by 1 m. This finding led to a meticulous excavation, as if the tomb of a great king lay below. The process began with excavation of half the pit to reveal its contents and expose any strata (distinct layers). There being no obvious stratification, the soil was removed in 10 cm levels and set aside for later screening. At 60 cm below the ground surface, Hunter came across a layer of thin slate slabs across the entire bottom of the level. This was no natural feature. Could human remains lie beneath the slate pavement or was the pavement just part of an old construction? There was only one way to find out.

The slabs were removed so that the excavation could continue. At the 80-cm level, the archaeologists found human lower legs—bones and some soft tissues—still covered in clothing. The excavation was continued to the bottom of the grave around the remains, and then the other half of the pit was removed, leaving only a small vertical section, called a baulk, that doc-umented the stratification. After being recorded, the baulk was removed, which completely exposed the body and the bottom of the pit, the latter covered in a thin layer of gooey clay. The body and the base of the pit were recorded in a plan drawing and extensively photographed. There was little mystery as to the woman's cause of death, asphyxiation, for a rope was found around her neck.

Back in the laboratory, the remains were identified as those of the missing woman. The husband agreed to a plea bargain and was sentenced to prison for manslaughter. Hunter was not required to testify in court because the husband admitted his guilt, so compelling was the archaeological evidence. Had the case gone to trial, Hunter would have been asked to explain the archaeological process that led to the discovery of the body and its removal from the grave.

In other cases, the soil of the grave, especially samples taken near the body and processed in the laboratory, can yield pollen and other plant parts, insects, and animal bones that might indicate the time of death or burial and perhaps the place where the murder occurred. In addition, sifting the entire contents of the pit might turn up cigarette butts or items lost while the grave was being dug or filled, perhaps implicating the perpetrator. Any footprints found on the bottom of the grave can be compared to a suspect's shoes. And traces on the side of the burial pit can help identify the original tool(s) used to dig it, which may match a suspect's shovel.

Television shows have raised the viewing public's awareness about the contributions that forensic anthropologists and archaeologists make to criminal investigations. These shows are so successful that juries now expect investigations to meet the highest professional standards. This ensures that law enforcement agencies will continue to consult forensic archaeologists for help in finding human remains and in acquiring potentially significant evidence from gravesites. Such participation relegates the relatively recent Cummins Prison experience to an ancient era.

I thank John R. Hunter for comments on this chapter.

26

A Nazi-Era Mass Grave in Ukraine

FORENSIC ARCHAEOLOGY's most challenging and emotionally draining projects are mass graves, places where multiple individuals were buried at about the same time.[1] Prehistoric and historical archaeologists have long excavated mass graves resulting from battles and epidemics. But in recent decades, archaeologists have also been tasked with locating and excavating mass graves holding the victims of political executions as well as genocide in its many ethnic, religious, and political variants.[2]

Such excavations, especially those containing partially decomposed bodies, present a host of problems. There may be unexploded ordnance that requires specialist assistance. Some mass graves are buried under mountains of garbage containing toxic chemicals and noxious waste; others contain their own hazardous materials, including malodorous gases emanating from decomposing bodies. In these cases, fieldworkers wear protective clothing, boots, and respirators, and, of course, they shower and change clothing before returning to camp. Beyond the physical discomforts, archaeologists may have to keep reporters and photographers at bay as well as handle the victims' grieving relatives. If an excavation takes place in a town whose residents are hostile to the project, a security force is needed to protect the evidence and the archaeologists.

Mass graves of genocide may contain women and young children, perhaps tortured or mutilated. Archaeologists who have only excavated skeletons may be traumatized by having to unearth the decaying corpses of innocent victims of mindless violence; some field workers may require psychological counseling, especially if they develop symptoms of post-traumatic stress.

And even the seasoned excavator of mass graves cannot entirely avoid the psychological pain. As experienced forensic archaeologists have remarked, "Excavating a mass grave is a bizarre experience."[3]

Little did Australian archaeologist Richard Wright suspect that one day he would be having this bizarre experience. The story begins after World War II when many nations, including Australia, accepted immigrants displaced both by the war and the formation of the Eastern Bloc. Among the tens of thousands of immigrants arriving in Australia, several hundred had been Nazis and Nazi collaborators. While these people should have been barred from entering the country, the screening process was inadequate. Subsequently, the Australian government received credible reports from several organizations about these "war criminals" but took no action, dismissing the reports as Communist disinformation.[4]

Yet, finally responding to political pressure, in 1987 Australia established a special investigation unit (SIU) to identify residents who might have committed war crimes during World War II. Two years later, Parliament authorized the prosecution of war-crime suspects. After poring through old accounts, in 1990 the SIU arrested Ukrainian immigrant Ivan Polyukhovich, an Australian citizen since 1958, and charged him with the murder of Jews in and near Serniki, Ukraine, in September 1942.

At the time of the murders, which had been well attested after the war by eyewitnesses, Serniki was under German occupation. The Germans had begun to implement the "Final Solution," their plan for the total elimination of Jews. At Serniki, they began on a "small" scale in 1941, killing around 100 people.[5] The following year, with the alleged complicity of some local Ukrainians, the Germans herded the remaining Jews, perhaps 1,000 people, into a large pit and murdered those who did not escape into the forest. Polyukhovich was a Ukrainian forestry worker who, witnesses said, participated in the massacre and chased down and shot some escapees.

To forestall a "Holocaust denial" defense—the claim that the horrendous events did not take place—the Federal Attorney General's office sent teams of researchers to comb through historical sources in Germany, Russia, and Ukraine. They found no specific information about a massacre at Serniki. Whether such documents never existed or were destroyed is a moot point: the alleged incident lacked rigorous historical documentation. However, the prosecution had taken the precaution of also sending a team to Serniki to search for and excavate mass graves related to the massacre.

This team was headed by Richard Wright, a Cambridge-trained archaeologist at the University of Sydney who specialized in computer modeling and reconstructing past environments. Wright in 1990 had no experience in forensic archaeology, much less in excavating a mass grave—few archaeologists did—but he was a quick study, able to choose recovery techniques appropriate for the field conditions. Also on the team were Detective Sergeant David Hughes, an expert in crime-scene investigations, Godfrey Oettle, a forensic pathologist, and other Australians, including Wright's wife Sonia, also an archaeologist.[6]

An eyewitness, who had been forced to help refill the large burial pit after the massacre, led Wright to the grave's general location. Wright inferred from the disturbed soil, which contained lumps of subsoil clay, that this place was the mass grave.[7] Work was carried out in collaboration with the Soviet Union, which governed Ukraine at that time. The Soviet workers quickly began excavating one side of the grave with power equipment. On the other side, Wright proceeded more deliberately, carefully outlining the pit's boundaries. The huge burial pit, doubtless also dug originally with power equipment, measured 40 m by 5 m.[8]

Bodies were buried deeply: the first ones showed up 2 m below the present ground surface. The archaeologists used a bulldozer to remove the overburden to within about 20 cm. Then Wright and his crew used shovels to expose the human remains, completing the exposure with paintbrushes. Wright called the exposure of the bodies "gruesome," for some corpses retained soft tissue and hair.[9]

To prevent massive disturbance to bodies in the uppermost layer, lower layers were not exposed. And, respecting the wishes of Serniki villagers, Wright exhumed only a very few bodies for the pathologist to examine. The pathologist did the bulk of his work on the massive exposure of bodies at the gravesite itself.[10] In total, he recorded 553 bodies: 407 women, 98 men, and 48 indeterminate sex; 63 victims were less than 10 years old. The vast majority had been shot in the head, the remainder clubbed to death.[11]

Artifacts recovered from the grave included clothing, shoes, a watch, a comb still attached to hair, an artificial leg, bullets, and cartridge cases. When the cartridge cases were cleaned, stamped impressions could be discerned indicating manufacture in Germany during the years 1939, 1940, and 1941. This was important evidence as it showed that the massacre had to have occurred in 1941 or later. Counting the rings in a pine tree that had grown over the grave yielded 29 rings, which meant that the massacre predated 1961. Another attempt to push back the latest possible date depended on radiocarbon dating of hair samples. Results indicated that the people had lived (and died) before large-scale testing of nuclear bombs—ca. 1952—raised the radiocarbon content of the atmosphere.[12]

In a fascinating book on the Serniki massacre and subsequent trial of Polyukhovich in Australia, David Fraser drew a contrast between scholarly standards for accepting an inference—such as the date of an event—and standards of proof in a legal context.[13] Because of the risk that an innocent person might be convicted, legal proof employs very high standards, as illustrated by the dating of the massacre. An archaeologist or historian might assume that the German troops would not have run the risk of using old cartridges, and so the massacre would have taken place sometime in 1941 or 1942. In a court of law, however, such an inference was questionable: the legally defensible date—*from the archaeological evidence alone*—would be 1941–1952, despite its apparent absurdity.

Several historians as well as Wright testified at Polyukhovich's trial. Although the historians could not confirm through official records that a massacre had taken place at Serniki, they did provide evidence of general German policies in occupied Ukraine and brought to light other documented massacres. Despite gaps in the historical record, the archaeological evidence of the massacre was so overwhelming that the defense did not dispute it. In fact, the defense stipulated that at Serniki a massacre of no fewer than 550 Jews had occurred in September 1942 in conformity with Germany's Final Solution policy.[14] This move was calculated to head off accusations that the defense was denying that the Holocaust took place, which might have alienated the jury. Instead of Holocaust denial, the defense team employed a more effective legal strategy that turned on a different denial: they claimed that Polyukhovich did not commit the murders, for he was a victim of mistaken identity.

The prosecution imported aged witnesses from the Ukraine to attest to the events of 1942 and identify Polyukhovich as a perpetrator. Difficulties in translating the questions posed to the witnesses and their answers weakened the prosecution's case. Also, inconsistencies and gaps in the witnesses' stories gave the defense many openings to question whether Polyukhovich was in fact the forest worker they had seen killing Jews so many decades earlier. This was a crucial uncertainty that archaeology could not remedy.

Reasonable doubts having been raised about Polyukhovich's guilt, he was found innocent. The truth may never be known.

The Polyukhovich trial and those of two other alleged war criminals in Australia ended in acquittals; the SIU was soon disbanded and the enabling legislation repealed. However, the SIU's investigation set an important precedent that has been followed around the globe. Investigative teams seeking and excavating mass graves now routinely include archaeologists.[15] Since Serniki, dozens of similar investigations have been undertaken in such places as Rwanda, the former Yugoslavia, Guatemala, Argentina, and Iraqi Kurdistan; and, in some of the resulting trials archaeologists furnished important testimony.[16] Wright himself became a noted forensic archaeologist and has participated in other investigations. And artifacts recovered during the Serniki excavation are on permanent exhibition at the Sydney Jewish Museum.[17]

27

Recovery of Missing American Military Personnel

THE U.S. MILITARY employs archaeologists and funds many archaeological projects. Most of the archaeological work satisfies the requirements of environmental and historic preservation laws, such as inventorying archaeological resources on an Army or Air Force base. But one agency—the Joint POW/MIA Accounting Command (JPAC)—has a special mission: recover and identify missing Americans who served in the country's many wars.[1] JPAC's missions span the globe and focus on World War II, the Korean and Vietnam "conflicts," and even the Cold War.

JPAC's Central Identification Laboratory is "the largest forensic anthropology laboratory in the world."[2] Located at Joint Base Pearl Harbor–Hickam in Hawaii, the Laboratory maintains a staff of more than 75 scientists, most of whom are forensic anthropologists and archaeologists. There are also specialists in military hardware, including the all-important categories of life-support equipment and aircraft technology.

When a service person goes missing, the military begins a case file that remains open, even after the person is declared dead, until that person is identified. The laborious investigations, which often last years, may include excavations where burials are suspected and, often, where military planes have crashed, as in Vietnam, Papua New Guinea, and South Korea. Each year, the Laboratory identifies the remains of between 50 and 100 Americans. A positive identification brings closure, both for the government and surviving family members. The following case study shows that achieving such closure involves arduous fieldwork under difficult conditions and the collaboration of many specialists, usually in a joint operation with another country.

Sometime in 1968 during the Vietnam War, an RF-4C Phantom II carrying a pilot and navigator left Udorn airbase in Thailand on a mission to cross Laos and photograph targets in North Vietnam. The RF-4C was a fighter jet reconfigured with aerial sensors instead of armaments; it was highly maneuverable with a top speed approaching Mach 2 and a range in excess of 1,500 miles.[3] On this mission, radio contact was lost, and the plane did not return on schedule or land at another base; perhaps it had been hit by artillery fire or a surface-to-air missile. In any event, somewhere there was a crash site and possibly the remains of two airmen. The RF-4C's planned flight path was searched, but no trace of the plane could be found. Two decades later, in collaboration with the Vietnamese government, a more intensive search was undertaken, but still no wreckage was spotted.

A joint team of U.S. investigators and Laotian officials also questioned villagers about possible crash sites in Vilabouli District, Savannakhet Province, Laos (officially, the Lao People's Democratic Republic). In one village, several people recalled seeing a plane with a pointy nose go down nearby. The team went to the crash site, about 5 km from a village near the Vietnam border. A few large pieces of the plane, including a wing, engine, and landing gear, remained on the surface, but there were no traces of the airmen or of life-support gear.

Over the next two decades, beginning in 1991, joint American-Laotian archaeological teams carried out several survey and excavation projects at the crash site. In 2001, a survey team recovered several engine data plates whose serial numbers confirmed the wreckage as the lost RF-4C. Another team found two pieces of life-support gear, indicating that at least one airman was aboard when the plane crashed. It was also learned from villagers that the site had been scavenged somewhat, both by Laotians and Vietnamese, purportedly for artifacts but not human remains; traces of digging were also observed.

Since the crash site might contain human remains, two major excavation projects were undertaken despite numerous logistical and research design problems. It was in a remote area, about 5 km from the nearest unimproved road and 32 km from base camp, on a steep slope supporting dense jungle vegetation. A survey team also noted the presence of leeches. Adding to the challenges, the crash had cut a swath through the trees and undergrowth, creating a scar and exposing the ground to erosion, which had almost certainly carried and buried some debris down slope. To increase accessibility, a patch of jungle was cleared for a helicopter pad.

Archaeologists on the first excavation project in 2009 recorded aircraft pieces visible on the surface, cleared more jungle immediately surrounding the crash scar, and delineated the site's boundaries using a metal detector.[4] Covering about 1000 m², the site was gridded into 4 m by 4 m squares, five of which were excavated with hand tools down to pre-crash strata. Some excavation units reached a depth of more than 1 m and contained soil and artifacts that had slid or washed downhill. Passing all soil through quarter-inch mesh screen, the archaeologists were able to recover many small artifacts.

Items from each square were bagged for identification by pertinent specialists. Among the finds were highly fragmented personal life-support equipment, including parachute parts, an oxygen hose, a flotation cell, and pieces of G-suits, the inflatable trousers that prevent blood from pooling in the abdomen and legs when the wearer experiences high-G forces. But the most poignant finds were several tiny bone fragments, one of which was determined in the Laboratory to have come from a human femur; the remaining two fragments were too small for identification. The artifacts and human bone clinched the inference that at least one airman had gone down with the plane.

A year or two later, archaeologists returned to the site, seeking more human remains.[5] An additional 15 squares were excavated, bringing the total excavated area to about one-third of the site. Dozens of artifacts were found, including more fragmented life-support equipment. These were inventoried and analyzed at the Life Science Equipment Laboratory at Wright–Patterson Air Force Base. The investigators found two examples of several items, which led to the conclusion that both pilot and navigator lost their lives in the crash.

The findings provided a measure of closure for the military, but connecting the bone fragments with one of the lost men would provide closure for his surviving kin. Even a tiny scrap of bone could be buried with full military honors, but could any of the bone be associated with the pilot or navigator? Only DNA analysis could provide the answer.

While the two small bone fragments could not be analyzed for DNA, the femur fragment, measuring only 3.0 cm by 2.2 cm, yielded a sequence of mitochondrial DNA (which is inherited only from the mother). Further analyses were carried out at the Armed Forces DNA Identification

Laboratory in Rockville, Maryland. Researchers sequenced the mitochondrial DNA from the femur fragment and compared it to the sequences of family members of both men. There was a match with the brother of one airman, and the family was notified.

Because the second airman could not be identified, the archaeologists recommended that further excavations be carried out. After all, there was a chance that more human bone might be found in unexcavated portions of the site.

The JPAC's involvement with this remote crash site in the mountains of Laos lasted for more than two decades, requiring several surveys as well as two major excavations. As a result of this arduous process, the aircraft was identified, the two airmen were shown to have perished in the crash, and the remains of one man were identified. This long-term project not only plugged a hole in military records, but also provided some finality for at least one family.

I thank Gregory L. Fox, Supervisory Archaeologist and Laboratory Manager, and Thomas D. Holland, Scientific Director, both of JPAC, who graciously supplied unpublished reports on this case. Gregory L. Fox also commented on a draft of this chapter. The documents I received were redacted to protect the privacy of surviving family members of the airmen and to safeguard other sensitive information. Because case numbers, authors, and most dates were redacted from the reports, I am unable to provide complete bibliographic information (an ellipsis in a reference indicates a redaction).

X

EXPANDING
THE SOCIAL SCIENCES

ARCHAEOLOGY IS UNIQUE among the social sciences because its major source of evidence about human behavior, past and present, is material culture. Archaeologists have shown that research on material culture in modern, industrial societies furnishes new generalizations about human behavior and thus contributes to the social sciences. Archaeology's footprint here goes well beyond these significant studies: other social scientists have also adopted our material culture approach. Not only have some social scientists acquired the "archaeological gaze"—seeing societies as people and things interacting incessantly at all social scales—but they also use archaeological methods to gather and analyze data.

In 1973, William L. Rathje, a Mayanist at the University of Arizona, founded the iconic Garbage Project. Generalizing from the findings of the Garbage Project, Rathje was the first archaeologist to make sustained contributions to the social sciences. He argued that household garbage was a *material* indicator of certain behavior patterns inaccessible through interviews and questionnaires, the traditional techniques for obtaining social science data. Among the project's important—but counterintuitive—findings was the discovery that shortages of particular food items lead to more wastage of those items. The Garbage Project also did "front door, back door" studies, comparing interview data with garbage from the same households. These studies revealed patterned discrepancies such as the tendency to over-report the consumption of healthful foods. The Garbage Project's perspective appealed to corporations and U.S. government agencies, which supported the research for more than two decades. Because the Garbage Project was so novel and successful, Rathje became a media star, the spokesman for an artifact-based archaeology of the present day that yields important generalizations about human behavior.

In recent decades, intrepid investigators on the fringes of every social science began to study material culture, many no doubt influenced by the

Garbage Project. Material culture studies are not limited to garbage, but include investigations of artifacts used in households, businesses, public places, and so forth. One of the most intriguing studies was done by a multidisplinary team at UCLA, which included archaeologist Jeanne Arnold. Supported by the Sloan Foundation, The Everyday Lives of American Families Project aimed to learn about actual behavior in urban, middle-class households. Each of 32 households was subjected to a week of intensive video recording, digital photography, and interviews with adults and children talking about their things and rooms. From analyses of the data, researchers extracted eight major themes about middle-class life, including the saturation of houses with material culture, "vanishing leisure," "kitchens as command centers," and "Master Suites as Sanctuaries." The themes were presented in a lavishly illustrated book, *Life at Home in the Twenty-First Century*.

Despite heavy policing by the U.S. Border Patrol, the border between Mexico and the United States is crossed illegally every day. Migrants who hike across the Southern Arizona desert during the summer cannot carry enough water and place themselves at great risk of hyperthermia, dehydration, and other serious conditions. What kinds of material culture do the migrants bring along to help them avoid such conditions and evade the Border Patrol? These are among the questions asked by Jason De León, an anthropologist at the University of Michigan who was trained in Mesoamerican archaeology. Through his Undocumented Migration Project, he surveyed migrant trails in Arizona, recording the abundant material culture that migrants left behind in their trek northward; in Mexico, he also interviewed would-be and returned migrants. He learned that the choices of material culture—black clothing, cheap sneakers, black water bottles—made to evade the Border Patrol had the unintended effect of increasing the migrants' risk of hyperthermia and dehydration. This poor trade-off, De León suggests, stems from mythology and folk knowledge that, nonetheless, give migrants confidence in the face of uncertainty.

28

The Garbage Project

EVEN BEFORE HE FINISHED his Harvard dissertation on the Classic Maya of Central America, William L. Rathje was hired in 1971 by the anthropology department at the University of Arizona. In the next few years, he published many scholarly articles on the Maya, some with memorable titles such as "Praise the Gods and Pass the Metates," and "Last Tango in Mayapan." His fresh ideas on trade, religion, and other topics established a new agenda for Maya research. By the time he was 30 years old, Rathje had become the preeminent young Mayanist. Then something unexpected happened.

A brilliant teacher of undergraduates, Rathje had assigned an open-ended term paper to one of his first archaeology classes. He received many interesting papers, but two in particular grabbed his attention. The students had surreptitiously collected garbage from street-side trash bins at several houses in two neighborhoods, one wealthy, the other poor. The students' simple analyses hinted that different neighborhoods discard different items.[1] Rathje grasped the possibility that research on household garbage might yield new insights into modern human behavior. After all, if we can learn about ancient societies from their garbage, then we should also be able to learn about modern societies from *their* garbage.[2] What's more, no other social or behavioral scientists had staked out garbage as a research topic. Ignoring snickers from some archaeologists, Rathje founded the Garbage Project in 1973, also known as the *Le Projet du Garbàge*.[3]

Rathje conceived the Garbage Project as a versatile research tool in search of applications—any applications. In his words, "The primary goal of the Garbage Project is to explore the potential contributions of refuse research by providing valuable data to as many researchers and policy planners in as many areas of interest as possible."[4] Because the Garbage Project offered a unique window into actual human behavior, he argued, its findings could serve as a baseline for predicting the effects of a new activity or technology, perhaps helping to prevent such tragedies as "urban renewal projects that create slums, toys that harm children, cleaning products that pollute, medicines that cause disease, energy-saving devices that use more energy, and fail-safe devices that fail."[5] Rathje pursued his vision relentlessly, convincing researchers across the academy and in the business world—as well as policy makers—that the Garbage Project might answer some of their pressing questions.

With the collaboration of the City of Tucson Sanitation Division, which owned the trash bins and their contents, Rathje secured samples of household garbage from different neighborhoods. Bags of garbage were delivered to the Sanitation Division's maintenance yard for sorting, counting, and weighing of individual items. On a lengthy form, the sorters tallied the contents of each household's trash and entered the numbers into a computer database. To preserve the anonymity of the families, the sorters recorded no names or addresses. Sorting became much more convenient when, a decade later, garbage was delivered to the University of Arizona campus.[6]

The sorters were student volunteers in archaeology classes. Wearing gloves, they pawed through everything from half-eaten T-bone steaks to rotting fruit and disposable diapers. This was not glamorous work, but Rathje's ability to recruit dozens of students, year after year for more than two decades, testifies to his passion for the project and the ability to communicate its importance to would-be volunteers. And it helped that he was a gregarious and charismatic leader. Aware that his own management skills were sketchy, however, Rathje put the project's daily operations in the hands of Wilson Hughes, his capable codirector and field supervisor.

Because the Garbage Project required ongoing funding, Rathje spent much time writing grant proposals to government agencies and soliciting contracts from businesses. Here too, he was very successful, winning support from the National Science Foundation, Department of Agriculture, Environmental Protection Agency, and the National Cancer Institute. He also obtained contracts with dozens of companies including Frito-Lay, Miller Brewing, and Procter and Gamble.

By the late 1970s, Maya archaeology had taken a back seat to garbage studies in Rathje's research. When archaeologists began to realize that his move to garbage was not a brief dalliance but a committed relationship, some were appalled and wondered why he would "throw away" his Harvard degree and stellar career as a Mayanist. But Rathje wanted to make his mark in the world, and for him the world of Maya archaeology was, perhaps, a little too small.

Rathje was especially eager for the Garbage Project to help remake social science by documenting many aspects of human behavior more accurately than the recollections and attitudes obtainable through interviews and questionnaires. It is well known that these venerable social-science tools are subject to all kinds of errors and biases. After all, people cannot recall all of their activities; they may mislead, lie, and be mistaken; and they may shape their responses to meet what they believe are the researcher's expectations. Though smelly and gross, garbage data do not suffer from such problems and can furnish evidence of many behaviors in *material* form. In addition, Rathje believed that long-term records of household garbage might reveal unsuspected behavioral trends. And they did.

Beginning in the spring of 1973, the United States experienced a beef shortage that lasted through September; many cuts were scarce and prices spiked. Rathje wondered if the Garbage Project could detect whether the shortage had caused a change in the amount of beef wasted. Fortunately, as he later noted, meat packaging is "labeled with the type of cut, the weight, the price, and the date."[7] The data were recorded for a period of 15 months but results were very puzzling. During the shortage period, 9 percent of the beef brought into the house was wasted, but after the shortage the wastage dropped to 3 percent. When beef was in short supply, Rathje suggested, people bought larger amounts than usual as well as unfamiliar cuts. Maybe some of the beef couldn't be stored or prepared effectively, and so wastage increased. The findings led to the "First Principle of Food Waste:... *the more you eat the same things day after day—the less food you waste.*"[8] While this is a simple principle, it has profound implications for managing household purchases: variety may be the spice of life, but in the case of food it comes at a price.

Another study relating to household management examined package sizes. A widely accepted hypothesis, one that had never been tested on *material* evidence, was that poor households buy items—from rice to laundry detergent—in smaller packages than wealthy ones, and so the poor pay more per ounce of contents. The period of rampant inflation and stagnant wages during the mid and late 1970s provided an opportunity to test this hypothesis. Focusing on canned foods, the Garbage Project found that wealthy households bought more large cans, and poor ones bought more small ones. Because the hypothesis was supported, Rathje developed one of its implications about proposed product-disposal charges that some communities were considering at that time. He counseled that this seemingly beneficial move might have a "disproportionate impact on the poor" because their purchases involved more packaging material per ounce of contents.[9]

In addition to sorting garbage by neighborhood, the Garbage Project conducted "front door, back door" studies. The idea was to compare data from interviews and questionnaires with garbage from the same households. In seeking permissions for these studies, the Garbage Project found that most people didn't mind having their garbage analyzed but many objected to the interviews.[10] Fortunately, the Garbage Project was able to enroll enough willing families.

Front door, back door studies led Rathje to identify a "Good Provider Syndrome": people overreport the use of fresh ingredients in meals cooked at home and underreport the amount of prepared (ready-to-eat) foods they buy. He also identified a "Lean Cuisine Syndrome." Influenced by media accounts of healthful diets, "People consistently underreport the amount of regular soda, pastries, chocolate, and fats that they consume; they consistently overreport the amount of fruits and diet soda." The discrepancies were dramatic: candy was underreported by 80 percent and cottage cheese was overreported by 311 percent.[11] Such findings on diet—along with many more—were of special interest to the U.S. Department of Agriculture, which funded some of the studies.

During the Garbage Project's long life, Rathje expanded it to other cities in the United States. He also did more typical archaeology, excavating samples from deep in landfills. The excavations were supported by federal agencies and cities interested in learning about landfill contents so they could develop policies to reduce the amount of material going into them. The excavation tools included backhoe and bucket auger, the latter a machine that could penetrate to a depth of 100 feet, grab a sample of garbage, and bring it to the surface. The samples were dated (1952–88) on the basis of newspapers and other artifacts, and "sorted into as many as 35 material composition/type categories that were recorded by weight, volume, and moisture content."[12]

One bombshell finding of the landfill excavations was the limited amount of biodegradation taking place. Laboratory experiments had shown that bacteria would rapidly degrade organic items such as paper, food waste, and lawn clippings, a process that generates methane. Yet, measurements of methane coming from landfills were always much lower than laboratory-based predictions. The Garbage Project explained this discrepancy, finding that organic materials in landfills were decomposing slowly if at all. A sample of deposits predating 1975 had "more than 25 percent recognizable and readable paper items."[13] Rathje was especially fond of displaying a decades-old hotdog that was still recognizable. Moisture content is the most important factor affecting decomposition, but even in rainy regions the moisture in rapidly buried garbage, covered with a thick layer of soil, is too low to promote much decay. This discovery had an obvious implication: develop better recycling policies and practices, and many cities did.

Because the Garbage Project's findings were so compelling, often surprising, and relevant to present-day concerns, Rathje attracted an enormous amount of media attention. For three decades, the Garbage Project received more publicity than any other University of Arizona research project. To millions of Americans, he was the public face of archaeology, highly visible on television and radio, in newspapers and magazines, and as a keynote speaker at business conventions. He even testified before Senate committees in Washington. And, often with collaborators, he published Garbage Project findings in many journals, delivered numerous invited talks at professional meetings, and briefed dozens of governmental agencies—federal, state, and local—that had solicited his advice on garbage-related topics.

Yet, although the value of Rathje's approach was apparent to researchers in many universities, companies, and governmental agencies, American archaeologists were slow to give the Garbage Project much respect. The snickering eventually subsided, as archaeologists came to see that, owing to Rathje, their discipline was making contributions to the social sciences that were unexpected, significant, and widely known. Today, almost every introductory textbook on archaeology includes a section lauding Rathje and the Garbage Project. In addition, books in other social sciences point to the Garbage Project as a new kind of "nonreactive" measure for monitoring behavior. In one of his last projects, Rathje was the consulting editor to the massive *Encyclopedia of Consumption and Waste: The Social Science of Garbage*.[14] And Mayanists still draw inspiration from Rathje's early work.

This chapter is adapted from Schiffer (2015).

29

The "Material-Culture Turn" in the Social Sciences

FOR A GROWING NUMBER of social scientists, the study of material culture has become an important part, if not the core concern, of their research projects. But it wasn't always so. In contrast to archaeology, other social sciences lack a *necessity* to engage material culture, and so it has been neglected as a source of data about human behavior. Instead, cultural anthropologists, sociologists, cultural geographers, social psychologists, and others have relied mainly on interviews, questionnaires, and highly contrived experiments for learning about people's behavior, thoughts, and beliefs.[1] The "material-culture turn" in the social sciences, which began in the 1970s, came about in part because these traditional data-gathering techniques had reached their limits of usefulness as measures of what people *actually do*. More importantly, social scientists were becoming familiar with—and applying—archaeological perspectives on human behavior and material culture.[2]

Social scientists could learn about the potential usefulness of an archaeological approach in many ways. Since the 1960s, archaeology courses have enjoyed great popularity in universities, enrolling a cross-section of future social scientists. By reading archaeological textbooks, perhaps as undergraduates, these students became sensitized to the myriad kinds of behavioral information that research on artifacts might yield. Later, as professionals carving out new research niches, some consulted archaeological publications that contained conceptual tools for artifact studies. Another source of inspiration was archaeologist William L. Rathje's Garbage Project, publicized extensively in virtually all mass media beginning in the mid-1970s.[3]

Finally, several leading material-culture researchers had archaeological training. Richard R. Wilk is an economic anthropologist whose insights into household consumption patterns and village economics are influencing many disciplines. Until his last years of graduate school, Wilk was a Mayan archaeologist who had co-authored articles with Rathje and other archaeologists.[4] Perhaps the most influential figure in material culture studies is Daniel Miller, a cultural anthropologist and author of about two dozen books, including the eminently readable *Stuff.*[5] Trained at Cambridge University as an archaeologist, Miller has done ethnographic fieldwork around the world, from London to the Solomon Islands, examining the use and meaning of objects from fashions to cell phones.[6] In the Department of Anthropology at University College, London, Miller and colleagues—several also have archaeological backgrounds—produce a host of innovative studies that attract interest across the social sciences. They also edit the *Journal of Material Culture*, an interdisciplinary forum.

As Miller aptly observed, "Material culture thrives as a rather undisciplined substitute for a discipline: inclusive, embracing, original, sometimes quirky researches and observations."[7] But it remains in this disciplinary limbo because the organization of social sciences in universities has ossified, allowing no room to establish departments of material-culture studies. Today, material-culture researchers thrive on the fringes of all disciplines that deal with people; even so, the center of gravity remains archaeology, the only social science that teaches people how to study material culture from all times and places. As a case in point, *The Oxford Handbook of Material Culture Studies*, published in 2010, is a weighty tome of 28 chapters.[8] The organizers and editors, Dan Hicks and Mary C. Beaudry, are both archaeologists, but a fair sprinkling of chapter authors come from cultural anthropology, geography, sociology, and communications.

Archaeology continues to nurture material-culture studies with an outpouring of theoretical works and creative case studies, especially on industrial societies.[9] Meanwhile, other social scientists, imbued with the "archaeological gaze," have struck out in new directions. Thus, *The Oxford Handbook of The Archaeology of the Contemporary World*, another massive book, contains chapters by researchers in several disciplines willing to publish under the archaeology umbrella. The book includes a breathtaking diversity of topics, as in media and global network technologies, Silicon Valley, afterlives of artifacts, and archaeology of the Space Age.[10] The intellectual vitality of these chapters is almost palpable.

What is the "archaeological gaze" and how does it differ from the shared gaze of other social sciences? When envisioning an entire society, a small group, or even a family, social scientists focus on social interaction: people talking to each other, deploying their cultural beliefs, attitudes, and values in relation to their socioeconomic class, race, gender, ethnicity, religion, neighborhood, and so forth. In contrast, archaeologists envision groups at all social scales as consisting of activities of every kind in which people *and material culture* interact continuously. There is no such thing as "social" interaction per se, because people never interact with each other in the absence of material culture. And those artifacts, such as makeup, clothing, cooking utensils, tools, furniture, and structures, are as necessary for activity performance as the people themselves.[11] In short, the archaeological gaze fosters an appreciation for the pervasiveness and importance of material culture in all activities, whether applying makeup, praying in church, or dancing. Social scientists who share our gaze acknowledge that *every research question about human behavior must have a material-culture component.* A telling comment comes from Tim Dant, a British sociologist:

> As archaeologists and anthropologists have long recognized, material culture provides evidence of the distinctive form of a society. It provides this evidence because it is an integral part of what that society is; just as the individual cannot be understood independently of society, so society cannot be grasped independently of its material stuff.[12]

But, he adds, mainstream sociology still takes "a largely agnostic view of the role of material objects in the life of societies."[13]

Some chapters in the Oxford Handbooks mentioned above are coauthored by archaeologists and researchers in other social sciences. Such collaborations have resulted in novel and significant projects. I now turn to one of these, on material life at home, which was part of a larger UCLA project on the Everyday Lives of American Families, funded for a decade by the Alfred P. Sloan Foundation. The foundation was interested in "understanding the busy lives of working families in the United States."[14] Researchers included professors and students of archaeology, cultural anthropology, and linguistics. Leading the research team on material culture was archaeologist Jeanne E. Arnold.[15]

This project provided the first thorough and well-documented study of people and artifacts in present-day American homes, yielding insights into post-purchase consumer behavior. Thanks to copious records of economic transactions in the United States today, researchers have information about the kinds and quantities of things that people buy and bring into the home. However, after products enter homes, social scientists are stymied because interviews and questionnaires cannot answer basic questions about actual behavior, such as,

> How do people interact with these household objects in everyday life? Which objects do they find meaningful? Are Americans burdened by their material worlds? Which key spaces inside the house serve as the main stages on which U.S. family activities unfold?[16]

The only way to answer these questions is to enter homes and observe and record people interacting with their objects.

Thirty-two middle-class families took part in this project, opening their homes "to a week of filming and detailed photography of their houses and possessions" from 2001 to 2005.[17] The families were homeowners, had young children in school, lived in southern California, and were ethnically and occupationally diverse. Thirty households were headed by two adults, both of whom had essentially full-time jobs outside the home. The research team compiled an "archive of 20,000 digital images, dozens of maps, thousands of scanned observations, and 1,500 hours of videotaped daily activities."[18] This wealth of data was enriched further by recordings of adults and children talking about the meanings of their rooms and things. The project's findings have been published in articles and in a book, *Life at Home in the Twenty-First Century*, lavishly illustrated with color images of home interiors.

The bulk of the book consists of eight chapters, each of which develops a "theme" pertaining to "middle-class life at home." The massive data sets that Arnold and her colleagues compiled are the foundation for discussing the themes in some detail. A brief summary of those fascinating themes follows.[19]

Material Saturation. Homes are stuffed with objects to the point of saturation, an intense clutter that some women find stressful. Amidst the clutter there are still places to display meaningful objects, which reflect family history and interests, including photographs, souvenirs, toys, and trophies. There may be no room in the garage for cars because it has been colonized by the overflow of household goods.

Food, Food, Food. Few meals are prepared from fresh ingredients; family members often eat dinners at different times in different rooms. There is extensive storage of canned and frozen foods.

Vanishing Leisure. Cluttered home offices signal declining adult leisure time indoors; outdoors, there are many leisure-related amenities from pools to swing sets to barbeque equipment, but they are seldom used.

Kitchens as Command Centers. The focus of domestic life is the kitchen, where the day's activities are coordinated and scheduled. In addition to displaying colorful magnets, the refrigerator's door is a billboard for event reminders, phone numbers, invitations, and so on. On kitchen tables and counters are stored "keys, cell phones, chargers, PDAs, backpacks, and lunch boxes," ready to be carried off in the morning.

Bathroom Bottlenecks. Older homes may have too few bathrooms to accommodate the morning time crunch when two adults are hurriedly preparing for work and children are getting ready for school.

Master Suites as Sanctuaries? These large bedrooms, sometimes with adjoining walk-in closets and bathrooms, tend to be clutter-free. Although envisioned as sanctuaries for the adults, they are seldom used as retreats.

Plugged In. Electronic gadgets are ubiquitous in homes and "both isolate and unite family members in work and play."

My Space, Your Space, Our Space. "Walls and shelves are lined with photos, heirlooms, awards, mementos, and children's artwork." The families also display objects that express their "affiliation with various nations, religions, pop culture icons, and sports heroes." Children brand their bedrooms with "names on doors, walls, and furniture."

Readers who, as children or parents, were (or are) members of middle-class families, similar to those who took part in the project, will recognize themes that match their own memories. We could surely offer anecdotes about how American homes overflow with material culture but still have space to display meaningful objects or whose kitchens are command centers, but social science demands that conclusions rest on hard evidence, not anecdotes. Accordingly, Arnold and colleagues grounded these themes in nuanced and often quantitative analyses of the project's unique data sets. By documenting peoples' actual relationships to material culture, this project has created a unique account of middle-class human behavior.

Today, social scientists in every discipline perform creative and insightful studies of material culture. Archaeologists in particular are developing new conceptual tools, which may be taken up by other social scientists and used in case studies. And we continue to enter domains of human life previously unexposed to the archaeological gaze, such as processes of artifact design, homelessness, and even the Burning Man festival in Nevada.[20]

30

Undocumented Migrants
Face the Arizona Desert

THE CONTEMPORARY BORDER between Mexico and the United States became fixed in Arizona only after the Gadsden Purchase was ratified in 1854. Culturally and environmentally, this border is wholly arbitrary. After all, many families of Hispanic and Indian heritage have members on both sides. Passage across the border was once largely unhindered, allowing family members to assemble for holidays and other occasions. The situation has changed drastically in recent decades: the U.S. government made legal and illegal crossings much more difficult by vastly expanding the number of Border Patrol agents, building a steel fence across part of the southwestern border, and intensifying security at ports of entry. These measures have forced undocumented migrants to choose routes in remote and more dangerous locations in the Sonoran Desert.

Migrants heading to the United States to join or rejoin family members, obtain work, or escape persecution in their homelands have found the going rough. The migrants pay huge fees to smugglers (*coyotes*) and may be robbed multiple times along the way. Once the border is reached, the rest of the trip (up to 70 miles) has to be made on foot. In the hottest months from May to September, people attempting this hike of three or more days endure temperatures in excess of 100°F, and hundreds die of hyperthermia annually.[1] In addition, Border Patrol agents who are poorly trained and lack adequate supervision have killed and wounded migrants, occasionally before they entered Arizona. To locate migrants, the Border Control employs technologies such as motion and sound detectors, aerial drones, and infrared cameras.

Since 2009, Jason De León has directed the Undocumented Migration Project (UMP), focusing on people crossing between Sonora, Mexico, and southern Arizona. De León is an anthropologist at the University of Michigan with training in both sociocultural anthropology and archaeology. Prior to working on the UMP, he took part in archaeological projects, including Ph.D. research on the obsidian tool industries of the Olmec of southern Mexico and has published papers on Mesoamerican prehistory. Not surprisingly, in studying immigrants he employs techniques of data gathering from both cultural anthropology and archaeology. UMP's goals include documenting the daily realities of the migrant experience and demonstrating "the effectiveness of using an archaeological approach to understand an ongoing and clandestine social process."[2]

One of the project's first tasks was to survey the artifact-littered migrant trails northwest of Nogales, a city bisected by the border. UMP researchers mapped dozens of "migrant stations" along the trails "where people rest, eat, change clothes" and deposit clothing, water bottles, and other artifacts.[3] Some migrant stations have accumulated huge artifact deposits.

Researchers also interviewed hundreds of migrants in Nogales and Altar, Mexican towns from which many people depart for Arizona. Interviews, informal and semistructured, were conducted with people about to cross or recently deported from the United States. These interviews have enabled De León to identify a "border crossing industry" consisting of "smugglers, criminals, vendors, and manufacturers who profit by robbing and selling products and services to migrants."[4] Vendors offer products they claim are essential for a safe crossing (Figure 30.1).

Despite individual variation in purchases, much migrant material culture exhibits a common pattern. Items conforming to the pattern are dark-colored clothing; inexpensive sneakers and boots; high-salt foods such as crackers and tuna fish; water and hydration drinks in plastic bottles; first-aid items such as gauze and painkillers; extra socks; and a backpack. Also helpful is a small mirror that can be used in an emergency to summon the Border Patrol. Purchasing decisions are influenced by two major requirements: evading detection by the Border Patrol's surveillance technologies and staying alive in the desert.

Shoes, clothing, and water bottles dramatically materialize the suffering that migrants endure while crossing the desert. Water is a vital necessity, but no one can carry enough for the entire journey in the summer—an estimated

FIGURE 30.1. Shop in Altar, Mexico, offering products to migrants headed to Arizona (courtesy of Jason De León).

5 gallons. An adult can tote just one or two one-gallon plastic water bottles, along with food and other items. The artifact deposits at migrant stations include large quantities of small water bottles, suggesting that many people carry less than a gallon. When bottled water runs out, some people risk ill-ness by drinking from cattle tanks that dot the landscape. Migrants believe that in contrast to light-reflecting white bottles dark bottles will be harder for Border Patrol agents to see. Thus, people may paint the bottles black or cover them with black plastic or dark fabric. Responding to consumer de-mand, bottling plants in Altar began making black plastic bottles in late 2009.

Science tells us that black bottles absorb heat better than white bottles, thus raising the water temperature. UMP researcher Steven Ritchey per-formed an experiment to learn the extent of this difference. He placed white and black water-filled bottles in the sun from 7:30 AM to 4:30 PM. The air temperature at 4:30 was 100.7°; the white bottle was 112.8° and the black bottle 126.3°.[5] While dark bottles may marginally reduce a person's visibility, they are an unwise choice for hydration, especially for someone carrying a heavy backpack over rugged and rocky terrain.

A 36-year-old man, who had carried only one gallon of water, described hyperthermia's effects: "My heart was pounding and I started to see things. I was delirious. I was hallucinating. I was looking at the trees but I was seeing houses and cities all around me."[6]

And he survived.

UMP's study of use wear on hundreds of recovered shoes furnished poignant evidence as to the effects of footwear on feet. Many migrants believe that sneakers are the most appropriate footwear for people trying to look inconspicuous in the United States. They wear cheap Chinese or Mexican knock-offs of better-made and more expensive brands; the inferior products are prone to wear out quickly and sometimes come apart.[7] And, if purchased new, they may not have been broken in before the journey. These problems lead to blisters that are apt to pop, bleed, and become dirty and infected. Bloody socks and gauze as well as shoes with holes testify to these problems. Enduring what may be severe pain, people trudge onward in a reserve pair of shoes, in shoes with a jury-rigged repair, or perhaps barefoot. It is doubtful that sneakers render migrants less conspicuous in the United States, but it is certain that ill-fitting and poorly made shoes make the journey a test of pain tolerance.

Migrants also believe that dark clothing helps them to evade the Border Patrol, especially at night. A typical migrant's apparel consists of "darkly colored clothes, usually black T-shirts, dark denim jeans, and dark sweatshirts." Owing to their colors and fabrics, these kinds of clothes add greatly to a migrant's heat burden and accelerate dehydration and hyperthermia. Predictably, clothing and backpacks found at migrant stations "emit intense perspiration odor and display large, crystalline sweat stains."[8] Warm bodies are of course highly visible to the Border Patrol's infrared cameras, day or night. And dark clothing is in effect a uniform that alerts the Border Patrol and robbers that the wearer is probably an undocumented migrant, not a hiker.

Of course, inquiring minds want to know: why do migrants buy products that are largely ineffective as camouflage and increase their suffering? Despite the journey's dangers and difficulties, most migrants do not die in the desert. In later crossings, survivors may tell would-be migrants that dark clothing and water bottles helped them get past the Border Patrol, thus spreading and reinforcing erroneous beliefs. Migrants may not possess the scientific information needed to refute these claims. In addition, vendors offer such products, and so migrants may assume they are effective. De León suggests that the chaotic process of border crossing is generally burdened by much mythology and folk knowledge. These beliefs are comforting and maintain an illusion of control in the face of an uncertain outcome which, in the final analysis, "is strongly determined by tenacity and luck" and other intangibles.[9]

The Undocumented Migration Project has provided a stark description of the suffering endured by migrants in southern Arizona. Ethnographies, previous social-science studies, and government reports provided background and context for De León's archaeological research. But he emphasizes that the material culture of migrants, recovered and analyzed using archaeological techniques, "can help us better see many of the intimate details of this suffering that, because of its pervasiveness, complexities and subtleties, can be difficult to document using ethnography alone."[10]

I thank Jason De León for helpful comments on this chapter.

XI

CONTRIBUTING TO THE PHYSICAL SCIENCES AND ENGINEERING

ARCHAEOLOGY HAS A SMALL but significant footprint in chemistry, physics, material sciences, and engineering. Excavations often turn up objects and materials whose compositions or manufacture processes are at first unknown. In collaboration with physical scientists, archaeologists solve these puzzles. Those solutions contribute to archaeology and, sometimes, other sciences. Archaeological objects have also been used to validate and calibrate new dating techniques, such as radiocarbon dating, which is widely used not only in archaeology but also in physical and environmental sciences. Well-dated artifacts can furnish information about rates of material deterioration, which is useful in designing artifacts and in developing effective methods of waste disposal.

Many researchers have sought to learn the composition and manufacture processes of Maya blue, a lovely pigment that the ancient Maya painted on many objects used in ritual contexts. The first studies eliminated the obvious possibilities: the pigment was not a copper mineral or iron silicate. It was also learned that the major constituent of Maya blue is palygorskite, a white clay. But what pigment was added to the clay to create blue? Chemical orthodoxy prescribed that the pigment had to be an *inorganic* compound. After studying samples of Maya blue closely, Anna O. Shepard, a specialist in archaeological ceramics, offered the bold conjecture that the colorant was *organic*. Through experiments, several researchers succeeded in replicating Maya blue using indigo, a vibrant blue pigment derived from the plant genus, *Indigofera*. Because its composition is unique, Maya blue has attracted the attention of physical scientists. They have shown that the indigo is actually incorporated into the unusual crystal structure of palygorskite clay, which creates a kind of material new to science.

Archaeologists played a critical role in helping chemist Willard Libby develop and validate radiocarbon dating, an accurate and versatile technique for assigning ages to organic materials. Long incubating the idea of a dating technique based on radiocarbon, a carbon isotope that he believed was produced in the atmosphere, Libby took up the challenge in earnest after World War II. His work showing that, yes, the atmosphere does contain radiocarbon attracted the interest and financial support of the Viking Fund, a foundation for anthropological—especially archaeological—research. With this support, Libby and colleagues shored up the basic science underlying the potential dating technique. To show that radiocarbon dating measured time, Libby acquired hundreds of known-age specimens of wood, seeds, and other organic materials from archaeologists and dated them. These studies showed that the new technique did measure time, but it needed some tweaking to improve accuracy. Now calibrated with tree-ring-dated wood, radiocarbon dating is a workhorse of modern science.

Archaeologists have helped countries solve research problems posed by the accumulation of radioactive wastes from nuclear power plants. In designing multi-barrier systems for waste disposal, engineers have turned to archaeologists, seeking to learn whether specific containment materials would be durable over several millennia. In England, archaeometallurgist R. F. Tylecote visited museums looking for traces of corrosion on archaeological metal specimens of known age. He learned that lead and bronze survive very well. Danièle Foy and Marie-Pierre Jézégou's excavation of a two-millennia-old shipwreck off the coast of France supplied specimens of bulk glass to nuclear researchers. Studied in detail, the specimens illuminated the deterioration processes of glass and helped researchers to build, validate, and calibrate a general model of glass deterioration. In the United States, the government tapped archaeologist Maureen Kaplan to advise on the best way to mark a waste disposal site to discourage intruders. Her recommendations were based on a careful consideration of sites that had survived largely intact for many millennia.

31

The Mysterious Pigment

Maya Blue

ARCHAEOLOGISTS SOMETIMES recover enigmatic artifacts whose materials and manufacture processes have no modern counterparts. Faced with a puzzling artifact, they may do experiments to recreate it. Another strategy is to send it to specialists who have an interest in archaeology as well as advanced training in chemistry, physics, or materials science. Known as archaeometrists, these specialists employ scientific instruments that can furnish unique evidence of an artifact's composition and perhaps of its manufacture process. Occasionally, however, an artifact is so unusual that even archaeometrists are stumped for many years. One such artifact was made by the Prehispanic Maya of lowland Mesoamerica.

The Maya are famed for their monumental temples, lavishly appointed burials, and exquisite jade artifacts. They also invented a lovely pigment, called Maya blue, that was painted mainly on objects in ritual contexts such as murals, sculptures, pottery, and human sacrifices (see book cover). It took archaeometrists decades to identify Maya blue's composition and manufacture process. So unexpected were their findings that Maya blue continues to attract the interest of chemists and materials scientists.

An obvious hypothesis was that the pigment came from a blue copper mineral such as ultramarine or azurite, but a chemical analysis in 1931 found that Maya blue contained no copper.[1] In further analyses, chemist Gregory P. Baxter identified aluminum, silicon, calcium, and iron, all common elements in clays. Among these elements, only iron compounds can impart a blue color, and so it was suggested that Maya blue owes its hue to an iron silicate. But Maya blue didn't resemble the blue hue of iron silicate minerals.[2]

Research on the Maya blue mystery ramped up in the 1950s and 1960s, attracting many new researchers. An important contributor was Anna O. Shepard; trained as a ceramic scientist, she worked at the Carnegie Institution analyzing archaeological ceramics. Shepard was adept at using a technique called petrographic analysis, which enabled her to identify microscopically, in a thin slice of pottery, the minerals present in sand or crushed rock added as temper. Knowing where the minerals occur naturally in the environment, she could infer whether the pot had been made locally or was imported. Early in her career, Shepard analyzed pottery from several prehistoric pueblos in northern New Mexico. The mineral inclusions indicated that much pottery had been traded long distances, a finding that contradicted the traditional belief in the self-sufficiency of individual pueblos. Southwestern archaeologists were very slow to accept her findings.[3]

Shepard also worked on Maya ceramics, which gave her the opportunity to investigate Maya blue. Examining a thin section of the puzzling pigment through her petrographic microscope, she wrote that it "appears in flocks lacking a definite particle size and shape," and did not correspond to any known mineral. The source of the blue color remained unknown.[4]

Rutherford J. Gettens, a chemist and pigment authority at the Smithsonian's Freer Gallery of Art, also took up the Maya blue problem. He learned through x-ray diffraction, a technique for characterizing crystals at the scale of atoms and molecules, that the clay in Maya blue was the mineral palygorskite, which occurs in the Maya area.[5] This was an important finding, but palygorskite is white, not blue.

Hoping to learn about the properties of Maya blue, Gettens scraped small samples from a prehistoric incense burner and placed them separately in containers of "concentrated nitric acid, concentrated hydrochloric acid, aqua regia, concentrated sulphuric acid, 5% sodium hydroxide." The results were astounding: even after 18 hours of immersion in these liquids, the color held fast. These tests allowed Gettens to conclude that "the blue is an integral part of the mineral base, not a superficially attached dye." It seemed evident that no organic colorant, such as a plant extract, could survive these brutal tests. He offered the tentative conclusion that "Maya blue is an *inorganic* pigment."[6]

Commenting on Gettens's findings in 1962, Shepard assessed several hypotheses about the pigment's composition and, one by one, dismissed the inorganic alternatives. Against prevailing chemical orthodoxy, she proposed the radical hypothesis, "Maya blue is a clay-organic complex with an organic colorant in an inorganic base" of palygorskite clay.[7] Shepard also noted that this clay has an unusual structure for a clay mineral because its molecules are not plate-like but fibrous.

Shepard's hypothesis received support from the experiments of clay chemist H. van Olphen. In the Yucatan, still home to many Maya, there are native plants of the genus *Indigofera* that yield the blue dye known as indigo after processing. Mixing palygorskite clay with both synthetic and natural indigo, van Olphen arrived at two recipes that yielded a substance similar in color and chemical properties to Maya blue. The key to making his facsimile Maya blue was the use of "less than 0.5 percent" indigo and heating the powder "for several days at 75°C or preferably at 105° to 150°C." But how heating worked its magic remained a puzzle.[8] He also showed that Maya blue could not be made from typical platy clay minerals; palygorskite's fibrous structure, which Shepard had identified, was necessary. He speculated that the indigo molecules resided only on the clay particles' "external surfaces."[9] However, van Olphen used materials in his experiments that the ancient Maya lacked: acetone and sodium hydrosulfite. While van Olphen had increased the likelihood that Maya blue was, as Shepard had boldly proposed, a "clay-organic complex," details of the Maya process for making this blue were still unknown.

In 1980 a medical doctor with chemistry expertise and an interest in archaeology, Edwin R. Littmann, published a troubling finding: indigo could not be found in x-ray diffraction analyses of Maya blue. Presumably its low concentration fell below the technique's detection limits.[10] He next turned to replication experiments, learning that the source of indigo's color, indican, is easily extracted "by steeping the leaves and stems in warm water."[11] Next, Littmann tested both synthetic and natural indigo, employing several heating regimes. Adding natural indigo extract to powdered palygorskite clay and boiling the mixture, he obtained several shades of blue, but only after adding a small amount of dilute hydrochloric acid. The ancient Maya, he concluded, could have used natural acids available to them. Littmann's replications provided several plausible recipes for processing the indigo and combining it with palygorskite to produce a stable blue pigment.

Although van Olphen and Littman had shown, generally, how Maya blue could have been made, a big scientific mystery remained: how could an *organic* substance, a mere plant extract, resist prolonged attack by the strongest acids and most caustic bases? Apparently, unknown chemistry was at work. In recent years, physical scientists have taken up this intriguing problem. Applying new scientific instruments for characterizing materials, they have teased out the secret of Maya blue's microstructure and its incredible durability.

A team of Italian researchers, led by Giacomo Chiari of the University of Turin's Department of Mineralogy and Petrology, analyzed Maya blue, calling it "the most stable pigment ever produced."[12] Resolving one of Littman's concerns, infrared spectroscopy and photoluminescence spectroscopy "unequivocally revealed the presence of indigo in both the antique pigment and in the synthetic one."[13] Using powder synchrotron diffraction and molecular modeling, the team also showed that moderate heating of the clay enabled indigo to create the necessary chemical bonds in the clay's fibrous channels.

About the same time, German chemists led by Dirk Reinen at Philipps University in Marburg used experiments and optical spectroscopy to show that indigo molecules were actually incorporated into the clay's crystal lattice.[14]

Not surprisingly, these highly technical studies have been of more interest to physical scientists than to archaeologists. A case in point: Antonio Doménech and his team of analytical chemists at the University of València, in Spain, have specialized in studies of Maya blue, publishing many articles in physical science journals. This interest persists because, according to the Doménech team, Maya blue is a "nanostructured polyfunctional hybrid organic–inorganic material" *of a kind new to modern science.*[15]

Clearly, analyses of archaeological finds can sometimes result in challenges to conventional knowledge in the physical sciences. After all, in the early 1930s, when studies of Maya blue began, no chemist or materials scientist predicted from its chemical properties that the coloring agent was an organic substance. When Anna O. Shepard took up the Maya blue problem in the early 1960s, she was able to dismiss the inorganic candidates, concluding that only one possibility—though highly improbable—was left: an organic colorant. Experiments by others soon confirmed her conjecture. More recent analyses of Maya blue have shown it to be a new kind of material, one that is keeping some chemists and material scientists busy as they create new science.

32

Radiocarbon Dating

By ASSIGNING AGES to once-living materials, radiocarbon dating has been a boon to many sciences, including geology, oceanography, geophysics, hydrology, atmospheric science, and paleoclimatology. The technique makes it possible to date environmental events, including some volcanic eruptions; the formation of groundwater reservoirs; the creation of soil horizons; and the end of the last glaciation. Thanks to radiocarbon dating, scientific knowledge of environmental processes has grown phenomenally.

Archaeology has of course reaped enormous benefits from radiocarbon dating, for its use has revolutionized many prehistoric chronologies around the globe, from the first Americans to the last Neanderthals. It is less well known that archaeologists played pivotal roles in developing and validating radiocarbon dating, helping to transform a theoretical possibility into a workhorse of modern science.

During the late 1940s, Willard F. Libby and colleagues invented radiocarbon dating for which he alone received the Nobel Prize in Chemistry in 1960.[1] He was trained in physical chemistry at UC-Berkeley, earning a Ph.D. in 1933. At Berkeley, Libby fashioned instruments that could detect minute amounts of low-energy radiation. During the war, Libby moved to Columbia University where, as a participant in the Manhattan Project, he helped develop the gaseous diffusion process that produced enriched uranium-235 for the bomb that destroyed Hiroshima. After the war, Libby became a professor at the University of Chicago.

In 1946, Libby theorized that cosmic-ray neutrons bombarding the atmosphere generate a radioactive form of carbon.[2] Radiocarbon atoms, he posited, would then combine with oxygen to form carbon dioxide, which is taken up by plants. Because animals ingest plants, they also acquire radiocarbon. The ratio of radiocarbon (^{14}C) to stable carbon (^{12}C) in all living things should equal that ratio in the atmosphere (about one part in a trillion). Since dead organisms no longer take up ^{14}C, their stock of it continuously declines through radioactive decay. Decaying atoms emit electrons (beta particles), the decay rate depending on radiocarbon's half-life—the number of years it takes for half the ^{14}C atoms in a sample to decay. Thus, increasingly old samples would have less and less ^{14}C and thus a declining ratio of ^{14}C to ^{12}C. Drawing on his prewar experience, Libby calculated that the tiny amount of radiation given off by living matter would be detectable.

Although radiocarbon in organic matter was still unconfirmed, Libby had already contemplated a project to create a dating technique. In late 1946, he shared his vision with others, including James Arnold, a physical chemist, who would soon be assisting in the research. Arnold mentioned the dating project to his father, a lawyer who had an abiding interest in Egyptian archaeology. A. S. Arnold then talked to a friend, Ambrose Lansing, Director of the Metropolitan Museum of Art in New York. Excited by the possibilities, Lansing sent James Arnold a package containing some Egyptian specimens he hoped could be dated, and James passed them on to Libby. There was no dating technique yet, so Libby set the specimens aside, noting how easily archaeological samples could be obtained.[3]

In early 1947, Libby and colleagues announced in *Science* that they had found radioactivity in living matter and confirmed that the source was ^{14}C. The half-life of ^{14}C, not precisely known but estimated to be around 5,000 years, led to the momentous claim that it would be possible to determine the "ages of various carbonaceous materials in the range of 1,000–30,000 years," assuming that radiocarbon was produced in the atmosphere at a constant rate.[4] Such dating would depend on measuring the ratio of ^{14}C to ^{12}C in archaeological specimens of wood, seeds, and other organic material. They reported that development of this technique was being explored. One of the greatest remaining challenges was to increase the sensitivity of the radiation detector so that it could measure the minute amount of beta particles emitted by ^{14}C in ancient specimens.

Just after this paper was published, Paul Fejos, a Hungarian anthropologist and Director of the Viking Fund for anthropological research, learned about Libby's dating work. Under Fejos's leadership, the Viking Fund (now called the Wenner–Gren Foundation for Anthropological Research) took a special interest in funding risky but potentially game-changing projects. Fejos visited Libby at Chicago and offered support for the dating project.[5] In November of 1947, Libby received the first grant from the Viking Fund; eventually he would receive a total of $35,545 (a huge sum then—more than $500,000 in 2014 dollars).[6]

Libby soon visited New York at Fejos's invitation and lectured at a Viking Fund Supper Conference about radiocarbon dating and its archaeological implications. The audience of more than 100 included distinguished archaeologists and anthropologists from many institutions. Although some expressed skepticism about the intrusion of physics into archaeology, most knew that a technique capable of dating organic materials anywhere in the world and reaching back tens of thousands of years was the holy grail for prehistorians. In discussions after the lecture, Libby learned that archaeologists were hungry for dates that his hypothetical technique might furnish. Early encounters with archaeologists—including others at Chicago—no doubt buttressed Libby's belief in the potential utility of radiocarbon dating.[7]

The Viking Fund grants enabled studies to solidify radiocarbon dating's scientific foundation. The technique's feasibility depended on whether ^{14}C in the atmosphere mixed uniformly throughout the world. It turned out that radiation measurements on wood from South America, south and west Asia, and Australia were reasonably uniform across 14 specimens.[8] This pillar of radiocarbon dating seemed well established, though the sample size was small.

And what about radiocarbon's half-life? Obviously, an accurate value was needed. The Libby team's measurements at Argonne National Laboratory in Chicago put the half-life at 5720±47.[9]

As Libby refined the beta counter's design, he knew that radiocarbon dating would have to be validated on samples of known age. Clearly, collaboration with archaeologists would be essential. An early move was to hire James Arnold in order to interact with archaeologists. To promote this collaboration, the American Anthropological Association, later joined by the Geological Society of America, established a committee on radiocarbon dating. The three archaeologists and one geologist on the committee worked closely with Libby's group, especially Arnold, by "selecting samples for measurement, advising on priorities, and lending a friendly ear in troubled periods."[10]

In the earliest collaboration, archaeologists helped Libby secure a small sample of wood specimens from four sites in Egypt and one in Syria, all of which had been independently dated by historical evidence. The oldest specimen was from Egypt, and the radiocarbon date placed it in the middle of the 3rd millennium BC. Also analyzed were two pieces of wood independently dated by tree-ring analysis. Reported in late 1949 in a table and graph, the results showed a very good agreement between the known ages and the radiocarbon dates, perhaps too good to be true.[11] In the next year or so, Libby's lab ran hundreds of dates on specimens archaeologists supplied.

The first fruits of this collaboration were published in 1951 as a Memoir of the Society for American Archaeology.[12] This report is significant, not only because it was the first list of dates made publicly available to the archaeological community but also because it testifies to Libby's utter dependence on the archaeologists tapped by the committee to provide and interpret specimens. The contributors were a who's who of mainly American archaeologists and included New World and Old World specialists who took time away from other research to participate in Libby's project; there were also geological contributions.[13] The publication included 266 radiocarbon dates, some of them bearing on the most intriguing chronological problems in prehistory, including the first occupancy of the New World, painting of the Lascaux caves in France, and the earliest agriculture in several regions.

The dozen or more specialists assessed the dates in their regions of expertise, creating minichapters that comprised a majority of the report. After considering the assessments, the committee concluded that "the method is valid and that the dates are accurate within the expectable error."[14] This seminal publication demonstrated that the radiocarbon technique did measure time—though coarsely. Future progress, the committee noted, would depend "upon the success of continued collaboration between physicists, archaeologists, geologists, botanists and others."[15]

That radiocarbon dating was still a work in progress was widely understood, especially by Libby. In fact, he preferred not to give dates to archaeologists, but the need to correlate the dates with contextual information, which only archaeologists could interpret, made this impossible. Libby no doubt regretted the confusion that resulted from prematurely released dates, some of which were later retracted.[16]

Prehistorians who had no other way to date their archaeological sequences were delighted—and sometimes surprised—by their specimens'

ages. Archaeologists who worked with *independently* dated sequences, however, were less pleased because many radiocarbon dates were anomalous, a
problem that came into sharper focus in the 1950s as the technique's precision
was improved. What's more, the anomalies seemed to have a pattern: radiocarbon dates from the 3rd millennium (BC), mainly from Egypt, tended to
be too young.[17] According to Egyptologists, who had figured out how the
ancient solar and lunar calendars worked, their historical dates were fairly
secure because they were based on concordances among dated king lists
and calibrated with astronomical references to major events such as solar
eclipses.[18]

Interest in fundamental physical processes along with the growing number of anomalous dates from historical contexts encouraged several geoscientists to take up the problem and, in the late 1950s, they began to discern
the cause.[19] Employing tree-ring-dated samples supplied by the Laboratory
of Tree-Ring Research at the University of Arizona, including specimens of
bristlecone pine, the geoscientists' research undermined Libby's assumption
that ^{14}C production in the atmosphere had remained constant over time.
Happily, this dark cloud had a silver lining, for the problem pointed to its
own solution: a calibration curve could be constructed from a long series of
radiocarbon-dated tree rings.[20]

Libby himself was reluctant to give up the assumption of constant ^{14}C
production, even though geoscientists had identified mechanisms that could
account for variation in this rate, including changes in solar activity and in
the Earth's magnetic field. In his 1967 "history of radiocarbon dating," Libby
discussed the new work, and even advocated use of the recent calibration
curve for the last 2,000 years. But, noting the troubling anomalies in older
BC dates, which also afflicted a new date-series from Egypt, he opined, "It is
conjectural whether the deviation is real, or whether the Egyptian historical
dates are incorrect, or possibly both." As for the equally anomalous radiocarbon dates on tree-ring samples, he claimed "the Bristle Cone Pine dating
technique remains to be established to the point of certainty needed."[21]
Libby was implying that Egyptologists and tree-ring specialists might not
know their business.

Work to reconcile radiocarbon dates with Egyptian calendrics continues.
A recent paper has shown that the greatest source of persistent anomalies
is dates on wood and charcoal, which tend to suffer from an "old wood"
problem caused, in some cases, by long-lived trees or reuse of old wood.[22]

Curiously, Libby deemed wood and charcoal highly appropriate for dating, probably because these materials are abundant in many sites.[23]

In recent decades, many laboratories have run massive numbers of dates on known-age tree-ring samples from the United States and Europe, which has led to the creation of reliable calibration curves that extend to about 12,000 years ago. A few laboratories have exploited other independently datable materials, such as laminated lake sediments and coral, to construct much longer calibration curves. Columbia University's Lamont–Doherty Earth Observatory, for example, has crafted one reaching back 55,000 years.[24]

Radiocarbon dating has advanced greatly since Libby's pioneering work, making it exceedingly versatile and accurate. It is now indispensable for research across academic and applied sciences. The profusion of dating facilities around the world indicates its importance. Recently, the journal *Radiocarbon* listed 48 countries with laboratories, the vast majority affiliated with universities or government agencies; the United States alone has 16 facilities, including several commercial ones.[25] Of course, when important university laboratories were established early on in the United States in Arizona, Pennsylvania, and Michigan, archaeologists played instrumental roles.[26]

Although applications of radiocarbon dating appear in dozens of journals, from *Quaternary Geochronology* to *Chemical Geology*, *Radiocarbon* remains a major outlet for cutting-edge research across all radiocarbon-using disciplines. In recent decades, however, archaeologists' contributions to *Radiocarbon* have often been dwarfed in number by those of other researchers. It is doubtful that the latter are aware that an anthropological research foundation aided the technique's development and that archaeologists were central in validating it.

I thank Iain Davidson for calling my attention to this example and commenting on this chapter.

33

Nuclear Waste Disposal

DISPOSAL OF "HIGH-LEVEL" radioactive wastes from nuclear power plants is a persistent problem in countries where reactors have been running for decades. In the United States, vast amounts of wastes are stored "temporarily" in cooling ponds at commercial reactor sites. But temporary has apparently lapsed into permanent because specialized underground repositories are unavailable. People opposed to repositories believe that they will leak radiation and pollute nearby land, air, and water. Although decades ago nuclear experts in several countries designed promising multi-barrier systems to contain high-level wastes, local opposition to these facilities remains strong.

A multi-barrier system is designed to isolate nuclear wastes for millennia. First, radioactive materials are incorporated into blocks of borosilicate glass. Second, the glass blocks are encased in metal containers. Third, the metal containers are buried in a geologically stable environment, perhaps surrounded by a layer of clay or concrete. Fourth, the site is conspicuously marked to warn or ward off intruders.

To help design each barrier and predict its effectiveness, governments have conducted and contracted for thousands of technical studies. *Laboratory* experiments on the deterioration of borosilicate glass and on the corrosion of container materials, such as lead and copper, indicate that these materials are quite durable and have led to optimistic predictions about the long-term safety of repositories. But even nuclear researchers admit to some uncertainties. To bolster confidence in their predictions, nuclear establishments in several countries have turned to archaeology, acquiring ancient

232   CHAPTER 33

artifacts along with information about their recovery, dating, and provenance (place of origin).

In the late 1970s British Nuclear Fuels, Ltd., a company owned by the UK government, hired R. F. Tylecote to assess which metals might be suitable for waste containers. A metallurgist at the University of Newcastle-upon-Tyne, Tylecote was no ordinary metals expert, for he was a founder of archaeo-metallurgy. This subdiscipline employs research tools of the material sciences to infer the life histories of metal objects recovered archaeologically. Like archaeometallurgists of today, Tylecote even took part in excavations.

In search of millennia-old metal artifacts, Tylecote visited many museums. Before examining an artifact, he had to obtain the museum's permission to cut and polish a small piece so that he could view it through a metallographic microscope. With light reflected from the specimen's surface, he measured the penetration of corrosion and identified any changes in the metal's crystalline structure.

Tylecote examined dozens and dozens of artifacts, and his findings were informative. Lead weights from a shipwreck that sank in the Thames River in London, during the second century AD, showed little deterioration.[1] He also studied lead from older Mediterranean wrecks and Roman water pipes, which supported his conclusion that this metal, which often develops a protective patina, survives for millennia.[2] Tylecote found that bronze artifacts also showed good durability, such as those found in a Middle Bronze Age shipwreck (ca. 1200–900 BC), near the Dover cliffs, which were only slightly corroded.[3] On the basis of his extensive studies, Tylecote recommended that waste containers be made of bronzes with a high tin content (and few impurities) or of pure lead.

Owing to its brittleness, glass may not seem like the best material for the primary barrier, but borosilicate glass has desirable properties. Ordinary glass, including that made in ancient Greece and Rome, is composed of silicon dioxide (from quartz sand), lime, and a flux such as potassium or sodium compounds that lowers the melting point of quartz (1700° C). Melting these materials in a furnace produced raw glass that was remelted, usually at workshops in different locations, and crafted into bottles, bowls, and so on. On the other hand, borosilicate glass was not manufactured until the 20th century. It contains boron as the flux along with silicon dioxide (the glass former) and is more resistant to certain chemical attacks than ordinary glass. Borosilicate glass also expands very little when heated and so is ideal

0   5   10 cm

Emb 0140

FIGURE 33.1. Block of Roman glass recovered from the ship *Ouest-Embiez 1* (courtesy of the Ministère de la Culture et de la Communication, Département des Recherches Archéologiques Subaquatiques et Sous-Marines, Marseille, France).

for making oven-top cookware and telescope mirrors. It is also excellent for incorporating heat-producing nuclear wastes.

How durable, nuclear researchers asked, would borosilicate glass be over millennia? Fortunately, archaeological glass helped to answer that question. Researchers believe that ancient glass artifacts can be used as "analogs" for borosilicate glass despite differences in chemical composition. Thus, nuclear researchers tested their deterioration models on millennia-old glass.[4] Let us turn to a recent project that took advantage of the serendipitous find of 1,800 year-old glass.

Around the beginning of the 3rd century AD, a Roman ship loaded with lovely glass vessels, window panes, and tons of raw glass chunks (Figure 33.1) foundered in the treacherous seas near the island of Ouest Embiez along France's Mediterranean coast. Discovered by a diver in 1993, the wreck was partially excavated several years later by French archaeologists Danièle Foy and Marie-Pierre Jézégou.[5] They had their work cut out for them: the ship, named *Ouest-Embiez 1*, was resting at a depth of 55 m, which limited dives to

20 minutes, and there were strong winds and currents. In addition, a layer of sediment covering the cargo had to be removed with trowels and a water dredge.[6] Overcoming the difficulties, the archaeologists recovered a large sample of the cargo from the earliest known merchant ship of its kind.

Once in the laboratory, samples of finished products and raw glass underwent chemical analyses to determine their provenance.[7] The archaeologists concluded that the raw glass was most likely made in the Syria-Palestine area, but the ship's destination—perhaps glass workshops in France—remains unknown.[8]

The significance of the *Ouest-Embiez 1*'s cargo didn't end with the light it shed on Roman trade. The large chunks of raw glass, with a dense network of cracks formed during cooling in the furnace, were an excellent analog for borosilicate glass because it, too, forms cracks during manufacture. In a moist environment, such as the sea or a leaky nuclear repository, cracks allow the entry of chemical compounds that may cause deterioration.

Accounts of the *Ouest-Embiez 1* and its spectacular cargo were carried in French newspapers. These reports attracted the interest of nuclear researchers who asked for and received samples of the raw glass.[9] Focusing a battery of high-tech analytical tools on the cracks, they identified mechanisms of deterioration and observed that some mechanisms, shared with borosilicate glass, were self-limiting.[10] In fact, the cracks exhibited little deterioration.

A few years later, the same researchers built these mechanisms into a deterioration model that included information about glass composition and burial environment. The model simulated the degree of long-term deterioration for several glass recipes under various conditions. Because the model's predictions matched the condition of the *Ouest-Embiez 1* glass, researchers confidently concluded that borosilicate glass would contain radioactive wastes for thousands of years.[11] This strong claim could not have been made without benefit of a well-documented archaeological analog that enabled both identification of deterioration mechanisms and testing of the predictive model.

Finally, there is the matter of how to warn people, up to 10 millennia in the future, not to disturb repositories. This issue became pressing because the U.S. government was developing an experimental repository in a deep salt deposit in southeastern New Mexico.[12] In 1990, a multidisciplinary panel was commissioned to come up with suggestions.[13] One of the panel's members was archaeologist Maureen Kaplan, already a leading authority on the disposal of nuclear waste.[14] Drawing lessons from archaeological sites, Kaplan's insights are reflected in the panel's final report.

Kaplan focused on sites that had survived relatively intact for thousands of years. Stonehenge and the Egyptian pyramids clearly indicate that massive stone monuments can withstand the onslaughts of deterioration processes—even assaults by later peoples—for 4,000 years or more. The Parthenon (a stone structure on the Acropolis in Athens) once held several bronze shields, but in later years these valuable metals were scavenged and reused. Using such materials would not be a wise move. The Great Wall of China, she noted, required constant maintenance, an undesirable feature for a marking system.

Building on these lessons, Kaplan offered sensible recommendations. The marking system should consist of a ring of monoliths made of granite or basalt—two extremely durable kinds of stone—large enough to enclose the repository's footprint. The monoliths should be polished to shed water and be tapered to discourage reuse as building materials. They should stand *at least* 10 to 12 feet tall and carry carved inscriptions—not metal plaques— in six widespread languages from several linguistic families, augmented by symbols; both inscriptions and symbols should be readable at eye level. She assumed that literate societies would survive for thousands of years and be able to translate the warnings. After all, she pointed out, with the Rosetta Stone it took "twenty-five years to read the hieroglyphs, but the [ancient] Greek could be read immediately."[15]

As of mid-2014, the issue of repository markers is moot. The United States did build a $4 billion facility at Yucca Mountain, Nevada, to handle commercial nuclear wastes, but its status remains in limbo owing to political wrangling. And, according to *BBC News*, "not a single country worldwide has an operational underground repository"—more than a half century after the first commercial reactors began generating electricity and radioactive waste.[16] In some countries, however, vast amounts of high-level wastes have been incorporated into borosilicate glass.

Regardless of the fate of nuclear wastes, archaeologists have helped to shore up the science underlying waste containment and the marking of repositories. Archaeological analogs also continue to be important in recent studies of steel and concrete.[17] In addition, textbooks on nuclear waste disposal mention the relevance of archaeological analogs.[18] Finally, the nuclear establishment exploits analogs in educating the public. John P. Sokol, a public relations official with Westinghouse, a manufacturer of nuclear reactors, remarked that analogs "make a presentation more interesting," spicing up a purely theoretical talk. And audiences put off by abstract timeframes relate easily to 2000-year-old glass or metal objects from the Roman Empire.[19]

XII

BOLSTERING BIOLOGICAL SCIENCES

ONE OF ARCHAEOLOGY'S advantages over other human sciences is time depth, which gives us access to information about the deep past beyond historical records. Time depth is essential for answering some questions that biological scientists ask about relationships among people, plants, and animals. Often in collaboration with biologists, archaeologists provide well-dated specimens and inferences about their societal and environmental contexts. Archaeobotanists specialize in the recovery and analysis of plant remains, whereas animal remains are the province of zooarchaeologists.

Archaeobotanist Bruce D. Smith, a researcher at the Smithsonian Institution, tracked down the earliest domesticated sunflowers. Although early sunflower shells and seeds had been found before in the eastern United States, the problem was to determine *rigorously* whether they were wild or domesticated (wild sunflower seeds are smaller than cultivated varieties). Smith obtained a reference collection of hundreds of wild sunflowers from a wildlife refuge far from modern fields, thus avoiding hybrid varieties. After charring the shells and seeds so that they would be comparable to archaeological specimens, he measured their dimensions. Smith then turned to several early sites in the eastern U.S., measuring the sunflower specimens and comparing them to those in the reference collection. He was able to show convincingly that domesticated sunflowers were present at around 5,000 BP in central Tennessee.

Zooarchaeologists increasingly play important roles in conservation biology. On the basis of well-dated faunal remains from archaeological and paleontological sites, zooarchaeologists can establish the prehistoric distribution of a species and set it into its—possibly changing—environmental context. Such analyses provide conservation biologists and wildlife managers with information relevant for making decisions. A major advocate for "applied zooarchaeology," R. Lee Lyman did a fascinating study of pygmy rabbits.

The rabbits occurred in a small part of the Columbia Basin in Washington State, where their numbers were declining precipitously, and in a larger area that encompasses parts of several other states in the Great Basin. Lyman's research showed that the pygmy rabbit population once had a continuous distribution. Efforts to restore the pygmy rabbit population in the Columbia Basin through captive breeding and release failed. Lyman had suggested simply transferring rabbits from the Great Basin population to the Columbia Basin. This recommendation was finally followed. The pygmy rabbits are slowly making a comeback, but their long-term prospects are uncertain.

Human bodies contain astonishing numbers of bacteria, viruses, and other microbiota. Recent research in microbiology has shown that some species are symbiotic, serving functions that enhance human health, while others cause disease. Much can be learned about microbiota from studies of modern human populations in various parts of the world, but archaeology also makes contributions because questions about "ancestral" microbiota require ancient specimens. An important source of evidence on ancestral microbiota is coprolites (ancient feces or archaeo-poop), which are sometimes found in dry caves, waterlogged deposits, and mummies. In an analysis of six coprolites from several sites, Raul Y. Tito and colleagues showed that a new species of *Treponema*, whose close relatives cause such diseases as syphilis and yaws, may also aid the digestion of whole grains. Another fascinating study, conducted by Raul J. Cano and colleagues, studied a large sample of coprolites from two contemporary prehistoric cultures in Puerto Rico, Huecoid and Saladoid; they found that the two cultures differed in diet and also in microbiota.

34

Origin of the Domesticated Sunflower

PEOPLE DEPEND ON fruits, vegetables, and grains for food, but few of these plants are "natural." Rather, domesticated plants (domesticates or cultivars) are artifacts because natural selection *and cultural selection* have created their genomes. During the millennia before genetic engineering came along, humans domesticated dozens of species by exerting selective pressures through planting, harvesting, storage, and cooking activities. Depending on the plant and its cultural context, these activities favored characteristics such as frost tolerance, greater seed or fruit size, longer shelf life, and palatability. As a result, genes responsible for favored characteristics became more prevalent with each generation, and this process eventually created a plant unknown in the wild. Such is evolution.

For centuries, botanists have wondered where and when particular species were domesticated. Before the mid-twentieth century, they acquired clues from the geographical distributions of modern plants. Swiss botanist Augustin de Candolle pioneered these efforts, but the most ambitious researcher was the Russian botanist Nikolai Vavilov. On the basis of prodigious fieldwork around the world in the early twentieth century, Vavilov identified "centers" of domestication, regions where a group of domesticated plants had arisen independently of other centers.[1] His main evidence was the diversity of modern varieties of each crop plant. According to Vavilov, domestication took place in the region of greatest variation. In one of his last works, he listed eight centers, each consisting of a dozen or more domesticates: South Mexican and Central American, South American, Mediterranean, Middle Eastern,

Ethiopian, Central Asiatic, Indian, and Chinese.[2] The South Mexican and Central American center, for example, included maize (corn), several kinds of beans, sweet potato, papaya, cherry tomato, grain amaranth, and cacao (the source of chocolate).

The geographical inferences of de Candolle, Vavilov, and others were just plausible hypotheses until archaeobotanists began to accumulate evidence on early domestication. Archaeobotanists, also known as paleoethnobotanists, are a particular kind of scientist—usually an archaeologist—who studies plant remains from sites. As such, in addition to archaeological and botanical expertise, archaeobotanists are skilled at identifying charred and fragmentary plant parts.[3] Archaeobotanists build inferences about all human uses of plants, from diet to ritual; they also help reconstruct past environments and illuminate the prehistory of domesticates.

In some regions, archaeobotanists have tentatively answered the where and when questions and revised Vavilov's domestication centers. Vavilov was an insightful researcher, and a fair number of his hypotheses about specific plants have turned out to be approximately correct. However, not all domesticated plants originated in centers, and he failed to identify several centers.

An important center Vavilov missed is eastern North America, where four domesticated plants evolved: marshelder (*Iva annua*), chenopod (*Chenopodium berlandieri*), squash (*Curcurbita pepo* ssp. *ovifera*), and sunflower (*Helianthus annuus*). Marshelder and chenopod are no longer cultivated, but squash (which was independently domesticated in another center) and sunflower are today grown throughout the world.

The sunflower is much more than a tasty snack food or birdseed, for it has many modern uses. Sunflower kernels yield a healthful oil used in cooking and salad dressings; and finely ground kernels are made into a spread that can substitute for nut butters. There are also ornamental, medicinal, and industrial uses, including livestock feed.[4] In the United States alone, the value of the sunflower crop approaches $750 million.[5]

The eastern North American center was brought into sharp focus by archaeobotanist Bruce D. Smith, a curator at the Smithsonian Institution who specializes in the prehistory of the eastern United States. Building on the foundation laid by other researchers, Smith pulled together information buried in technical reports and presented a strong case for this center.[6] His work on the sunflower, in particular, illustrates the difficulties in distinguishing domesticates from their wild ancestors and in dating their early history.

Almost 70 species of the sunflower genus, *Helianthus,* grow wild throughout North America, but their disks—the central part holding the seeds—are seldom more than a few inches in diameter, and the seeds are small. In contrast, the disks of some modern commercial varieties (*Helianthus annuus*) can approach a foot in diameter and hold many hundreds of large seeds. Archaeobotanists should be able to use seed size (shell or kernel) to identify domesticated sunflowers, but it's not so simple.

Think about preservation. Throughout the eastern U.S., uncharred seeds rarely survive because abundant rainfall keeps soils moist much of the time, creating ideal conditions for decay organisms. Although dry caves and rockshelters have yielded caches of uncharred seeds and other plant parts, such sites are rare.[7]

When burned in an oxygen-starved atmosphere, plant parts are charred (or carbonized). *Charred* plant parts usually survive in moist soil, but recovery is difficult because they are fragile and hard to separate from the soil by hand. When inferring prehistoric diets became a high priority in the 1960s, American archaeologists began to use a technique called flotation. Originally, an old laundry tub, bucket, or infant bathtub was filled with water and the soil sample gradually poured in and gently stirred. Since plant parts have a lower specific gravity than water, they floated to the surface and could be skimmed with a fine mesh sieve. After drying, the plant parts were identified under a microscope. In recent decades, archaeologists have abandoned their makeshift flotation setups in favor of commercial machines that, among other features, recycle the water—a blessing in arid lands.

Applied to soil samples from hearths, house floors, and middens, flotation has generated a vast amount of new evidence on domestication. What's more, the recovered plant materials can now be dated directly by Accelerator Mass Spectrometry, a relatively new radiocarbon technique that requires only a small amount of material: even one tiny seed can be dated. Direct dating also eliminates errors that can arise when associated material, not the plant itself, is the basis of a date.

Yet, despite the widespread use of flotation, sunflower seeds have not been recovered in abundance from early sites. The largest sample comes from the Marble Bluff site, a rock-shelter in the Arkansas Ozarks. Excavations there in 1934 turned up hundreds of charred seeds of many species, including sunflower, stored in woven bags.[8] But were they domesticates? Before prehistoric sunflower seeds can be compared with modern ones on the basis of size, an archaeobotanist must deal with several complications.

The first complication is that wild sunflowers may not be so wild after all: they can be pollinated by cultivated varieties in nearby fields, producing hybrids with larger seeds. To eliminate this possibility, Smith formed a "reference class" of wild sunflower seeds from the DeSoto National Wildlife Refuge in Iowa. Grown far from modern fields, these specimens are believed to be uncontaminated by domesticates. Equally important was the genetic relationship between the DeSoto sunflowers and domesticated varieties. Although varieties of wild sunflowers abound, genetic analyses showed that the DeSoto population most closely represents the ancestral sunflowers from which the domesticates evolved.[9]

The second complication is that charring causes plant parts to shrink, and so rules out the *direct* comparison of size measurements on charred and uncharred specimens. In previous experiments, investigators had charred *cultivated* sunflower kernels and shells to establish shrinkage percentages, which varied widely. For example, shell length ranged from 12–22 percent, and width from 22–28 percent.[10] These values were turned into conversion factors and applied to charred archaeological specimens in order to estimate their original dimensions.

Wary of using conversion factors based on cultivated sunflowers, Smith made use of DeSoto specimens. In the oxygen-starved atmosphere of a muffle furnace, he charred 100 DeSoto shells and obtained lower shrinkage values: 2–12 percent length and 4–26 percent width. Allowing for the considerable variation in shrinkage, Smith deemed the charred DeSoto specimens an appropriate reference class whose dimensions could be compared directly with those of charred archaeological specimens.

Smith next turned to the prehistoric sunflowers. Archaeobotanist Gayle Fritz had previously measured specimens from the Marble Bluff site and concluded that they were domesticates. Smith measured 259 shells from Marble Bluff and compared them with those in the DeSoto reference class. In length and overall size (length times width), 97 percent of the Marble Bluff shells were larger than any in the reference class.[11] Fritz's conclusion was dramatically reaffirmed. What's more, the botanical specimens from Marble Bluff have been well dated to around 3000 BP (BP = before present).

Thus, by extending the work of earlier researchers, especially Charles B. Heiser Jr. and Richard Yarnell, Smith showed that these complications can be handled, making it possible to say with near certainty whether prehistoric sunflower specimens were wild or domesticated.

Although there is no doubt that Indians in the eastern U.S. had domesticated sunflowers by 3000 BP, the beginning of the process is murky, owing to the scarcity of pre–3000 BP specimens. The oldest ones come from the Koster site, in Illinois, which yielded two shells and one kernel. With estimated ages of 6500–6000 BP and 8500 BP, the shells were clearly wild, but the dimensions of the single kernel, dated to about 5900–5800 BP, are intermediate between wild and domesticated. One ambiguous kernel cannot clinch the case for domestication being that early.

In the many millennia between Koster and Marble Bluff, there are only 15 specimens from five sites. Among these, the best case for pre–3000 BP domestication comes from the Hayes site in central Tennessee, where six kernels were recovered. All six are longer than those in the DeSoto reference class, but one kernel's overall size suggests that it may be from a wild plant. A kernel was direct-dated to around 4840 BP. On the basis of this evidence, Smith concluded that the sunflower had been domesticated by this time.

Smith highlighted the urgent need to recover more sunflower seeds from pre–5000 BP contexts. He also raised the possibility that museums might hold unidentified or unreported specimens that fall into the temporal gap between Koster and Hayes. Perhaps archaeobotanists will be encouraged to pore over old archaeological collections and turn up some treasures.

The sunflower case shows us that inferences about a plant's domestication will change if earlier specimens, perhaps in nearby regions, are discovered. Thus, the earliest dated specimen does not necessarily pinpoint the time and place where domestication *first* occurred, especially in poorly known regions. As for the sunflower, the strongest inference supportable with current evidence is that *by this time* (5000 BP) people *in this place* (central Tennessee) were making use of the domesticated variety. In the following millennia, sunflowers would be cultivated much more widely in the eastern United States and elsewhere in North America.

Archaeobotanists have established numerous strong inferences about the domestication of more than 100 species worldwide. These findings are a significant contribution to botany, as can be seen in the many books, articles, and web sites on plant history and geography. More than that, our growing

FIGURE 34.1. Left to right: teosinte, a teosinte-corn hybrid, and modern corn (Wikimedia Commons; John Doebley, photographer).

knowledge of domestication is a convincing demonstration that, over many thousands of years, humans have had a major impact on plant evolution. In cases more extreme than the sunflower, as in corn (*Zea mays*), the ancestral plant (teosinte) and the domesticated varieties are so dissimilar as to appear completely unrelated (Figure 34.1). Many more surprising inferences can be expected in the decades ahead because archaeobotany is a young specialty facing wide gaps in the archaeological record.

I thank Bruce D. Smith for comments on this chapter.

35

The Pygmy Rabbit and Applied Zooarchaeology

ZOOARCHAEOLOGISTS, who study animal bones and other faunal remains from archaeological sites, are an unusual breed of scientist. When driving on country roads they brake for animals—dead animals. After pulling over, they wrestle the wretched critters into their cars and resume driving. And then it gets strange. One zooarchaeologist takes the carcass home and buries it in his yard; another puts it into a big metal drum teeming with a colony of voracious dermestid beetles; and a third plops it into a pot of boiling water with a dash of soap. What's going on? The three zooarchaeologists are using different methods to remove soft tissues so that they can make a *reference specimen*, which consists of bones and teeth alone.[1]

A reference (or comparative) collection of many species, which may include male and female as well as young and old specimens, is essential for identifying archaeological bones, especially small pieces, and for teaching zooarchaeology. Even the most experienced researcher consults a reference collection when facing an unfamiliar fragment. Not surprisingly, zooarchaeologists are always on the lookout for new specimens to expand their collections.

Before the middle of the twentieth century, many American archaeologists paid little attention to animal bones. At best, they boxed up the bones from a site and shipped them to a kindly paleontologist or zoologist, hoping to get them identified for free. In return, the archaeologist might eventually receive a list of the species in the boxes, which could be included as an appendix to the excavation report.

These informal collaborations ended in the 1970s. The main reason was the emergence of the first generation of archaeologists actually trained as zooarchaeologists. They showed that analyses of animal bones could yield a host of important inferences about past human behavior and the natural environment. Another reason was a vast increase in archaeological funding in Western countries, which made it possible to hire zooarchaeologists for major projects.

Zooarchaeology is now a demanding and prestigious specialty. It is demanding because, in addition to building and working with reference collections, zooarchaeologists have archaeological expertise and may have received training in paleontology and zoology. In fact, their research often straddles these disciplines. Zooarchaeology is prestigious because, in the last few decades, it has produced an impressive array of *new* information about the past obtainable in no other way.

Where bone is recovered in ample quantities, zooarchaeologists may build inferences about hunting strategies and behavior, carcass processing and transport of parts, sharing of meat, seasonal use of sites, bone as a raw material for making artifacts, ritual activities, domesticated versus wild animals, ethnic food preferences, and so forth. In addition, zooarchaeological studies furnish information about a past environment, especially long-term changes in a species' abundance and geographic distribution. Such environmental inferences also enable zooarchaeologists to contribute to conservation biology.[2]

With roots in ecology, conservation biology is a relatively new interdisciplinary science, a response to the increasing awareness that humans are devastating the planet. The aim is to provide decision-makers with information to manage environmental resources, whether one species or an entire ecosystem. In the United States, decision-makers are usually officials who administer government land within agencies such as the National Park Service, Forest Service, Bureau of Land Management, and Department of Defense. Indian tribes may also manage environmental resources on their reservations.

Decision-makers confront wildlife management issues such as: (1) should an introduced (nonnative) species be eradicated? (2) Should a species' population, which grew uncontrollably because of hunting restrictions, be greatly reduced? (3) Can the loss of a species be prevented? (4) Should a species that disappeared be reintroduced? Such questions imply that, prior to recent times and especially before human impacts on ecosystems, an environment had a "natural" or "pristine" state, a return to which is desired. Such idealized states are referred to as *benchmarks*. The conservation biologist's job is to provide decision-makers with information, such as whether a given benchmark is realistic and whether a particular intervention is likely to achieve the benchmark.[3]

But a benchmark rests on assumptions about a past environment. For example, eradicating an introduced species from an area assumes that it had never been there. Likewise, reintroducing a species assumes that it had once been a long-term resident. Many benchmarks assume that an environment has remained stable for centuries or even millennia. With information about past species and environments, zooarchaeologists and conservation biologists can evaluate these assumptions and determine a benchmark's feasibility. The next step is to offer plans for achieving *feasible* benchmarks.[4] Increasingly, zooarchaeologists are even making their own recommendations.

Donald K. Grayson, long-time researcher in the Burke Museum at the University of Washington, is one of the pioneers of modern zooarchaeology in the United States.[5] Integrating paleontology, mammalogy, and archaeology, his projects are relevant to conservation biology. One of Grayson's major study areas is the Great Basin.

The Great Basin is a distinct region that encompasses parts of many western states. It consists of lowland basins separated by mountain ranges of varying extent and altitude. Because mountaintops receive much more rain and snow than the intervening basins, their upper reaches boast forests and animals not found at lower levels. These relatively lush zones are known as "sky islands."

To test a model about the changing geographic distributions of small mammals in the Great Basin, such as pika, marmot, bushy-tailed woodrat, and golden-mantled ground squirrel, Grayson examined paleontological and archaeological records from 25 deeply stratified cave and rockshelter sites.[6] In general, he found that during the late Pleistocene, the lowlands were wetter and more hospitable to the little animals. Later, during the Holocene era (ca. 12,000 years ago to the present), episodic environmental changes caused many small animals in the lowlands to disappear, but they tended to survive in some of the sky islands. Grayson concluded that his findings have "clear implications for the management of high altitude environments in the Great Basin."[7]

Although Grayson did not further develop these implications, R. Lee Lyman, one of Grayson's students, did. A zooarchaeologist at the University of Missouri, Lyman in 1996 argued convincingly that faunal analysis is relevant to conservation biology, especially wildlife management, and even gave this new orientation a name: "applied zooarchaeology."[8] Lyman suggested that applied zooarchaeologists could address questions such as, "What species are native and occurred in an area in the past…? What species are exotic, or have been introduced by human agency…? What kinds of changes to ecological communities have been caused by humans?"[9] In addition, he illustrated applied research with intriguing examples drawn from his own and others' projects.

In working out the implications of Grayson's findings, Lyman employed the insights of island biogeographers. In the smallest sky islands, animal populations are especially vulnerable to *extirpation*, a term that means *local* extinction. This vulnerability arises because small mammals with their narrow ecological niches are very sensitive to environmental change and to random decreases in population size. Addressing conservationists' concerns about their survival, Lyman considered two ways to increase populations: enlarge the sky islands or provide wildlife corridors to connect them. He judged that neither alternative was feasible. Rather, the animals' best hope for survival is to prevent people from degrading their precious habitats.

Lyman does much of his work in the Intermountain West, which includes parts of the Great Basin. We will consider one of his case studies there, the pygmy rabbit (*Brachylagus idahoensis*).[10] The pygmy rabbit is aptly named: individuals usually weigh about a pound and are cute beyond description. This rabbit occurs today in two separate locations: the northern Great Basin location, which is large and includes "portions of four states: northern Nevada, western Utah, southern Idaho and southeastern Oregon"; and the Columbia Basin in Washington, which is much smaller.[11] The Columbia Basin population of pygmy rabbits has been declining precipitously. This reduction in numbers is of great concern because small populations lose genetic diversity and so are highly susceptible to extirpation.

How did the Columbia Basin population become isolated and so vulnerable? To help answer this question, Lyman sought evidence for pygmy rabbits in archaeological and paleontological sites in central Washington. He rummaged through faunal reports, contacted colleagues for leads, and examined museum collections. Eventually, he identified their bones in two paleontological and 11 archaeological sites. An important finding was that some occurred in locations beyond their reported historical range.[12] Evidently, the pygmy rabbit's prehistoric range in Washington was once larger.

To understand their decline, Lyman focused on the pygmy rabbit's re-source needs. It turns out that its major habitat is "dense stands of big sage-brush," which are the rabbit's prime food source and provide shelter from predators.[13] Again seeking clues from the past in floral and faunal remains, Lyman learned that the environment had changed during the Holocene. In earlier times—from the late Pleistocene into the Holocene—big sagebrush communities were more widespread than at present, and so were pygmy rabbits. In all likelihood, then, the animal's habitat had once stretched con-tinuously from central Washington to the northern Great Basin. Around 4,500 years ago, changes in precipitation patterns caused big sagebrush com-munities to begin contracting. The rabbits followed, becoming in central Washington an isolated and scattered population that could easily die out. In more recent times, human activities accelerated the decline of the rabbit's habitat through open-range grazing and clearing land for crops.[14]

By 1990, the estimated population of pygmy rabbits in the Columbia Basin had dwindled to fewer than 250 individuals. In 1993, the Washington Wildlife Commission listed it as an endangered species, and properly so, because such a small population could rapidly succumb to "fire, disease, intense predation, and the random variation in birth and death rates, [and] sex ratios."[15]

In 1995, the Washington Department of Fish and Wildlife developed a "Recovery Plan for the Pygmy Rabbit." Prepared by Kelly R. McAllister, it drew upon Lyman's findings. McAllister chose as the benchmark the res-toration of the pygmy rabbit's range and population to former levels. Spe-cifically, the plan sought to achieve "a minimum population of 1,400 adult pygmy rabbits" distributed among several areas in the Columbia Basin.[16] To achieve this goal, the plan offered a broad spectrum of detailed interventions to maintain and expand the habitat. McAllister proposed that the rabbit's range could be expanded by identifying lands having favorable soil condi-tions; some areas could be restored and vacant lands colonized. To say the least, the plan was ambitious and potentially costly.

A year later, Lyman himself proposed ways to promote the rabbit's sur-vival. While emphasizing the need to maintain the existing big sagebrush habitats in central Washington, he suggested importing individuals from southeastern Oregon to augment the rabbit population.[17] McAllister had also mentioned the possibility of transplanting pygmy rabbits from the northern Great Basin but did not stress this option.[18]

McAllister's plan, updated several times, was never fully implemented. The pygmy rabbit population continued to decline, losing more genetic diversity along the way. In response to the immediate threat of extirpation, the Department of Fish and Wildlife began a captive breeding program in 2001, but it was plagued with problems. Not until six years later were any captive rabbits released, and none of the 20 animals "survived beyond a year."[19] The reduced genetic diversity had degraded the population's vitality so that the rabbits didn't breed like rabbits. In the meantime, the federal government listed the Columbia Basin pygmy rabbit as an endangered species.

By 2004, the pygmy rabbit's population had very likely reached zero and its reintroduction—recovery was no longer an option—demanded desperate measures. At last, a relocation program, as championed by Lyman, was put into action. A collaborative effort among several state agencies and other organizations led to the adoption of multiple measures for transplanting pygmy rabbits from other states, which included breeding them first in enclosures. In the period 2011–13, 384 offspring were placed into the Sagebrush Flat Wildlife Area of the Columbia Basin. Continuous monitoring of the new population suggests that the reintroduction is enjoying some success, but the original benchmark is a distant goal.[20] And in the background is the nagging fear that no intervention can compensate, *over the long run*, for the environmental changes that caused the rabbit's isolation and slow decline in the first place. To maintain a population in the Columbia Basin, pygmy rabbits may have to be introduced repeatedly.

During the two decades since Lyman's seminal article appeared, many archaeologists have done applied zooarchaeology, tackling challenging projects and publishing their findings in journals read by conservation biologists and wildlife managers.[21] Underscoring the importance of such projects, government agencies are increasingly funding them. In a recent book, Lyman and his student, Steve Wolverton, showcased a sample of projects that have contributed to conservation biology.[22] In every project, the zooarchaeologist's information about a species' past population and distribution lays a foundation for setting realistic benchmarks and making sound management decisions. And let us not forget that this research depends on the ability to identify animals from bones and teeth—a skill hard won through collecting and studying reference specimens.

I thank R. Lee Lyman for comments on a previous draft.

36

Microbiota of the Human Gut and Coprolites

THE HUMAN BODY is an ecosystem containing thousands of poorly known, microscopic species (microbes) that live on us and in us. Abundant in well-known places such as the mouth and gut, they are also found wherever microbiologists look, from armpits to ear canals to genitals. What's more, nonhuman cells in our bodies outnumber human ones by more than 10 to 1.[1] Until very recently, our tiny fellow travelers were little studied because most of them cannot be cultured in the laboratory. Happily, new techniques of DNA extraction and analysis have made their genomes accessible for research, ushering in an era of exciting new findings. Some microbes cause disease, but others are symbiotic and promote mental and physical health.[2]

Investigating the *microbiota*—the entirety of our microscopic, nonhuman inhabitants—is now high-priority science, attracting government funding in many countries. Researchers are revealing how the composition of the microbiota varies among individuals and societies, zones of the body, and stages of life; and correlations are turning up between the microbiota and diet and disease. But there is one family of questions that microbiologists alone are unable to answer. (1) How have "humans and microbes coevolved in response to different environments...including responses to both natural and cultural change" over millennia?[3] (2) To what extent were people in prehistoric and early historic societies afflicted with parasites and other pathogens? And (3) which groups of microbes composed the microbiotas of ancestral human populations? Archaeologists are helping to answer these questions by providing specimens for analysis from well-understood contexts and collaborating with biologists.

Collaboration is the key word here because studies of archaeological microbiota require a team, sometimes a huge one. An important research paper of 2012 has 32 authors from more than a dozen institutions in seven countries, including the School of Archaeology and Ancient History at the University of Leicester in the UK, and the Department of Prehistory and Archaeology at the University of Valencia in Spain.[4]

Because millennia-old human bodies seldom survive with soft tissues intact, obtaining microbiota from archaeological sites can be difficult. Fortunately, microbes occur in the tartar on teeth and in coprolites (old feces or archaeo-poop). Studies of tartar are just beginning, but coprolite analysis in search of microorganisms has a decades-long history. Accordingly, this chapter is about coprolite studies and their intriguing findings.[5]

Coprolites are found mainly in dry caves and rockshelters and in mummies. In these contexts, the coprolites are dry and brittle, and must be handled carefully and packaged in sterile forensic bags to prevent contamination from the modern environment—and from researchers. The real fun begins in the laboratory because desiccated coprolites have to be rehydrated. This usually calls for treatment with a dilute aqueous solution of trisodium phosphate.[6] Rehydration restores not only a coprolite's texture but also its smell. On the other hand, coprolites found in waterlogged latrines and privies, and bodies in bogs, retain their original characteristics.

In the earliest coprolite studies, researchers using microscopes identified food remains along with parasites and pathogens.[7] By 1990, archaeobiologists had identified a roster of creepy parasitic worms in coprolites from the Old and New Worlds, including "nematodes (roundworms), trematodes (flukes), cestodes (tapeworms), and acanthocephalans (thorny-headed worms)," as well as hookworms and pinworms, the latter an indicator of unsanitary living conditions.[8] Human ancestors around the globe carried a heavy parasite load.

During the past two decades, diagnostic tests have identified microbe-specific proteins in coprolites. Using fluorescent microscopy and monoclonal antibodies, researchers found the single-cell parasites *Cryptosporidium*, *Giardia*, and *Cyclospora* in millennia-old coprolites from Peru.[9] All three can cause nasty bouts of diarrhea.

Research on microbiota accelerated with the advent of DNA sequencing, but it hasn't been easy. DNA consists of very long chains of base pairs (adenine-guanine, cytosine-thymine) that encode genes and form the core of the familiar double helix. After cell death, DNA degrades into ever-shorter stretches of base pairs. Adding to the difficulties, environmental microbes colonize coprolites and introduce their own DNA. Thus, obtaining ancient DNA depends on the use of sensitive extraction techniques that also screen out contaminants. Because the extracted DNA occurs in minute quantities, it must be amplified using the polymerase chain reaction (PCR). Bases in the amplified DNA fragments are then sequenced and joined into longer sequences through computer algorithms. The reconstructed sequences are in turn compared to digitized sequences of DNA from a reference library of known microbes. When there is a match, the mystery microbe is identified. Use of these techniques in coprolite analysis has led to the identification of both parasitic and nonparasitic microbes.[10]

A family of techniques known as "next generation sequencing," or mass sequencing, has recently made it possible to specify the *entire* DNA content of the microbiota—the *microbiome*. To fund, hasten, and coordinate research using next generation sequencing, in 2007 the U.S. National Institutes of Health established the Human Microbiome Project. The project "aims to develop tools and datasets for the research community for studying the role of these microbes in human health and disease." The first phase characterized microbiomes on mucosal surfaces such as the gut, mouth, and nasal passages. The second phase produced datasets on the "biological properties" of the microbiome and focused on diseases.[11] A similar project in Europe is the Metagenomics of the Human Intestinal Tract (MetaHIT).

Fecal samples from modern societies as well as ancient coprolites have yielded to next generation sequencing. An early finding, augmenting the previous work with microscopes, is that parasites were common in many prehistoric and early historic societies, especially roundworm species transmitted through contaminated soil. These parasites have been found in "80% of human coprolites in European archeological sites and in 100% of those from medieval times."[12] Summarizing coprolite research as of 2013, Sandra Appelt reports that a host of pathogens have been detected.[13] In her analysis of a fourteenth-century coprolite from Belgium, she found viruses and even two genera of bacteria that cause systemic infections, *Bartonella* and *Bordetella*; some species of the latter are responsible for whooping cough.[14]

Next generation sequencing has also shown that the modern human gut contains seven main phyla of microorganisms.[15] All seven have been found in coprolites from diverse times and places, but they—and many less-common microbes—occur in varying proportions. What causes these differences?

Analyses of modern feces have shown that diet has the greatest influence on the composition of the gut's microbiota and is especially sensitive to "the proportion of proteins, carbohydrates, and insoluble fiber in the diet."[16] *Bacteroides* seems to be prevalent in diets high in animal protein and fats, but carbohydrate-dominant diets favor *Prevotella*. These findings remind us that groups of microbes in the healthy gut, as in any ecosystem, play important roles. On the basis of the known functions of genes, researchers suggest that the microbiota aid in "digesting food, producing hormones and vitamins, participating in human metabolism, keeping weight in check, and affecting brain chemistry."[17] As biologists learn more about gene functions, it will become possible to determine the symbiotic roles that specific microbes play. Some microbes suspected to be pathogens may turn out to be symbiotic in healthy people, as the following example shows.

Knowledge of gene functions enabled a recent project to offer a surprising hypothesis about *Treponema*, a genus of spirochete bacteria, some of whose species cause yaws and syphilis. Carlotta De Filippo and her Italian and Belgian colleagues compared microbiomes of 15 healthy children in Florence, Italy, and 15 healthy children in a rural village in Burkina Faso (West Africa). *Treponema* occurred in the African feces but not in the Italian ones. The researchers noted that *Treponema* (and other microbes) have genes that enable fermentation of "undigested dietary fiber, resistant starch, and other components of whole grains."[18] The African children were also free from noninfectious diseases of the colon. The findings of De Filippo's group raised an obvious question: did *Treponema* occur in prehistoric contexts and in other parts of the world?

This question was answered by research in the Molecular Anthropology/Ancient DNA Laboratory at the University of Oklahoma. Raul Y. Tito and colleagues analyzed six coprolites from three sites: Hinds Cave (ca. 8000 BP) in the U.S. Southwest; Caserones (ca. 1600 BP) in northern Chile; and La Cueva de los Chiquitos Muertos in Rio Zape (ca. 1400 BP), northern Mexico.[19] Significantly, Tito's team found *Treponema berlinense* (a newly defined species) in the Mexican coprolites. This discovery supports the hypothesis that, in some traditional rural communities where whole grains were an important part of the diet, a species of "*Treponema* may enhance the host's ability to extract nutrients from fibrous foods and may provide anti-inflammatory capability."[20] Despite its sinister relatives, *Treponema berlinense* may have coevolved with humans, providing mutual benefits, but disappeared wherever the human diet became dependent on processed grains or other low-fiber foods.

Studies of feces and coprolites are showing that modern urban diets, overuse of antibiotics, limited contact with animals, and effective sanitation have changed the human microbiota from ancestral states. I emphasize *states*, plural, because prehistoric societies had varied diets and so had varied microbiota. Such variation shows up even on a small geographic scale. Raul J. Cano and his colleagues analyzed an unusually large sample of coprolites (n = 34) from Vieques Island, Puerto Rico, representing two archaeological cultures that coexisted during the first millennium A D. Their study showed that the Huecoid and Saladoid cultures had significantly different diets and microbiota, including parasites.[21]

Given the wide variation in ancestral diets and microbiota, can we expect any generalizations to survive future research? Yes. We can say with confidence that the parasite load in ancestral societies was large but has diminished in modern urban contexts. It is also clear that many ancestral populations had symbiotic microbes that, among other functions, helped people to digest high-fiber foods. We moderns tend to lack many of these microbes and so suffer from allergies and other inflammatory diseases. As more is learned about the microbiota—ancient and modern—and their gene functions, new treatments such as fecal transplantation that administer health-promoting bacteria without increasing the parasite load may come into widespread use.[22]

XIII

FURNISHING TOOLS FOR ENVIRONMENTAL SCIENCES

MANY ARCHAEOLOGICAL sites contain environmental materials, including animal bones and teeth, mollusk shells, insects, wood, leaves, seeds, pollen, soils, flood sediments, and volcanic ash. Such materials provide valuable evidence about past environmental events and processes. When datable, environmental materials from stratified sites or a long sequence of sites make it possible to monitor environmental change. This information is useful, not only to archaeologists, but also to environmental scientists—geologists, climatologists, zoologists, and botanists. Not surprisingly, there is much collaboration among archaeologists and environmental scientists, especially when they share an interest in reconstructing environmental change and learning about human impacts such as deforestation or a mass extinction of animals.

Astronomer A. E. Douglass established dendrochronology (tree-ring dating) at the University of Arizona. Seeking to build a tree-ring chronology, he started with living trees and moved back in time, noting the sequence of wide and narrow rings. To extend the chronology, Douglass worked with archaeologists in the American Southwest where many ruins contained roof beams. Archaeologists supplied Douglass with a wealth of wood specimens that became the foundation of the first important tree-ring chronology. This chronology permitted Douglass to date some of the Southwest's most spectacular ruins, such as Pueblo Bonito, and pinpointed the Great Drought of the thirteenth century. Douglass trained other dendrochronologists and established the Laboratory of Tree-Ring Research (LTRR) at the University of Arizona. Early on, Douglass also invented the science of dendroclimatology—using tree rings to infer past environmental conditions such as rainfall and streamflow. A researcher at the LTRR, Edmund Schulman, pioneered methods for estimating streamflows, bringing to fruition Douglass's vision for dendroclimatology.

Archaeological sites may contain evidence for dating a specific environmental event. Sunset Crater, a cinder cone near Flagstaff, Arizona, was believed to be fairly recent owing to its relatively uneroded slopes. Not until the advent of tree-ring dating, however, was it possible for researchers at the Museum of Northern Arizona to assign a calendar age to its eruption. Founded in 1928 by Harold S. Colton and Mary-Russell Ferrell Colton, the museum's research focus was the prehistory of the Flagstaff region. Taking advantage of the growing number of pit-houses with tree-ring dates, Colton charged archaeologist John C. McGregor with dating the eruption. Drawing on tree-ring dates from houses that pre- and post-dated the eruption, McGregor came up with a date in the late ninth or early tenth century A D. A decade later, Colton placed the eruption in the mid- to late-eleventh century. In recent years, other researchers have revised the date slightly, but there is little doubt that Sunset Crater was born in the late eleventh century. The environmental history of the Flagstaff area now boasts a well-dated cinder cone of recent vintage, stories of whose eruption survive in legends of the Hopi Indians.

An enduring mystery of modern science is the relation of humans to the mass extinction of American megafauna such as mammoths, horses, and giant beavers at the end of the Pleistocene. Zoologist Paul S. Martin offered the "overkill hypothesis," which asserts that after humans entered the New World they killed off many large mammals. Numerous scientists have marshaled evidence for and against the overkill hypothesis, and it remains in a state of uncertainty. An ironclad case that traditional, preindustrial peoples can cause mass extinctions comes from Polynesia. In a century or two after arrival in New Zealand, ancestors of the modern Māori had driven about 10 species of large birds, known as moas, to extinction. Ornithologist and zooarchaeologist David W. Steadman examined the faunal records from many other Pacific islands, finding a consistent pattern of mass bird extinctions linked to human activities. Traditional peoples were clearly not always wise stewards of their environment, for they eliminated species by preying on them, introducing new animals, and reducing the habitats of native species.

37

Tree-Ring Dating and Dendroclimatology

TREE-RING DATING, or dendrochronology, was developed during the early twentieth century in the American Southwest. In prehistoric ruins where roof beams survive, it is often possible now to pin down the exact year when a structure was built. The stockpiling of beams, repair episodes, and other behaviors may also be inferred from tree rings and assigned a calendar age. Archaeologists promoted the development of tree-ring dating and supplied much of the labor for constructing the first important chronology.[1] And tree-ring dating makes possible dendroclimatology, an important tool for reconstructing past environments.

Tree-ring dating is not available universally. This can result from unfavorable climate, unsuitable tree species, poor wood preservation, or lack of local tree-ring research. Where tree-ring dating is feasible, chronologies not only provide dates but, through dendroclimatology, make significant contributions to geology, hydrology, meteorology, and climatology.[2]

Dendrochronology is grounded in basic biological processes. Trees add a new growth ring annually whose characteristics, such as width, density, and chemical composition, are determined by prevailing environmental conditions including available moisture and temperature. In the arid American Southwest, trees close to perennial streams, where water is plentiful year after year, are "complacent," meaning their rings don't vary. But it's a different story for trees far from streams: when rainfall is abundant, a thick ring grows; in drought years, only a thin ring. These "sensitive" trees make possible tree-ring dating.

Andrew Ellicott Douglass was an astronomer whose career took an interesting turn. After leaving the Lowell observatory in Flagstaff, Arizona, he was hired in 1906 by the University of Arizona in Tucson. He was keen to study the influence of solar phenomena on Earth's climate, hoping to detect the 11-year sunspot cycle in tree-ring patterns. In pursuing this interest, Douglass established a long chronology for the giant sequoia of California's Sierra Nevada Mountains and also worked on ponderosa pine from northern Arizona. In these studies he developed the method of *crossdating*, which is the foundation of all tree-ring chronologies.

For crossdating, Douglass obtained ring samples from sensitive trees growing in a single environment. Having experienced the same moisture conditions, these living trees have identical sequences of wide and narrow rings. This ring sequence of known age, anchored to the present, is the foundation of the chronology. To extend this chronology back in time, Douglass sought older trees whose ring sequences overlapped with the modern sequence and, farther back in time, with each other. Redundancy—several overlapping specimens for any given time interval—ensured that the chronology achieved certainty, a feature Douglass insisted was essential for dendrochronology's credibility.

In a seminal paper in 1914, Douglass showed how to infer an area's rainfall history from tree rings. Significantly, he demonstrated that there was "much agreement" between a curve of annual rainfall and a curve of ring widths between 1867 (when weather records began) and 1910 for Prescott, Arizona.[3] This paper inaugurated the science of dendroclimatology, which today aims to understand past environmental variability in order to make predictions regarding the frequency, severity, and duration of droughts and floods and other phenomena.

Although dendroclimatology was Douglass' lifelong passion, he became interested in dating archaeological wood after receiving a letter from Clark Wissler. A curator in the American Museum of Natural History in New York, Wissler was an authority on Indian tribes of the northern Great Plains and also had archaeological interests.[4] Wissler wanted to learn about the cultural changes that led to the historic tribes, but he was frustrated by the lack of accurate prehistoric chronologies. After reading Douglass's paper, Wissler grasped the possibility that a long tree-ring chronology could be used to date wood from prehistoric sites, allowing calendar ages to replace speculation in studies of culture change.

FIGURE 37.1. Pueblo Bonito, Chaco Canyon National Historical Park, New Mexico (Wikimedia Commons; Bob Adams, photographer).

Wissler asked Douglass if tree rings could be used in the manner he had envisioned. Douglass answered yes, and together they sketched out a project. Wissler channeled resources to the project through his Huntington Survey of the Southwest, which had a large archaeological component that aimed to determine the "time-relations" of prehistoric sites.[5] He instructed his archaeologists in the field, especially Nels C. Nelson and Earl H. Morris, to collect wood and charcoal from sites they were digging. As a result, many specimens came to Douglass for crossdating and chronology building, analyses that Wissler's project also partially bankrolled.[6] But more than five years of effort did not produce a long prehistoric chronology, and thus many ruins, especially the most spectacular ones in Mesa Verde National Park and Chaco Canyon, remained undated. Funding for the tree-ring project dried up.

Neil M. Judd, an archaeologist at the Smithsonian Institution, helped to put the project back on track.[7] Judd was doing fieldwork in Chaco Canyon whose massive, multistory pueblo ruins had entranced generations of visitors. Through Judd's efforts, the Smithsonian and the National Geographic Society (NGS) funded Douglass's studies of southwestern wood. Not surprisingly, a major goal of the National Geographic Society was to date Chaco Canyon ruins, particularly the 800-room Pueblo Bonito (Figure 37.1).

During the 1920s, Douglass and colleagues, especially archaeologist Lyndon Hargrave, mounted seven expeditions to obtain wood, three of them funded by NGS. By crossdating roof beams from Pueblo Bonito and other sites, Douglass built a "floating" chronology that in 1926 consisted of 235 years.[8] The problem was to close the gap between the floating and modern chronologies. With wood from historic sites, including old Hopi pueblos, Douglass in 1928 extended the modern chronology back to AD 1260. The floating chronology now reached 590 years and encompassed cliff dwellings at Mesa Verde, but the gap persisted.[9] Douglass suspected that the gap was fairly narrow and even had in mind dates for Pueblo Bonito. However, he would say nothing until tree-ring specimens could bridge the gap with certainty, for Douglass's policy was *never* to disclose dates that were merely likely or tentative.[10]

By this time, archaeologists had worked out relative sequences of ceramic types for many regions in the northern Southwest. Thus Hargrave could predict from their ceramics which sites might yield promising pieces of wood.[11] For NGS's Third Beam Expedition, Douglass hired one of his recent students, archaeologist Emil W. Haury, to assist Hargrave.

With four sites targeted on the basis of ceramics, Hargrave and Haury headed to northern Arizona.[12] Their first stop was the Whipple Ruin in the small town of Show Low, where the team established camp in a nearby hotel. The site seemed unpromising because it had been partially looted, stone-robbed, and modified by modern features and trash. Even so, a crew was hired and put to work digging for charred wood. Several days of effort yielded only tiny pieces of charcoal, not the long ring series needed. On June 22, the very day that Douglass and Judd joined the team in the field, workers found a large piece of a fragile beam. After the log was carefully treated and wrapped, Douglass tried to match its ring series with paper plots of the floating and modern chronologies but said nothing.

That evening the team gathered in the hotel living room where Douglass sat at a table covered with chronology plots and charred wood. After a long silence, the astronomer—founder of two sciences and part-time archaeologist—spoke. His words, Haury recalled decades later, were spellbinding: "There was no gap at all." The two chronologies had in fact overlapped, but only by 26 years, too few to ensure that the ring patterns, though similar, covered the same time interval. Luckily the beam, designated HH-39 (for Hargrave and Haury), had a long series of rings that greatly overlapped both chronologies. It "established the bridge." Douglass then supplied dates for other ruins, including Pueblo Bonito, which "was occupied in the 11th and early 12th centuries."[13] Back in Tucson, Douglass assigned Haury to check the entire chronology, and he of course found it correct.[14]

In December 1929, *National Geographic Magazine* published an article by Douglass describing the expeditions, trumpeting the news about the breakthrough, and furnishing dates for spectacular sites. He also emphasized that trees tell the story of climate through ring widths, and so identified years of severe drought as well as the persistent "Great drought of 1276–1299."[15]

During the 1930s, Douglass trained several archaeology students as dendrochronologists. Working mainly at other institutions, they furnished dates for archaeological wood and created refined regional chronologies. Although the University of Arizona was hardly a research powerhouse in the 1930s, Douglass's tree-ring triumph, news of which traveled quickly, garnered favorable publicity and raised the university's international profile. After all, until Douglass, *no one had ever assigned accurate calendar years to any prehistoric behavior*. As the university's first world-class scientist, Douglass had some clout. And so, when he suggested that university administrators create a permanent unit for the study of tree rings, they agreed.

The Laboratory of Tree-Ring Research (LTRR) was established in 1937 as an autonomous department, headed by Douglass. Some of the initial funds for the LTRR came from the Anthropology Department, whose recently appointed head was none other than Emil W. Haury.[16] And let us not forget that Douglass's major accomplishment—providing calendar ages for important prehistoric ruins—resulted from a 15-year collaboration with archaeologists and led to the founding of the LTRR. To this day, the LTRR conducts cutting-edge research in dendrochronology and dendroclimatology.

Dendroclimatology came into its own after World War II, thanks largely to the work of Edmund Schulman, who was hired by the LTRR in 1939. With encouragement from Douglass, Schulman began a challenging project to learn if tree-ring chronologies could be used to reconstruct stream runoff. Should this be possible, the findings would have enormous implications for hydrology—the study of water resources—particularly in arid lands where rainfall, and thus runoff, varies greatly from year to year.

Schulman focused on the Colorado River, a major source of water for hydroelectric power, irrigation, and domestic and industrial uses. His fieldwork was partially funded by an interested party, the Los Angeles Bureau of Power and Light, which received electricity from Boulder (now Hoover) Dam on the Colorado. A compact signed in 1922 by the nine states of the Colorado River watershed had divided up the water according to a formula based on annual streamflow measurements. Unfortunately, no reliable streamflow records predated 1900, and so the compact relied solely on data from the previous two decades. Hoping to extend the streamflow record by many centuries, Schulman collected ring samples and created chronologies for the Colorado's major tributaries.

Using the brief historical streamflow records, Schulman showed that tree rings correlated with rainfall and runoff in the tributaries and in the Colorado itself. This finding validated the use of tree rings as a proxy measure of streamflow. Next he estimated the frequency of droughts—years of below-average streamflow—by employing his 658-year chronology for the entire Colorado River basin. The results were stunning: "One out of every six years tends to be either an extreme or moderate drought year." The same proportion also held for "years of excess."[17] Schulman noted that some droughts were persistent, such as one lasting from 1573 to 1593. Later investigators at the LTRR called attention to an ominous pattern: the Colorado River compact was based on two decades of *above-average* streamflow, suggesting that a persistent drought in the future might create severe water shortages and cause conflicts within and among states.[18]

Schulman is also well known for his discovery that the bristlecone pine, which grows at high elevation in the arid White Mountains of eastern California and Nevada, among other places, can live longer than 4,000 years. Many trips to the White Mountains supplied Schulman with enough specimens to build a millennia-long record of rainfall variation.[19] In the 1960s, cuts from dated pieces of bristlecone pine and other species became the foundation of the first calibration curves to correct systematic errors in radiocarbon dating.[20]

Dendroclimatology is an important and well-funded offspring of tree-ring dating and has many applications. As global warming has accelerated in recent decades, reconstructing rainfall and streamflow from tree rings has become a high priority around the world for water managers and users.[21] Modern streamflow reconstructions employ complex statistics and simulation modeling to enable probabilistic predictions. Even so, these sophisticated reconstructions rest on a foundation of regional tree-ring chronologies, built with principles devised by Douglass and refined in collaboration with southwestern archaeologists. And let us not forget the pivotal role that archaeology played in establishing the LTRR, whose major focus during recent decades has been dendroclimatology.

38

Dating Sunset Crater

HUMANS SELDOM see the birth of a volcano, but the prehistoric ancestors of the Hopi Indians witnessed this terrifying event. In the high country of northern Arizona, near the San Francisco Mountains and 15 miles northeast of Flagstaff, a miles-long fissure opened in the earth. A new volcano burst forth and rapidly reached a height of 1,000 feet (Figure 38.1). Called Sunset Crater, this cinder cone stands out among many hundreds in the region because its orange rim appears to be in perpetual sunset.[1]

Weeks of earthquakes probably preceded its emergence. Then, the volcano belched ash high in the sky, oozed two distinct lava flows, set fires, and blanketed hundreds of square miles of forest and high desert with a layer of ash and cinders. People in the immediate area gathered up a few possessions and abandoned their villages, leaving homes and fields to suffer complete destruction. The "lava fire fountain" would have been visible at night for many dozens of miles, and the towering ash plume could have been seen during the day hundreds of miles away.[2]

The fiery emergence of a new mountain deeply impressed the Indian eyewitnesses, and their stories were passed down from generation to generation. Mennonite missionary H. R. Voth, who was fluent in the Hopi language, recorded the story of a growing fire visible near the San Francisco Mountains that forced evacuations and consumed villages. This disaster, according to the Hopi tale, was punishment for immoral behavior, especially that of women who were gambling rather than taking care of their children.[3]

When did this event occur? Lacking a long calendar, the Hopi can't answer this question. But it is a question of great interest to geologists,

FIGURE 38.1. Sunset Crater, Arizona (courtesy of the National Park Service).

archaeologists, and other scientists who reconstruct the environmental history of the Flagstaff region. In the early twentieth century, there was no scientific way to assign a calendar age to the eruption. At best, researchers could estimate a crater's *relative* age by comparing its degree of weathering to that of other craters.[4] In 1907, famed Harvard geographer Douglas W. Johnson observed that Sunset Crater had experienced little erosion and so suggested that it was fairly recent, but he did not guess its age.[5] Archaeologists at the Museum of Northern Arizona (MNA) in Flagstaff finally took up the dating challenge.[6]

MNA was established in 1928 by Philadelphians Mary-Russell Ferrell Colton, an accomplished landscape painter, and her husband Harold S. Colton, a zoology professor at the University of Pennsylvania.[7] The wealthy Coltons had fallen in love with the region after honeymooning in Flagstaff and, in 1926, moved there permanently. With support from prominent members of the community, they built a natural history museum that encompassed archaeology, geology, zoology, and ethnology. Harold S. Colton would make published contributions to all these fields, but his special passion was archaeology. Even before the founding of MNA, he had recorded sites around Flagstaff. Mary-Russell was the museum's curator of ethnology and established annual shows of Hopi and Navajo art that helped Indian artists achieve international acclaim. Through the lobbying efforts of the Coltons and other locals, President Hoover designated Sunset Crater Volcano a National Monument in 1930.

Tree-ring dating of ruins came to fruition in 1929, which enabled the dating of prehistoric construction events—especially in the Flagstaff region. But could this new tool date Sunset Crater? That question was answered by an accidental discovery. In 1930, MNA was hosting Australian artist H. Neville-Smith, who came to paint the handsome volcano. MNA's curator of geology, Lionel F. Brady, drove him to the vicinity of the crater and, while waiting for the painting to be finished, Brady happened upon some prehistoric sherds lying on the cinder layer.[8] Informed of the discovery, Colton suspected that the sherds had been moved upward by tree fall and that a site lay below. Digging beneath the cinders revealed the remains of two pit-houses—semisubterranean, earth-covered, wooden structures—typical of pre-Pueblo construction.[9] Evidently, these pit-houses and others nearby had been abandoned before the eruption. Without a doubt, people had been present when Sunset Crater emerged. Tree-ring evidence from buried pit-houses, Colton believed, could contribute to dating this extraordinary event.

During the next half-dozen years, Colton's field teams, under the able direction of Lyndon Hargrave, found and excavated more sites, 112 in all, within and beyond the cinder-covered zone. MNA researchers recorded the stratigraphic relationships between cinder layers and structural remains, collected pottery and other artifacts, and saved charcoal pieces for tree-ring dating. Although few pieces of charcoal yielded dates, Colton believed that there was enough evidence to take a stab at dating the volcano. He assigned the task to John C. McGregor, who had received training in dendrochronology from A. E. Douglass at the University of Arizona.

Working with a *provisional* sequence of local pottery types, McGregor compared sites from within and beyond the cinder zone, inferring that some of the latter were occupied before the eruption and others after it. At that time, 16 sites yielded a total of around 80 tree-ring dates. This seems like a large number of dates, but it isn't: many dated specimens were missing outer rings, and so estimating the year the tree was felled for structural material was an exercise in guesswork. On the basis of pottery distributions, stratigraphy, and tree-ring dates, McGregor inferred that the "eruption took place sometime very near 885 AD, but it might conceivably have been as early as 860 AD, or as late as 910 AD."[10]

Despite McGregor's valiant attempt to integrate several lines of weak evidence, his dates led to troubling inconsistencies with other regional archaeological data that would not be resolved for a decade. During the interim, MNA archaeologists excavated more sites, refined the pottery types and sequence, and obtained additional tree-ring dates. Deciding that it was time to redate Sunset Crater, Harold S. Colton tackled the task himself in 1945.[11]

Among tree-ring dated sites, the strongest evidence came from those buried by cinders and those yielding sherds of Sunset Red, a pottery type containing cinder temper. Sites covered with a layer of cinders uniformly lacked sherds of Sunset Red, indicating that their occupation was pre-eruption; sites containing sherds of Sunset Red must have been occupied post-eruption. These inferences were reasonably consistent with the occurrences of other pottery types, now fairly well dated, at those sites.

Colton recognized the significance of this simple pattern for interpreting the tree-ring dates. The volcano's birth could be bracketed by the latest dates from pre-eruption sites and the earliest dates from post-eruption sites. Studying his tables of tree-ring dates, Douglass concluded, "The eruption must have taken place after 1046 AD, and certainly before 1071 AD."[12] (In a footnote to Colton's 1945 paper, McGregor gave his blessing to the new date.)

Since 1945, revisiting the dating of Sunset Crater has become a cottage industry. Even with a score of archaeologists, geologists, and dendrochronologists weighing in, uncertainties remain. Some researchers narrowed Colton's date range or fixed on a specific year, usually AD 1064–65, 1067, or 1068.[13] Recently, Mark D. Elson and colleagues at Desert Archaeology in Tucson, Arizona, assessed many new lines of evidence. They contend that the eruption most likely began between 1085 and 1090.[14] There are also questions about the eruption's duration because the complex stratification of cinders and lava deposits indicates that the eruption was episodic.[15] At present, we don't know whether the eruptions took place over weeks, months, or years. Even if the eruptions lasted for a long period, researchers agree that they *began* sometime during the later decades of the eleventh century. On a geological timescale, however, discrepancies of a few years—or even a few decades—matter little.

Although the emergence of a new volcano is a rare event, eruptions of existing volcanoes are fairly common in many parts of the world, as are forest fires and floods. The study of human responses to changing landscapes has become an important part of regional archaeology, made possible because cultural materials lie on, in, and under geological deposits.[16] Accordingly, throughout much of the twentieth century, specialists with expertise in both archaeology and geology—called *geoarchaeologists*—have become essential members of research teams, identifying and dating environmental processes. Geoarchaeological studies contribute to archaeology and geology by reconstructing the changing environmental stage on which human dramas played out. Not surprisingly, the effects of volcanism on human populations have been of special interest, even in MNA's early work.[17]

Many years of MNA research had filled in the outlines of prehistory in the Flagstaff region, laying a foundation for inferences about changes in landscape use. On this foundation, Colton built a scenario about how some of the cinder-covered land acted as a mulch, which encouraged farmers to recolonize the area. In Colton's view, this led to "a veritable land rush."[18] A thin layer of cinders does help retain moisture for plant growth, but some archaeologists believe that it was the religious significance of the new volcano or climate change that drew settlers in droves. These explanations for partial resettlement of the cinder-covered zone are not mutually exclusive.[19]

Sunset Crater is one of the American volcanoes featured in a recent book, *The Volcano Adventure Guide*, because it formed in "a single eruption or series of related eruptions."[20] The author, Rosaly Lopes, is a distinguished planetary geologist and volcanologist who fully credits archaeologists with having figured out that the volcano was born in the late eleventh century. Clearly, no environmental history of the Flagstaff region would be complete without mentioning Sunset Crater and archaeology's role in dating its birth.

I thank Christian E. Downum for discussing the dating of Sunset Crater.

39

Mass Extinctions of Animals:
The Human Role

AT THE LA BREA TAR PITS in Los Angeles, visitors can view life-size models of enormous animals and learn about them in the adjacent Page Museum. The models represent animals that became mired in the tar pools thousands of years ago and couldn't escape. Known as "megafauna," mammoths and mastodons, giant beavers and sloths, and horses and saber-toothed cats once roamed much of the Americas during the Pleistocene, the last epoch of great glaciers. But within 2,000 years after the Pleistocene ended (about 10–12,000 years ago), the megafaunal species all disappeared in an unusually rapid episode of mass extinction.[1] Environmental scientists want to know what happened to these fascinating creatures, as well as the victims of other mass extinctions. Archaeologists are helping find the answers.

The end of the Pleistocene also marked extinctions of megafauna in parts of the Old World and Australia, whose fossils began turning up in the eighteenth century. At first, some investigators doubted that extinction had taken place. Thomas Jefferson in 1799 wrote that these strange animals probably existed somewhere on Earth but hadn't been seen yet. When extinction was acknowledged during the nineteenth century, a few researchers fingered catastrophes such as the biblical deluge, others invoked the changing post-Pleistocene environment, and some cited human activity.[2] But not until the twentieth century did a researcher build a *strong* argument for holding humans responsible.

Paul S. Martin was a zoologist with wide-ranging interests in ecology, paleontology, archaeology, and beyond.[3] He spent his professional career in the Department of Geosciences at the University of Arizona where he trained students, collaborated with colleagues, and authored one of the most influential ideas of twentieth-century science: the "overkill hypothesis."

Martin developed this hypothesis in a 1973 paper in the prestigious journal *Science*, where it was noticed by researchers in many disciplines.[4] What had impressed Martin most was the apparent coincidence between the megafaunal extinctions and the arrival in the New World of the first humans. He argued that the megafauna had no experience with humans, and so were naïve prey that hunters could approach and dispatch. Thriving on the abundance of meat, populations grew rapidly, spread out in a wave from Alaska, and colonized all of North and South America in about a millennium. As the wave passed, so too did the superabundance of food, because overkill had eliminated the prey species. According to Martin, the slaughter must have begun immediately after humans entered the New World. Thus, if humans came before about 12,000 years ago, then the extinctions would have occurred earlier.

Martin marshaled many lines of evidence in support of his hypothesis, including well-dated "kill" sites in Arizona and New Mexico, where stone tools and mammoth bones indicated that the large animals had met their fate at human hands. But he was aware that much more archaeological and paleontological research would be needed to establish overkill as *the* extinctions' cause, given that the environment was changing at the same time.

Provoked by Martin's ideas, scientists in many disciplines offered evidence for and against the overkill hypothesis. Several archaeologists reported new sites, including Monte Verde in Chile and Meadowcroft Shelter in Pennsylvania, suggesting that people had colonized the New World between 14,000 and 17,000 years ago.[5] Other objections were raised on the basis of the extinction patterns: vulnerable prey animals became extinct but so too did large carnivores that were probably not hunted. Over the decades, partly in response to the many critics, Martin and his supporters elaborated the overkill hypothesis and attempted to deal with conflicting evidence. Dating of the pre-12,000 BP materials was disputed, as was the association of dated materials with human activities. And of course it was suggested that large carnivores died out because their prey were gone. Despite Martin's 2005 book vigorously defending overkill, the hypothesis remains mired in controversy.[6]

Perhaps the overkill hypothesis was overly ambitious for it attempted to explain—with one dramatic process—the loss of diverse species on a hemispheric scale. Even so, Martin's work generated a vast amount of high-quality research and stimulated the study of other, more recent mass extinctions. Above all, it suggested that *traditional peoples*, even hunter-gatherers, were not necessarily wise stewards of their environments. This possibility encouraged scientists to consider human activities as a possible cause of prehistoric mass extinctions.

To learn whether traditional peoples could cause mass extinctions, researchers require simple cases in small study areas such as islands, preferably over time periods when environmental change was limited. Investigators working in Polynesia, on widely scattered island groups in the South Pacific, have compiled excellent case studies on this issue.

New Zealand consists of two large islands located east of Australia. Together, they comprise about 104,000 square miles. The size of Colorado, New Zealand was the last large land mass on Earth to be colonized by humans. Because New Zealand was isolated for millions of years, distinctive plants and animals evolved there, including about 10 species of large, flightless birds found nowhere else. Known as moas, the largest species was 10–12 feet tall and weighed around 550 lbs (Figure 39.1). Ecologically, the moas filled herbivore niches because New Zealand's native fauna lacked land mammals (except bats). When Europeans arrived, they found *no* living moas but did encounter numerous Māori people, whose vibrant culture endures.

The archaeology of moa sites began with the work of Julius von Haast, a German immigrant trained in geology who founded the Canterbury Museum in Christchurch, New Zealand. In the late 1860s, Haast excavated in Glenmark swamp, which contained moa bones estimated at more than 1,000 birds. The bones' geological context suggested to Haast that the birds were of glacial (Pleistocene) age. He argued that, like the megafauna of the Old World, the moas had disappeared at the end of the Pleistocene. Haast held humans responsible for slaughtering the moas because the islands lacked other predators. The Moa hunters, he argued further, came before the Māori and, like the moas, disappeared. In 1869, excavations in a site on the Rakaia River revealed burned moa bones associated with stone tools and ovens. Clearly, people had feasted on the big birds.[7]

Haast's later excavations at Moa-Bone Point Cave seemingly shored up the inference that the Moa hunters were an indigenous group that had lived, and died, before the arrival of the seafaring Māori.[8] One of Haast's assistants, Alexander McKay, claimed instead that the Moa hunters were actually

FIGURE 39.1. Richard Owen and a skeleton of the largest moa species
(Owen 1879, Plate XCVII).

ancestors of the Māori because no evidence pointed to a gap in human occupation.[9] The disagreement between Haast and McKay was the first major
controversy in New Zealand science, but Haast eventually conceded that
there was continuity from Moa hunters to Māori.[10]

During the twentieth century, hundreds of moa-hunter sites were excavated, yielding large assemblages of bones, tools, and other artifacts, allowing archaeologists to flesh out the lifeway of the first New Zealanders.[11]
The ancestral Māori ate many moas, but did they actually cause the birds'
extinction? Answering this question with certainty requires a great many
accurate radiocarbon dates from early settlements. As these dates began to

accumulate, one finding soon became apparent: the moa hunters were not of Pleistocene age, but were much more recent. By the end of the century, large numbers of radiocarbon dates had reliably fixed the Polynesian colonization of New Zealand at A D 1230–80, which strongly suggested that the moas had vanished in a mere century or two. Nailing down this rapid extinction, New Zealand paleoecologists created a model of human population growth and moa hunting that showed the birds becoming extinct within 50–150 years after the Polynesians arrived (from Tahiti).[12] Because there are no competing hypotheses, archaeologists and environmental scientists agree that humans extinguished the moas.

The moa case leaves no doubt that a traditional society can cause a mass extinction. But was this case a fluke, perhaps merely reflecting an unusual relationship between ancestral Māori and big birds? Fortunately, other Pacific islands have provided additional examples of mass extinctions, and these have been well researched by environmental scientists and archaeologists. The foremost authority on these extinctions is David W. Steadman, a paleo-biologist at the Florida State Museum specializing—as an ornithologist and zooarchaeologist—in birds. His interest in mass extinctions is not surprising; after all, he is a student of Paul S. Martin.

Through his own excavations and those of others, Steadman has analyzed tens of thousands of archaeological bird bones from many dozens of Pacific, mainly Polynesian, islands.[13] From the Cook Islands to Hawaii, from the Society Islands to the Marquesas, from Samoa to Easter Island, Steadman's findings are uniformly grim: "Bones identified from archaeological sites show that most species of land birds and populations of seabirds on those islands were exterminated by prehistoric human activities. The loss of birdlife in the tropical Pacific may exceed 2,000 species."[14] Among the birds lost were *flightless* ducks, geese, ibises, and rails that had adapted, in the absence of land mammals, to untapped resources. There were also exotic species of pigeons, owls, doves, parrots, crows, and many others.[15] And as in New Zealand, it was especially the large, flightless species that disappeared rapidly after humans arrived.

In order to remove lingering doubts about whether humans were responsible for the carnage, Steadman examined data on bird extinctions from the Galapagos Islands, in the eastern Pacific. These islands are best known for their unique fauna such as giant tortoises and, of course, Darwin's finches. The Galapagos fauna have survived because people never settled the islands prehistorically. As such, the abundant fossil record—about a half million bones have been recovered from lava tubes—can be used to calculate a "natural" rate of vertebrate extinction. In a 4,000-year-period before Europeans arrived, Steadman estimates that three or fewer vertebrate species were lost.[16] In contrast, for islands occupied by humans prehistorically, the extinction rate is many hundreds, perhaps thousands, of times greater. That these rates are so high for so many far-flung island groups confirms that the extinctions did not result from natural processes.

Fine-grained research on fossil and archaeological bird assemblages has pinpointed processes that brought about the loss of specific species.[17] It turns out that exploiting birds for food was only one cultural process at work. In the course of colonization, Polynesians introduced domesticated animals to the islands—chickens, pigs, and dogs—as well as fellow travelers, rats. These animals preyed on, and competed for food and living space with, the native fauna and may have passed diseases to them. Polynesians themselves altered the natural environment through deforestation and agriculture, thus eliminating habitats for many land birds. These findings suggest that the term "overkill," while an attention-grabber, is somewhat misleading because human predation is just one cultural process that may lead to extinctions.

Pacific islands vary in topography, size, soils, climate, degree of isolation, plant and animal diversity, and also in their histories of colonization. As a result, each island tends to have its own extinction pattern. To tame this variation, Steadman and Martin built a model that includes both environmental and cultural factors that can, in principle, account for the onset and rate of an island's loss of species.[18] Working out the implications of their model for continent-wide processes, they insist that the overkill hypothesis does explain the megafaunal extinctions in the Americas. Other researchers disagree.

The major cause of mass extinctions in the modern world, besides overkill of land and sea animals, is the degradation and loss of habitats brought about by deforestation, expansion of agriculture (especially monoculture), extraction of petroleum and minerals, global warming, and pollution of land, air, and water. Introduced species also take a toll. The saddest example in the United States is the passenger pigeon. At the beginning of the nineteenth century, there were hundreds of millions of these handsome birds in the Midwest, but they were doomed by overzealous hunting and habitat reduction. The last one, named Martha, died in the Cincinnati Zoo in 1914.[19] Environmental scientists have learned from archaeological research that traditional societies also degraded natural environments and were agents of mass extinctions.

We still don't know if humans caused the disappearance of the American megafauna at the end of the Pleistocene, but perhaps archaeological discoveries will one day help solve that mystery.[20]

I thank David W. Steadman for comments on this chapter.

XIV

REVEALING OUR PREHISTORIC PAST

AMONG ALL THE SCIENCES, only archaeology can provide evidence about the entirety of the deep human past, beginning with the earliest ape-like creatures that lived millions of years ago, to the first agricultural societies, to the rise of ancient cities. The findings of prehistory give archaeology its most significant and influential footprint in the modern world. Educated people in industrial societies are aware that archaeologists have pieced together the human past before history, and many are familiar with some of the findings. Although the details of prehistory are far from complete, archaeologists and collaborators have tracked general trends in human evolution; identified original centers that sired agriculture and domesticated plants and animals; and reconstructed life in a multitude of ancient cities in both the Old and New Worlds.

Researchers have reconstructed the general course of human (hominin) evolution, which depends on the discovery and excavation of rare sites that are hundreds of thousands or even millions of years old. Investigated by archaeologists and biological anthropologists, these sites may yield tools, fossil hominins, or both. The first discoveries, of Neanderthals, were made in Europe in the mid-nineteenth century, followed shortly by what are now called *Homo erectus* in East Asia. In the early twentieth century, Southern African limestone deposits disgorged fossils of even more ape-like hominins, known collectively as australopithecines. Perhaps the most *culturally* significant discovery was made by Mary and Louis Leakey in East Africa in 1959. Although merely a robust australopithecine, the fossil's excavation was documented in film and publicized around the world in *National Geographic* and other print and electronic media, turning Louis Leakey into a star and fastening peoples' attention on the facts of human evolution. Because new fossils are still being found, details of the hominin family tree remain in flux. But the major trends are well documented: humans walked upright and used tools more than a million years before their brain expanded.

Researchers have long been interested in the shift in human subsistence from exploiting wild plants and animals to depending almost entirely on domesticated species. Foraging lifeways persisted for millions of years, yet in a short time after the close of the Pleistocene, about 12,000 years ago, "original centers" of agriculture sprang up in the Old and New Worlds. Archaeologists have documented around a dozen original centers and identified their major cultivated species. Most recently, Tim Denham's excavations at the Kuk Swamp site verified earlier speculations that New Guineans had been farming thousands of years ago. New Guinea was in fact an original center where taro, greater yam, bananas, and sugarcane were domesticated. Today archaeologists wonder why foragers would become farmers. We know that this was a very slow process, probably triggered by different causes in different regions. We also know that early farmers were imperialists, for their growing populations had budded off, as emigrants sought new fields and pastures and spread agricultural lifeways far and wide.

The variety of lifeways that arose in ancient cites is illustrated by Tikal in Central America and Mohenjo–Daro in South Asia. Tikal is a vast culturally modified landscape that sprawls amidst a tropical forest. Along with massive limestone temples and palaces, Tikal's residents built dams, reservoirs, and other features to ensure a steady supply of water during the dry season. The city was ruled by a dynasty of kings whose tenures and accomplishments were recorded on stone stelae, most of which can now be read. It is believed that a severe drought caused Tikal and many other Maya cities to be abandoned in the late ninth century AD. In stark contrast to Tikal, Mohenjo–Daro is a compact city with deeply stratified deposits of mud-brick and brick architecture. No kings or other leaders have been discerned, but planned streets, wells, and sewers indicate that the leadership was effective. There was a writing system, but it has not been deciphered. No temples have been found, and seemingly life in Mohenjo–Daro had a commercial character. The city was abandoned around 1900 BC, and the cause is still debated.

40

In the Beginning

THE JUDEO-CHRISTIAN Genesis story is one of many colorful origin myths found worldwide. Such stories vary greatly, but all respond to the question: where did we come from? Origin myths testify to human curiosity and creativity, reflect the cultures in which they arose, and are meaningful to believers. The processes of science have also created an origin story that gives meaning to human lives. It does not rest on faith in supernatural beings but on evidence provided by biological anthropologists and archaeologists that situates us in the natural world.[1]

Scientific alternatives to the Genesis story arose in the early nineteenth century, culminating in Charles Darwin's *On the Origin of Species by Means of Natural Selection* (1859) and *The Descent of Man* (1871). According to Darwin, species evolved gradually through natural selection, not divine acts. Going further, he claimed humans and anthropoid apes, such as the gorilla and chimpanzee, had a common ancestor in Africa, a claim that made pious people angry and indignant. Where, critics demanded, were the telltale fossils having features of both humans and apes, the so-called "missing links" that evolution supposedly required? And how could the slow process of evolution have taken place when, according to biblical scholars, Earth was scarcely 6,000 years old? Fortunately for the credibility of evolutionary science, by the end of the nineteenth-century fossils were turning up and geologists and physicists had dramatically extended the age of the Earth.

Geology is based on uniformitarianism, a principle promoted by Charles Lyell in 1830 that links the present to the past.[2] Uniformitarianism declares that observable processes, such as erosion, volcanic eruptions, and the movement of glaciers, also took place in the past and created modern landforms. Thus, erosion by the Colorado River made the Grand Canyon, erupting volcanoes built the Hawaiian Islands, and the movement of glaciers produced Minnesota's 10,000 lakes. Because most geological processes observable today act very slowly, geologists and physicists at the end of the nineteenth century estimated that creating the surface of the Earth would have taken 100 million years.[3]

Geologists also constructed a long sequence of epochs in Earth's history. Accurate ages have been determined for the four most-recent epochs, all of which are relevant to human evolution. Dates are expressed as millions of years ago (mya):[4]

Holocene   .01 mya to present
Pleistocene 2.3 mya to .01 mya
Pliocene   5.3 mya to 2.3 mya
Miocene   23 mya to 5.3 mya

Human remains from the Holocene and late Pleistocene are mainly *Homo sapiens*. During the nineteenth and early twentieth centuries, earlier Pleistocene deposits yielded finds of human-like fossils. In the late twentieth century, important fossils have also been found in Pliocene and even late Miocene deposits.

What were these early human-like ancestors like? Did they have large brains? Did they walk on all fours? Did they make tools? And when and where did they live? Archaeological finds have enabled researchers to answer these questions.

The first human-like fossil was discovered just before Darwin's *Origin* was published. Found buried in a cave in the Neander Valley of Germany, it was named Neanderthal (or Neandertal). Descriptions of the skull and several other bones sparked spirited debates about the fossil's age and relation to modern humans. The bones were compared with those of western Europeans and members of so-called "primitive races," and differences were found. But did these differences justify naming a distinct and older species? On this issue, C. Carter Blake in 1864 was uncertain but nonetheless suggested *Homo neanderthalensis*, a species name that has gone in and out of fashion.[5]

In later decades, excavations encountered more Neanderthal fossils, which led to a fuller description. They were shorter than modern humans

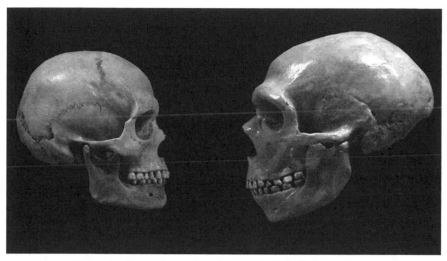

FIGURE 40.1. Plastic replicas of a modern human skull (left) and a Neanderthal skull (right) in the Cleveland Museum of Natural History (Wikimedia Commons; Dr. Mike Baxter, photographer).

and *much* stockier, but they clearly walked on two legs. Their faces were wide with an imposing nose, the forehead was sloped, and the back of the skull had a bun-shaped protrusion (Figure 40.1). Surprisingly, their brain size— estimated from the volume of the skull—was equal to ours. Neanderthals also had some ape-like features, including a massive jaw and brow ridge (the continuous bone above the eyes).

Neanderthals used fire and made a variety of stone and bone tools. They were omnivores and hunted large game; and there is some evidence that they buried their dead.

Since the first discoveries, the name Neanderthal has evoked a cartoonish image of a lumbering and dim-witted creature. One early researcher even believed that Neanderthals were idiots, perhaps dying like hermits in their caves.[6] Although Neanderthals had a brain of ample size, William King, a professor at Queen's University in Ireland, believed that "the thoughts and desires which once dwelt within it never soared beyond those of the brute."[7] He concluded in 1864 that Neanderthals were not *Homo sapiens*. To this day, the cognitive abilities of Neanderthals are vigorously debated.

We now know that Neanderthals lived during the late Pleistocene, from about 300,000 to 35,000 years ago, and the last ones were confined to a small part of Europe. Although many researchers believe they died out, perhaps outcompeted by modern *Homo sapiens*, there is an ironic twist to their presumed demise. Recently, biological anthropologist Svante Pääbo and an international team of more than 50 researchers sequenced a Neanderthal genome. Building on this remarkable feat, they showed that the genomes of modern Europeans and Asians contain about 1–2 percent Neanderthal genes.[8]

Although Neanderthals would stand out in any crowd today, they are too much like us to qualify as the missing link, much less the earliest hominins. Hominins, by the way, include our close relatives and direct ancestors that lie on the human family tree after it split from the other anthropoid apes. It is now believed that this split, from chimpanzees, occurred in the late Miocene between 8 and 5 mya.

And so the search continued for fossils that might help fill out the early part of our family tree. A Dutch anatomist, zoologist, and naturalist Eugène Dubois made the next significant discovery. He became interested in human evolution and wanted to vindicate Darwin by finding the missing link. Believing that fossils of these creatures might be found in the tropics, Dubois joined the army and obtained a post in the Dutch East Indies (now Indonesia). In Java, he searched for promising sites in caves and near rivers. In 1890–91, he found a new ape-like fossil, which he named *Pithecanthropus erectus*. It had a huge brow ridge, sloping forehead, and receding chin—yet walked erect. Its brain was small but larger than those of gorilla and chimpanzee. Dubois was certain that he had found the missing link, but even after seeing the bones many researchers had doubts.[9]

Today, many more of these hominins have been discovered in East Asia, Europe, and Africa. They are known as *Homo erectus* and are likely ancestral both to modern humans and to Neanderthals (Figure 40.2). *Homo erectus* had a good run throughout the Pleistocene, as fossils have been dated from about 1.8 mya to about .2 mya.[10] They were skilled hunters who may have used spears and possibly fire.

The stone tools made by *Homo erectus* are fairly common in much of the Old World. Perhaps the most characteristic tool is the "handaxe," used for working wood and digging up edible roots but probably not felling trees (Figure 40.3).[11] The handaxe was also a convenient source of raw material: sharp flakes could be easily chipped off and used for cutting and scraping plant and animal materials. Portable and versatile, the handaxe was the Paleolithic equivalent of the Swiss Army Knife.

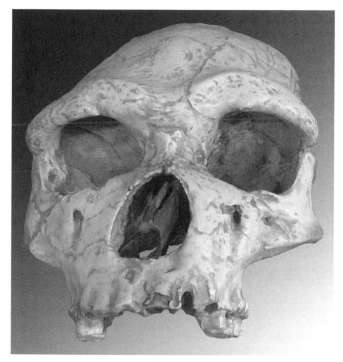

FIGURE 40.2. *Homo erectus* skull from Tautavel, France
(Wikimedia Commons; Ciell, photographer).

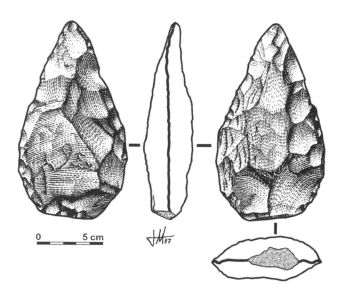

FIGURE 40.3. Drawing of a handaxe found near the Esla River, Spain (Wikimedia
Commons; José-Manuel Benito, artist).

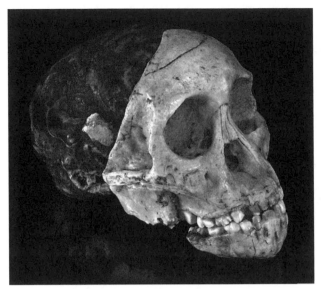

FIGURE 40.4. Cast of the "Taung Child," an *Australopithecus africanus*, in the University of Witwatersrand, Johannesburg, South Africa (Wikimedia Commons; Didier Descouens, photographer).

The ancestral status of *Homo erectus* gained plausibility after the discovery of an even more ape-like species. Raymond Dart, an anatomist at the University of Witwatersrand in Johannesburg, South Africa, didn't actually find or excavate the fossils himself: they came from a limestone quarry and had been liberated from the stone by blasting. Fortunately, Dart was able to examine a few fossils from the site and identified them as anthropoid apes. This discovery was extraordinary because no anthropoid fossils had been found before in Southern Africa.[12]

And then it got even better. Another fossil from a quarry in Taung consisted of a large part of a child's face, lower jaw and teeth, and a piece of brain-shaped limestone that had accreted in the skull's interior postmortem (Figure 40.4).[13] After making detailed anatomical comparisons, Dart concluded in 1925 that the tiny fossil had come from "an extinct race of apes *intermediate between living anthropoids and man*."[14] To this new species of "ape-man," surely a missing link, he gave the name *Australopithecus africanus*.

Dart's interpretations were challenged, but in the next few decades they gained support from other researchers, especially Robert Broom, who explored the limestone quarries of Southern Africa and recovered more fossils.[15] Several resembled *Australopithecus africanus*, but others were different enough to be called a new species, *Australopithecus robustus* (or *Paranthropus robustus*). *Africanus* was small and dainty; *robustus* was larger and robust. Both had tiny brains and many other anthropoid features, yet jaws, teeth, some aspects of the skull, and the ability to walk erect were human-like.

Together, these two species are referred to as australopithecines, and some researchers inferred that the dainty one was a human ancestor. Unfortunately, beyond educated guesses, these fossils could not be dated apart from vague placement in the Pleistocene. And, at the time of discovery in the 1940s, they had not been found associated with stone tools.

After the Second World War, researchers began to make monumental hominin discoveries in East Africa, and it all began at Olduvai Gorge, which runs along the eastern edge of the Serengeti Plain in Tanzania. Olduvai Gorge is a special locality because erosion created massive exposures of Pleistocene layers that contain human fossils and include "living floors"—places where early hominins butchered game and deposited stone tools and animal bones. These traces of biology and behavior, as well as numerous animal fossils, were exposed not by blasting but by meticulous archaeological excavation at many sites. Olduvai Gorge is also special because it was being worked at a time when the new medium of television brought its discoveries into homes around the world. Extensive coverage of excavations there created a celebrity archaeologist, Louis S. B. Leakey, and primed public interest in human evolution.

Leakey was born in Kenya, son of English missionaries who worked with the Kikuyu tribe, Kenya's largest. More than an African by accident of birth, Leakey was fluent in the Kikuyu language and was an initiated member of the tribe. He studied archaeology and anthropology at Cambridge University, earning the Ph.D. at age 27.[16]

Like Darwin, Leakey believed that humankind originated in Africa, a belief buttressed by the australopithecine discoveries. He visited Olduvai Gorge in 1931 with his first wife Frida and a German colleague. There, they found simple stone tools but no hominins. From time to time, he returned to Olduvai with his second wife Mary. A talented artist who illustrated Louis's first book, Mary also had archaeological experience and an uncanny knack for spotting fossils. She became a distinguished archaeologist.

The Leakeys' decades of intermittent fieldwork in Olduvai Gorge had failed to turn up early hominin fossils, but that was about to change. On

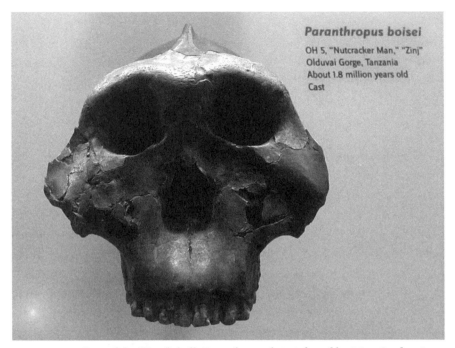

Paranthropus boisei

OH 5, "Nutcracker Man," "Zinj"
Olduvai Gorge, Tanzania
About 1.8 million years old
Cast

FIGURE 40.5. Cast of the "Zinj" skull, *Paranthropus boisei*, found by Mary Leakey in Olduvai Gorge, in the National Museum of Natural History, Smithsonian Institution (photograph by the author).

July 17, 1959, as Louis lay in bed with the flu, Mary decided to explore on her own a site in an early Pleistocene layer known as Bed I, where many stone tools and animal fossils had been seen on the surface. There she made the discovery of a lifetime. In her own words: "One scrap of bone that caught and held my eye was not lying loose on the surface but projecting from underneath.... I carefully brushed away a little of the deposit, and then I could see part of two large teeth in place in the upper jaw."[17] This exposure was enough to confirm that she had found part of a very ancient skull. She hurried back to camp and told Louis the good news. Miraculously recovering from the flu, he hopped out of bed and accompanied Mary to the site. After inspecting the skull, they covered it carefully and waited for the arrival of Des Bartlett to film the excavation.

They unearthed the skull with great care and searched the area around it for additional fragments, of which there were many; the major part missing was the lower jaw. Although Louis named the fossil *Zinjanthropus boisei*,[18] most specialists declared it an *Australopithecus robustus* or, more recently, *Paranthropus boisei* (Figure 40.5).

The film showed the excavation of the skull along with Louis's captivating interviews and publicized this important find. Most importantly, the discovery of "Zinj" focused the public's attention on the fossil evidence for human evolution. Publicity also opened the door for long-term support from the National Geographic Society and other funding agencies. They were eager to contribute because the living floor on which Zinj was found promised to reveal details of australopithecine behavior.

The stone tools on the Zinj floor were very simple, little more than cobble choppers and flake knives. Australopithecines may have done some hunting, but they also ate plants and practiced scavenging, using their rudimentary tools to extract the last pieces of meat and bone marrow from a carcass after lions and hyenas had finished.

But how old were the tools and Zinj? The answer came from J. F. Evernden and G. H. Curtis, geoscientists at the University of California, Berkeley. Having learned about Zinj, they were eager to apply the new technique of potassium-argon dating to the layers of volcanic tuff associated with Bed I at Olduvai. In 1961, they reported the stunning result: the Zinj living floor "was approximately 1.75 million years old," near the beginning of the Pleistocene.[19]

The Leakeys soon found many more early hominins, and their successes encouraged other researchers, including their son Richard, to explore new regions of east and central Africa. Archaeological expeditions to Ethiopia, Kenya, and Chad found dozens of Pleistocene, Pliocene, and even late Miocene sites, many of them datable by potassium-argon. Excavations produced a cornucopia of hominin fossils and often stone tools, some of the latter dating to 3.4 mya.[20] These projects led to the naming of more than a dozen new species, drawing attention to an unexpectedly complex pattern of human evolution.

Until the early 1960s, the human family tree had seemed simple: *Australopithecus africanus* evolved into *Homo erectus,* which evolved into *Homo sapiens* (*Australopithecus robustus* and *Homo neanderthalensis* were sometimes shown as evolutionary dead ends). Today's family tree has numerous new species and many branches that died out—a very bushy tree.[21] And, seemingly, every researcher applies different names to the same fossils and constructs a different family tree.

Even so, recent discoveries support the most basic evolutionary pattern: hominins made tools and walked upright more than a million years before the brain's enlargement. Today researchers debate about which selective pressures eventually resulted in brain expansion and modern *Homo sapiens*'s vast cognitive abilities. Was it tool making, planning hunting and foraging trips, intricate social interactions, avoiding predators, or some combination of these thinking-intensive activities? Right now, we don't know. Such uncertainties are the lifeblood of science because they stimulate new research projects.

Although our family tree remains a work in progress, dozens of well-dated fossils and associated artifacts make the fact of human evolution scientifically indisputable. Even so, some people cling to their origin myths and deny human evolution. That no amount of scientific evidence can modify these beliefs frustrates researchers, especially in the United States, where anti-evolutionists have influenced state and local educational policies on, for example, the contents of K–12 textbooks. For some people, the story of human origins written by scientists is not as compelling or comforting as ancient myths.

41

From Foragers to Farmers

IN MODERN WESTERN DIETS, few foods are caught or collected in the wild; but it wasn't always so. Archaeology has shown that no more than 15,000 years ago, long after modern *Homo sapiens* had evolved, all groups got their food from foraging (also known as hunting and gathering). A major archaeological interest is to provide evidence of, and explain, the transition from foraging to farming. Since the middle of the twentieth century, there have been many exciting discoveries.

The first region to be intensively investigated was the "fertile crescent" in the Near East, which includes large parts of modern Syria and Iraq. Because this region supported civilizations from about 5,000 BP (before present) onward, archaeologists suspected that early agriculture would be found there too. And it was.

The archaeological evidence was convincing because, under cultural selection in agricultural societies, species become *domesticated*, undergoing evolutionary changes that distinguish them from their wild ancestors.[1] Using flotation on soil from dozens of early sites in and near the fertile crescent, archaeologists have recovered abundant seeds; and screening the soil has added to the yield of animal bones. Analyzed by archaeobotanists and zooarchaeologists, respectively, these remains testify to the presence of agricultural societies by 9,000 BP. Well-known sites such as Jarmo, Çayönü, and Jericho have produced clear evidence for domesticates including wheat, barley, chickpeas; and cattle, sheep, goats, and pigs.

Before domesticated species evolved in the Near East, foragers there were managing wild species, a practice that reaches back to at least 10,500 BP.[2]

Management includes activities such as watering, weeding, and moving plants; and tending, taming, and protecting animals.[3] At that time, managed species did not yet exhibit evolutionary changes, and so archaeologists have to rely on subtle evidence such as traces of gardens and the age and sex ratios of animals.

The management and eventual domestication of many species, along with irrigation and other new technologies, made possible the growth of cities and complex societies in the Near East. Millennia before the Sumerians, Assyrians, and Babylonians appeared, the earliest farmers were, in a sense, imperialists. Their productive agriculture spurred population growth, especially in villages occupied year-round. And, compared to foraging, farming could support many more people in a given land area. These growing communities budded off, sending migrants to other regions in search of arable land and pastures. Migrants carried the group of Near Eastern domesticates westward, reaching Greece and Italy by 8,000 BP and Spain and Portugal by at least 7,500 BP.[4]

The Near East is one of more than a dozen *original centers* of agriculture, where groups of plants and sometimes animals were domesticated independently of other such centers.[5] Archaeologists have identified the domesticates of other original centers, including Mesoamerica (maize, squash, avocado, etc.), South America (chili peppers, common bean, potato, sweet potato; llama, alpaca, guinea pig, etc.), China (rice, peach, pear, several varieties of millet; chicken, pig, etc.), and Africa (yam, sorghum, several varieties of millet, etc.). In every original center, domestication continued for thousands of years and brought new species under human control. In Mesoamerica, for example, later additions included tobacco, agave, and cacao.

Archaeologists have recently identified two new original centers: eastern North America and New Guinea. The New Guinea findings are especially intriguing because they came as a big surprise.

After Greenland, New Guinea is the second largest island in the world, slightly bigger than the state of Texas. It lies amidst many smaller islands just northeast of Australia in the Melanesian culture area. New Guinea is very mountainous, and so there is much altitude-based environmental variation that sustains a breathtaking diversity of native plants and animals.[6]

Humans first settled New Guinea more than 40,000 years ago. In the island's rich environment, foraging societies thrived, eventually developing into more than 1,000 tribes speaking as many languages. When Westerners

FIGURE 41.1. Group of Koyari chiefs, New Guinea, ca. 1890 (*Popular Science*, September 1890, p. 611).

first made contact with New Guineans, they found the populous peoples actively practicing agriculture supplemented with foraging. Many traditional tribes survived into the twentieth century, still making pottery and stone tools, building thatch houses, and warring with each other (Figure 41.1).

New Guinea attracted cultural anthropologists who wanted to study apparently pristine tribal societies before they were devastated by disease, corporations, occupying governments, and missionaries. Margaret Mead wrote one of the most famous—and now most controversial—New Guinea ethnographies, based on fieldwork among the Arapesh, Tchambuli, and Mundugumor tribes. In *Sex and Temperament in Three Primitive Societies* (1935), Mead asserted that sex roles were culturally determined, as shown by tribal differences in male and female dominance patterns; this finding became a key tenet of modern feminism. Since Mead's death in 1978, her ethnographic work has been criticized and is no longer accepted as authoritative.

Although cultural anthropologists were drawn early on to the exoticism of New Guinea, archaeologists did not arrive in appreciable numbers until recent decades. Obviously, doing survey and excavation in a mountainous, tropical environment presents logistical challenges; and preservation of organic remains is usually poor. But there are other reasons for the neglect. Unlike peoples in the Near East, China, and Mesoamerica, indigenous New Guineans established no cities, states, or civilizations and remained in the "stone age" well into the twentieth century. Thus, archaeologists did not expect that New Guinea was an original center of agriculture. Subtle racism may have played a role too, for New Guineans are as black as Africans. In any event, New Guinea was not regarded as a place with great archaeological promise.

But sometimes our expectations turn out to be wrong.[7]

New Guinea prehistory began to gain traction in the late twentieth century, especially as Australian archaeologists sought connections between Aborigine peoples and New Guineans. Tim Denham, an archaeologist at Australian National University (ANU) in Canberra, specializes in geoarchaeology. By analyzing soils and sediments, he learns how people interacted with their environment over time, which sets the stage for investigating early agriculture.

Following in the footsteps of his mentor, ANU archaeologist Jack Golson, Denham embarked on a multidisciplinary project in the late 1990s at the Kuk Swamp site, located in the Upper Wahgi Valley of the New Guinea Highlands (on the Papua side of the island). At first glance, the Kuk Swamp site may seem unpromising, for it apparently lacks houses and other visible traces of domestic life. Rather, it consists of mounds, extensive ditches, and other odd landscape features. Yet Golson's earlier fieldwork there had shown that these features were artificial earthworks: ditches to drain fields and earthen platforms for planting.[8] Without much evidence, Golson claimed that these features supported very early agriculture. Denham aimed to evaluate Golson's shaky claim on the basis of microbotanical remains and radiocarbon dates, hoping to learn what was grown there and when.

Denham reconstructed the changing environment in and near the site and conducted extensive excavations of the earthworks. Dozens of trenches intercepted house sites and furnished cross-sections of the earthworks, revealing original ground surfaces. Several phases of construction were identified, beginning with Phase 1 at about 10,000 BP. Even at this early time, wild plants were being managed, as indicated by pits as well as holes for posts and stakes. According to Denham and colleagues, "These features are consistent with planting, digging, and tethering of plants…in a cultivated plot" that was burned over periodically.[9] Burning maintained grassland vegetation, fostering an island of arable land in a forest.

Although cultivated plants per se were not preserved at the Kuk Swamp site, their distinctive microscopic traces were. Phase 2, which began about

7,000–6,500 BP, held an abundance of banana phytoliths (silica structures that form in and around cells) as well as yam and taro oxalate crystals extracted from the working edges of stone tools. These impressive finds, along with the extensive earthworks, are interpreted as the beginning of deliberate planting and propagation of staple crops.[10]

So far, the Kuk Swamp site has furnished the earliest evidence of agriculture in New Guinea, but other projects have recovered traces of different plants that were domesticated later.[11] The four major domesticates are taro, greater yam, bananas, and sugarcane, all bountiful sources of carbohydrates. Clearly, New Guinea was an original center of agriculture where several crops of modern worldwide importance were domesticated.

Why did foragers in the Near East, Mesoamerica, New Guinea, and other original centers become farmers? Archaeologists have offered many explanations to account for the transition that created original centers, but even today none is widely accepted. Let us begin with an incomplete explanation, move to one that is clearly wrong, and end with a general scenario of what might have taken place.

It is striking that the dozen or so original centers all developed between about 12,000 and 6,000 BP, after the close of the Pleistocene when sea levels rose (as glaciers melted) and new communities of plants and animals arose in many regions. That the original centers appeared soon after these environmental changes hints that the processes were related, but was this a causal relationship? Some archaeologists claim it was, yet can't explain how the environmental changes led directly to the original centers or why earlier episodes of melting glaciers produced no agricultural societies. Even so, environmental processes at the end of the Pleistocene probably figured somehow in the emergence of the original centers. Perhaps the changes in plant and animal communities—loss of some species, gain of others—led in some regions to experiments in managing resources, especially in regions where human populations were growing.

The most fanciful explanation is the "genius model," still found in mass media even though archaeologists debunked it long ago.[12] It goes something like this: a genius carefully observes nature for a long time and makes a remarkable "discovery": how plants and animals reproduce. The genius then spreads the word among members of the community and soon everyone is planting seeds and herding animals. Agriculture is born. What makes this model so laughable is the assumption that it took a genius to figure out the facts of life. We are confident that foragers understood reproduction in nature and were satisfied to harvest what nature provided.

The genius model also assumes that farming is inherently superior to foraging. And so, as soon as foragers learned about farming, they would adopt this new lifeway. In many regions of the Old and New Worlds, however, foragers knew about farming because their neighbors practiced it, yet they continued to hunt and gather. Even in North America foragers persisted well into the nineteenth century in California, Alaska, the Pacific Northwest, the Great Basin, Canada, and northwest Mexico, to name a few. Although foraging in some regions is a very demanding lifeway, even in these areas it is far from the bleak, hand-to-mouth existence that smug, shopping-cart-pushing moderns might imagine.

Understanding of actual forager lifeways comes from ethnographic, ethnohistorical, and ethnoarchaeological studies.[13] A salient fact about foragers is that there were as many different lifeways as groups. Every environment has a distinctive climate, whether it is a Brazilian rainforest, the Kalahari Desert, or the Canadian Arctic, and that environment also has unique plant and animal communities. In order to procure particular species, foragers employed appropriate technologies at specific times in specific places.[14] Some groups established a village and remained there year-round—sea-oriented societies in the Northwest Coast of North America, for example. Other groups moved often from camp to camp, such as the Aborigines of the Western Desert of Australia. Many groups, including some California tribes, alternated seasonally between coastal villages for acquiring marine resources and inland villages for harvesting acorns and game.

Most foraging societies required a great deal of territory to sustain their relatively small populations. A foraging territory had to be large enough to include distant resources such as sheep in the mountains or shellfish along the shore, as well as sacred springs and mountaintops.

Foraging is an effective lifeway as long as the environment doesn't change too rapidly.[15] But even the most stable environment can suffer sporadic drought, flooding, or temperature extremes, reducing the availability of some resources. Perhaps management and eventually domestication developed as people tried out various strategies to mitigate such extreme events. It is also possible that population growth or changes in plant and animal communities during the late Pleistocene led to management of some resources.

Whatever kicked off the process in a given region, the first peoples who began managing plants, such as moving them to new areas, weeding, watering, or encouraging their growth with fire, were not trying to become farmers. Rather, they were trying to maintain their foraging lifeway. Through trial and error, they learned that some management strategies were effective, and these were adopted. From then on, as population grew imperceptibly, generation after generation, cultural selection resulted in species being slowly domesticated, increasingly more important in the diet and more dependent on people for their propagation. These "farmers" inherited the effects of small decisions accumulated over many centuries, set in motion by the first people to establish new relationships with plants (and sometimes animals) so they could continue as foragers.

Modern explanations for original centers point out that it took a millennium or more for peoples to transition from managing wild plants to relying heavily on domesticates. The genius model and its major implication (farming is superior to foraging) obviously do not satisfy this requirement, but the above scenario does—even though it can't specify what kicked off the process in any region.

It is easier to explain why societies both nearby and far from the original centers adopted agriculture. After all, these transformations are still going on, and the causes are similar in premodern and modern times: encroachment on foraging territories. When agricultural societies colonize foraging territories by establishing settlements, fields, plantations, lumbering operations, and so forth in locations of critical resources, the result for foragers is hardship. Groups experiencing these impacts face a palette of unpleasant choices: become farmers, obtain government support, or submit to wage labor in mines and plantations (often a form of slavery). In some regions, these choices are rendered moot by genocide. The encroachment process began with emigration from the original centers, but recent episodes of colonization by empires of East and West alike have drastically reduced the number of foraging societies left on Earth.

But once agriculture became established in any area, groups were usually receptive to experimenting with new crops, regardless of their source. That's why most societies today cultivate combinations of plants and animals domesticated in many regions.

The unexpected discovery that New Guinea was an original center suggests that there may be more surprises ahead, as archaeologists search for early agriculture in other regions where complex societies did not develop. Much remains to be learned. We don't know the origins of many ancient domesticated species, and we are far from figuring out what kicked off the transition to agriculture in particular regions. Archaeologists are actively seeking evidence to resolve these issues. Greater knowledge of the diverse origins of agriculture won't put more wild things in supermarkets, but it helps us to appreciate that the creation of our modern world of domesticated plants and animals has been a panhuman process.

42

The Urban Revolution

IN REGIONS OF highly productive agriculture, some tribal villages grew large and became the basis of a new—some say revolutionary—kind of existence: urban life. Modern societies could not exist without cities, but archaeologists have shown that the roots of apparently indispensable cities lie in the ancient past.

The earliest cities developed in the Near East during the fourth millennium BC, with Uruk of Sumer among the first.[1] Pioneering cities in Asia, Europe, Africa, and the Americas were commonly followed by dozens more. A versatile lifeway, ancient cities arose independently in deserts, tropical forests, and other environments, their populations varying from a few thousand people to perhaps 200,000.[2] Many ancient cities endured for centuries, some for millennia, and a few such as Erbil in Kurdistan are still inhabited.[3] When a region's cities are finally abandoned, however, the lifeways of the people change dramatically.

For archaeologists, a city is a large settlement having (1) much occupational specialization, part-time and full-time; (2) well-defined political structure and leadership roles; (3) social stratification with elites and commoners; (4) specialized, nonresidential buildings; (5) public works such as canals, reservoirs, and roads; and (6) local, regional, and interregional exchange. These characteristics all have implications for material culture and thus the archaeological record.

Exchange networks enabled cities to import raw materials and products to satisfy subsistence, economic, and social needs. Social needs were especially demanding because the elite had special artifact requirements. The king, royal family, and court functionaries, for example, had to acquire foods, clothing, ornaments, housing, and tombs that uniquely embodied and symbolized their social status, distinguishing them from commoners. In some regions, social needs stimulated the development of new technologies such as pyramid construction in Egypt and Mesoamerica, copper metallurgy in the Near East and Peru, and ceramic armies in China.[4] In many cities, products that met social needs were supplied through a mix of exchange activities, local craft production, and conquest.

Cities often waged war against each other, forming ever-changing alliances and, in some regions, incorporating many other cities and villages into one imperialist polity such as the Roman and Inka empires. At some point in the growth of a city or empire, record keeping may have become essential, leading to the creation of writing systems or other technologies for tracking economic transactions. And with a writing system, elites could inscribe their achievements on documents and monuments.

Every early city invites this question: how did it develop from farming villages? This question is difficult, perhaps impossible, to answer, but questions about how a city was organized and functioned are just as intriguing. The latter questions often begin as puzzles whose solutions give insights into the many ways that people created unique and long-lived urban communities.

But the puzzles of ancient cities aren't easily solved. Fieldwork is challenging. In Near Eastern cities, commoners' houses were made of mud brick. After such houses decayed or were razed, people built new ones on top of the debris. Centuries of occupation resulted in a large mound, called a *tell*, that could reach 100 feet in height. Cities that mainly grew outward not upward, such as Chan Chan on the coast of Peru or Teotihuacán in the Valley of Mexico, seem more tractable but like tells they require large-scale (and very expensive) field projects lasting decades.

Despite the challenges of investigating ancient cities, archaeologists continue tackling them and reporting impressive discoveries. Let us turn to Tikal, a Maya city in Mesoamerica, and Mohenjo–Daro, a Harappan city in South Asia. As different as two cities can be, they illustrate a few of the vast possibilities of urban life realized in the ancient world.

Beginning in the first millennium BC, during the Preclassic period, the ancient Maya built cities in the tropical forests of Central America, from the Yucatán Peninsula to the Pacific Coast, encompassing parts of

FIGURE 42.1. Left, Temple 1 at Tikal, Guatemala; right, the royal palace (Wikimedia Commons; chensiyuan, photographer).

modern Mexico, Guatemala, and other countries. During the Classic Period, ca. AD 200–900, dozens of new cities were established, their temples rising high above the jungle floor. From the end of the Classic period into the Postclassic (AD 900–1600), all cities were abandoned, but the Maya did not disappear. The Maya remained a vibrant people but gave up city life, turning to villages and the practice of shifting cultivation (moving fields every few years), a land-hungry form of farming that limits a settlement's size and a region's population density.

Besides building monumental temples and palaces (Figure 42.1), the ancient Maya created a calendar, astronomy, mathematics, and a writing system. Inscriptions appear on pottery and upright carved stones called *stelae*, on murals painted in caves and stone structures, and in the few surviving books the Spanish conquerors didn't burn. Archaeologists and other scholars have succeeded in translating the glyphs—individual symbols—and now more than 90 percent of the inscriptions can be read.

The inscriptions, which include dates in the Maya calendar, make clear that the Maya were organized as city-states ruled by hereditary kings who "possessed economic, religious, and political power reinforced by a belief that they ruled with the support and approval of the Maya gods."[5] The stelae commemorate events in the lives of named kings and two queens whose reigns can be dated because researchers, drawing on early historic sources, have correlated the Maya and modern calendars. But the inscriptions are silent as to how the Maya wrested a living from the tropical forest. Long-term, multidisciplinary research at Tikal, one of the largest and most majestic Maya cities, has helped to solve this puzzle.

Under the direction of William R. Coe, the University of Pennsylvania Museum began a decade-long field project at Tikal in 1956 that cost almost $1 million. The first major task was to map the core area—about 6 square miles.[6] Next, after clearing away jungle, almost 350 structures were excavated. Finally, survey and excavations were done outside the core area.

Earlier archaeologists believed that the ancient Maya, like their descendants, practiced shifting cultivation (also known as slash-and-burn agriculture), growing maize, beans, and squash in temporary fields cleared by burning. However, large clusters of temples, palaces, and other city-like constructions in Tikal's core countered that belief. Could these monumental structures have been, as some archaeologists surmised, vacant ceremonial centers occasionally visited for religious rituals? Clues to solving this puzzle lay beyond the city core in Tikal's "sustaining area."

In fieldwork directed by William A. Haviland, the crew laid out four radial strips, 500 m wide and 12 km long. Originating at the Great Plaza in the core area, the strips went outward in the four cardinal directions. Pedestrian surveys of these strips, a horrific task in the jungle, recorded 1,430 structures and 265 subterranean storage pits (*chultuns*). The density of structures and pits declined gradually with distance from the Great Plaza, indicating that the core and sustaining area had been a single urban landscape of around 165 km^2. Test excavations in more than 100 structures showed that the sustaining area contained commoner residences, each consisting of several thatch structures on a raised platform. In 1969, Haviland extrapolated from the new field data to a "conservative" population estimate for Tikal of 49,000 people.[7] Clearly, the core and sustaining area together had supported a huge resident population, laying to rest the curious notion of a vacant ceremonial center.

Solving this puzzle led to a new one: shifting cultivation alone could not have sustained that many people. How did they survive? During the following decades projects at Tikal and other Maya cities answered the question by investigating environmental change, land use, agricultural practices, and diet.

Many ancient cities were founded near perennial streams or rivers that supply water for drinking, food preparation, and other activities, but the closest river to Tikal is almost 30 km away. And although the average annual rainfall exceeds 0.8 m, it rains very little during winter. To ensure a reliable, year-round water supply, the Maya became sophisticated hydraulic engineers and landscape architects.[8]

Tikal is situated on a series of limestone ridges interspersed with swampy depressions known as *bajos*. The first settlers occupied a ridge with a spring, which they dammed. As the city grew, gated dams were also placed across three seasonal streams (*arroyos*). At least nine major reservoirs were dug above the *bajos* to receive the impounded water, their walls plastered to reduce seepage. Before water entered several reservoirs, it was filtered through a bed of sand. Digging the reservoirs in turn liberated vast amounts of limestone that went into building temples and palaces.

The residents of Tikal also transformed their biotic environment through agricultural and forest-management practices. Fruit trees were cultivated, especially in the core area, and other trees were sustainably harvested for firewood and construction materials. Although household gardens were abundant throughout Tikal, the sustaining area grew much staple food. Like many ancient cities in tropical areas, Tikal incorporated its agricultural hinterland.[9]

Tikal's occupation lasted more than a millennium, its final stela erected in AD 869, but soon afterward the city was truly vacant. What happened?

Researchers have recently concluded that in Tikal's largely artificial environment the population had a sustainable lifeway—as long as there was no drastic environmental change.[10] Drawing on several lines of environmental evidence, including tree rings and oxygen-isotope measurements on the annual carbonate deposits of speleothems (stalagmites), archaeologists have converged on a tentative explanation. It seems that the late ninth century was beset by a series of harsh and persistent droughts that must have caused devastating famines, leading to death and emigration. The droughts also convinced commoners that the kings' rituals to bring rain were ineffective.[11] Loss of faith in rulers and in their water- and fertility-obsessed religion led to strife and hastened the exodus to dispersed villages. These days, Tikal is a national park and major tourist attraction.

FIGURE 42.2. Partial view of Mohenjo–Daro, Pakistan; reconstruction is visible on the tops of some walls (Wikimedia Commons; Usman Ghani, photographer).

While Tikal was a low-density city spread over a huge cultural landscape, Mohenjo–Daro was much smaller and more compact at around about 3 km².[12] Located on the floodplain of the Indus River, Mohenjo–Daro is one of the largest sites of the Harappan culture, whose village-farming and herding roots reach back to about 7000 BC.[13] The Harappan culture occupied a huge region on the floodplains of the Indus and Sarasvati Rivers that included parts of present-day India and Pakistan.

Mohenjo–Daro, in modern Pakistan, was repeatedly flooded and covered with Indus River sediments. New construction built on the old, forming a tell consisting of several separate mounds, with the earliest occupations inaccessible below the present-day water table. Some mounds have a wall and gate that archaeologist Jonathan M. Kenoyer suggests kept out raiders and regulated the coming and going of traders. There is no evidence of warfare.[14]

Several major excavations have taken place since Mohenjo–Daro's discovery in 1922. Early projects removed massive amounts of sediment to expose thick-walled buildings of mud bricks and fired mud bricks (Figure 42.2). Uniformity of bricks in *several* standard sizes and similarities in construction techniques suggest that the city's brick makers and masons were specialists. One of the earliest cities in the world built according to a plan,

Mohenjo–Daro was laid out in a north-south rectangular grid with rows of structures opening onto streets.[15] The last urban occupation at Mohenjo–Daro dates from about 2600 to 1900 BC and is known as the Mature Harappan; after this time, Harappan urban life ended.

In contrast to Tikal, Mohenjo–Daro's subsistence base was readily inferred, but the functions of some structures and the nature of leadership remain puzzles.

Subsistence depended on domesticated plants and animals, including barley, wheat, lentils, peas, various vegetables, water buffalo, cattle, sheep, and goats. Mohenjo–Daro's residents also hunted and fished. The proportion of food obtained locally versus trade with nearby small towns and villages is unknown.[16]

Most houses consisted of several rooms and a courtyard, and some had a second story or roof patio. A few houses were much larger than others, most likely elite residences, possibly palaces. There are two architectural oddities: a single structure with 156 rooms, sometimes referred to as the "college," and a huge, one-room building known as the "Great Hall," the latter interpreted by some as a granary or warehouse.[17] Archaeologists don't know whether these structures served religious, political, or commercial functions.

Mohenjo–Daro had plenty of water, easily reached from the shallow water table through elegant brick-lined wells. Abundant wells served domestic needs, and houses even included bathing platforms and toilets. Ceramic pipes conveyed wastewater to the public sewer, which ran in covered channels through the streets and emptied outside the city. There was also a large structure known as the "great bath" because its walls were lined with asphaltum; the floors were almost impermeable, and it had a drain. Apparently, residents were fastidious. In fact, the Mohenjo–Daro water supply and sewer system were marvels of civil engineering unequaled in Western countries until the late nineteenth century.[18]

Clues to a city's social and political organization often come from tombs and cemeteries, but none have been found at Mohenjo–Daro. Relevant information may eventually be gleaned from the Harappan writing system, which consists of at least 400 different symbols, many found on seals used to stamp clay and seal containers and storerooms. Symbols were also inscribed on ornaments, bone tools, and other artifacts. While the writing system has resisted decipherment, researchers infer commercial functions for the seals. Kenoyer suggests that animal motifs that sometimes accompany inscriptions may "represent powerful clans or officials who controlled trade and political organization." Perhaps a city-state, Mohenjo–Daro may have been ruled not by a monarch but by "groups of competing elites, such as landowners, merchants and ritual specialists."[19] In any event, the city plan and extensive public works indicate that Mohenjo–Daro had effective leadership.

Exchange activities were important in the city's life, enabled by standardized stone weights. Mohenjo–Daro-made products were widely traded and included artifacts of copper (and possibly other metals), shell, stone beads, and ceramic and steatite seals, all made by specialists.[20] Potters had the fast wheel and fashioned a variety of handsome vessels. For transporting products within and beyond the city, traders used two-wheel oxcarts and perhaps pack animals; for coastal and riverine trade, Harappans used boats.[21]

Although Mohenjo–Daro and contemporary Harappan cities were abandoned around 1900 BC, the people continued living in more than a thousand small villages with an agrarian lifeway. There are many scenarios to explain the complete de-urbanization of Harappan culture. These include catastrophic flooding, the Indus River changing course, the Sarasvati River drying up, and climate change, but none is widely accepted.[22] Perhaps, Kenoyer suggests, an environmental disaster "led to the disruption of agriculture and the eventual breakdown of trade and political networks."[23]

People in early cities like Tikal and Mohenjo–Daro developed dams, reservoirs, sewage systems, wells, masonry, metallurgy, and other technologies that would become foundations of modern urban life. With sufficient multidisciplinary efforts these developments can be understood, which helps archaeologists—and popularizers of our research—to link the past and present. Understanding the growth and abandonment of ancient cities along with details of ethnicity, economy, religion, environmental impacts, and social and political organization presents puzzles that keep archaeologists digging despite the difficulties.

Notes

Preface

1. Several other books have also taken this tack (e.g., Feder 1999; Little 2002; Sabloff 2008).

Introduction

1. Squier and Davis 1848.
2. I count the U.S. National Museum and the Bureau of American Ethnology as parts of the Smithsonian (Schiffer 2009).
3. http://www.encyclopediavirginia.org/Jefferson_s_Mound_Archaeological_Site, accessed 23 April 2015.
4. On the Wrights and the Maya Revival Style, see Braun (1993).
5. http://en.wikipedia.org/wiki/Pyramid_power, accessed 10 April 2015.
6. Go to "Stonehenge art" in Google images.
7. Braun 1993.
8. http://en.wikipedia.org/wiki/Michael_Crichton, accessed 27 May 2015.
9. Schablitsky 2007.
10. http://en.wikipedia.org/wiki/Indiana_Jones_%28franchise%29, accessed 10 April 2015.

Chapter 1

1. Silverberg (1968) reviews the mound builder controversy.
2. Powell 1894:XL.
3. Powell 1894:XLI.
4. Squier and Davis 1848:301.
5. Powell 1894:XLIV.
6. Thomas 1894:688.
7. See also Thomas (1885:65).
8. Powell 1894:XLVIII.
9. Willey and Sabloff 1993.

Chapter 2

1. DeCosta 1890.
2. Morison 1971:37.

3. Rafn 1838.
4. Bancroft 1879:6.
5. Marie Brown 1887; DeCosta 1890; Horsford 1892; Hovgaard 1914.
6. Anne Stine Ingstad 1977, 2001; Kay 2012
7. The experts: William E. Taylor Jr., National Museum of Canada; Henry B. Collins, Smithsonian Institution; Junius Bird, American Museum of Natural History.
8. Helge Ingstad 1964:712.
9. Helge Ingstad 1964:708.
10. Wallace (2005) and Kay (2012) synthesize the archaeological evidence.
11. Nydal 1989.
12. McGhee 1984:4
13. Wallace 1990:166; see also Hovgaard 1914:xv.

Chapter 3

1. Garfinkel et al. 2012.
2. Levy, Najjar, and Higham 2010.
3. Ben-Yosef et al. 2010; Levy, Najjar, and Ben-Yosef 2014.
4. Levy, Ben-Yosef, and Najjar 2012.
5. Hauptmann 2007.
6. Levy et al. 2004, Levy, Najjar, and Ben-Yosef 2014.
7. Levy et al. 2004.
8. Levy et al. 2008.
9. Levy et al. 2004; Levy et al. 2005; Levy, Najjar, and Higham 2010.
10. For example, Fantalkin, Finkelstein, and Piasetzky 2011; Finkelstein and Singer-Avitz 2009.
11. For example, Friedman et al. 2008.

Chapter 4

1. Nathan Richards 2008.
2. Chaffin 2008:170–72.
3. www.NUMA.net, accessed 9 June 2014.
4. Conlin and Russell 2006, 2010.
5. Hicks and Kropf 2002 (245–46) discount some explanations.
6. Information in this and the following two paragraphs comes from http://www.nps .gov/archeology/cg/sum_fa_2001/hunley.htm, accessed 9 June 2014 and http:// www.hunley.org/main_index.asp?CONTENT=LAB, accessed 11 June 2014.
7. Mardikian 2004.
8. Chaffin 2008:233–34; Jacobsen 2005:14–15.
9. Hicks and Kropf 2002:249.
10. Jacobsen, Blouin, and Shirley 2012.
11. Chaffin 2008:234; Jacobsen 2005:15.
12. Jacobsen 2005:8–9.

13. Jacobsen 2005:13.
14. Ragan 1995:182.
15. Hicks and Kropf 2002:247–48.
16. Chaffin 2008:250–51.
17. Eric Powell 2013:47.

Chapter 5

1. Hume 1964:216.
2. Barka, Ayres, and Sheridan 1984:8.
3. Some sources state 1956.
4. Watkins and Hume 1967:91.
5. Barka 1973.
6. Barka, Ayres, and Sheridan 1984:270–71.
7. Barka, Ayres, and Sheridan 1984:3.
8. Gooch, quoted in Barka, Ayres, and Sheridan 1984:5.
9. Barka, Ayres, and Sheridan 1984:11.
10. Barka, Ayres, and Sheridan 1984:48.
11. Barka, Ayres, and Sheridan 1984:27.
12. McCartney and Ayres 2004.
13. McCartney and Ayres 2004.
14. Barka, Ayres, and Sheridan 1984:92. My estimate of this quantity of vessels is based on valuations of pottery in the probate inventory of Rogers's estate.
15. Barka, Ayres, and Sheridan 1984:176.
16. Barka, Ayres, and Sheridan 1984:96.
17. Barka, Ayres, and Sheridan 1984:144.
18. Watkins and Hume 1967:83.
19. Hume, in Watkins and Hume 1967.
20. Barka 1973; Barka, Ayres, and Sheridan 1984.
21. Barka, Ayres, and Sheridan 1984:280.
22. Barka, Ayres, and Sheridan 1984:564.
23. Barka (2004) has color illustrations of the pottery and kilns.

Chapter 6

1. http://www.wsmr.army.mil/PAO/Trinity/Pages/default.aspx, accessed 5 March 2015.
2. On the archaeology of the Trinity site: Duran and Morgan (1995), Merlan (1997), and Slater (1996).
3. Delgado, Lenihan, and Murphy (1991) did an archaeological survey and assessment of these ships.
4. Beck 2002:65.
5. Beck 2001, 2002:75; William Johnson 2002a.
6. Jones, Bullard, and Beck 2006:1–2.

7. Beck 2002:69.
8. Beck 2001.
9. William Johnson 2002b.
10. General information on Project Rover comes from Dewar (2004).
11. Bussard and DeLauer 1958:1–3.
12. I have left out several other projects (see Dewar 2004).
13. Quotes in this paragraph are from Drollinger, Goldenberg, and Beck (2000b:7).
14. For a video of the demolition of R-MAD, see http://www.youtube.com/watch?v=xvC1rc3Sd4M, accessed 24 June 2015.
15. Beck et al. 1996.
16. Drollinger, Goldenberg, and Beck 2000b:14.
17. Drollinger, Goldenberg, and Beck 2000a.
18. Spence 1968.
19. Dewar 2004.
20. McAvennie (2004) investigated the supposed crash site.

Part 3
1. Harrison 2009, 2013.

Chapter 7
1. Page 1910.
2. Page 1910:24.
3. Grabitske 2003–04.
4. Information on the history of archaeology at Mount Vernon comes from Pogue 2006.
5. Pogue 2006:171.
6. Bessey and Pogue 2006.
7. Pogue (2004, 2011) furnishes information about the history of the distillery.
8. Pogue 2011:11; White 2004.
9. The historical materials—manuals and Washington's records—are discussed by Breen 2004.
10. Breen 2004.
11. Pogue 2011:200.
12. Christensen 2004.
13. Breen (2004), Breen and White (2006), and Pogue (2011:126–34) describe the excavations.
14. Breen and White 2006:216–17.
15. White 2004.
16. Pogue 2011:190.
17. Pogue 2011:204–05.
18. Pogue 2011:201–09.

19. http://www.mountvernon.org/the-estate-gardens/distillery/george-washing
tons-rye-whiskey-and-straight-rye-whiskey/?utm_source=Mount+Vernon&utm
_campaign=9a525ac7ad-DecWhiskeySale_Dec2014&utm_medium=email&utm
_term=0_0a9fb91d40-9a525ac7ad-231858653, accessed 2 December 2014.
20. http://www.deathandtaxesmag.com/196185/george-washingtons-95-whiskey
-might-taste-like-crap/, accessed 29 March 2014; http://www.drinkupny.com
/Hillrock_Estate_Distillery_George_Washington_Rye_p/s1384.htm, accessed
29 March 2014.

Chapter 8
Unless otherwise noted, information in this chapter comes from Bank of Cyprus
Cultural Foundation 1987; Costello 2011; Soren 1985; and Soren and James 1988.
1. Costello 2011:47
2. Soren and James 1988:76.
3. Soren and James 1988:85.
4. Soren and James 1988:78.
5. Costello 2011.
6. This information is from my field diary; see also Soren and James (1988:115).
7. Soren and James 1988, after page 82.
8. David Soren (personal communication, February 2014) told me about the post-
excavation life history of Room 8. Kourion Museum at Episkopi: http://www
.mcw.gov.cy/mcw/DA/DA.nsf/All/21E14D80F55D8539C22571990020DC5C
?OpenDocument, accessed 3 March 2014.
9. Costello (2011:38) mentions the alternate dating.
10. http://www.visitcyprus.com/wps/portal, accessed 25 February 2014.
11. Bryant and Shales 2010.

Chapter 9
1. de Valbourg 1719:282.
2. Johnson and Manget 1783.
3. Samuel Clemens to Olivia L. Clemens, 25 December 1873. http://www.mark
twainproject.org/, accessed 13 February 2014.
4. Sprules 1884.
5. Richards 2011:3.
6. Schlanger (1992:97) defines "persistent place."
7. Unless otherwise noted, this drastically simplified sketch of Stonehenge's life
history is based on Darvill (2005, 2010) and Richards (2011). Other useful works
include Bender (1998), Chippindale (2012), and Souden (1997).
8. Richards and Whitby 1997.
9. D. Jones 2008.
10. Pearson and the Stonehenge Riverside Project 2011.

11. Baxter and Chippindale 2002:151.
12. Mason and Kuo 2008. Mason and Kuo 2008.
13. Baxter and Chippindale 2002, 2005.
14. Atkinson 1987.
15. Richards 2011. http://www.english-heritage.org.uk/publications/stonehenge -teachers-kit/, accessed 19 February 2014.
16. Stone and Feather 2005.
17. http://www.english-heritage.org.uk/daysout/properties/stonehenge/, accessed 19 February 2014.
18. Darvill 2005.
19. Young, Chadburn, and Bedu 2009.

Chapter 10

1. Brown and Cooper 1990:8.
2. Fairbanks 1974; Ascher and Fairbanks 1971.
3. Orser (1990) and Singleton (1995) synthesize the first generation of studies on the archaeology of plantation slavery; see also Leland Ferguson (1992).
4. Brown and Cooper 1990:10.
5. Brown and Cooper 1990.
6. McDavid 1997.
7. Kenneth Brown reports that the abandonment date is now believed to be "1887 or very early 1888" (personal communication, 19 December 2014).
8. Brown and Cooper (1990) discuss the formation processes of the cabins.
9. Brown and Cooper 1990:16.
10. Brown and Cooper 1990:16–17.
11. Brown and Cooper 1990:17. Kenneth Brown (1994, 2004, 2011) discusses other artifacts employed in ritual activities and their connections to West Africa.
12. McDavid 1997:114.
13. McDavid 1997:115.
14. McDavid 1997:117.
15. McDavid 1997:120.
16. McDavid 1997:123.
17. McDavid 1997:124.
18. McDavid 1997:124.
19. McDavid 1997:128, emphasis mine.
20. McDavid 2011.
21. http://www.visitlevijordanplantation.com/index.aspx?page=12, accessed 22 June 2015.
22. http://www.webarchaeology.com/html/Default.htm3, accessed 3 December 2014.
23. McDavid 2000:230, 2002:304, 2011.
24. Demographic data support this (Brown 1994).
25. http://www.webarchaeology.com/html/abandonm.htm, accessed 3 December 2014.

26. Carol McDavid also created a website aimed at archaeologists: http://intarch.ac
.uk/journal/issue6/mcdavid/toc.html, accessed 3 December 2014.

Chapter 11

1. Background information on the site and excavations: Samuels and Daugherty
(1991), Daugherty (1988), Daugherty and Kirk (1976), and https://content.lib
.washington.edu/cmpweb/exhibits/makah/arch.html, accessed 12 Nov 2014.
2. Quotes: Bowechop and Erikson 2005:266.
3. Daugherty and Kirk 1976:73; see also Ames (2006).
4. Daugherty and Kirk 1976:73; quote on p. 74.
5. Ledford 1993.
6. Archambault (1993); Fuller and Fabricius (1992).
7. Patricia Erikson 2005:276.
8. Ledford 1993.
9. Samuels and Daugherty 1991.
10. Huelsbeck 1988; Sepez 2008.
11. J. Friedman 1975.
12. Croes 1977:iv.
13. Mauger 1991.
14. Samuels and Daugherty 1991:21.
15. Archambault 1993:13.
16. Bowechop and Erikson 2005:264.
17. Quote: www.Makahmuseum.com, accessed 14 November 2014; see also Renker
and Arnold (1988) and Erikson, Ward, and Wachendorf (2002).
18. Archambault 1993:13.
19. Arnold, quoted in R. Friedman (1995:18), emphasis mine; see also Renker and
Arnold (1988).

Chapter 12

1. Field 1940; Shaw 1960.
2. Ebighgbo (2001) is an ethnographic example from Nigeria.
3. Field 1940:6.
4. Shepherd 2002.
5. Ogundiran 2005.
6. MacDonald 2013.
7. Shaw 1960, 1967.
8. Shaw 1960:164.
9. Shaw 1960:165, 1967:72.
10. Shaw 1960:165.
11. Shaw 1970.
12. Lawal 1973; Posnansky (1973) was also critical of the dating.
13. Shaw 1975.
14. McIntosh and McIntosh 1988.

15. The quotes: Craddock et al. 1997:405, 426; see also Chikwendu et al. 1989.

16. Information in this paragraph comes from MacDonald (2013), McIntosh (2013), Pamela Jane Smith (2014), and Pamela Jane Smith, personal communication, 1 December 2014.

17. The book: Shaw 1977; quote: Alexander 1978:145.

18. McIntosh 2013.

19. Quote: McIntosh 2013, see also MacDonald 2013.

20. A video on the proceedings: https://www.youtube.com/watch?v=gvRwiUVh FsM&feature=youtu.be, accessed 11 November 2014.

21. http://www.mcdonald.cam.ac.uk/events/Memorial-service, accessed 2 November 2014.

22. https://groups.google.com/forum/#!topic/wief/lXoQNZozO-o, accessed 7 November 2014.

Chapter 13

1. Background information comes from Ludlow Collective (2001), McGuire and Larkin (2009), McGuire and Reckner (2002, 2003), McGuire (2008:188–221), and Saitta (2007). Saitta (2005) details the strike's background.

2. See also Atalay et al. (2012) and Stottman (2011).

3. Larkin and McGuire 2009:xv.

4. McGuire and Larkin 2009:17.

5. McGuire and Reckner 2002.

6. McGuire 2004.

7. McGuire 2004.

8. McGuire and Larkin 2009:5, 14–16.

9. McGuire and Larkin 2009:4.

10. Saitta 2005:379.

11. The preceding three paragraphs condense and paraphrase McGuire and Larkin (2009:18–20); see also Saitta 2005.

Chapter 14

1. Zimmerman and Welch 2006.

2. Albertson 2009.

3. Zimmerman, Singleton, and Welch 2010:446.

4. This discussion is liberally paraphrased from Zimmerman, Singleton, and Welch 2010:447.

5. Zimmerman and Welch 2011:81.

6. Zimmerman, Singleton, and Welch 2010:449–51.

7. Valado 2006:11.

8. Valado 2006:278-82.

9. Valado and Amster 2012; this book has a massive bibliography of research on homelessness. On ethical issues, see also Kiddey and Schofield 2011.

10. Zimmerman, Singleton, and Welch 2010:444.

11. Zimmerman, Singleton, and Welch 2010:444.
12. Zimmerman, Singleton, and Welch 2010:446, 447; Zimmerman and Welch 2011:81–82.
13. Zimmerman 2013.
14. Albertson 2009.
15. Zimmerman and Welch 2006, 2011.
16. Zimmerman 2013:348.
17. Zimmerman, Singleton, and Welch 2010:453.
18. Kiddey and Schofield 2011:19.
19. Kiddey and Schofield 2011:19. This project is documented in several YouTube videos.
20. Kiddey 2014.

Chapter 15

1. For examples of conventional explanations, see Basalla (1988:200), Flink (1970:240), Scharff (1991:44), Volti (1990:44).
2. An introduction to behavioral archaeology is Schiffer (2010).
3. Kimes and Clark 1989.
4. On varieties of the performance matrix, see Schiffer (2011).
5. Schiffer, Butts, and Grimm 1994.
6. E.g., Hugill 1996.
7. Kirsch 2000; Mom 2004.
8. Schiffer 1995.
9. Schiffer 2000a.
10. Schiffer 2000b.
11. http://www.worldcat.org/title/taking-charge-the-electric-automobile-in-amer ica/oclc/29598437&referer=brief_results, accessed 26 January 2014.

Chapter 16

1. Weber and Wahl 2006.
2. Crabtree 1968.
3. Crabtree 1968:472.
4. On the two Crabtree surgeries: Schwartz (1981). Quote from Buck 1982:268.
5. *Washington Post* 1981, C-13.
6. Scott and Scott 1982:1051–52.
7. http://newsletter.wsu.edu/chronicle/07may/daugherty.html, accessed 24 June 2015.
8. Buck 1982:269.
9. Disa, Vossoughi, and Goldberg 1993:887.
10. Washington Post 1981, C-13; Schwartz 1981.
11. McIlrath 1984.
12. Brochure in "Ray Harwood's Journal," http://monache.blogspot.com/2010/05 /aztecnics-alternative-edge.html, accessed 30 October 2013.

13. Errett Callahan (personal communication, 26 October 2013) confirmed that the major market, especially for knives, is collectors. He also mentioned the sale of blades to Green.
14. Information about this project comes from J. Jeffrey Flenniken, personal communication, 23 October 2013.
15. According to McIlrath (1984:30), "An FDA spokesman said that 'until and unless there begin to be reports of adverse reactions, the only requirement the blade manufacturers would need to meet is registration and compliance with good manufacturing practice regulations.'" But who would determine the "good" practices?
16. Sheets 1993.
17. Information in this paragraph comes from Payson D. Sheets, personal communications, 13–14 October 2013.
18. http://www.fluther.com/13416/whats-the-deal-with-obsidian-scalpels/, accessed 1 November 2013.
19. http://www.finescience.com/Special-Pages/Product-Search.aspx?searchtext=obsidian%20scalpels, accessed 30 October 2013.

Chapter 17
1. Bandy 2005:271.
2. Erickson 1998:34.
3. Erickson 1998: 38; contributors in Minnis (2014) discuss possibilities for cultivating ancient and extinct crops.
4. Swartley 2000:159.
5. Janusek and Kolata 2004:419.
6. Janusek and Kolata 2004:420–21.
7. These findings come from Erickson (1998:34) and Janusek and Kolata (2004:409).
8. On crop rotation and fallowing, Swartley 2000:161–62.
9. Bandy 2005:274.
10. On the outside funders, Swartley 2000:126.
11. Swartley 2000:4–5, 126.
12. Erickson 1998:39.
13. Bandy 2005:274.
14. Swartley (2000) made many of these points in fleshing out the context of the raised-field projects.
15. Schumacher 1973.
16. Peru: Erickson 1998:39; Bolivia: Swartley 2000:130.
17. Erickson 1998:40; Swartley 2000:22.
18. Swartley 2000:5.
19. Swartley 2000:iii.
20. Bandy 2005:274.
21. Swartley 2000:29, 159, 178.

22. Swartley 2000:178–79.
23. Swartley 2000:124–26.
24. Bandy 2005.
25. Boserup 1974; Bandy 2005.
26. Swartley 2000:155–56.
27. Renard et al. 2012.

Chapter 18

1. Hough 1932.
2. Fewkes 1898:650–51; much of the Nampeyo story comes from Frisbie (1973) and Kramer (1996).
3. Traugott (1999:11) calls attention to the role of the Old Cuñopavi vessels in Nampeyo's development.
4. Wyckoff 1983.
5. Traugott 1999.
6. Wade 1988.
7. Information on Maria comes from Spivey (2003), Peterson (1989), and Gridley (1974:105–18).
8. Woodbury 1994.
9. Clemmer 2008.
10. Edelman 1979:312.
11. Brody 1979:605–06.
12. Peterson 1984.
13. Zega 2001.
14. Jacobs 1998; Mullin 1992.
15. Edelman 1979.

Chapter 19

1. Thomas King 2013 is a guide to federal CRM laws.
2. The term "cultural resources" takes in more than archaeological sites and artifacts, but here I deal only with archaeological resources.
3. Hardesty and Little (2009) provide guidance on assessing significance.
4. The term "environmental impact statement" became "environmental statement" and now "environmental assessment." I use the original term.
5. Schiffer and Gumerman (1977) is a guide for applying NEPA to archaeological resources.
6. Schiffer 1979.
7. McGimsey and Davis (1977) discuss the major kinds of CRM projects and the corresponding reports.
8. McGuire and Schiffer 1982.
9. Schiffer and Wells 1982.
10. Cheryl Blanchard, personal communication, 7 May 2014.

11. https://www.dodlegacy.org/legacy/index.aspx, accessed 10 May 2014.
12. Eidenbach et al. 1996.
13. Eidenbach et al. 1996:1
14. Eidenbach et al. 1996:137–44
15. Enscore 1998:25.

Chapter 20
1. Trigger 1984.
2. An important exception—and there were others—was Indian land-claim cases.
3. Tribal Historic Preservation Officers were authorized by a 1992 amendment to the National Historic Preservation Act.
4. For example, Powell, Garza, and Hendricks 1993.
5. Watkins 2005.
6. Stapp and Burney 2002:4.
7. For histories of the Seminoles, see e.g., Covington (1993) and Sturtevant (1971).
8. Cypress 1997.
9. James E. Billie, quoted in Cypress 1997:159.
10. Cypress 1997:157.
11. http://www.stofthpo.com/Tribal-Archaeology-Seminole-Tribe-FL-Tribal-Historic-Preservation-Office.html, accessed 24 May 2014.
12. Maureen Mahoney, Seminole Tribal Archaeologist, personal communication, 21 May 2014.
13. http://www.stofthpo.com/Archaeometry-Seminole-Tribe-FL-Tribal-Historic-Preservation-Office.html, accessed 24 May 2014.
14. http://www.stofthpo.com/Architectural-History-Seminole-Tribe-FL-Tribal-Historic-Preservation-Office.html, accessed 26 May, 2014. Some information in this paragraph comes from Seminole Tribe 2013.
15. Information in this paragraph comes from Department of the Interior 2008, Section 7.
16. Department of the Interior 2008, Section 8, p. 5.
17. Academic studies of Seminole archaeology include Bell (2004), Robert S. Carr (2012), and Weisman (2007, 2012).
18. Paul Backhouse, personal communication, 27 May 2014.

Chapter 21
1. Cressey and Anderson 2006:9–12.
2. Cressey and Anderson 2006:14.
3. http://alexandriava.gov/historic/archaeology/default.aspx?id=28168, accessed 15 April 2014.
4. http://alexandriava.gov/historic/archaeology/default.aspx?id=28146, accessed 16 April 2014.
5. http://alexandriava.gov/historic/archaeology/default.aspx?id=46284, accessed 16 April 2014.

6. Cressey and Vinton 2007:395; Cressey 2005; Cressey, Reeder, and Bryson 2003; Appler 2012.
7. http://alexandriava.gov/historic/archaeology/default.aspx?id=33900, accessed 30 April 2014.
8. Cressey 2002.
9. Cressey et al. 1982.
10. Cressey 1993.
11. Cressey and Vinton 2007:404–09.
12. http://alexandriava.gov/FreedmenMemorial, accessed 3 May 2014.
13. On St. Augustine: Appler 2013.

Chapter 22

1. Pinkoski 2008.
2. U.S. Government 1980. Unless otherwise noted, this source provided information about the commission's founding and operations. The National Indian Law Library has links to original source material on these cases: http://www.narf.org/nill/resources/icc.htm, accessed 24 August 2014.
3. U.S. Government 1980:10.
4. Paraphrased from U.S. Government 1980:10.
5. Zedeño, Austin, and Stoffle 1997.
6. Ray 2006.
7. According to Ray (2006:257), Kroeber introduced the term tribelet.
8. Kroeber 1925.
9. This immensely complex case (see, e.g., Shipek 1989) has been simplified here.
10. Heizer and Kroeber 1976:40.
11. Ray 2006:260–61.
12. Ray 2006:266–67.
13. Heizer and Kroeber 1976:41.
14. Heizer and Kroeber 1976:42.
15. Heizer and Kroeber 1976:44.
16. Heizer and Kroeber 1976:47–48.
17. Heizer and Kroeber 1976:48.
18. Heizer and Kroeber 1976:48–49.
19. Heizer and Kroeber 1976:50.
20. Heizer and Kroeber 1976:51.
21. Heizer and Kroeber 1976:39–40.
22. Beals 1985; see also Ray 2006.
23. Quotes are from Beals 1985:147.
24. Ferguson 2014:247.
25. Beals 1985. The federal attorney, Ralph A. Barney (1955), even published an article in *Ethnohistory*, encouraging anthropologists to become involved in the commission's proceedings.
26. Ray 2006.

27. Harkin 2010.
28. U.S. Government 1980:21.
29. Sutton 1985.
30. Ray 2006:272; Heizer and Kroeber 1976.
31. U.S. Government 1980:21.

Chapter 23

1. Robert F. Carr and Case 2005; Seeman 1979.
2. http://www.j-and-dee-artifacts.com/woodland_period.htm, accessed 11 August 2014.
3. 16 U.S.C. 470ee(c).
4. Tomak 1994:5.
5. Munson, Jones, and Fry 1995:136.
6. Tomak 1994.
7. Mackey 2006:50.
8. All known GE Mound artifacts were analyzed and reported by Tomak (1994). A later analysis of GE Mound materials is Seeman (1995).
9. Munson, Jones, and Fry 1995:137.
10. McAllister and McManamon 2007.
11. Munson, Jones, and Fry 1995:150.
12. Munson, Jones, and Fry 1995:148–51.
13. See, for example, Fisher (2013). Munson, Jones, and Fry (1995) detail the pushback from collectors and looters; quote is from p. 145.
14. Mackey 2006:54.
15. Seeman 1995.

Chapter 24

1. Quotes from Brodie and Renfrew (2005:346).
2. Coggins 1972.
3. http://portal.unesco.org/en/ev.php-URL_ID=13039&URL_DO=DO_TOPIC &URL_SECTION=201.html, accessed 4 September 2014.
4. http://en.wikipedia.org/wiki/List_of_national_museums, accessed 7 September 2014.
5. 19 U.S.C. 2601, amended 1987.
6. 19 U.S.C. 2605.
7. http://eca.state.gov/cultural-heritage-center/cultural-property-protection/bilateral-agreements, accessed 6 September 2014.
8. http://eca.state.gov/cultural-heritage-center/cultural-property-protection/process-and-purpose/cultural-property-advisory, accessed 4 September 2014.
9. Gerstenblith interviewed by Rachel Metea, https://www.youtube.com/watch?v=yX5vKIDomm4, accessed 6 September 2014.
10. See Gerstenblith 2012.

11. Brodie and Renfrew 2005:346.
12. http://eca.state.gov/files/bureau/bzmou2013.pdf, accessed 6 September 2014.
13. http://www.cbp.gov/about/labs-scientific-svcs/org-operations, accessed 7 September 2014.
14. http://www.ice.gov/news/releases/0902/090211laredo.htm, accessed 7 September 2014.
15. http://illicitculturalproperty.com/tag/ebay/, accessed 7 September 2014.
16. 18 U.S.C. 2314 and 2315.
17. Gerstenblith 2002.
18. Gerstenblith 2002; see also Lufkin 2002.
19. http://caselaw.findlaw.com/us-2nd-circuit/1456261.html, accessed 4 September 2014. See also Lufkin 2003.
20. Brodie 2006.
21. Luke and Kersel 2012:81.
22. Brodie and Renfrew 2005.

Chapter 25

1. Morse, Crusoe, and Smith 1976.
2. Powers and Sibun 2013; Sigler-Eisenberg 1985.
3. Morse, Crusoe, and Smith 1976.
4. Bass and Birkby 1978.
5. Dupras et al. 2011; Hunter and Cox 2005; Hunter, Roberts, and Martin 1996; Hunter, Simpson, and Colls 2013; Morse, Duncan, and Stoutamire 1984.
6. Killam 2004:7.
7. Ubelaker and Hunt 1995.
8. http://archive.wbir.com/news/local/10news_at_five/article/139066/173/Your-Stories-Dr-Bill-Bass, accessed 25 November 2013.
9. Hunter (1994) is an early review article on forensic archaeology in Britain.
10. This case is liberally paraphrased from Hunter and Cox (2005:121–22).

Chapter 26

1. This chapter draws heavily on Wright, Hanson, and Sterenberg 2005.
2. Haglund, Connor, and Scott 2001; Schmitt 2002.
3. Wright, Hanson, and Sterenberg 2005:157.
4. Fraser 2011:51–54.
5. Bevan 1994:56.
6. Bevan 1994:53.
7. Bevan 1994:54.
8. Wright 1995.
9. Wright 1995:41.
10. Wright, Hanson, and Sterenberg 2005:146.
11. Bevan 1994:59.

12. Wright 1995:42.
13. Fraser 2011.
14. Fraser 2011:133.
15. Fraser 2011:304.
16. Stover and Ryan 2001.
17. http://www.sydneyjewishmuseum.com.au/Exhibitions/Permanent-Exhibtions/default.aspx, accessed 12 December 2013.

Chapter 27
1. Hoshower 1998.
2. http://www.jpac.pacom.mil/index.php?page=mission_overview&size=100&ind=0, accessed 30 November 2013.
3. http://www.marchfield.org/rf4c.htm, accessed 1 December 2013.
4. JPAC n.d.a.
5. JPAC n.d.b.

Chapter 28
1. Rathje and Murphy 1992:20.
2. Rathje and Murphy 1992:11.
3. Rathje 1974.
4. Rathje 1984:12.
5. Rathje 1984:10.
6. Rathje and Murphy 1992:63.
7. Rathje and Murphy 1992:60.
8. Rathje and Murphy 1992:62.
9. Rathje and Murphy 1992:66.
10. Rathje and Murphy 1992:67.
11. Rathje and Murphy 1992:70–71; quote on p. 70.
12. Rathje et al. 1992:439.
13. Rathje et al. 1992:442.
14. Zimring 2012.

Chapter 29
1. Cultural anthropologists also employed participant observation, but mainly in traditional, small-scale societies.
2. On the "material-culture turn," see Hicks (2010).
3. The first archaeological book on "modern" material culture was Gould and Schiffer (1981).
4. Wilk and Cliggett (2007) is his most well known book.
5. Miller 2010.
6. Miller (1985) is based on his archaeological doctoral dissertation.

7. Daniel Miller 2010:1.

8. Hicks and Beaudry 2010.

9. Examples include Buchli and Lucas (2001); Gould (2007); Gould and Schiffer (1981), Graves-Brown (2000); Harrison and Schofield (2010); Hodder 2012; Olsen (2010), Schiffer (2011, 2013); Schiffer and Miller (1999); Skibo and Schiffer (2008).

10. Graves-Brown, Harrison, and Piccini 2013.

11. Daniel Miller 1985; Schiffer and Miller 1999.

12. Dant 1999:2.

13. Dant 1999:2.

14. Arnold et al. 2012:12.

15. Arnold et al. 2012.

16. Arnold et al. 2012:3.

17. Arnold et al. 2012:6.

18. Arnold et al. 2012:3.

19. Quotes in this paragraph and in the themes come from Arnold et al. (2012:14–16).

20. Artifact design: Schiffer (2011, chapter 8); Skibo and Schiffer (2008); Homelessness: Zimmerman and Welch (2011); Burning Man Festival: Carolyn White (2013).

Chapter 30

1. De León 2012:480.

2. De León 2012:478.

3. De León 2012:478; Gokee and De León 2014.

4. De León 2012:482.

5. Data in De León 2012:486, 488.

6. Raul, quoted in De León 2012:486.

7. Images of shoes: De León 2012:491, 2013:333.

8. Both quotes in this paragraph: De León 2012:489.

9. De León 2013:492.

10. De León 2012:341.

Chapter 31

1. Merwin 1931.

2. Gettens 1962.

3. Bishop and Lange 1991.

4. Shepard, quoted in Gettens (1962:558).

5. Gettens 1962. In early publications, the clay is called attapulgite.

6. Quotes from Gettens (1962), pp. 561–62 (emphasis mine).

7. Shepard 1962:565.

8. van Olphen 1966:645.

9. van Olphen 1966:645.

10. Littman 1980.

11. Littmann 1982:405.

12. Chiari, Giustetto, and Ricchiardi 2003:21.

13. Chiari, Giustetto, and Ricchiardi 2003:22.

14. Reinen, Köhl, and Müller 2004.

15. Doménech et al. 2009:2371.

Chapter 32

1. Seaborg 1981.

2. Libby 1946.

3. Marlowe 1980.

4. E. C. Anderson et al. 1947:577.

5. Marlowe 1980.

6. Personal communication, Mark Mahoney, Wenner–Gren Foundation, 17 June 2014.

7. Marlowe 1980, 1999.

8. Libby, Anderson, and Arnold 1949.

9. Engelkemeir et al. 1949. Curiously, this half-life is closer to the modern value (5730) than the one chosen by convention for calculating raw radiocarbon dates (5568).

10. Libby 1955:v.

11. Arnold and Libby 1949. Were these dates cherry-picked from several runs of the same specimen?

12. Frederick Johnson 1951a; Libby (1952, 1955) also published lists of dates, and this became standard practice among the dozens of radiocarbon laboratories founded during the 1950s and 1960s.

13. Among the contributors were Frank H. H. Roberts, Jr., Robert F. Heizer, James B. Griffin, William A. Ritchie, Robert J. Braidwood, Hallam L. Movius Jr., and 11 others (Johnson 1951a).

14. Frederick Johnson et al. 1951:59.

15. Frederick Johnson et al. 1951:62.

16. Frederick Johnson (1951b:3) mentions retracted dates.

17. H. S. Smith 1964.

18. Edwards 1970.

19. E.g., Suess 1961.

20. Bucha and Neustupny 1967; Stuiver and Suess 1966.

21. Libby 1967, both quotes on p. 22; see also Libby 1963.

22. Dee et al. 2012. On the general problem of old wood, see Schiffer (1986).

23. Libby 1955:44, 1967:15–16.

24. http://radiocarbon.ldeo.columbia.edu/research/radiocarbon.htm, accessed 19 June 2014.

25. *Radiocarbon* 55(4), 2013.

26. Taylor 1987:167–68.

Chapter 33

1. Tylecote 1977.
2. Tylecote 1983.
3. Tylecote 1979.
4. Ball 2003; Kaplan 1980; Kaplan and Mendel 1982; Römich 2003.
5. Foy and Jézégou 2004.
6. Mardikian and Girard 2010.
7. Foy, Thirion-Merle, and Vichy 2004.
8. Fontaine and Foy 2007.
9. Marie-Pierre Jézégou, personal communication, 25 September 2014.
10. Verney-Carron, Gin, and Libourel 2008.
11. Verney-Carron, Gin, and Libourel 2010:8; see also Poinsott and Gin 2011.
12. This facility is known as the Waste Isolation Pilot Plant (WIPP). The first archaeologist to be consulted on these issues was William L. Rathje (1977).
13. Trauth, Hora, and Guzowski 1993.
14. Kaplan 1980, 1982, 1986.
15. Kaplan 1986:266.
16. Broomby 2014.
17. L'Hostis, Foct, and Dillmann 2008; Neff et al. 2010.
18. Miller et al. 1990; Ojovan and Lee 2014.
19. Sokol 1983; see also Smellie, Karlsson, and Alexander 1997; Winograd 1986.

Chapter 34

1. Vavilov 1992.
2. http://en.wikipedia.org/wiki/Center_of_origin, accessed 8 December 2014.
3. Archaeobotanists also identify pollen, plant crystals, and phytoliths: see Pearsall 2000; Piperno 2006.
4. http://www.motherearthliving.com/natural-health/the-many-uses-of-sunflowers.aspx#axzz3MOECMMUW, accessed 19 December 2014.
5. http://www.agmrc.org/commodities__products/grains__oilseeds/sunflower-profile/, accessed 19 December 2014.
6. Bruce Smith 2006; see also Minnis 2003.
7. Miksicek 1987.
8. Bruce Smith 2014.
9. Bruce Smith 2014:61–62.
10. Bruce Smith 2014:65.
11. Bruce Smith 2014:65.

Chapter 35

1. Some sources on zooarchaeology: Reitz and Wing (2008); Russell (2012).
2. Lyman 2006.
3. Lyman 2006.

4. Lyman 1996, 2006; Wolverton and Lyman 2012a.
5. His classic work on methods is Grayson (1984).
6. Grayson 1987.
7. Grayson 1987:373.
8. Lyman 1996; see also Lyman (2012) which introduces the broader term "applied palaeozoology."
9. Lyman 1996:1.
10. Lyman 1991.
11. Lyman 1996:113.
12. Lyman (2004) reported more archaeological occurrences of pygmy rabbits outside their historic range.
13. Lyman 1991:110.
14. This paragraph closely paraphrases Lyman (1996:113, 2006:14).
15. Kelly McAllister 1995:vii.
16. Kelly McAllister 1995:vii.
17. Lyman 1996:113; he later reiterated the need to preserve habitat (Lyman 2004).
18. Kelly McAllister 1995:33.
19. http://wdfw.wa.gov/conservation/pygmy_rabbit/, accessed 12 January 2014.
20. http://wdfw.wa.gov/conservation/pygmy_rabbit/, accessed 12 January 2014; see also Hannan 2013.
21. Some examples: Campbell and Butler 2010; Etnier 2007; Etnier and Fowler 2010; Murray 2008.
22. Wolverton and Lyman 2012b.

Chapter 36

1. Harper and Armelagos 2013:142.
2. Ursell et al. 2013.
3. Tito et al. 2012:2.
4. Warinner et al. 2014.
5. Several recent works on dental plaque: Warinner et al. 2014; Warinner, Speller, and Collins 2014.
6. Appelt 2013:16–17.
7. Reinhard and Bryant 1992.
8. Reinhard and Bryant 1992:253.
9. Ortega and Bonavia 2003.
10. Appelt 2013:19–20, 47–48.
11. http://commonfund.nih.gov/hmp/index, accessed 30 December 2014.
12. Appelt 2013:23.
13. Appelt 2013:61.
14. Appelt et al. 2014.
15. *Firmicutes, Bacteroides, Actinobacteria, Fusobacteria, Proteobacteria, Verrumicrobia* and *Cyanobacteria*; Appelt 2013:22.

16. Harper and Armelagos 2013:143.
17. Harper and Armelagos 2013:144.
18. De Filippo et al. 2010:14694.
19. Tito et al. 2012:2.
20. Tito et al. 2012:5.
21. Cano et al. 2014.
22. Sharon Levy 2013; Ursell et al. 2013.

Chapter 37
1. Nash (1999:67). I relied heavily on this book.
2. Dean 1997:50–52.
3. Douglass 1914:108.
4. Freed and Freed 1992.
5. Wissler 1921:13.
6. Nash 1999:32–35.
7. Nash 1999:35–40.
8. Nash 1999:43.
9. Nash 1999:43–45, 53. Douglass (1929:742) gives the 1260 date.
10. Nash 1999:16.
11. Nash 1999:50.
12. Haury (1962) is an account of closing the gap; Douglass's (1929:767) version differs in some details.
13. Haury 1962:13.
14. Nash 1999:72.
15. Douglass 1929:751.
16. Creasman et al. 2012; Webb 2002:58–74.
17. Schulman 1945:43.
18. Treeflow.info, accessed 4 July 2014.
19. Straka 2008.
20. Leavitt and Bannister 2009.
21. Meko and Woodhouse 2011.

Chapter 38
1. John Wesley Powell, director of the U.S. Geological Survey, named it "Sunset Mountain" in 1892 (Colton 1945b:7).
2. Elson et al. 2002.
3. Voth 1905:241–44.
4. Colton 1937; Robinson 1913.
5. Douglas Johnson 1907.
6. Downum (1988) has researched MNA's projects to date Sunset Crater in great depth. A recent synthesis is Elson (2011).
7. Colton 1953; Horstman 1984.

8. Colton 1945b; Nash 1999:145; Reid and Whittlesey 1997:207–08.
9. Colton 1945b.
10. McGregor 1936:24. Colton (1932) had inferred that the eruption occurred during Pueblo II, in the range AD 700–875.
11. Colton 1945a.
12. Colton 1945a:352.
13. Downum 1988:258.
14. Elson 2011:128.
15. Holm and Moore 1987.
16. The classic work on environmental archaeology is Butzer (1971); see also Reitz and Shackley 2012.
17. Modern volumes include Grattan and Torrence 2007; Sheets and Grayson (1979).
18. Colton 1945b:12. This hypothesis appears first in Colton (1932).
19. Kirk Anderson 2003; Elson et al. 2002; Ort et al. 2008.
20. Lopes 2005:146.

Chapter 39

1. Faith and Surovell 2009.
2. For nineteenth-century explanations of the extinctions, see Grayson (1980).
3. Donlan and Greene 2011.
4. Martin 1973; see also Mosimann and Martin 1975.
5. Meltzer 2009.
6. Martin 2005.
7. Information in this paragraph comes from Cooper (2011:41–43, 46).
8. Cooper 2011:48–49.
9. Cooper 2011:51–52.
10. Thode 2009.
11. Anderson 1989; Duff 1950.
12. Dating: Wilmshurst et al. (2011); simulations: Holdaway and Jacomb (2000).
13. Steadman 1989, 1995.
14. Steadman 1995:1123; see also Steadman 1997.
15. James et al. 1987.
16. Steadman 1995:1128.
17. Boyer 2008.
18. Steadman and Martin 2003.
19. http://www.audubonmagazine.org/articles/birds/why-passenger-pigeon-went -extinct, accessed 29 September 2014.
20. Haynes 2009.

Chapter 40

1. Wood 2010.
2. Grayson 1983.

3. http://www.scientificamerican.com/article/how-science-figured-out-the-age-of-the-earth/, accessed 26 January 2015.
4. http://www.stratigraphy.org/ICSchart/ChronostratChart2014-02.jpg, accessed 29 January 2015.
5. Blake 1864:clv.
6. Blake 1864.
7. William King 1864:96.
8. Green et al. 2010; Sankararaman et al. 2012.
9. Dubois 1896.
10. I ignore *H. floresiensis*.
11. Keeley 1977.
12. Dart 1925.
13. Known as the Taungs child, this skull was found in Bechuanaland (Dart 1940).
14. Dart 1925:195, emphasis in original.
15. Broom 1943.
16. http://en.wikipedia.org/wiki/Louis_Leakey, accessed 25 January 2015.
17. Mary Leakey 1984:120–21.
18. L. S. B. Leakey 1959.
19. L. S. B. Leakey, Evernden, and Curtis 1961; see also Evernden and Curtis 1965.
20. Wood and Lonergan 2008.
21. Wood and Lonergan 2008; Wood and Richmond 2000.

Chapter 41

1. See Zeder (2012) for changes in domesticated animals.
2. Zeder 2011.
3. Harris 2007.
4. Gignoux, Henn, and Mountain 2011; Zeder 2008.
5. Some researchers use potentially misleading terms such as "pristine" or "primary" to designate original centers.
6. http://en.wikipedia.org/wiki/New_Guinea, accessed 5 February 2015.
7. Some ideas in this paragraph come from Cowan and Watson (2006).
8. Denham, Haberle, and Lentfer 2004.
9. Denham et al. 2003:191.
10. Fullagar et al. 2006; Haberle et al. 2011.
11. Denham 2011.
12. Hayden 1993:221–23 debunks the genius model.
13. For archaeological syntheses of hunter-gatherer lifeways, see, e.g., Bettinger (1991) and Kelly (1995).
14. Terrell et al. 2003.
15. The following scenario draws inspiration from Barker (2006), Bellwood (2004), Cowan and Watson (2006), Denham and Haberle (2008), Harris (2007), Terrell et al. (2003), Zeder (2008, 2011, 2012).

Chapter 42

1. https://en.wikipedia.org/wiki/Uruk, accessed 13 February 2015.
2. http://en.wikipedia.org/wiki/List_of_largest_cities_throughout_history, accessed 13 February 2015.
3. For examples, see Monica Smith (2003).
4. On social needs and technology, see Schiffer (2011).
5. Sharer 2012:30.
6. Robert F. Carr and Hazard 1961.
7. Haviland 1969.
8. The following discussion draws on Harrison (2012), Isendahl (2012), Lentz, Dunning, and Scarborough (2015), Lucero et al. (2014), and Scarborough et al. (2012).
9. Fletcher 2009.
10. Lentz, Dunning, and Scarborough 2015; Lentz et al. 2012.
11. Moyes et al. 2009.
12. Tikal cultural landscape: Fletcher 2009; Isendahl 2012.
13. Possehl 1997.
14. Kenoyer 2015:415.
15. Stanislawski 1946.
16. Kenoyer 2015.
17. Possehl 1997.
18. Gray 1940; Webster 1962.
19. Quotes in this paragrah: Kenoyer 2011:41.
20. On Harappan metallurgy: Kenoyer and Miller 1999.
21. Kenoyer 2013.
22. Madella and Fuller 2006; Possehl 1997.
23. Kenoyer 2015:426.

References

Albertson, N.

2009   Archaeology of the Homeless. *Archaeology* 62(6):42–3.

Alexander, John

1978   Review of "Unearthing Igbo–Ukwu: Archaeological Discoveries in Eastern Nigeria." *Man* 13:144–145.

Ames, Kenneth M.

2006   The Place of Ozette in Northwest Coast Archaeology. In *Ozette Archaeological Project Research Reports*, Vol. III: *Ethnobotany and Wood Technology*, edited by David L. Welchel, pp. 9–24. Washington State University, Department of Anthropology, Reports of Investigations 68.

Anderson, Atholl

1989   *Prodigious Birds: Moas and Moa-Hunting in Prehistoric New Zealand*. Cambridge University Press, Cambridge.

Anderson, E. C., W. F. Libby, S. Weinhouse, A. F. Reid, A. D. Kirshenbaum, and A. V. Grosse

1947   Radiocarbon from Cosmic Radiation. *Science* 105:576–577.

Anderson, Kirk

2003   Sunset Crater and Cinder Mulch Agriculture. *Archaeology Southwest* 17(1):8.

Appelt, Sandra

2013   Paléomicrobiologie des Coprolithes. Ph.D. dissertation, Faculty of Medicine, Aix-Marseille University, France.

Appelt, Sandra et al.

2014   Polyphasic Analysis of a Middle Ages Coprolite Microbiota, Belgium. *PLoS One* 9(2):e88376.

Appler, Douglas R.

2012   Municipal Archaeology Programs and the Creation of Community Amenities. *The Public Historian* 34:40–67.

2013   Tracing the Roots of Municipal Archaeology in St. Augustine, Florida: The Story of How 'The Oldest City' Connected Archaeology, Local Government, and the Public. *Public Archaeology* 12(1):7–26.

Archambault, JoAllyn

1993   American Indians and American Museums. *Zeitschrift für Ethnologie* 118:7–22.

Arnold, Jeanne E., Anthony P. Graesch, Enzo Ragazzini, and Elinor Ochs
2012   *Life at Home in the Twenty-First Century: 32 Families Open Their Doors.* Cotsen Institute of Archaeology Press, University of California at Los Angeles.

Arnold, J. R. and W. F. Libby
1949   Age Determinations by Radiocarbon Content: Checks with Samples of Known Age. *Science* 110:678–680.

Ascher, Robert and Charles H. Fairbanks
1971   Excavation of a Slave Cabin, Georgia, U.S.A. *Historical Archaeology* 5:3–17.

Atalay, Sonya, Lee Rains Clauss, Randall H. McGuire, and John R. Welch (editors)
2012   *Transforming Archaeology: Activist Practices and Prospects.* Left Coast Press, Walnut Creek, CA.

Atkinson, Richard J. C.
1987   *Stonehenge and Neighboring Monuments.* English Heritage, London.

Ball, Philip
2003   To the Heart of Glass. *Nature* 421:783–784.

Bancroft, George
1879   *History of the United States of America from the Discovery of the Continent* Vol. 1. Rev. ed. Little, Brown, Boston.

Bandy, Matthew S.
2005   Energetic Efficiency and Political Expediency in Titicaca Basin Raised Field Agriculture. *Journal of Anthropological Archaeology* 24:271–296.

Bank of Cyprus Cultural Foundation
1987   *A Guide to Kourion.* Bank of Cyprus Cultural Foundation in Collaboration with the Department of Antiquities, Nicosia.

Barka, Norman F.
1973   The Kiln and Ceramics of the "Poor Potter" of Yorktown: A Preliminary Report. In *Ceramics in America,* edited by Ian M. G. Quimby, pp. 291–318. University of Virginia Press, Charlottesville.
2004   Archaeology of a Colonial Pottery Factory: The Kilns and Ceramics of the "Poor Potter" of Yorktown. *Ceramics in America 2004,* pp. 15–47.

Barka, Norman F., Edward Ayres, and Christine Sheridan
1984   The "Poor Potter" of Yorktown: A Study of a Colonial Pottery Factory. *Yorktown Research Series* 5.

Barker, Graeme
2006   *The Agricultural Revolution in Prehistory: Why Did Foragers Become Farmers?* Oxford University Press, Oxford.

Barney, Ralph A.
1955   Legal Problems Peculiar to Indian Claims Litigation. *Ethnohistory* 2:315–325.

Basalla, G.
1988   *The Evolution of Technology.* Cambridge University Press, Cambridge.

Bass, William M., III and Walter Birkby
1978   Exhumation: The Method Could Make the Difference. *FBI Law Enforcement Bulletin* 47(7):6–11.

Baxter, Ian and Christopher Chippindale

2002   From "National Disgrace" to Flagship Monument: Recent Attempts to Manage the Future of Stonehenge. *Conservation and Management of Archaeological Sites* 5:151–184.

2005   Managing Stonehenge: The Tourism Impact and the Impact on Tourism. In *International Cultural Tourism: Management, Implications, and Cases*, edited by Marianna Sigala and David Leslie, pp. 137–150. Elsevier, Amsterdam.

Beals, Ralph L.

1985   The Anthropologist as Expert Witness: Illustrations from the California Indian Land Claims Case. In *Irredeemable America: The Indians' Estate and Land Claims*, edited by Imre Sutton, pp. 139–156. University of New Mexico Press, Albuquerque.

Beck, Colleen M.

2001   Applying Archaeological Theory to Nuclear Testing Sites. In *Eureka: The Archaeology of Innovation & Science. Proceedings of the 29th Annual Chacmool Conference*, edited by R. Harrison and R. M. Gillespie, pp. 267–284. Archaeological Association of the University of Calgary, Calgary, AB.

2002   The Archaeology of Scientific Experiments at a Nuclear Testing Ground. In *Matériel Culture: The Archaeology of Twentieth-Century Conflict*, edited by John Schofield, William G. Johnson, and Colleen M. Beck, pp. 65–79. Routledge, New York.

Beck, Colleen M., Harold Drollinger, Robert Jones, Diane Winslow, and Nancy Goldenberg

1996   A Historical Evaluation of the Engine Maintenance Assembly and Disassembly Facility, Area 25, Nevada Test Site, Nye County, Nevada. Desert Research Institute, Cultural Resources Reconnaissance, Short Report SR082696-1.

Bell, Christine

2004   Investigating Second Seminole War Sites in Florida: Identification Through Limited Testing. M.A. thesis, Department of Anthropology, University of South Florida.

Bellwood, Peter

2004   *First Farmers: The Origins of Agricultural Societies*. Oxford University Press, Oxford.

Bender, Barbara

1998   *Stonehenge: Making Space*. Berg, Oxford.

Ben-Yosef, Erez, Thomas E. Levy, Thomas Higham, Mohammad Najjar, and Lisa Tuaxe

2010   The Beginning of Iron Age Copper Production in the Southern Levant: New Evidence from Khirbat al-Jariya, Faynan, Jordan. *Antiquity* 84:724–746.

Bessey, S. Fiona and Dennis J. Pogue

2006   Blacksmithing at George Washington's Mount Vernon. *Archaeological Society of Virginia, Quarterly Bulletin*, December, pp. 176–195.

Bettinger, Robert L.

1991   *Hunter-Gatherers: Archaeological and Evolutionary Theory.* Plenum, New York.

Bevan, David

1994   *A Case to Answer For: The Story of Australia's First European War Crimes Prosecution.* Wakefield Press, Adelaide.

Bishop, Ronald L. and Frederick W. Lange (editors)

1991   *The Ceramic Legacy of Anna O. Shepard.* University Press of Colorado, Boulder.

Blake, C. Carter

1864   On the Alleged Peculiar Characters, and Assumed Antiquity of the Human Cranium from the Neanderthal. *Journal of the Royal Anthropological Society of London* 2:cxxxix–clvii.

Boserup, Ester

1974   *The Conditions of Agricultural Growth.* Aldine, Chicago.

Bowechop, Janine and Patricia Pierce Erikson

2005   Forging Indigenous Methodologies on Cape Flattery. *American Indian Quarterly* 29:263–273.

Boyer, Alison G.

2008   Extinction Patterns in the Avifauna of the Hawaiian Islands. *Diversity and Distributions* 14:509–517.

Braun, Barbara

1993   *Pre-Columbian Art and the Post-Columbian World.* Harry N. Abrams, New York.

Breen, Eleanor E.

2004   Whiskey on the Rocks: Excavating and Interpreting the Archaeological Remains of George Washington's Distillery. Paper presented at the 2004 Annual Conference of the Society for Historical Archaeology, St. Louis, MO.

Breen, Eleanor E. and Esther C. White

2006   "A Pretty Considerable Distillery": Excavating George Washington's Whiskey Distillery. *Quarterly Bulletin of the Archaeological Society of Virginia* 61(4): 209–220.

Brodie, Neil

2006   The Plunder of Iraq's Archaeological Heritage, 1991–2005, and the London Antiquities Trade. In *Archaeology, Cultural Heritage, and the Antiquities Trade,* edited by Neil Brodie, Morag M. Kersel, Christina Luke, and Kathryn Walter Tubb, pp. 206–226. University of Press of Florida, Gainesville.

Brodie, Neil and Colin Renfrew

2005   Looting and the World's Archaeological Heritage: The Inadequate Response. *Annual Review of Anthropology* 34:343–361.

Brody, J. J.

1979   Pueblo Fine Arts. In *Handbook of North American Indians, Volume 9: Southwest,* edited by Alfonso Ortiz, pp. 603–608. Smithsonian Institution, Washington, D.C.

Broom, Robert

1943   An Ankle-Bone of the Ape-Man, *Paranthropus robustus*. *Nature* 152:689–690.

Broomby, Rob

2014   How France is disposing of its nuclear waste. BBC News: Science & Environ-
        ment, 4 March. http://www.bbc.com/news/science-environment-26425674,
        accessed 25 September 2014.

Brown, Kenneth L.

1994   Material Culture and Community Structure: The Slave and Tenant Commu-
        nity at Levi Jordan's Plantation, 1848–1892. In *Slave Society and Domestic Econ-
        omy in the American South*, edited by Larry E. Hudson, pp. 95–118. University
        of Rochester Press, Rochester, NY.

2004   Ethnographic Analogy, Archaeology, and the African Diaspora: Perspectives
        from a Tenant Community. *Historical Archaeology* 38:79–89.

2011   BaKongo Cosmograms, Christian Crosses, or None of the Above: An Ar-
        chaeology of African American Spiritual Adaptations into the 1920s. In *The
        Materiality of Freedom: Archaeology of Postemancipation Life*, edited by Jodi A.
        Barnes, pp. 209–227. University of South Carolina Press, Columbia.

Brown, Kenneth L. and Doreen C. Cooper

1990   Structural Continuity in an African-American Slave and Tenant Community.
        Historical Archaeology 24:7–19.

Brown, Marie A.

1887   *The Icelandic Discoverers of America*. Gilbert and Rivington, London.

Bryant, Sue and Melissa Shales

2010   *Frommer's Cyprus Day by Day*. Wiley, Chichester, UK.

Bucha, V. and E. Neustupny

1967   Changes of the Earth's Magnetic Field and Radiocarbon Dating. *Nature* 215:
        261–263.

Buchli, Victor and Gavin Lucas (editors)

2001   *Archaeologies of the Contemporary Past*. Routledge, London.

Buck, Bruce A.

1982   Ancient Technology in Contemporary Surgery. *Western Journal of Medicine*
        136:265–269.

Bussard, R. W. and R. D. DeLauer

1958   *Nuclear Rocket Propulsion*. McGraw-Hill, New York.

Butzer, Karl W.

1971   *Environment and Archaeology*. 2nd ed. Aldine, Chicago.

Campbell, Sarah K., and Virginia L. Butler

2010   Archaeological Evidence for Resilience of Pacific Northwest Salmon Popula-
        tions and the Socioecological System Over the Last ~7,500 Years. *Ecology and
        Society* 15(1):17.

Cano, Raul J. et al.

2014   Paleomicrobiology: Revealing Fecal Microbiomes of Ancient Indigenous
        Cultures. *PLoS One* 9(9):e106833.

Carr, Christopher and D. Troy Case (editors)

2005   *Gathering Hopewell: Society, Ritual, and Ritual Interaction.* Kluwer/Plenum, New York.

Carr, Robert F. and James E. Hazard

1961   Map of the Ruins of Tikal, El Peten, Guatemala. *University of Pennsylvania Museum Monographs, Tikal Reports* 11.

Carr, Robert S.

2012   *Digging Miami.* University Press of Florida, Gainesville.

Chaffin, Tom

2008   *The H. L. Hunley: The Secret Hope of the Confederacy.* Hill and Wang, New York.

Chiari, Giacomo, Roberto Giustetto, and Gabrielle Ricchiardi

2003   Crystal Structure Refinements of Palygorskite and Maya Blue from Molecular Modelling and Powder Synchrotron Diffraction. *European Journal of Mineralogy* 15:21–33.

Chikwendu, V. E.

1989   Nigerian Sources of Copper, Lead and Tin for the Igbo–Ukwu Bronzes. *Archaeometry* 31:27–36.

Chippindale, Christopher

2012   *Stonehenge Complete.* 4th ed. Thames & Hudson, New York.

Christensen, Kim

2004   Tourists, Schoolchildren, and Liquor Lobbyists: The Various Publics of the Mount Vernon Distillery Site. Paper presented at the 2004 Annual Conference of the Society for Historical Archaeology, St. Louis, MO.

Clemmer, Richard O.

2008   The Leisure Class versus the Tourists: The Hidden Struggle in Collecting of Pueblo Pottery at the Turn of the Twentieth Century. *History and Anthropology* 19:187–207.

Coggins, Clemency

1972   Archaeology and the Art Market. *Science* 175:263–266.

Colton, Harold S.

1932   The Effect of a Volcanic Eruption on an Ancient Pueblo People. *Geographical Review* 22:582–590.

1937   The Basaltic Cinder Cones and Lava Flows of the San Francisco Mountain Volcanic Field. *Museum of Northern Arizona Bulletin* 10.

1945a   A Revision of the Date of the Eruption of Sunset Crater. *Southwestern Journal of Anthropology* 1:345–344.

1945b   Sunset Crater. *Plateau* 18(1):7–14.

1953   History of the Museum of Northern Arizona. *Plateau* 24:1–8.

Conlin, David L. and Matthew A. Russell

2006   Archaeology of a Naval Battlefield: H. L. Hunley and USS Housatonic. *International Journal of Nautical Archaeology* 35(1):20–40.

2010   Maritime Archaeology of Naval Battlefields. In *The Historical Archaeology of Military Sites: Method and Topic*, edited by Clarence R. Geier, Lawrence E. Babits, Douglas D. Scott, and David G. Orr, pp. 39–56. Texas A&M University Press, College Station.

Cooper, Elaine M.

2011   Julius Haast and the Canterbury Museum and Māori. M.A. thesis, Massey University, Palmerston North, NZ.

Costello, Benjamin IV

2011   An Analysis of the Architecture and Material Culture from the Earthquake House at Kourion, Cyprus. Ph.D. dissertation, Department of Classics, SUNY Buffalo.

Covington, James W.

1993   *The Seminoles of Florida*. University Press of Florida, Gainesville.

Cowan, C. Wesley and Patty Jo Watson

2006   Some Concluding Remarks. In *The Origins of Agriculture: An International Perspective*, edited by C. Wesley Cowan, Patty Jo Watson, and Nancy L. Benco, pp. 207–212. University of Alabama Press, Tuscaloosa.

Crabtree, Don E.

1968   Mesoamerican Polyhedral Cores and Prismatic Blades. *American Antiquity* 1968:446–478.

Craddock, Paul T. et al.

1997   Metal Sources and the Bronzes from Igbo–Ukwu, Nigeria. *Journal of Field Archaeology* 24:405–429.

Creasman, Pearce P., Bryant Bannister, Ronald H. Towner, Jeffrey S. Dean, and Steven W. Leavitt

2012   Reflections on the Foundation, Persistence, and Growth of the Laboratory of Tree-Ring Research, Circa 1930–1960. *Tree-Ring Research* 68(2):81–89.

Cressey, Pamela J.

1993   *To Witness the Past: African American Archaeology in Alexandria*. City of Alexandria, Virginia.

2002   *Walk and Bike the Alexandria Heritage Trail: A Guide to Exploring Virginia Town's Hidden Past*. Capital Books, Sterling, VA.

2005   Community Archaeology in Alexandria, Virginia. In *Unlocking the Past: Celebrating Historical Archaeology in North America*, edited by Lu Ann De Cunzo and John H. Jameson Jr., pp. 97–102. University Press of Florida, Gainesville.

Cressey, Pamela J. and Margaret J. Anderson

2006   *Alexandria, Virginia*. Oxford University Press, New York.

Cressey, Pamela J., Ruth Reeder, and Jared Bryson

2003   Held in Trust: Community Archaeology in Alexandria, Virginia. In *Archaeologists and Local Communities: Partners in Exploring the Past*, edited by Linda Derry and Maureen Mallow, pp. 1–18. Society for American Archaeology, Washington, D.C.

Cressey, Pamela J., John F. Stephens, Steven J. Shepard, and Barbara H. Magid
1982   The Core-Periphery Relationship and the Archaeological Record in Alexandria, Virginia. In *Archaeology of Urban America: The Search for Pattern and Process*, edited by Roy S. Dickens Jr., pp. 143–173. Academic Press, New York.

Cressey, Pamela J. and Natalie Vinton
2007   Smart Planning and Innovative Public Outreach: The Quintessential Mix for the Future of Archaeology. In *Past Meets Present: Archaeologists Partnering with Museum Curators, Teachers, and Community Groups*, edited by John H. Jameson Jr. and Sherene Baugher, pp. 393–410. Springer, New York.

Croes, Dale R.
1977   *Basketry from the Ozette Village Archaeological Site: A Technological, Functional, and Comparative Study*. Ph.D. dissertation, Department of Anthropology, Washington State University, Pullman.

Cypress, Billy L.
1997   The Role of Archaeology in the Seminole Tribe of Florida. In *Native Americans and Archaeologists: Stepping Stones to Common Ground*, edited by Nina Swidler, Kurt E. Dongoske, Roger Anyon, and Alan S. Downer, pp. 156–160. AltaMira, Walnut Creek, CA.

Dant, Tim
1999   *Material Culture and the Social World: Values, Activities, Lifestyles*. Open University Press, Buckingham, UK.

Dart, Raymond A.
1925   *Australopithecus africanus*: The Man-Ape of South Africa. *Nature* 115:195–199.
1940   The Status of Australopithecus. *American Journal of Physical Anthropology* 26:167–186.

Darvill, Timothy
2005   (compiler and editor) *Stonehenge World Heritage Site: An Archaeological Research Framework*. English Heritage and Bournemouth University, London and Bournemouth.
2010   *Prehistoric Britain*. 2nd ed. Routledge, London.

Daugherty, Richard D.
1988   Problems and Responsibilities in the Excavation of Wet Sites. In *Wet Site Archaeology*, edited by Barbara A. Purdy, pp. 15–30. Telford Press, Caldwell, NJ.

Daugherty, Richard D. and Ruth Kirk
1976   Ancient Indian Village Where Time Stood Still. *Smithsonian* 7(2):68–75.

Dean, Jeffrey S.
1997   Dendrochronology. In *Chronometric Dating in Archaeology*, edited by R. E. Taylor and Martin J. Aitken, pp. 31–64. Plenum, New York.

DeCosta, B. F.
1890   *The Pre-Columbian Discovery of America by the Northmen with Translations from the Icelandic Sagas*. 2nd ed. J. Munsell, Albany, NY.

Dee, M. W., J. M. Rowland, T. F. G. Higham, A. J. Shortland, F. Brock, S. A. Harris, and C. Bronk Ramsey
2012   Synchronising Radiocarbon Dating and the Egyptian Historical Chronology by Improved Sample Selection. *Antiquity* 86:868–883.
De Filippo, Carlotta et al.
2010   Impact of Diet in Shaping Gut Microbiota Revealed by a Comparative Study in Children from Europe and Rural Africa. *Proceedings of the National Academy of Sciences* 107:14691–14696.
De León, Jason
2012   "Better to be Hot than Caught": Excavating the Conflicting Roles of Migrant Material Culture. *American Anthropologist* 114:477–495.
2013   Undocumented Migration, Use Wear, and the Materiality of Habitual Suffering in the Sonoran Desert. *Journal of Material Culture* 18:321–345.
Delgado, James P., Daniel J. Lenihan, and Larry E. Murphy
1991   *The Archeology of the Atomic Bomb: A Submerged Cultural Resources Assessment of the Sunken Fleet of Operations Crossroads at Bikini and Kwajalein Atoll Lagoons, Republic of the Marshall Islands.* U.S. National Park Service, Southwest Cultural Resources Center, Professional Papers 37.
Denham, Tim
2011   Early Agriculture and Plant Domestication in New Guinea and Island Southeast Asia. *Current Anthropology* 52:S379–S395.
Denham, Tim P. et al.
2003   Origins of Agriculture at Kuk Swamp in the Highlands of New Guinea. *Science* 301:189–193.
Denham, Tim P., Simon Haberle, and Carol J. Lentfer
2004   New Evidence and Revised Interpretations of Early Agriculture in Highland New Guinea. *Antiquity* 78:839–857.
Denham, Tim and Simon Haberle
2008   Agricultural Emergence and Transformation in the Upper Wahgi Valley, Papua New Guinea, During the Holocene: Theory, Method and Practice. *The Holocene* 18:481–496.
Department of the Interior
2008   National Register of Historic Places Registration Form for the Seminole Red Barn, Glades County, Florida. United States Department of the Interior, National Park Service, Washington, D.C.
de Valbourg, Henri Misson
1719   [1698] *M. Misson's Memoirs and Observations in His Travels over England. With Some Account of Scotland and Ireland* (translated from the French by Mr. Ozell). London.
Dewar, James A.
2004   *To the End of the Solar System: The Story of the Nuclear Rocket.* University of Kentucky Press, Lexington.

Disa, Joseph J., Jafar Vossoughi, and Nelson H. Goldberg
1993   A Comparison of Obsidian and Surgical Steel Scalpel Wound Healing in
        Rats. *Plastic and Reconstructive Surgery* 92.5:884–887.
Doménech, Antonio, María Teresa Doménech-Carbó, Manuel Sánchez del Rio,
María Luisa Vázquez de Agredo Pascual, and Enrique Lima
2009   Maya Blue as a Nanostructured Poly-Functional Hybrid Organic-Inorganic
        Material: The Need to Change Paradigms. *New Journal of Chemistry* 33:
        2371–2379.
Donlan, C. Josh and Harry W. Greene
2011   Paul S. Martin (1928–2010): Luminary, Natural Historian, and Innovator.
        PLoS Biology 9(2):e1001016.
Douglass, Andrew E.
1914   A Method for Estimating Rainfall by the Growth of Trees. *Carnegie Institution
        of Washington Publication* 192, pp. 101–121.
1929   The Secret of the Southwest Solved by Talkative Tree Rings. *National
        Geographic Magazine* 56(6):736–770.
Downum, Christian E.
1988   *"One Grand History": A Critical Review of Flagstaff Archaeology, 1851 to 1988.*
        Ph.D. dissertation, University of Arizona. University Microfilms, Ann
        Arbor, MI.
Drollinger, Harold, Nancy Goldenberg, and Colleen M. Beck
2000a   An Historical Evaluation of the R-MAD Building in Area 25 for Planned Ac-
        tivities Associated with the Environmental Management Decontamination
        and Decommissioning Program, Nevada Test Site, Nye County, Nevada.
        Desert Research Institute, Cultural Resources Reconnaissance Short Report
        SR022900-1.
2000b   An Historical Evaluation of the Test Cell C Facility for Characterization Ac-
        tivities Associated with Decontamination and Decommissioning, Area 25,
        Nevada Test Site, Nye County, Nevada. Desert Research Institute, Cultural
        Resources Reconnaissance, Short Report SR021500-1.
Dubois, Eugène
1896   On Pithecanthropus Erectus: A Transitional Form Between Man and the
        Apes. *Journal of the Anthropological Institute of Great Britain and Ireland*
        25:240–255.
Duff, Roger
1950   *The Moa-Hunter Period of Maori Culture.* Canterbury Museum Bulletin 1,
        Department of Internal Affairs, Wellington, NZ.
Dupras, John J. Schulz, Sandra M. Wheeler, and Lana J. Williams
2011   *Forensic Recovery of Human Remains: Archaeological Approaches.* 2nd ed. CRC
        Press, Boca Raton, FL.
Duran, Meliha S. and Beth Morgan (editors)
1995   Trinity at Fifty: The Archaeology of Trinity Site National Historic Landmark,

White Sands Missile Range, Socorro County, New Mexico. Human Systems Research, White Sands Missile Range Archaeological Report No. 95-08. Tularosa, NM.

Ebighgbo, Chris N.

2001 Art of Bronze Casting in Nigeria: Continuity and Change. *USO: A Nigerian Journal of Art* 1:106–114.

Edelman, Sandra K.

1979 San Ildefonso Pueblo. In *Handbook of North American Indians, Volume 9: Southwest*, edited by Alfonso Ortiz, pp. 308–316. Smithsonian Institution, Washington, D.C.

Edwards, I. E. S.

1970 Absolute Dating from Egyptian Records and Comparison with Carbon-14 Dating. *Philosophical Transactions of the Royal Society of London, Series A*, Vol. 269:11–18.

Eidenbach, Peter L., Richard L. Wessel, Lisa M. Meyer, and Gail C. Wimberly

1996 *Star Throwers of the Tularosa: The Early Cold War Legacy of White Sands Missile Range*. Human Systems Research, Report No. 94-22, White Sands Missile Range Archaeological Report, No. 96-12. Tularosa, NM.

Elson, Mark D. (editor)

2011 Sunset Crater Archaeology: The History of a Volcanic Landscape. *Center For Desert Archaeology, Anthropological Papers* 37.

Elson, Mark D., Michael H. Ort, S. Jerome Hesse, and Wendell A. Duffield

2002 Lava, Corn, and Ritual in the Northern Southwest. *American Antiquity* 67:119–135.

Engelkemeir, Antoinette G., W. H. Hamill, Mark G. Inghram, and W. F. Libby

1949 The Half-Life of Radiocarbon (C^{14}). *Physical Review* 75:1825–1833.

Enscore, Susan I.

1998 *Operation Paperclip at Fort Bliss: 1945–1950*. Pamphlet, Conservation Division, Fort Bliss, TX.

Erickson, Clark

1998 Applied Archaeology and Rural Development: Archaeology's Potential Contribution to the Future. In *Crossing Currents: Continuity and Change in Latin America*, edited by Michael B. Whiteford and Scott Whiteford, pp. 34–45. Prentice Hall, Upper Saddle River, NJ.

Erikson, Patricia Pierce

2005 Trends in Image and Design: Reflections on 25 Years of a Tribal Museum Era. *Histories of Anthropology Annual* 1:271–286.

Erikson, Patricia Pierce, Helma Ward, and Kirk Wachendorf

2002 *Voices of a Thousand People: The Makah Cultural and Research Center*. University of Nebraska Press, Lincoln.

Etnier, Michael A.

2007 Defining and Identifying Sustainable Harvests of Resources: Archaeological

Examples of Pinniped Harvests in the Eastern North Pacific. *Journal for Nature Conservation* 15:196–207.

Etnier, Michael A. and Charles W. Fowler

2010   Size Selectivity in Marine Mammal Diets as a Guide to Evolutionarily Enlightened Fisheries Management. *North American Journal of Fisheries Management* 30:588–603.

Evernden, J. F. and G. H. Curtis

1965   Potassium-Argon Dating of Late Cenozoic Rocks in East Africa and Italy. *Current Anthropology* 6:342–385.

Fairbanks, Charles H.

1974   The Kingsley Slave Cabins in Duval County, Florida, 1968. *Conference on Historic Sites Archeology Papers 1972*, Vol. 7:62–93.

Faith, J. Tyler and Todd A. Surovell

2009   Synchronous Extinction of North America's Pleistocene Mammals. *Proceedings of the National Academy of Sciences* 106:20641–20645.

Fantalkin, Alexander, Israel Finkelstein, and Eli Piasetzky

2011   Iron Age Mediterranean Chronology: A Rejoinder. *Radiocarbon* 53:179–198.

Feder, Kenneth L.

1999   *Lessons from the Past: An Introductory Reader in Archaeology*. Mayfield, Mountain View, CA.

Ferguson, Leland

1992   *Uncommon Ground: Archaeology and Early African America, 1650–1800*. Smithsonian Institution Press, Washington, D.C.

Ferguson, T. J.

2014   Archaeologists as Activists, Advocates, and Expert Witnesses. In *Transforming Archaeology: Activist Practices and Prospects*, edited by Sonya Atalay, Lee Rains Clauss, Randall H. McGuire, and John R. Welch, pp. 239–253.

Fewkes, J. Walter

1898   *Archeological Expedition into Arizona in 1895*. Seventeenth Annual Report of the Bureau of American Ethnology, 1895–1896, pp. 519–742.

Field, J. O.

1940   Bronze Castings Found at Igbo, Southern Nigeria. *Man* 40:1–6.

Finkelstein, Israel and Lily Singer-Avitz

2009   The Pottery of Khirbet en-Nahas: A Rejoinder. *Palestine Exploration Quarterly* 141:207–218.

Fisher, Jim

2013   *The GE Mound Case: The Archaeological Disaster and Criminal Persecution of Artifact Collector Art Gerber*. CreateSpace Independent Publishing Platform.

Fletcher, Roland

2009   Low-Density, Agrarian-Based Urbanism: A Comparative View. *Insights* 2(4):2–19.

Flink, J. J.
1970   *America Adopts the Automobile, 1895–1910*. MIT Press, Cambridge, MA.
Fontaine, Souen Deva and Danièle Foy
2007   L'Épave Ouest-Embiez 1, Var: Le Commerce Maritime du Verre Brut et Man-
        ufacturé en Méditerranée Occidentale dans l'Antiquité. *Revue Archéologique
        de Narbonnaise* 40:235–265.
Foy, Danièle and Marie-Pierre Jézégou
2004   Sous les Vagues le Verre: L'Épave Antique Ouest-Embiez 1. *Archéologia*
        407:22–33.
Foy, Danièle, Valérie Thirion-Merle, and Michèle Vichy
2004   Contribution à l'Étude des Verres Antiques Décolorés à l'Antimoine. *Revue
        d'Archéométrie* 28:169–177.
Fraser, David
2011   *Daviborshch's Cart: Narrating the Holocaust in Australian War Crimes Trials*.
        University of Nebraska Press, Lincoln.
Freed, Stanley A. and Ruth S. Freed
1992   *Clark Wissler, 1870–1947*. Biographical Memoir, National Academy of
        Sciences, Washington, D.C.
Friedman, Elizabeth S., Aaron J. Brody, Marcus L. Young, Jon D. Almer, Carlo U.
Segre, and Susan M. Mini
2008   Synchrotron Radiation-Based X-Ray Analysis of Bronze Artifacts from an
        Iron Age Site in the Judean Hills. *Journal of Archaeological Science* 35:1951–
        1960.
Friedman, Janet Patterson
1975   *The Prehistoric Uses of Wood at the Ozette Archaeological Site*. Ph.D. disserta-
        tion, Department of Anthropology, Washington State University, Pullman.
Friedman, Roger
1995   Return to Ozette. *Federal Archeology* 7(4):16–19.
Frisbie, Theodore R.
1973   The Influence of J. Walter Fewkes on Nampeyo: Fact or Fancy? In *The Chang-
        ing Ways of Southwestern Indians: A Historic Perspective*, edited by Albert H.
        Schroeder, pp. 231–244. Rio Grande Press, Glorieta, NM.
Fullagar, Richard, Judith Field, Tim Denham, and Carol Lentfer
2006   Early and Mid Holocene Tool-Use and Processing of Taro (*Colocasia escu-
        lenta*), Yam (*Dioscorea sp.*) and Other Plants at Kuk Swamp in the Highlands
        of Papua New Guinea. *Journal of Archaeological Science* 33:595–614.
Fuller, Nancy J. and Susanne Fabricius
1992   Native American Museums and Cultural Centers: Historical Overview and
        Current Issues. *Zeitschrift für Ethnologie* 117:223–237.
Garfinkel, Yosef, Katharina Streit, Saar Ganor, and Michael G. Hasel
2012   State Formation in Judah: Biblical Tradition, Modern Historical Theories,
        and Radiometric Dates at Khirbet Qeiyafa. *Radiocarbon* 54:359–369.

Gerstenblith, Patty

2002   United States v. Schultz. *Culture Without Context* 10: Spring.

2012   *Art, Cultural Heritage, and the Law: Cases and Materials.* 3rd ed. Carolina Academic Press, Durham, NC.

Gettens, Rutherford J.

1962   Maya Blue: An Unsolved Problem in Ancient Pigments. *American Antiquity* 27:557–564.

Gignoux, Christopher R., Brenna M. Henn, and Joanna L. Mountain

2011   Rapid, Global Demographic Expansions After the Origins of Agriculture. *Proceedings of the National Academy of Sciences* 108:6044–6049.

Gokee, Cameron D. and Jason De León

2014   Sites of Contention: Archaeological Classification and Political Discourse in the US–Mexico Borderlands. *Journal of Contemporary Archaeology* 1:135–165.

Gould, Richard A.

2007   *Disaster Archaeology.* University of Utah Press, Salt Lake City.

Gould, Richard A. and Michael B. Schiffer (editors)

1981   *Modern Material Culture: The Archaeology of Us.* Academic Press, New York.

Grabitske, David M.

2003–04 First Lady of Preservation: Sarah Sibley and the Mount Vernon Ladies Association. *Minnesota History*, Winter 2003–04, pp. 407–416.

Grattan, John and Robin Torrence (editors)

2007   *Living Under the Shadow: Cultural Impacts of Volcanic Eruptions.* Left Coast Press, Walnut Creek, CA.

Graves-Brown, Paul (editor)

2000   *Matter, Materiality and Modern Culture.* Routledge, London.

Graves-Brown, Paul, Rodney Harrison, and Angela Piccini

2013   *The Oxford Handbook of the Archaeology of the Contemporary World.* Oxford University Press, Oxford.

Gray, Harold F.

1940   Sewerage in Ancient and Mediaeval Times. *Sewage Works Journal* 12:939–946.

Grayson, Donald K.

1980   Vicissitudes and Overkill: The Development of Explanations of Pleistocene Extinctions. *Advances in Archaeological Method and Theory* 3:357–403.

1983   *The Establishment of Human Antiquity.* Academic Press, New York.

1984   *Quantitative Zooarchaeology: Topics in the Analysis of Archaeological Faunas.* Academic Press, Orlando, FL.

1987   The Biogeographic History of Small Mammals in the Great Basin: Observations on the Last 20,000 Years. *Journal of Mammalogy* 68:359–375.

Green, Richard E. et al.

2010   A Draft Sequence of the Neandertal Genome. *Science* 328:710–722.

Gridley, Marion E.

1974   *American Indian Women.* Hawthorn Books, New York.

Haberle, Simon G., Carol Lentfer, Shawn O'Donnell, and Tim Denham
2011   The Paleoenvironments of Kuk Swamp from the Beginnings of Agriculture in the Highlands of Papua New Guinea. *Quaternary International* 249: 129–139.
Haglund, William D., M. Connor, and Douglas D. Scott
2001   The Archaeology of Contemporary Mass Graves. *Historical Archaeology* 35:57–69.
Hannan, Richard R.
2013   Endangered and Threatened Wildlife and Plants; Recovery Plan for the Columbia Basin Distinct Population Segment of the Pygmy Rabbit (*Brachylagus idahoensis*). *Federal Register* 78(15):4865–4866.
Hardesty, Donald L. and Barbara J. Little
2009   *Assessing Site Significance: A Guide for Archaeologists and Historians.* 2nd ed. AltaMira, Lanham, MD.
Harper, Kristin N. and George J. Armelagos
2013   Genomics, the Origins of Agriculture, and Our Changing Microbe-Scape: Time to Revisit Some Old Tales and Tell Some New Ones. *American Journal of Physical Anthropology* 57:135–152.
Harkin, Michael E.
2010   Ethnohistory's Ethnohistory. Creating a Discipline from the Ground Up. *Social Science History* 34:113–128.
Harris, David R.
2007   Agriculture, Cultivation and Domestication: Exploring the Conceptual Framework of Early Food Production. In *Rethinking Agriculture: Archaeological and Ethnoarchaeological Perspectives*, edited by Tim Denham, José Iriarte, and Luc Vrydaghs, pp. 16–35. Left Coast Press, Walnut Creek, CA.
Harrison, Peter D.
2012   A Marvel of Maya Engineering: Water Management at Tikal. *Expedition* 54(2):19–26.
Harrison, Rodney
2009   (editor) *Understanding the Politics of Heritage.* Manchester University Press, Manchester.
2013   *Heritage: Critical Approaches.* Routledge, New York.
Harrison, Rodney and John Schofield
2010   *After Modernity: Archaeological Approaches to the Contemporary Past.* Oxford University Press, Oxford.
Hauptmann, A.
2007   *The Archaeo-Metallurgy of Copper—Evidence from Faynan, Jordan.* Springer, New York.
Haury, Emil W.
1962   HH-39: Recollections of a Dramatic Moment in Southwestern Archaeology. *Tree-Ring Bulletin* 24(3–4):11–14.

Haviland, William A.

1969   A New Population Estimate for Tikal, Guatemala. *American Antiquity* 34:429–433.

Hayden, Brian

1993   *Archaeology: The Science of Once and Future Things.* W. H. Freeman, New York.

Haynes, Gary (ed.)

2009   *American Megafaunal Extinctions at the End of the Pleistocene.* Springer, New York.

Heizer, Robert F. and Alfred L. Kroeber

1976   For Sale: California at 47 Cents per Acre. *Journal of California Anthropology* 3(2):38–65.

Hicks, Brian and Schuyler Kropf

2002   *Raising the Hunley: The Remarkable History and Recovery of the Lost Confederate Submarine.* Ballantine Books, New York.

Hicks, Dan

2010   The Material-Culture Turn: Event and Effect. In *The Oxford Handbook of Material Culture Studies,* edited by Dan Hicks and Mary C. Beaudry, pp. 25–98. Oxford University Press, Oxford.

Hicks, Dan and Mary C. Beaudry (editors)

2010   *The Oxford Handbook of Material Culture Studies.* Oxford University Press, Oxford.

Hodder, Ian

2012   *Entangled: An Archaeology of the Relationships Between Humans and Things.* Wiley-Blackwell, Oxford.

Holdaway, R. N. and C. Jacomb

2000   Rapid Extinction of the Moas (Aves: Dinornithiformes): Model, Test, and Implications. *Science* 287:2250–2254.

Holm, Richard F. and Richard B. Moore

1987   Holocene Scoria Cone and Lava Flows at Sunset Crater, Northern Arizona. *Geological Society of America, Centennial Field Guide—Rocky Mountain Section,* pp. 393–397.

Horsford, Eben N.

1892   *The Landfall of Leif Erikson, AD 1000, and the Site of His Houses in Vineland.* Damrell and Upham, Boston.

Horstman, E.

1984   Mary-Russell Ferrell Colton. *Plateau* 56(1):23.

Hoshower, L. M.

1998   Forensic Archeology and the Need for Flexible Excavation Strategies: A Case Study. *Journal of Forensic Sciences* 43:53–56.

Hough, Walter

1932   Biographical Memoir of Jesse Walter Fewkes, 1850–1930. *Biographical Memoirs,* National Academy of Sciences, 15(9):259–283.

Hovgaard, William
1914   *The Voyages of the Norsemen to America.* The American-Scandinavian Foundation, New York.

Huelsbeck, David R.
1988   Whaling in the Precontact Economy of the Central Northwest Coast. *Arctic Anthropology* 25:1–15.

Hugill, Peter J.
2006   Review of *Taking Charge: The Electric Automobile in America,* by Michael Brian Schiffer. *Technology and Culture* 37:379–381.

Hume, I. Noël
1964   Archaeology: Handmaiden to History. *The North Carolina Historical Review* 41:214–225.

Hunter, John R.
1994   Forensic Archaeology in Britain. *Antiquity* 68:758–769.

Hunter, John R. and Margaret Cox
2005   *Forensic Archaeology: Advances in Theory and Practice.* Routledge, New York.

Hunter, John R., Charlotte Roberts, and Anthony Martin
1996   *Studies in Crime: An Introduction to Forensic Archaeology.* Batsford, London.

Hunter, John R., Barrie Simpson, and Caroline Sturdy Colls
2013   *Forensic Approaches to Buried Remains.* Wiley-Blackwell, Chichester, West Sussex.

Ingstad, Anne Stine
1977   *The Discovery of a Norse Settlement in America: Excavations at L'Anse Aux Meadows, Newfoundland, 1961–1968* (translated by Elizabeth Seeberg). Universitetsforlaget, Oslo.
2001   The Excavation of a Norse Settlement at L'Anse aux Meadows, Newfoundland. In Helge Ingstad and Anne Stine Ingstad, *The Viking Discovery of America,* pp. 141–169. Checkmark, New York.

Ingstad, Helge
1964   Vinland Ruins Prove Vikings Found the New World. *National Geographic* 126:708–734.

Isendahl, Christian
2012   Agro-Urban Landscapes: The Example of Maya Lowland Cities. *Antiquity* 86:1112–1125.

Jacobs, Margaret D.
1998   Shaping a New Way: White Women and the Movement to Promote Pueblo Indian Arts and Crafts, 1900–1935. *Journal of the Southwest* 40:187–215.

Jacobsen, Maria
2005   H. L. Hunley Project: 2004 Archaeological Findings and Progress Report. Department of Defense, Legacy Resource Management Program, Project 04–106.

Jacobsen, Maria, Vincent Y. Blouin, and William Shirley
2012   Does Erosion Corrosion Account for Intriguing Damage to the Civil War
        Submarine *H. L. Hunley? Marine Technology Society Journal* 46(6)38–48.
James, Helen F. et al.
1987   Radiocarbon Dates on Bones of Extinct Birds from Hawaii. *Proceedings of the
        National Academy of Sciences* 84:2350–2354.
Janusek, John W. and Alan L. Kolata
2004   Top-Down or Bottom-Up: Rural Settlement and Raised Field Agriculture
        in the Lake Titicaca Basin, Bolivia. *Journal of Anthropological Archaeology*
        23:404–430.
Johnson, Douglas W.
1907   A Recent Volcano in the San Francisco Mountain Region, Arizona. *Bulletin of
        the Geographical Society of Philadelphia* 5:146–151.
Johnson, Frederick (assembler)
1951a   Radiocarbon Dating: A Report on the Program to Aid in the Development of
        the Method of Dating. *Society for American Archaeology Memoir* 8.
1951b   Introduction. In Johnson 1951a, pp. 1–4.
Johnson, Frederick, Froelich Rainey, Donald Collier, and Richard F. Flint
1951   Radiocarbon Dating, A Summary. In Johnson 1951a, pp. 58–62.
Johnson, William G.
2002a   Cultural Resources Management of the Cold War at the Nevada Test Site:
        Developing Significance Through a Particularist Strategy. In *Eureka: The Ar-
        chaeology of Innovation & Science,* edited by Roman Harrison, Milan Gillespie,
        and Meaghan Peuramaki-Brown, pp. 207–215. Archaeological Association of
        the University of Calgary, Calgary, AB.
2002b   Archaeological Examination of Cold War Architecture: A Reactionary
        Cultural Response to the Threat of Nuclear War. In *Matériel Culture: The Ar-
        chaeology of Twentieth Century Conflict,* edited by John Schofield, William G.
        Johnson, and Colleen M. Beck, pp. 227–235. Routledge, New York.
Johnson, Samuel and Jacques-Louis Manget
1783   *A Description of Stonehenge, Abiry, &c. in Wiltshire.* London.
Jones, D.
2008   New Light on Stonehenge. *Smithsonian* 39(7):36–46.
Jones, Robert C., Thomas F. Bullard, and Colleen M. Beck
2006   Historical Evaluation of U12b Tunnel Complex in Area 12, Nevada Test Site,
        Nye County, Nevada. Desert Research Institute, Historical Evaluation, Short
        Report HE050106-1.
JPAC Central Identification Laboratory
n.d.a   Search and Recovery Report...a RF-4C Crash Site Associated with...,
        Villabouli District, Savannakhet Province, Lao People's Democratic Repub-
        lic,...Through.... Unpublished report, JPAC Central Identification Labora-
        tory, Joint Base Pearl Harbor-Hickam, Hawaii.
n.d.b   Interim Search and Recovery Report..., an RF-4C Crash Site Associated

with…, Vilabouli District, Savannakhet Province, Lao People's Democratic Republic,…Unpublished Report, JPAC Central Identification Laboratory, Joint Base Pearl Harbor-Hickam, Hawaii.

Kaplan, M. F.

1980   Characterization of Weathered Glass by Analyzing Ancient Artifacts. In *Scientific Basis for Nuclear Waste Management*, Vol. II, edited by C. J. M. Northrup Jr., pp. 85–92. Plenum, New York.

1982   *Archaeological Data as a Basis for Repository Marker Design.* Office of Nuclear Waste Isolation Report ONWI-3541.

1986   Mankind's Future: Using the Past to Protect the Future: Archaeology and the Disposal of Highly Radioactive Wastes. *Interdiscipinary Science Reviews* 11:257–268.

Kaplan, M. F. and Mendel, J. E.

1982   Ancient Glass and the Safe Disposal of Nuclear Waste. *Archaeology* 35(4): 22–29.

Kay, Janet E.

2012   *Norse in Newfoundland: A Critical Examination of Archaeological Research at the Norse Site of L'Anse aux Meadows, Newfoundland.* BAR International Series 2339. British Archaeological Reports, Oxford.

Keeley, Lawrence H.

1977   The Functions of Paleolithic Flint Tools. *Scientific American* 237:108–126.

Kelly, Robert L.

1995   *The Foraging Spectrum: Diversity in Hunter-Gatherer Lifeways.* Smithsonian Institution Press, Washington, D.C.

Kenoyer, Jonathan M.

2011   Changing Perspectives of the Indus Civilization: New Discoveries and Challenges. *Puratattva* 41:1–18.

2013   Marine and Riverine Trade of the Indus Cities: Strategies for Research and Interpretation. In *Maritime Heritage of Indian Ocean*, edited by Alok Tripathi, pp. 61–87. Sharada, Delhi.

2015   The Indus Civilisation. *The Cambridge World Prehistory*, edited by Colin Renfrew and Paul Bahn, 1:407–432. Cambridge University Press, Cambridge.

Kenoyer, Jonathan M. and Heather M. -L. Miller

1999   Metal Technologies of the Indus Valley Tradition in Pakistan and Western India. *MASCA Research Papers in Science and Archaeology* 16:107–151.

Kiddey, Rachael

2014   Homeless Heritage: Collaborative Social Archaeology as Therapeutic Practice. Ph.D. dissertation, Department of Archaeology, University of York.

Kiddey, Rachael and John Schofield

2011   Embrace the Margins: Adventures in Archaeology and Homelessness. *Public Archaeology* 10:4–22.

Killam, Edward W.

2004   *The Detection of Human Remains.* 2nd ed. Charles C. Thomas, Springfield, IL.

Kimes, B. R. and H. A. Clark Jr.

1989   *Standard Catalog of American Cars, 1805–1942.* 2nd ed. Krause Publications, Iola, WI.

King, Thomas F.

2013   *Cultural Resource Laws and Practice.* 4th ed. AltaMira, Lanham, MD.

King, William

1864   The Reputed Fossil Man of the Neanderthal. *Quarterly Review of Science* 1:88–97.

Kirsch, David A.

2000   *The Electric Vehicle and the Burden of History.* Rutgers University Press, New Brunswick, NJ.

Kramer, Barbara

1996   *Nampeyo and Her Pottery.* University of New Mexico Press, Albuquerque.

Kroeber, Alfred L.

1925   *Handbook of the Indians of California.* Smithsonian Institution, Bureau of American Ethnology, Bulletin 78.

Larkin, Karin

2009   Archaeology and the Colorado Coalfield War. In *The Archaeology of Class War: The Colorado Coalfield Strike of 1913–1914,* edited by Karin Larkin and Randall H. McGuire, pp. 69–121. University Press of Colorado, Boulder.

Larkin, Karin and Randall H. McGuire (editors)

2009   *The Archaeology of Class War: The Colorado Coalfield Strike of 1913–1914.* University Press of Colorado, Boulder.

Lawal, Babatunde

1973   Dating Problems at Igbo–Ukwu. *The Journal of African History* 14:1–8.

Leakey, L. S. B.

1959   A New Fossil Skull From Olduvai. *Nature* 184:491–493.

Leakey, L. S. B., J. F. Evernden, and G. H. Curtis

1961   Age of Bed I, Olduvai Gorge, Tanganyika. *Nature* 191:478–479.

Leakey, Mary

1984   *Disclosing the Past.* Doubleday, New York.

Leavitt, Steven W. and Bryant Bannister

2009   Dendrochronology and Radiocarbon Dating: The Laboratory of Tree-Ring Research Connection. *Radiocarbon* 51:373–384.

Ledford, Janine

1993   A Lifetime With the Makah Collections. *Federal Archeology Report,* Summer, p. 5.

Lentz, David L., Nicholas P. Dunning, and Vernon L. Scarborough

2015   Defining the Constructed Niche of Tikal: A Summary View. In *Tikal: Paleoecology of an Ancient Maya City,* edited by David L. Lentz, Nicholas P. Dunning, and Vernon L. Scarborough, pp. 280–296. Cambridge University Press, Cambridge.

Lentz, David L. et al.

2012   Forests, Fields, and the Edge of Sustainability at the Ancient Maya City of Tikal. *Proceedings of the National Academy of Sciences* 111:18513–18518.

Levy, Sharon

2013   Ancient Gut Microbiomes Shed Light on Modern Disease. *Environmental Health Perspectives* 121(4):A118.

Levy, Thomas E., Russell B. Adams, Mohammad Najjar, Andreas Hauptmann, James D. Anderson, Baruch Brandl, Mark A. Robinson, and Thomas Higham

2004   Reassessing the Chronology of Biblical Edom: New Excavations and ^{14}C Dates from Khirbat en-Nahas (Jordan). *Antiquity* 78:865–879.

Levy, Thomas E., E. Ben-Yosef, and M. Najjar

2012   New Perspectives on Iron Age Copper Production and Society in the Faynan Region, Jordan. In *Eastern Mediterranean Metallurgy and Metalwork in the 2nd Millennium BC*, edited by V. Kassianidou and G. Papasavvas, pp. 197–214. Oxbow Books, Oxford.

Levy, Thomas E., Thomas Higham, Christopher Bronk Ramsey, Neil G. Smith, Erez Ben-Yosef, Mark Robinson, Stefan Münger, Kyle Knabb, Jürgen P. Schulze, Mohammad Najjar, and Lisa Tauxe

2008   High-Precision Radiocarbon Dating and Historical Biblical Archaeology in Southern Jordan. *Proceedings of the National Academy of Sciences* 105:16460–16465.

Levy, Thomas E., Mohammad Najjar, and Erez Ben-Yosef (editors)

2014   *New Insights into the Iron Age Archaeology of Edom, Southern Jordan.* Monumenta Archaeologica, Vol. 35. UCLA, Cotsen Institute of Archaeology Press, Los Angeles.

Levy, Thomas E., Mohammad Najjar, and Thomas Higham

2010   Ancient Texts and Archaeology Revisited—Radiocarbon and Biblical Dating in the Southern Levant. *Antiquity* 84:834–847.

Levy, Thomas E., M. Najjar, J. van der Plicht, N. G. Smith, H. J. Bruins, and T. Higham

2005   Lowland Edom and the High and Low Chronologies: Edomite State Formation, the Bible and Recent Archaeological Research in Southern Jordan. In *The Bible and Radiocarbon Dating—Archaeology, Text and Science,* edited by Thomas E. Levy and T. Higham, pp. 129–163. Equinox, London.

L'Hostis, V., F. Foct, and P. Dillmann

2008   Corrosion Behaviour of Reinforced Concrete: Laboratory Experiments and Archaeological Analogues for Long-Term Predictive Modelling. *Journal of Nuclear Materials* 379:124–132.

Libby, Willard F.

1946   Atmospheric Helium Three and Radiocarbon from Cosmic Radiation. *Physical Review* 69:671–672.

1952   *Radiocarbon Dating.* University of Chicago Press, Chicago.

1955   *Radiocarbon Dating.* 2nd ed. University of Chicago Press, Chicago.

1963   Accuracy of Radiocarbon Dates. *Science* 140:278–280.

1967   History of Radiocarbon Dating. In *Radioactive Dating and Methods of Low-Level Counting*, pp. 3–25. International Atomic Energy Agency, Vienna.

Libby, Willard F., E. C. Anderson, and J. R. Arnold

1949   Age Determination by Radiocarbon Content: World-Wide Assay of Natural Radiocarbon. *Science* 109:227–228.

Little, Barbara J. (editor)

2002   *Public Benefits of Archaeology*. University Press of Florida, Gainesville.

Littman, Edwin R.

1980   Maya Blue: A New Perspective. *American Antiquity* 45:87–100.

1982   Maya Blue—Further Perspectives and the Possible Use of Indigo as the Colorant. *American Antiquity* 47:404–408.

Lopes, Rosaly M. C.

2005   *The Volcano Adventure Guide*. Cambridge University Press, Cambridge.

Lucero, Lisa J. et al.

2014   Water and Landscape: Ancient Maya Settlement Decisions. In *The Resilience and Vulnerability of Ancient Landscapes: Transforming Maya Archaeology through IHOPE*, edited by Arlen F. Chase and Vernon L. Scarborough, pp. 40–42. *American Anthropological Association, Archeological Papers* 24.

Ludlow Collective

2001   Archaeology of the Colorado Coal Field War 1913–1914. In *Archaeologies of the Contemporary Past*, edited by Victor Buchli and Gavin Lucas, pp. 94–107. Routledge, London.

Lufkin, Martha B. G.

2002   End of the Era of Denial for Buyers of State-Owned Antiquities: United States v. Schultz. *International Journal of Cultural Property* 11:305–322.

2003   Criminal Liability for Receiving State-Claimed Antiquities in the United States: The 'Schultz' Case. *Art Antiquity and Law* 8(4):321–342.

Luke, Christina and Morag M. Kersel

2012   *U.S. Cultural Diplomacy and Archaeology: Soft Power, Hard Heritage*. Routledge, London.

Lyman, R. Lee

1991   Late Quaternary Biogeography of the Pygmy Rabbit (*Brachylagus idahoensis*) in eastern Washington. *Journal of Mammalogy* 72:110–17.

1996   Relevance of Faunal Analysis to Wildlife Management. *World Archaeology* 28:110–125.

2004   Biogeographic and Conservation Implications of Late Quaternary Pygmy Rabbits (*Brachylagus idahoensis*) in Eastern Washington. *Western North American Naturalist* 64:1–6.

2006   Paleozoology in the Service of Conservation Biology. *Evolutionary Anthropology* 15:11–19.

2012   A Warrant for Applied Palaeozoology. *Biological Reviews* 87:513–525.

MacDonald, Kevin C.

2013   Professor Thurstan Shaw CBE, FBA, FSA: A Personal Appreciation and
        Remembrance. *Azania: Archaeological Research in Africa* 48:426–433.

Mackey, Larry A.

2006   ARPA on Private Lands: The GE Mound Case. In *Presenting Archaeology in
        Court: Legal Strategies for Protecting Cultural Resources*, edited by Sherry Hutt,
        Marion Forsyth, and David Tarler, pp. 47–55. AltaMira, Lanham, MD.

Madella, Marco and Dorian Q. Fuller

2006   Palaeoecology and the Harappan Civilisation of South Asia: A Reconsider-
        ation. *Quaternary Science Reviews* 25:1283–1301.

Mardikian, Paul

2004   Conservation and Management Strategies Applied to Post-Recovery Analysis
        of the American Civil War Submarine *H. L. Hunley* (1864). *The International
        Journal of Nautical Archaeology* 33:137–148.

Mardikian, Paul and Pascale Girard

2010   18 Tons of Roman Glass Under the Sea: A Complex Conservation Puzzle.
        In *Glass and Ceramics Conservation 2010*, edited by Hannelore Roemich,
        pp. 110–118. Corning Museum of Glass, Corning, NY.

Marlowe, Greg

1980   W. F. Libby and the Archaeologists, 1946–1948. *Radiocarbon* 22:1005–114.

1999   Year One: Radiocarbon Dating and American Archaeology, 1947–1948. *Amer-
        ican Antiquity* 64:9–32.

Martin, Paul S.

1973   The Discovery of America. *Science* 179:969–974.

2005   *Twilight of the Mammoths: Ice Age Extinctions and the Rewilding of America.*
        University of California Press, Berkeley.

Mason, Peter, and I-Ling Kuo

2008   Visitor Attitudes to Stonehenge: International Icon or National Disgrace?
        Journal of Heritage Tourism 2(3):168–183.

Mauger, Jeffrey E.

1991   Shed-Roof Houses at Ozette and in a Regional Perspective. In *Ozette Archae-
        ological Project Research Reports*, Vol. I, *House Structure and Floor Midden*,
        edited by Stephan R. Samuels, pp. 29–169. Reports of Investigations 63,
        Washington State University, Pullman.

McAllister, Kelly R.

1995   *Washington State Recovery Plan for the Pygmy Rabbit.* Washington Depart-
        ment of Fish and Wildlife, Wildlife Management Program, Olympia.

McAllister, Martin E. and Francis P. McManamon

2007   *Technical Brief 20: Archeological Resource Damage Assessment: Legal Basis and
        Methods.* U.S. National Park Service Publications and Papers 120. http://digi
        talcommons.unl.edu/cgi/viewcontent.cgi?article=1119&context=natlpark,
        accessed 30 June 2016.

McAvennie, Mike

2004   *The Roswell Dig Diaries (Sci Fi Declassified)*. Pocket Books, New York.

McCartney, Martha W. and Edward Ayres

2004   Yorktown's "Poor Potter": A Man Wise Beyond Discretion. *Ceramics in America 2004*, pp. 48–59.

McDavid, Carol

1997   Descendants, Decisions, and Power: The Public Interpretation of the Archaeology of the Levi Jordan Plantation. *Historical Archaeology* 31:114–131.

2000   Archaeology as Cultural Critique: Pragmatism and the Archaeology of a Southern United States Plantation. In *Philosophy and Archaeological Practice: Perspectives for the 21st Century*, edited by Cornelius Holtorf and Håkan Karlsson, pp. 221–239. Bricoleur Press, Göteborg, Sweden.

2002   Archaeologies That Hurt; Descendants that Matter: A Pragmatic Approach to Collaboration in the Public Interpretation of African-American Archaeology. *World Archaeology* 34:303–314.

2011   Public Archaeology, Activism, and Racism: Rethinking the Heritage "Product." In *Archaeologists as Activists: Can Archaeologists Change the World?* edited by M. Jay Stottman, pp. 36–47. University of Alabama Press, Tuscaloosa.

McGhee, Robert

1984   Contact between Native North Americans and the Medieval Norse: A Review of the Evidence. *American Antiquity* 49:4–26.

McGimsey, Charles R., III and Hester A Davis (editors)

1977   *The Management of Archeological Resources: The Airlie House Report*. Special Publication of the Society for American Archaeology, Washington, D.C.

McGregor, John C.

1936   Dating the Eruption of Sunset Crater, Arizona. *American Antiquity* 2:15–26.

McGuire, Randall H.

1992   *A Marxist Archaeology*. Academic Press, San Diego, CA.

2004   Colorado Coalfield Massacre. *Archaeology* 57:62–70.

2008   *Archaeology as Political Action*. University of California Press, Berkeley.

McGuire, Randall H. and Karin Larkin

2009   Unearthing Class War. In *The Archaeology of Class War: The Colorado Coalfield Strike of 1913–1914*, edited by Karin Larkin and Randall H. McGuire, pp. 1–28. University Press of Colorado, Boulder.

McGuire, Randall H. and Paul Reckner

2002   The Unromantic West: Labor, Capital, and Struggle. *Historical Archaeology* 36:44–58.

2003   Building a Working-Class Archaeology: The Colorado Coal Field War Project. *Industrial Archaeology Review* 25:83–95.

McGuire, Randall, H. and Michael B. Schiffer (editors)

1982   *Hohokam and Patayan: Prehistory of Southwestern Arizona*. Academic Press, San Diego, CA.

McIlrath, Sharon

1984   Obsidian Blades: Tomorrow's Surgical Tools. *American Medical News*, 2 November, pp. 1, 29–30.

McIntosh, Susan Keech

2013   C. Thurstan Shaw. antiquity.ac.uk/tributes/shaw.html, accessed 6 November 2014.

McIntosh, Susan Keech and Roderick J. McIntosh

1988   From Stone to Metal: New Perspectives on the Later Prehistory of West Africa. *Journal of World Prehistory* 2:89–133.

Meko, David M. and Connie A. Woodhouse

2011   Application of Streamflow Reconstruction to Water Resources Management. In *Dendroclimatology: Progress and Prospects*, edited by Malcolm K. Hughes, Thomas W. Swetnam, and Henry F. Diaz, pp. 231–261. Springer, New York.

Meltzer, David J.

2009   *First Peoples in a New World: Colonizing Ice Age America*. University of California Press, Berkeley.

Merlan, Thomas

1997   The Trinity Experiments. Human Systems Research, White Sands Missile Range Archaeological Report No. 97-15. Tularosa, NM.

Merwin, H. E.

1931   Chemical Analysis of Pigments. In *The Temple of the Warriors at Chichen Itza, Yucatan*, edited by E. H. Morris, Jean Charlot, and A. A. Morris, p. 356. Carnegie Institution of Washington, Publication 406.

Miksicek, Charles H.

1987   Formation Processes of the Archaeobotanical Record. *Advances in Archaeological Method and Theory* 10:211–247.

Miller, Daniel

1985   *Artefacts as Categories: A Study of Ceramic Variability in Central India*. Cambridge University Press, Cambridge.

2010   *Stuff*. Polity Press, Cambridge, England.

Miller, William et al.

1990   *Geological Disposal of Radioactive Wastes and Natural Analogues: Lessons from Nature and Archaeology*. Elsevier, Oxford.

Minnis, Paul E.

2003   (editor) *People and Plants in Ancient Eastern North America*. Smithsonian Institution Press, Washington, D.C.

2014   (editor) *New Lives for Ancient and Extinct Crops*. University of Arizona Press, Tucson.

Mom, Gijs

2004   *The Electric Vehicle: Technology and Expectations in the Automobile Age*. Johns Hopkins University Press, Baltimore, MD.

Morison, Samuel E.

1971   *The European Discovery of America: The Northern Voyages,* AD *500–1600.* Oxford University Press, New York.

Morse, Dan, Donald Crusoe, and H. G. Smith

1976   Forensic Archaeology. *Journal of Forensic Sciences* 21:323–331.

Morse, Dan, Jack Duncan, and James Stoutamire (editors)

1984   *Handbook of Forensic Archaeology and Anthropology.* Rose Printing, Tallahassee, FL.

Mosimann, J. E. and P. S. Martin

1975   Simulating Overkill by Paleoindians. *American Scientist* 63:304–313.

Moyes, Holley, Jaime J. Awe, George A. Brook, and James W. Webster

2009   The Ancient Maya Drought Cult: Late Classic Cave Use in Belize. *Latin American Antiquity* 20:1750206.

Mullin, Molly H.

1992   The Patronage of Difference: Making Indian Art "Art, Not Ethnology." *Cultural Anthropology* 7:395–424.

Munson, Cheryl Ann, Marjorie Melvin Jones, and Robert E. Fry

1995   The GE Mound: An ARPA Case Study. *American Antiquity* 60:131–159.

Murphy, Larry E. (editor)

1996   *H. L. Hunley Site Assessment.* National Park Service, Submerged Cultural Resources Unit, Santa Fe, New Mexico.

Murray, Maribeth S.

2008   Zooarchaeology and Arctic Marine Mammal Biogeography, Conservation, and Management. *Ecological Applications* 18(2):S41–S55.

Nash, Stephen E.

1999   *Time, Trees, and Prehistory: Tree-Ring Dating and the Development of North American Archaeology, 1914–1950.* University of Utah Press, Salt Lake City.

Neff, Delphine et al.

2010   A Review of the Archaeological Analogue Approaches to Predict the Long-Term Corrosion Behaviour of Carbon Steel Overpack and Reinforced Concrete Structures in the French Disposal Systems. *Journal of Nuclear Materials* 402:196–205.

Noël Hume, Ivor

1964   Archaeology: Handmaiden to History. *The North Carolina Historical Review* 41:215–225.

Nydal, Reidar

1989   A Critical Review of Radiocarbon Dating of a Norse Settlement at L'Anse aux Meadows, Newfoundland Canada. *Radiocarbon* 31:976–985.

Ogundiran, Akinwumi

2005   Four Millennia of Cultural History in Nigeria (ca. 2000 BC–AD 1900): Archaeological Perspectives. *Journal of World Prehistory* 19:133–168.

Ojovan, M. I. and W. E. Lee
2014   *An Introduction to Nuclear Waste Immobilisation.* 2nd ed. Elsevier, Oxford.
Olsen, Bjørnar
2010   *In Defense of Things: Archaeology and the Ontology of Objects.* AltaMira, Lanham, MD.
Orser, Charles E., Jr.
1990   Archaeological Approaches to New World Plantation Slavery. *Archaeological Method and Theory* 2:111–154.
Ort, Michael H., Mark D. Elson, Kirk C. Anderson, Wendell A. Duffield, and Terry L. Samples
2008   Variable Effects of Cinder-Cone Eruptions on Prehistoric Agrarian Populations in the American Southwest. *Journal of Volcanology and Geothermal Research* 176:363–376.
Ortega, Y. R. and D. Bonavia
2003   Cryptosporidium, Giardia, and Cyclospora in Ancient Peruvians. *Journal of Parasitology* 89:635–636.
Owen, Richard
1879   *Memoirs on the Extinct Wingless Birds of New Zealand, Vol. 2.* John van Voorst, London.
Page, Thomas Nelson
1910   *Mount Vernon and Its Preservation: 1858–1910.* Knickerbocker Press, New York.
Pearsall, Deborah M.
2000   *Paleoethnobotany: A Handbook of Procedures.* 2nd ed. Academic Press, San Diego, CA.
Pearson, Mike Parker and the Stonehenge Riverside Project
2011   *Solving the Mysteries of the Greatest Stone Age Monument.* The Experiment, New York.
Peterson, Susan
1984   *Lucy M. Lewis, American Indian Potter.* Kodansha International, New York.
1989   *The Living Tradition of Maria Martinez.* Kodansha International, New York.
Pinkoski, Marc
2008   Julian Steward, American Anthropology, and Colonialism. *Histories of Anthropology Annual* 4:172–204.
Piperno, Dolores R.
2006   *Phytoliths: A Comprehensive Guide for Archaeologists and Paleoecologists.* AltaMira, Lanham, MD.
Pogue, Dennis J.
2004   Shad, Wheat, and Rye (Whiskey): George Washington, Entrepreneur. Paper presented at the 2004 Annual Conference of the Society for Historical Archaeology, St. Louis, MO.

2006   Archaeology at George Washington's Mount Vernon, 1931–2006. *Quarterly Bulletin of the Archaeological Society of Virginia* 61(4):165–175.

2011   *Founding Spirits: George Washington and the Beginnings of the American Whiskey Industry.* Harbour Books, Buena Vista, VA.

Poinsott, Christophe and Stéphane Gin

2011   Long-Term Behavior Science: The Cornerstone Approach for Reliably Assessing the Long-Term Performance of Nuclear Waste. *Journal of Nuclear Materials* 420:182–192.

Posnansky, Merrick

1973   Review of *Igbo Ukwu: An Account of Archaeological Discoveries in Eastern Nigeria*, by Thurstan Shaw. *Archaeology* 26(4):309–311.

Possehl, Gregory L.

1997   The Transformation of the Indus Civilization. *Journal of World Prehistory* 11:425–472.

Powell, Eric A.

2013   *Hunley* Decoded. *Archaeology* May/June, p. 47.

Powell, J. W.

1894   Report of the Director. In *Twelfth Annual Report of the Bureau of Ethnology, 1890–91*, pp. XIX–XLVIII. Government Printing Office, Washington, D.C.

Powell, Shirley, Christina Elnora Garza, and Aubrey Hendricks

1993   Ethics and Ownership of the Past: The Reburial and Repatriation Controversy. *Archaeological Method and Theory* 5:1–42.

Powers, Natasha and Lucy Sibun

2013   Forensic Archaeology. In *The Oxford Handbook of the Archaeology of the Contemporary World*, edited by Paul Graves-Brown, Rodney Harrison, and Angela Piccini, pp. 40–53. Oxford University Press, Oxford.

Rafn, Carl C.

1838   *America Discovered in the Tenth Century.* W. Jackson, New York.

Ragan, Mark K.

1995   *The Hunley: Submarines, Sacrifice, & Success in the Civil War.* Narwhal Press, Miami, FL

Rathje, William L.

1974   The Garbage Project: A New Way of Looking at the Problems of Archaeology. *Archaeology* 27:236–241.

1977   Public Acceptance of Radioactive Wastes Disposal: An Archaeologist's Perspective. In *Proceedings: A Workshop on Policy and Technical Issues Pertinent to the Development of Environmental Protection Criteria for Radioactive Wastes*, Albuquerque, New Mexico, April 12–14, pp. 3.39–3.45. U.S. Environmental Protection Agency, Office of Radiation Programs, Washington, D.C.

1984   The Garbàge Decade. *American Behavioral Scientist* 28:9–29.

Rathje, William and Cullen Murphy

1992   *Rubbish! The Archaeology of Garbage.* HarperCollins, New York.

Rathje, W. L., W. W. Hughes, D. C. Wilson, M. K. Tani, G. H. Archer, R. G. Hunt, and T. W. Jones

1992   The Archaeology of Contemporary Landfills. *American Antiquity* 57:437–447.

Ray, Arthur J.

2006   Historical Particularism and Cultural Ecology in Court. In *Central Sites, Peripheral Visions: Cultural and Institutional Crossings in the History of Anthropology*, edited by Richard Handler, pp. 248–274. University of Wisconsin Press, Madison.

Reid, Jefferson and Stephanie Whittlesey

1997   *The Archaeology of Ancient Arizona.* University of Arizona Press, Tucson.

Reinen, D., P. Köhl, and C. Müller

2004   The Nature of the Colour Centres in 'Maya Blue' — The Incorporation of Organic Pigment Molecules into the Palygorskite Lattice. *Zeitschrift für Anorganische und Allgemeine Chemie* 630:97–102.

Reinhard, Karl J. and Vaughn M. Bryant Jr.

1992   Coprolite Analysis: A Biological Perspective on Archaeology. *Archaeological Method and Theory* 4:245–288.

Reitz, Elizabeth J. and Myra Shackley

2012   *Environmental Archaeology.* Springer, New York.

Reitz, Elizabeth J. and Elizabeth S. Wing

2008   *Zooarchaeology.* 2nd ed. Cambridge University Press, Cambridge.

Renard, D., J. Iriarte, J. J. Birk, S. Rostain, B. Glaser, and D. McKey

2012   Ecological Engineers Ahead of their Time: The Functioning of Pre-Columbian Raised-Field Agriculture and its Potential Contributions to Sustainability Today. *Ecological Engineering* 45:30–44.

Renker, Ann M. and Greig W. Arnold

1988   Exploring the Role of Education in Cultural Resource Management: The Makah Culture and Research Center Example. *Human Organization* 47:302–307.

Richards, Julian

2011   *Stonehenge.* English Heritage, London.

Richards, Julian and Mark Whithy

1997   The Engineering of Stonehenge. *Proceedings of the British Academy* 92:231–256.

Richards, Nathan

2008   *Ships' Graveyards: Abandoned Watercraft and the Archaeological Site Formation Process.* University of Florida Press, Gainesville.

Robinson, H.

1913   The San Franciscan Volcanic Field, Arizona. *U.S. Geological Survey Professional Paper* 76.

Römich, Hannelore

2003   Studies of Ancient Glass and their Application to Nuclear-Waste Management. *Materials Research Society Bulletin* 28:500–504

Russell, Nerissa

2012   *Social Zooarchaeology: Humans and Animals in Prehistory*. Cambridge University Press, Cambridge.

Sabloff, Jeremy A.

2008   *Archaeology Matters: Action Archaeology in the Modern World*. Left Coast Press, Walnut Creek, CA.

Saitta, Dean F.

2005   Labor and Class in the American West. In *North American Archaeology*, edited by Timothy R. Pauketat and Diana DiPaolo Loren, pp. 359–385. Blackwell, Malden, MA.

2007   *The Archaeology of Collective Action*. University of Florida Press, Gainesville.

Samuels, Stephan R. and Richard D. Daugherty

1991   Introduction to the Ozette Archaeological Project. In *Ozette Archaeological Project Resarch Reports*, Vol. I, *House Structure and Floor Midden*, edited by Stephan R. Samuels, pp. 2–27, Reports of Investigations 63. Washington State University, Pullman.

Sankararaman, Sriram, Nick Patterson, Heng Li, Svante Pääbo, and David Reich.

2012   The Date of Interbreeding Between Neandertals and Modern Humans. *PLoS Genetics* 8:e1002947.

Scarborough, Vernon L. et al.

2012   Water and Sustainable Land Use at the Ancient Tropical City of Tikal, Guatemala. *Proceedings of the National Academy of Sciences* 109:12408–12413.

Schablitsky, Julie M. (editor)

2007   *Box Office Archaeology: Refining Hollywood's Portrayals of the Past*. Left Coast Press, Walnut Creek, CA.

Scharff, Virginia

1991   *Taking the Wheel: Women and the Coming of the Motor Age*. Free Press, New York.

Schiffer, Michael B.

1979   Some Impacts of Cultural Resource Management on American Archaeology. In *Archaeological Resource Management in Australia and Oceania*, edited by J. R. McKinlay and K. L. Jones, pp. 1–11. New Zealand Historic Places Trust Publication 11, Wellington.

1986   Radiocarbon Dating and the "Old Wood" Problem: The Case of the Hohokam Chronology. *Journal of Archaeological Science* 13:13–30.

1995   The Historical Context for Electric Car Commercialization. In *NESEA's Substainable Transportation and S/EV95, Proceedings*, pp. 7–15 to 7–18. Northeast Sustainable Energy Association, Greenfield, MA.

2000a   Why the Electric Automobile Lost Market Share. How Social Behavior Can Affect Product Technology. *IEEE Potentials* 19(5):40–53.

2000b   Indigenous Theories, Scientific Theories and Product Histories. In *Matter, Materiality and Modern Culture*, edited by Paul Graves-Brown, pp. 72–96. Routledge, London.

2009   Ethnoarchaeology, Experimental Archaeology, and the "American School." *Ethnoarchaeology* 1:7–26.

2010   *Behavioral Archaeology: Principles and Practice.* Equinox, London.

2011   *Studying Technological Change: A Behavioral Approach.* University of Utah Press, Salt Lake City.

2013   *The Archaeology of Science: Studying the Creation of Useful Knowledge.* Springer, Heidelberg.

2015   William L. Rathje, Father of Garbology. *Arizona Anthropologist* 25:78–86.

Schiffer, Michael B., Tamara C. Butts, and Kimberly K. Grimm

1994   *Taking Charge: The Electric Automobile in America.* Smithsonian Institution Press, Washington, D.C.

Schiffer, Michael B. and George J. Gumerman (editors).

1977   *Conservation Archaeology: A Guide for Cultural Resource Management Studies.* Academic Press, New York.

Schiffer, Michael B. and Andrea R. Miller

1999   *The Material Life of Human Beings: Artifacts, Behavior, and Communication.* Routledge, London.

Schiffer, Michael B. and Susan J. Wells

1982   Archaeological Surveys: Past and Future. In *Hohokam and Patayan: Prehistory of Southwestern Arizona,* edited by Randall H. McGuire and Michael B. Schiffer, pp. 345–383. Academic Press, San Diego, CA.

Schlanger, Sara

1992   Recognizing Persistent Places in Anasazi Settlement Systems. In *Space, Time, and Archaeological Landscapes,* edited by Jacqueline Rossignol and LuAnn Wandsnider, pp. 91–112. Plenum, New York.

Schmitt, S.

2002   Mass Graves and the Collection of Forensic Evidence: Genocide, War Crimes, and Crimes Against Humanity. In *Advances in Forensic Taphonomy,* edited by W. D. Haglund and H. H. Sorg, pp. 277–292. CRC Press, Boca Raton, FL.

Schulman, Edmund

1945   Tree-Ring Hydrology of the Colorado River Basin. *University of Arizona Bulletin* 16(4):1–51.

Schumacher, Ernst F.

1973   *Small Is Beautiful: A Study of Economics as if People Mattered.* Blond and Briggs, London.

Schwartz, J.

1981   A Touch of Glass. *Science 81* 2(1):79–80.

Scott, Michael J. and Michael J. Scott Jr.

1982   Obsidian Surgical Blades: Modern Use of a Stone Age Implement. *The Journal of Dermatologic Surgery and Oncology* 8:1050–1052.

Seaborg, Glenn T.

1981   Willard Frank Libby. *Physics Today* 34(2):92, 95.

Seeman, Mark F.

1979   *The Hopewell Interaction Sphere: The Evidence for Interregional Trade and Structural Complexity*. Indiana Historical Society, Indianapolis.

1995   When Words Are Not Enough: Hopewell Interregionalism and the Use of Material Symbols at the GE Mound. In *Native American Interactions: Multiscalar Analyses and Interpretations on the Eastern Woodlands*, edited by M. Nassaney and K. Sassaman, pp. 122–143. University of Tennessee Press, Knoxville.

Seminole Tribe

2013   Tribal Historic Preservation Office, 2013 Annual Report: *Sustaining Sovereignty*. Seminole Tribe, Big Cypress Reservation, FL.

Sepez, Jennifer

2008   Historical Ecology of Makah Subsistence Foraging Patterns. *Journal of Ethnobiology* 28:110–133.

Sharer, Robert

2012   Time of Kings and Queens. *Expedition* 54(1):26–35.

Shaw, Thurstan

1960   Bronzes from Eastern Nigeria: Excavations at Igbo–Ukwu. *Journal of the Historical Society of Nigeria* 2:162–165.

1967   The Mystery of the Buried Bronzes. *Nigeria Magazine* 92:55–74.

1970   *Igbo–Ukwu: An Account of Archaeological Discoveries in Eastern Nigeria*. Faber, London.

1975   Those Igbo–Ukwu Radiocarbon Dates: Facts, Fictions and Probabilities. *The Journal of African History* 16:503–517.

1977   *Unearthing Igbo–Ukwu: Archaeological Discoveries in Eastern Nigeria*. Oxford University Press, Ibadan, Nigeria.

Sheets, Payson D.

1993   Dawn of a New Stone Age in Eye Surgery. In *Archaeology: Discovering Our Past*, edited by Robert Sharer and Wendy Ashmore, pp. 108–110. McGraw-Hill, New York.

Sheets, Payson and Donald Grayson

1979   *Volcanic Activity and Human Ecology*. Academic Press, New York.

Shepard, Anna O.

1962   Maya Blue: Alternative Hypotheses. *American Antiquity* 27:565–566.

Shepherd, Nick

2002   The Politics of Archaeology in Africa. *Annual Review of Anthropology* 31:189–209.

Shipek, Florence C.

1989   Mission Indians and Indians of California Land Claims. *American Indian Quarterly* 13(4):409–420.

Sigler-Eisenberg, Brenda

1985   Forensic Research: Expanding the Concept of Applied Archaeology. *American Antiquity* 50:650–655.

Silverberg, Robert

1968   *Mound Builders of Ancient America: The Archaeology of a Myth.* New York
        Graphic Society, New York.

Singleton, Theresa A.

1995   The Archaeology of Slavery in North America. *Annual Review of Anthropology*
        24:119–140.

Skibo, James M. and Michael B. Schiffer

2008   *People and Things: A Behavioral Approach to Material Culture.* Springer, New
        York.

Slater, Mary

1996   *Integrity-Preservation Field Report: Trinity Ground Zero Area Instrument
        Shelters.* Human Systems Research, White Sands Missile Range Report
        No. 96-05. Tularosa, NM.

Smellie, John A. T., Fred Karlsson, and W. Russell Alexander

1997   Natural Analogue Studies: Present Status and Performance Assessment
        Implications. *Journal of Contaminant Hydrology* 26:3–17.

Smith, Bruce D.

2006   Eastern North America as an Independent Center of Plant Domestication.
        Proceedings of the National Academy of Sciences 103:12223-12228.

2014   The Domestication of *Helianthus annuus* L. (Sunflower). *Vegetation History
        and Archaeobotany* 23:57–74.

Smith, H. S.

1964   Egypt and C14 Dating. *Antiquity* 38:32–38.

Smith, Monica L. (editor)

2003   *The Social Construction of Ancient Cities*, edited by Monica L. Smith, pp. 1–36.
        Smithsonian Institution Press, Washington, D.C.

Smith, Pamela Jane

2014   Archaeology and Heritage in West Africa: Building Links and Capac-
        ity Through Thurstan Shaw's Legacy. *www.mcdonald.cam.ac.uk/.../shaw
        -programme*, accessed 1 November 2014.

Sokol, J. P.

1983   Oklo/Obsidian/Ancient Glasses: Applications to Nuclear Waste Public
        Information Programs. In *Waste Management '83: Waste Isolation in the U.S.,
        Technical Programs and Public Education*, edited by Roy G. Post, pp. 59–64.
        American Nuclear Society, La Grange Park, IL.

Soren, David

1985   An Earthquake on Cyprus: New Discoveries from Kourion. *Archaeology*
        38(2):52–59.

Soren, David and Jamie James

1988   *Kourion: The Search for a Lost Roman City.* Anchor Press, New York.

Souden, David

1997   *Stonehenge Revealed.* Facts on File, New York.

Spence, Roderick W. Spence
1968   The Rover Nuclear Rocket Program. *Science* 160:953–959.

Spivey, Richard L.
2003   *The Legacy of Maria Poveka Martinez*. Museum of New Mexico Press, Albuquerque.

Sprules, John
1884   *The Visitor's Illustrated Pocket-Guide to Stonehenge and the Salisbury Plain*. Oxford.

Squier, Ephraim G. and Edwin H. Davis
1848   Ancient Monuments of the Mississippi Valley, Comprising the Results of Extensive Original Surveys and Explorations. *Smithsonian Contributions to Knowledge* 1.

Stanislawski, Dan
1946   The Origin and Spread of the Grid-Pattern Town. *Geographical Review* 36:105–120.

Stapp, Darby C. and Michael S. Burney
2002   *Tribal Cultural Resource Management: The Full Circle to Stewardship*. AltaMira, Walnut Creek, CA.

Steadman, David W.
1989   Extinction of Birds in Eastern Polynesia: A Review of the Record, and Comparisons with Other Pacific Island Groups. *Journal of Archaeological Science* 16:177–205.
1995   Prehistoric Extinctions of Pacific Island Birds: Biodiversity Meets Zooarchaeology. *Science* 267:1123–1131.
1997   Human-Caused Extinction of Birds. In *Biodiversity II: Understanding and Protecting Our Biological Resources*, edited by Marjorie L. Reaka-Kudla, Don E. Wilson, and Edward O. Wilson, pp. 139–162. Joseph Henry Press, Washington, D.C.

Steadman, David W. and Paul S. Martin
2003   The Late Quaternary Extinction and Future Resurrection of Birds on Pacific Islands. *Earth-Science Reviews* 61:133–147.

Stone, Peter and Amanda Feather
2005   *Stonehenge: Information for Tutors and Students in Tourism Studies*. English Heritage, London.

Stottman, M. Jay (editor)
2011   *Archaeologists as Activists: Can Archaeologists Change the World?* 2nd ed. University of Alabama Press, Tuscaloosa.

Stover, Eric and Molly Ryan
2001   Breaking Bread with the Dead. *Historical Archaeology* 35:7–25.

Straka, Thomas J.
2008   Edmund P. Schulman (1908–1958). *Forest History Today*, Spring.

Stuiver, Minze and Hans E. Suess
1966   On the Relationship Between Radiocarbon Dates and True Sample Ages. *Radiocarbon* 8:534–540.

Sturtevant, William C.
1971   From Creek to Seminole. In *North American Indians in Historical Perspective*, edited by Eleanor B. Leacock and Nancy O. Lurie, pp. 92–128. Random House, New York.

Suess, Hans E.
1961   Secular Changes in the Concentration of Atmospheric Radiocarbon. In *Problems Related to Interplanetary Matter*. National Academy of Sciences, Nuclear Science Series Report No. 33, Publication 845, pp. 90–95. Washington, D.C.

Sutton, Imre
1985   Configurations of Land Claims: Toward a Model. In *Irredeemable America: The Indians' Estate and Land Claims*, edited by Imre Sutton, pp. 111–132. University of New Mexico Press, Albuquerque.

Swartley, Lynn
2000   Inventing Indigenous Knowledge: Archaeology, Rural Development, and the Raised Field Rehabilitation Project in Bolivia. Ph.D. dissertation, University of Pittsburgh, PA.

Taylor, R. E.
1987   *Radiocarbon Dating: An Archaeological Perspective*. Academic Press, New York.

Terrell, John E. et al.
2003   Domesticated Landscapes: The Subsistence Ecology of Plant and Animal Domestication. *Journal of Archaeological Method and Theory* 10:323–368.

Thode, Simon
2009   Bones and Words in 1870s New Zealand: The Moa-Hunter Debate Through Actor Networks. *The British Journal for the History of Science* 42:225–244.

Thomas, Cyrus
1885   Who Were the Mound Builders? Second Paper. *The American Antiquarian and Oriental Journal* 7(2):65–74.
1894   Report on the Mound Explorations of the Bureau of Ethnology. In *Twelfth Annual Report of the Bureau of Ethnology, 1890–91*, pp. 730. Government Printing Office, Washington, D.C.

Tito, Raul Y. et al.
2012   Insights from Characterizing Extinct Human Gut Microbiomes. *PLoS One* 7(12):e51146.

Tomak, Curtis H.
1994   The Mount Vernon Site: A Remarkable Hopewell Mound in Posey County, Indiana. *Archaeology of Eastern North America* 22:1–46.

Traugott, Joseph

1999   Fewkes and Nampeyo: Clarifying a Myth-Understanding. In *Native American Art in the Twentieth Century: Makers, Meanings, Histories*, edited by W. Jackson Rushing III, pp. 7–19. Routledge, London.

Trauth, Kathleen M., Stephen C. Hora, and Robert V. Guzowski

1993   Expert Judgment on Markers to Deter Inadvertent Human Intrusion into the Waste Isolation Pilot Plant. Sandia National Laboratories Report 92-1382, Albuquerque, NM.

Trigger, Bruce

1984   Alternative Archaeologies: Nationalist, Colonialist, Imperialist. *Man* 19: 355–370.

Tylecote, R. F.

1977   Durable Materials for Sea Water: The Archaeological Evidence. *The International Journal of Nautical Archaeology and Underwater Exploration* 6:269–283.

1979   The Effect of Soil Conditions on the Long-Term Corrosion of Buried Tin-Bronzes and Copper. *Journal of Archaeological Science* 6:345–368.

1983   The Behaviour of Lead as a Corrosion Resistant Medium Undersea and in Soils. *Journal of Archaeological Science* 10:397–409.

Ubelaker, D. H. and D. R. Hunt

1995   The Influence of William M. Bass III on the Development of American Forensic Anthropology. *Journal of Forensic Sciences* 40:729–734.

Ursell, Luke K. et al.

2013   Replenishing Our Defensive Microbes. *Bioessays* 35:810–817.

U.S. Government

1980   *United States Indian Claims Commission — Final Report*. U.S. Government Printing Office, Washington, D.C.

Valado, Martha Trenna

2006   Factors Influencing Homeless People's Perception and Use of Urban Space. Ph.D. dissertation, Department of Anthropology, University of Arizona, Tucson.

Valado, Trenna and Randall Amster (editors)

2012   *Professional Lives, Personal Struggles: Ethics and Advocacy in Research on Homelessness*. Lexington Books, Lanham, MD.

van Olphen, H.

1966   Maya Blue: A Clay-Organic Pigment? *Science* 154:645–646.

Vavilov, Nikolai

1992   *Origin and Geography of Cultivated Plants*. Cambridge University Press, Cambridge.

Verney-Carron, Aurelie, Stephane Gin, and Guy Libourel

2008   A Fractured Roman Glass Block Altered for 1800 Years in Seawater: Analogy with Nuclear Waste Glass in a Deep Geological Repository. *Geochemica et Cosmochimica Acta* 72:5372–5385.

2010   Archaeological Analogs and the Future of Nuclear Waste Glass. *Journal of Nuclear Materials* 406:365–370.

Volti, Rudi

1990   Why Internal Combustion? *American Heritage of Invention & Technology* 6(2)42–47.

Voth, Henry R.

1905   The Traditions of the Hopi. *Field Columbian Museum Publication* 96 (*Anthropological Series* VIII).

Wade, Edwin L.

1988   The Ethnic Art Market in the American Southwest. In *Objects and Others: Essays on Museums and Material Culture*, edited by George W. Stocking Jr., pp. 167–191. University of Wisconsin Press, Madison.

Wallace, Birgitta

1990   L'Anse aux Meadows: Gateway to Vinland. *Acta Archaeologica* 61:166–197.

2005   The Norse in Newfoundland: L'Anse aux Meadows and Vinland. *Newfoundland and Labrador Studies* 19(1):5–43.

Warinner, Christina et al.

2014   Pathogens and Host Immunity in the Ancient Human Oral Cavity. *Nature Genetics* 46:336–344.

Warinner, Christina, Camilla Speller, and Matthew J. Collins

2014   A New Era in Palaeomicrobiology: Prospects for Ancient Dental Calculus as a Long-Term Record of the Human Oral Microbiome. *Philosophical Transactions of the Royal Society B* 370:20130376.

Washington Post

1981   "Doctor, Archeologist Find New Use for Ancient Tool." 1 January, 1981.

Watkins, C. Malcolm and Ivor Noël Hume

1967   The "Poor Potter" of Yorktown. *United States National Museum, Bulletin 249*, Contributions from The Museum of History and Technology Paper 54, pp. 73–112.

Watkins, Joe

2005   Through Wary Eyes: Indigenous Perspectives on Archaeology. *Annual Review of Anthropology* 34:429–449.

Webb, George W.

2002   *Science in the American Southwest: A Topical History*. University of Arizona Press, Tucson.

Weber, J. and J. Wahl

2006   Neurosurgical Aspects of Trepanations from Neolithic Times. *International Journal of Osteoarchaeology* 16:536–545.

Webster, Cedric
1962   The Sewers of Mohenjo-Daro. *Journal of the Water Pollution Control Federation* 34:116–123.

Weisman, Brent R.
2007   Nativism, Resistance, and Ethnogenesis of the Florida Seminole Identity. *Historical Archaeology* 41:195–208.

2012   Chipco's House and the Role of the Individual in Shaping Seminole Indian Cultural Responses to the Modern World. *Historical Archaeology* 46:161–171.

White, Carolyn L.
2013   The Burning Man Festival and the Archaeology of Ephemeral and Temporary Gatherings. In *The Oxford Handbook of the Archaeology of the Contemporary World*, edited by Paul Graves-Brown, Rodney Harrison, and Angela Piccini, pp. 595–609. Oxford University Press, Oxford.

White, Esther C.
2004   Distilling the Future: Reconstructing Washington's Distillery. Paper presented at the 2004 Annual Conference of the Society for Historical Archaeology, St. Louis, MO.

Wilk, Richard R. and Lisa C. Cliggett
2007   *Economies and Cultures*. 2nd ed. Westview Press, Boulder, CO.

Willey, Gordon R. and Jeremy A. Sabloff
1993   *A History of American Archaeology*. 3rd ed. W. H. Freeman, New York.

Wilmshurst, Janet, Terry L. Hunt, Carl P. Lipo, and Athol J. Anderson
2011   High-Precision Radiocarbon Dating Shows Recent and Rapid Initial Human Colonization of East Polynesia. *Proceedings of the National Academy of Sciences* 108:1815–1820.

Winograd, Isaac J.
1986   *Archaeology and Public Perception of a Transscientific Problem—Disposal of Toxic Wastes in the Unsaturated Zone*. U.S. Geological Survey circular 990.

Wissler, Clark
1921   Dating Our Prehistoric Ruins. *Natural History* 21(1):13–26.

Wolverton, Steve and R. Lee Lyman
2012a   Introduction to Applied Zooarchaeology. In *Conservation Biology and Applied Zooarchaeology*, edited by Steve Wolverton and R. Lee Lyman, pp. 1–22. University of Arizona Press, Tucson.

2012b   (editors) *Conservation Biology and Applied Zooarchaeology*. University of Arizona Press, Tucson.

Wood, Bernard
2010   Reconstructing Human Evolution: Achievements, Challenges, and Opportunities. *Proceedings of the National Academy of Sciences* 107:8902–8909.

Wood, Bernard and Nicholas Lonergan
2008   The Hominin Fossil Record: Taxa, Grades, and Clades. *Journal of Anatomy* 212:354–376.

Wood, Bernard and Brian G. Richmond
2000   Human Evolution: Taxonomy and Paleobiology. *Journal of Anatomy* 196: 19–60.

Woodbury, Richard B.
1994   The Remarkable History of Edgar Lee Hewett's Ph.D. Dissertation. *Bulletin of the History of Archaeology* 4(1):2–4.

Wright, Richard
1995   Investigating War Crimes: The Archaeological Evidence. *The Sydney Papers* 7(3):39–43.

Wright, Richard, I. Hanson, and J. Sterenberg
2005   Mass Graves. In *Forensic Archaeology: Advances in Theory and Practice*, edited by John Hunter and Margaret Cox, pp. 137–158. Routledge, London.

Wyckoff, Lydia
1983   The Sikyatki Revival. In *Hopis, Tewas, and the American Road*, edited by Willard Walker and Lydia L. Wyckoff, pp. 67–93. Wesleyan University Press, Middletown, CT.

Young, Christopher, Amanda Chadburn, and Isabelle Bedu
2009   *Stonehenge: World Heritage Site Management Plan 2009*. English Heritage, London.

Zedeño, María Nieves, Diane Austin, and Richard Stoffle
1997   Landmark and Landscape: A Contextual Approach to the Management of American Indian Resources. *Culture & Agriculture* 19:123–129.

Zeder, Melinda A.
2008   Domestication and Early Agriculture in the Mediterranean Basin: Origins, Diffusion, and Impact. *Proceedings of the National Academy of Sciences* 105: 11597–11604.
2011   The Origins of Agriculture in the Near East. *Current Anthropology* 52:S221–S235.
2012   Pathways to Animal Domestication. In *Biodiversity in Agriculture: Domestication, Evolution, and Sustainability*, edited by P. Gepts et al., pp. 227–259. Cambridge University Press, Cambridge.

Zega, Michael E.
2001   Advertising the Southwest. *Journal of the Southwest* 43:281–315.

Zimmerman, Larry J.
2013   Homelessness. In *The Oxford Handbook of the Archaeology of the Contemporary World*, edited by Paul Graves-Brown, Rodney Harrison, and Angela Piccini, pp. 336–350. Oxford University Press, Oxford.

Zimmerman, Larry J., Courtney Singleton, and Jessica Welch
2010   Activism and Creating a Translational Archaeology of Homelessness. *World Archaeology* 42:443–454.

Zimmerman, Larry J. and Jessica Welch
2006   Toward an Archaeology of Homelessness. *Anthropology News*, February, p. 54.

2011   Displaced and Barely Visible: Archaeology and the Material Culture of
       Homelessness. *Historical Archaeology* 45:67–85.

Zimring, Carl A. (editor)
2012   *Encyclopedia of Consumption and Waste: The Social Science of Garbage.* SAGE,
       Thousand Oaks, CA.

About the Author

MICHAEL BRIAN SCHIFFER, an archaeologist, graduated with a BA in anthropology from UCLA in 1969 and earned his graduate degrees from the University of Arizona (MA 1972, PhD 1973). From 1975 to 2014 he served on the faculty of the University of Arizona, most recently as the Fred A. Riecker Distinguished Professor of Anthropology. He is currently a research associate in the Lemelson Center, National Museum of American History, Smithsonian Institution. His interests have included cultural resource management, formation processes of the archaeological record, experimental archaeology (ceramics), human (nonverbal) communication, technological change, materiality, and history of electrical science and technologies. His overarching interest is the development of method and theory in behavioral archaeology.

The author and wife Annette, hiking in Shenandoah National Park (photo by Adam J. Schiffer).

Among Schiffer's many books are *Behavioral Archaeology* (1976); *Formation Processes of the Archaeological Record* (1987); *The Portable Radio in American Life* (1991); *The Material Life of Human Beings* (1999); *Power Struggles: Scientific Authority and the Creation of Practical Electricity Before Edison* (2008); *Studying Technological Change: A Behavioral Approach* (2011); and *The Archaeology of Science: Studying the Creation of Useful Knowledge* (2013).

Index

Numbers in *italics* refer to figures, illustrations, or tables.